EMBARK ON A JOURNEY THROUGH UNCONDITIONAL LOVE, POWER, AND BETRAYAL!

How could an emperor like Napoleon Bonaparte be so captivated by the twenty-year-old Polish Countess Marie Walewska—admittedly a rare beauty but of minor nobility—that their affair would last through both his marriages? And if it wasn't romance that first drew Marie to Napoleon, what was it?

At just eight years old, Marie finds her life forever changed by the death of her father, killed in battle against the Russians. This tragedy sparks a deep, lifelong patriotism in her as Poland is fragmented and divided among Russia, Prussia, and Austria.

A fan of Napoleon since her school days, Marie eagerly seizes the opportunity to meet him when he passes through the former Poland, his intention to secure military support for his campaign to conquer Russia. She seeks only to express Poland's gratitude and hope he would restore the nation's independence. She never imagined a romantic entanglement. But Napoleon, taken with her patriotism, youth, and beauty, soon sets his sights on her—and begins a campaign to win her heart.

Though Marie resists, powerful forces pressure her—just as they had in her marriage—to give in to the emperor's desires.

Expect to be immersed in Marie's world, where love and loyalty collide amidst a galaxy of powerful aristocrats, politicians, and military leaders. You'll journey from Marie's manor house on the plains of Poland to cosmopolitan Warsaw, through grand palaces in Austria, France, and Italy—before sailing to the Island of Elba, where destiny awaits.

Theodora: actress, prostitute, mistress, feminist. And Byzantine Empress of the sixth-century Roman world. Stephen: handsome Syrian boy, wizard's apprentice, palace eunuch. And Secretary to the Empress. How does this unlikely pair become such allies that one day Empress Theodora asks Stephen to write her biography?

THE THEODORA DUOLOGY

FORTUNE'S CHILD

"A historical novel set in sixth-century Constantinople charts the extraordinary ascent of a woman from poverty to royal power. [This is] a meticulously researched historical account presented in the form of a thrilling political drama."

~Kirkus Reviews

**OVERALL GRAND PRIZE 2019
Best Book,
Chanticleer Int'l Book Awards**

TOO SOON THE NIGHT

Palace eunuch and secretary Stephen records Empress Theodora's life as she navigates wars, political and religious crises, a citywide rebellion, and the first world plague pandemic, all in a male-dominated world.

"A gorgeous tapestry of impeccable research and intricate worldbuilding."

~Kate Quinn, Author of *The Empress of Rome Saga* and *The Diamond Eye*

**Chaucer Grand Prize Winner, 2021
Chanticleer Int'l Book Awards
IPPI Bronze Medal Winner**

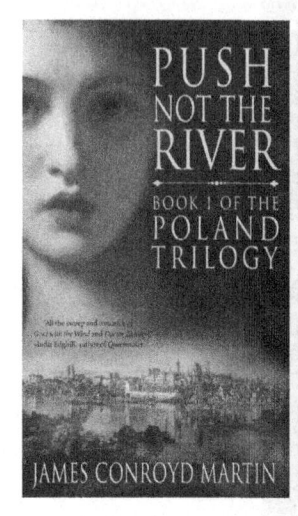

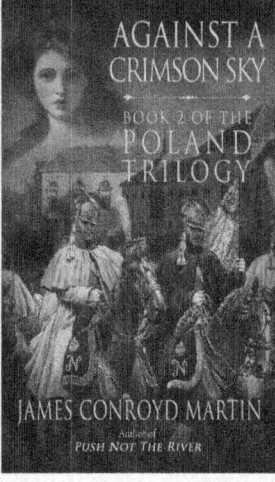

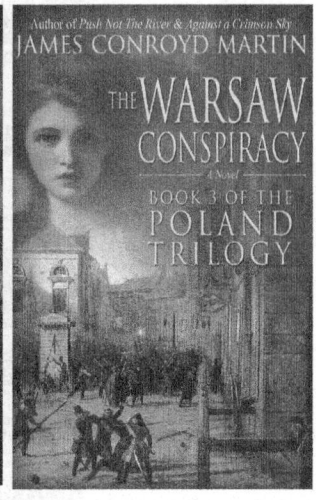

Check out The Poland Trilogy: https://goo.gl/93rzag

Based on the diary of a Polish countess who lived through the rise and fall of the Third of May Constitution years, 1791-94, **Push Not the River** paints a vivid picture of a tumultuous and unforgettable metamorphosis of a nation—and of Anna, a proud and resilient woman. **Against a Crimson Sky** continues Anna's saga as Napoléon comes calling, implying independence would follow if only Polish lancers would accompany him on his fateful 1812 march into Russia. Anna's family fights valiantly to hold on-to a tenuous happiness, their country, and their very lives. Set against the November Rising (1830-31), **The Warsaw Conspiracy** depicts partitioned Poland's daring challenge to the Russian Empire. Brilliantly illustrating the psyche of a people determined to reclaim independence in the face of monumental odds, the story features Anna's sons and their fates in love and war.

From the Author of The Poland Trilogy
JAMES CONROYD MARTIN

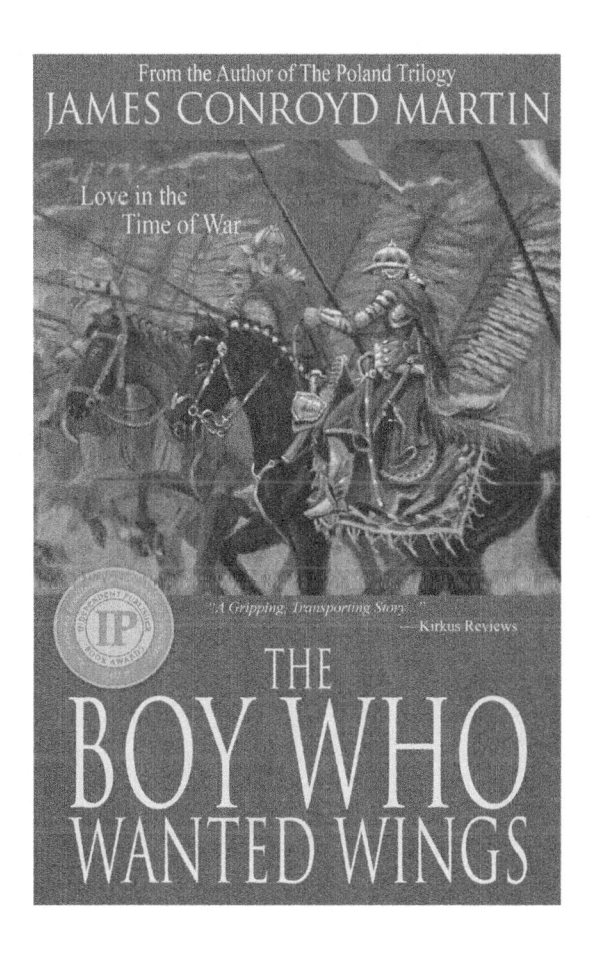

Love in the Time of War

"A Gripping, Transporting Story"
— Kirkus Reviews

THE BOY WHO WANTED WINGS

Aleksy, a Tatar raised by a Polish peasant family, wishes to become a Polish winged hussar, a Christian lancer who carries into battle a device attached to his back that holds dozens of eagle feathers. As a Tatar and as a peasant, this is an unlikely quest. When he meets Krystyna, the daughter of the noble who owns the land that his parents work, he falls hopelessly in love. But even though she returns his love, race and class differences make this quest as impossible as that of becoming a hussar. Under the most harrowing and unlikely circumstances, one day Aleksy must choose between his dreams.

An IPPI Gold Medal winner!

NAPOLEON'S SHADOW WIFE

— A Novel of Countess Marie Walewska —

JAMES CONROYD MARTIN

HUSSAR
QUILL PRESS

CHICAGO

Napoleon's Shadow Wife: A Novel of Countess Marie Walewska
Copyright 2025 by James Conroyd Martin Trust All rights reserved

First Print Edition: April 2025
Edited by Mary Rita Perkins Mitchell
Cover and formatting: Streetlight Graphics

Hardcover ISBN: 978-1-7340043-4-2
Paperback ISBN: 978-1-7340043-5-9

Art:
Front cover:
Young Woman Drawing
Marie-Denise Villers 1801
Public domain

First Consul Napoleon Bonaparte
Antoine-Jean Gros 1802
Public domain

Title Page and Print Back Cover:
Comtesse Marie Walewska
François Gérard 1810
Public domain

Print back cover
Napoleon at the Saint-Bernard Pass
Jacques-Louis David 1801
Public domain

No part of this book may be reproduced, scanned, or distributed in any printed or electronic form without permission. Please do not participate in or encourage piracy of copyrighted materials in violation of the author's rights. Thank you for respecting the hard work of this author.

While some characters are based on historical personages, this is a work of fiction.

Also By
James Conroyd Martin

Push Not the River
Against a Crimson Sky
The Warsaw Conspiracy
The Boy Who Wanted Wings
Fortune's Child
Too Soon the Night
Hologram: A Haunting

For my readers~
You have my heart.

Thank you for reading ***Napoleon's Shadow Wife!*** I hope you will reward me with a brief review at whatever venue you purchase books, and at Goodreads. Doing so is more important to an author than you might think. Another big help is to request an author's books at your local library. Thank you in advance!

Please subscribe to my **newsletter** for infrequent announcements: **http://www.JamesCMartin.com**

Follow/add me on Goodreads:
https://www.goodreads.com/author/show/92822.James_Conroyd_Martin

ACKNOWLEDGMENTS

I wish to express my sincere thanks to those who have supported me on this quest to make known Marie Walewska, a very important woman in Poland and European history. For exceptional editing skills, credit goes to Mary Rita Perkins Mitchell, as well as Pam Sourelis and Jessica Curtis. For website management I am in debt to Elizabyth Harrington, and for all things publishing, Glendon Haddix of Streetlight Graphics. For details relating to Poland and Polish culture, I thank Dr. Jacek Tylicki, Sophie Hodorowicz Knab and Lynn Dziadulewicz for their expertise. My fellow writers at Portland's 9-Bridges Downtown Saturday Meetups offered the most insightful critiques every week without fail. For sheer motivation, I thank Judi Free. And, as always, Scott Hagensee.

GLOSSARY

CZAPKA, CZAPKI (pl): A traditional Polish hat, usually four-cornered and made of felt, fur, or wool, and worn by people of different classes.

DOŻYNKI: Harvest Festival.

KARNAWAŁ: The festive season leading up to lent.

KOLACZ: A round, yeast-based cake-like bread made with various fillings and topped with decorations; it is shared at gatherings, like weddings.

KONTUSZ: A long, flowing coat or robe made of fine fabrics and worn by the Polish nobility.

KULIG: A horse-drawn sleigh ride through the countryside, often accompanied with music, singing, and other festivities.

OPLATEK: the thin wafer used in Poland and other countries at Christmas celebrations. The sharing of it fosters togetherness, highlighting family, peace, and love.

SZLACHTA: Poland's minor nobility who held a significant amount of political, social and economic power. Prior to the partitions of 1772-1795, they made up as much as 10% of the population.

STAROSTA: The chief administrator of a county in Poland.

WIGILIA: The traditional Christmas Eve (vigil) supper and celebration.

WYCINANKI: a traditional Polish folk art involving papercuttings, often created as decorations for homes, especially at Christmas and Easter.

ZUPAN: A long, fitted and usually highly decorated outer coat or robe, often layered over the kontusz, and worn by the Polish nobility.

Europe 1812

- ■ French Empire
- ▨ French Dependent States
- ▨ French Allies

NORWAY
North Sea
DENMARK
Dublin • UNITED KINGDOM
OLDENBURG
London
CONFEDERATION OF THE RHINE
Atlantic Ocean
Paris
FRENCH EMPIRE
KINGDOM OF ITALY
Corsica
Rome
Lisbon • PORTUGAL
Madrid • SPAIN
Sardinia
Mediterranean Sea
MOROCCO
ALGIERS
TUNIS

SWEDEN

Stockholm

Copenhagen

Baltic Sea

Riga

St. Petersburg

Moscow
Borodino

Tilsit
Niemen Wilno Smogoni Bobr Smolensk
Gdansk Voronovo Minsk Orsza
PRUSSIA Grodno Borisov Beresina

Poznan Vistula
Sochaczen Warsaw RUSSIAN EMPIRE
GRAND DUCHY
OF WARSAW
Kraków

Prague Kiev
Halicz Dnieper

Vienna AUSTRIAN Dniester
EMPIRE MOLDAVIA
Odessa

Bucharest
Danube

Black Sea

MONTENEGRO

Adriatic Sea OTTOMAN

KINGDOM
OF NAPLES
Naples Constantinople

EMPIRE

Sicily
KINGDOM
OF SICILY

N
W E
S

PART ONE

"Children are what you make them."
~Polish Proverb

1

Warsaw
Friday, 10 June 1803

"Come away from the window, Marie," Amelia said.

Marie Łączyńska stood in the small reception room, her gaze fixed on the stream of carriages queued up to collect young ladies going home for the summer. In little time, she and Amelia would leave their days at the convent finishing school behind them.

The sweet, rosy fragrance of peonies in full bloom wafted through the open window, filling Marie with a sudden euphoria—an intoxicating hint of freedom.

Countess Eliza Sobolewska entered the room. As if in support of Amelia's entreaty, she said, "Just step back a pace or two, Marie."

"Why should I?" Marie sang, still facing the window.

"Because," the countess warned, "Mother Abbess will look up, see you gawking with your nose at the window and scold you." The countess settled into a chair next to Amelia. She frequently visited the Convent of Our Lady of the Assumption at Mother Abbess Helena's invitation. Ten years older than Marie and Amelia, she served as a role model for young noble girls. Over the past three years, she had taken Marie under her wing, treating her more as an amusement than a trial—a term Mother Abbess occasionally employed, accompanied by a tsk or a scowl. The countess and Marie forged a friendship.

"Mother Abbess will say it's most undignified," Amelia added. "Isn't that right, Madame Eliza?"

"It is."

"Oh, everything's undignified in her view," Marie said, glancing back to admire the countess's emerald green silk dress. "I'll tell you what's undignified—it's these sack-like maroon uniforms and black wide-brimmed bonnets with nary a flower or ribbon. Well, since this is to be my last scold, I'm looking forward to it. You should be excited, too, Amelia. Our three-year sentence is at an end."

"What a way to talk!" the countess exclaimed.

Amelia clucked her tongue. "Oh, Madame Eliza, she thinks her looks will get her through anything. Don't you, Marie?"

Marie shrugged and smiled, her gaze returning to the window. Below, an open carriage carrying the buxom Kowalska twins and their large trunk was leaving the courtyard. No other carriage moved up to the *porte-cochere*, where Mother Abbess Helena was stationed.

Alarm set in. "No one's come from Kiernozia!" Marie cried. "Why hasn't Mother sent the carriage by now? If it doesn't come soon, we'll be travelling in the dark. —Sweet Jesus! What if she's ill? She mentioned having a cold in her last letter. What if—"

The countess immediately came to her side, gripping her hand and scanning the empty courtyard. "What are you thinking, Marie? Summer colds are common, not dangerous. Don't worry, the carriage will come."

Amelia joined them and peered out. "See there, Marie, Mother Abbess remains at her post. Don't lose faith."

"The wavy glass improves her looks," Marie said.

"Marie!" the countess chided. "That's unkind."

"Do you think so?" Marie asked, all innocence.

The three stood in silence for several minutes.

"There! Do you hear it?" Amelia cried. "Another carriage!"

"I *see* it, but that one's not from home, I can tell you," Marie said. "That's neither our carriage nor our horses, and it's certainly not our driver."

They leaned closer to the window as the convent groom unfolded the drop-down steps and opened the door for the uniformed occupant of the closed coach. "Look," the countess said, "it's a handsome student from the Collegium Nobilium. Do you recognize him, Marie?"

"*I do*," Amelia trilled. "I've seen him often enough in the village with his friends. It's your brother, Marie!"

"Teodor," Marie murmured, her alarm increasing. What could this unexpected appearance mean?

"Mother Abbess is motioning for us to come down," the countess said. "We *all* might be scolded now."

The three turned and made for the stairs, Marie trailing, her heart racing.

Downstairs, under the *porte-cochere*, Marie rushed toward her brother. "Teodor," she blurted, "what are you doing here?"

Dressed in his boarding school's dark blue uniform, Teodor stiffened and cast a quick, cautious glance at Marie's companions. Beneath his unruly mane of brown hair his brow furrowed slightly—a subtle signal Marie recognized as his way of saying, *not here, not now.*

Marie introduced her brother to Mother Abbess and the countess, and for the abbess's benefit, made certain to formally reintroduce him to Amelia Wozniak, who, despite lacking claim to nobility, had her tuition paid by Father Albin, the Kiernozia parish priest.

"Oh, Marie," Mother Abbess said.

Marie turned to her. "Yes?"

"Yes, *Mother Abbess*," she corrected.

"Yes, Mother Abbess," Marie repeated.

"Did you take those drawings of Napoleon Bonaparte off the wall in your room?"

"I did, Mother Abbess."

"Good! I do hope your artistry improves."

Marie managed a tight smile as the others bade farewell to the superior. Once the driver lashed Marie's and Amelia's valises to the roof and the countess gave him directions to her home, the four of them crowded into the coach. Marie and Teodor sat on the bench facing the countess and Amelia. "Madame Eliza lives here in Warsaw," Marie explained, "just a short distance away."

"I could have sent for a carriage, Marie," the countess said. "There was no cause to inconvenience everyone."

"Away, boys!" the driver called to his two-horse team, and the carriage began to roll.

"It's no inconvenience," Marie said, smiling. "I'll miss you, Madame Eliza. We'll write, and remember, you promised to visit me at Kiernozia!"

Marie felt Teodor's elbow nudge her slightly but paid no attention.

"I did and I will," the countess vowed.

"I think Mother Abbess had tears in her eyes when she bade us goodbye," Amelia said.

"There were no tears in her eyes when she said farewell to *me*," Marie countered. "Ha! Her lips were as dry as sand against my cheeks. Or perhaps that was her moustache."

"Why, Marie!" the countess chided, attempting to turn her impromptu laugh into a gasp.

"Well, you know it's true that she cares little for me."

Amelia laughed. "It's not like you haven't given her cause for the past three

3

years. And I heard that someone told her you were behind that little ruse in our final French class yesterday."

Marie giggled. "Is that why she questioned me? I'll wager it was one of the twins who told."

"Wait," Teodor said. "What's this? What did you do to the Mother Abbess, Marie? Out with it!"

"Never mind!"

"Indeed," the countess said. "I heard what went on, and it's shameful, Marie."

"I'll tell," Amelia offered.

Marie raised her hand in protest while trying to control her laughter. "No, you won't! I'll tell." She turned to her brother, securing his full attention. "You see, Teodor, Mother Abbess Helena prides herself on her French despite *never* having been to Paris. Even at her age, she insists on teaching that class. Why, it's merely classroom French she teaches. Teodor, if it weren't for our grounding in conversational French by Monsieur Chopin, I would be at a loss, should I ever find myself in polite society. He was an excellent tutor, Madame Eliza. I do miss him."

"The story!" Amelia pleaded.

"Well, all thirty-five of us must crowd into a long, narrow classroom. No one escapes French class. A good thing, too. It's the only tongue spoken at European courts. You see, the desks are made for two and placed close together, so there's only room for a narrow aisle along the side. That's where Mother Abbess patrols as we recite. Up and down, she marches, down and up."

"So," Amelia interjected, "yesterday, as we recited, those in the back of the room began to sing low, '*Ah, ça ira, ça ira, ça ira.*'"

Teodor's eyes lit up. "I know that tune! It's *Ça Ira*, a French revolutionary song."

"Indeed," Marie said, "and one perfect for our purposes, wasn't it, Amelia?"

Her friend nodded. "It was delicious."

"Mother Abbess is hard of hearing," Marie went on. "The singing grew louder until she finally heard it. Her head swiveled toward the students in the back, and her expression went from puzzled to furious. She flew like quicksilver to the rear of the room."

"And?" Teodor asked.

"And the singing there stopped and those of us at the front began to sing, '*Ah, ça ira, ça ira, ça ira.*'"

Teodor laughed. "And the nun raced to the front?"

Marie nodded. "Exactly! No one had ever seen her move so fast! By the time she got there, the singing began again at the back."

The coach slowed and came to a stop, still resounding with the laughter of its passengers.

Marie could scarcely contain herself. "And so, it went four or five more revolutions with her heavy heels thumping on the floorboards, to and fro. Mother Abbess was a blur of dark brown. Finally, she raced from the room."

Amelia put her hand to her mouth. "She thought she was going crazy or being visited by the devil. Her eyes were wild!"

"I think I know that devil personally," Teodor said, laughing.

"You are incorrigible, Marie," the countess said.

As the laughter lessened, they heard the driver lowering the steps.

"We've arrived at my home, it seems," the countess said, peering out the window and gathering up the folds of her dress.

When the driver opened the door, Teodor pivoted in his seat and jumped down to assist the countess in alighting from the coach.

Before the countess could exit, however, Marie reached her hand across and detained her. "Now, you *will* visit me at Kiernozia."

"I will."

"And," Marie said, "you promised once my schooling was behind me, I could call you Eliza, like we are friends."

The countess smiled. "Yes, you may. We *are* friends, Marie."

Marie released her now, and when the countess was on the ground and moving away, Marie called out: "Goodbye, *Eliza*!"

Scarcely missing a beat, Marie deftly took the countess's place next to Amelia. "I prefer to travel facing forward," she said, though her primary intent was to question her brother, vis à vis.

Teodor reentered the coach. "Marie, just who is this friend of yours, Madame Sobolewska? We just delivered her to the Branicki Palace."

"I know. It now belongs to the king's sister, Elżbieta Branicka, who installed Eliza and her mother in an apartment there."

"Tell him why, Marie," Amelia urged.

"You see, Teodor, Eliza's father was King Stanisław."

"What?"

"It's true!" Amelia chimed in. "Her mother did marry the king."

Teodor's eyes went wide. "How can that be? I've never heard of it."

"I'm not surprised, Teo," Marie said, employing his diminutive. She went on to explain that the king secretly wed Eliza's mother, Elżbieta Grabowska, in a morganatic marriage. "It's a Germanic concept whereby a noble may marry a commoner," Marie said with a shrug. "At least, her mother claims the king married her."

"Is there doubt?" Teodor asked.

"There are some doubters because she didn't voice her claim until after his death."

"Daughter of the king," Teodor said. "Imagine that! She certainly tried hard to appear disapproving of you. —Have you been in the Branicki Palace?"

"Yes, twice," Marie replied. "It's as luxurious as it appears from the outside. Eliza and her husband live there with two young daughters. They also have another residence in Paris."

"Do they?"

"Yes. Now—I want to know about Mother, Teodor."

"Mother?" Teodor leaned forward, his serious green eyes flicking toward Amelia then back to Marie in a cautionary way.

"Oh, you can talk in front of Amelia. I often confide in her."

Her brother nodded. "Mother is fine, Marie. She'll be delighted to have you home. For heaven's sake, what did you think?"

Marie took a defensive tone. "Your unexpected appearance gave me a fright. One never knows. Last month, one of our classmates, Eugenia, had her father come to collect her. Her mother had died quite unexpectedly."

"I see," Teodor said. "I'm sorry for making you worry."

"So—what is the purpose of this carriage? Where is ours—and our driver?"

"Mother sent word to the college for me to rent this and see to your return. She couldn't afford a driver any longer. Young Emeryk is in training to take his place."

"Our groom?"

"Yes. The estate is in disrepair. You must have noticed when you were home."

"Ah, that's why you nudged me. You think I shouldn't be inviting people there. You know, I haven't been home since Christmas, and what can one notice when there's nothing but three feet of snow all about?"

"Why didn't you go home at Easter? If you had, you would've noticed. Mother said it was your decision."

"I had French to study. Don't look at me like that. French is essential. And, to be honest, Madame Eliza led a dance class over the break."

Teodor exchanged his skeptical glance for one of understanding. "Ah, I see."

"Never mind that. Why couldn't Emeryk have taken the carriage to pick us up?"

"He's been made to carry other loads since Mother let the last of the field hands go."

"What—things are *that* bad? Oh, Teodor! I didn't know. Poor Mother!" Marie paused, appraising her brother. "Are you finished with your studies?"

"Finished? I am not. Don't think I can't see your mind at work. I won't be there to plant crops or mend the roof. I have every intention of slipping out of Poland at the right time and following Benedykt's path to Paris, where I, too, will emigrate and join General Napoleon's Polish legions."

"No! To follow Napoleon? You can't, Teodor!"

"Why not? What do you have against the little general? He's been named France's First Consul."

"I have nothing against him. Why, he's all but worshipped at school. Most of the girls believe he'll bring independence to Poland. Even the nuns praise him."

"You don't?"

"Of course, I hope they're right. I wish him success. But I worry for our brother. It's fortunate he's been posted in Milan and not been sent to the colony of Saint-Domingue to put down the revolution there. It's not gone well, by all accounts. Many Poles have died in combat or of tropical diseases. Despite that, Benedykt wrote saying he hoped to see action soon."

Teodor shrugged. "That's the way of soldiers. He's years older than us, so I think he knows his own mind."

"Don't you see that those islanders want independence, just like we do?"

Teodor did not respond.

Marie glanced over to see that Amelia was already dropping off to sleep. She lifted her gaze to her brother and leaned forward. "I'm worried for you, Teodor."

"I appreciate that, little sister, but you worry too much. Our brother is well trained and I will be, as well, so don't become a worrier."

"I'm younger by one year—just one!"

"Marie, you say you wish success for the Corsican. Tell me, has Mother Abbess taught you the word *velleity*?"

"No."

"Velleity describes a wish, Marie, but it's a wish that doesn't carry with it the *effort* it takes to attain it."

"An empty wish? You mean to say you would risk your life for Napoleon."

"I'd risk it to free Poland from foreign powers." Teodor's intensely green eyes held hers. "Just as Father did!"

The image of her father—killed nine years ago at the Battle of Maciejowice—struck Marie with painful clarity. She sat back against the hard bench, silenced, her sixteen-and-a-half-year-old heart aching.

In a short while, finding herself keeping company with two sleepers, she turned her head to stare out the window at the passing landscape.

Marie's most vivid memory of her father was of a perfect spring day when he had taken her by carriage to Warsaw. Entering the sprawling capital at the western gate had been thrilling, but when they stepped down from the carriage in the middle of Castle Square, just above the River Vistula, her heart soared at the wondrous sight of the bronze king atop Zygmunt's Column. "King Zygmunt carries a sword in one hand," her father said, "and a cross in the other. That's to show his courage in the fight against evil."

They walked over to the Royal Castle and then continued on foot the short distance to Market Square, passing great churches and the homes of nobles whom her father called *magnates*. As they came into the *rynek*, Marie became entranced by the spectacle of shops and stalls, the colors and rich aromas of food carts, the hubbub of shoppers, and then—the doll shop.

Smiling, her father opened the door and nodded for her to enter. "You're to choose one, Marysia," her father whispered, using her diminutive, "for your name day."

Marie gasped. "But my name day is a long time away, Papa."

"No, not so long. The middle of August, when we celebrate Mary's assumption into heaven. We are here, Marie, so we must take our chance now. I might have other duties come August."

Marie's heart raced with excitement at this sudden opportunity. Only later, much later, would she remember his caution about August. Indeed, by August he had been called to defend Poland.

She saw every variety of doll. Some were made of cloth, some wood, some terra cotta. Some depicted peasants, gypsies, Jews, nobles. All were colorful and charming.

And then she spied it. It was held upright on a little stand. Marie felt a lightness in her chest. It was the wooden doll of a noble lady with a painted face, glass eyes of blue, and real blonde hair tucked under an intricately shaped bonnet. She wore a gold silk dress that puffed out all around her, like a flower. Her tiny slippers were as red as her lips. Marie's gaze returned to the face. It seemed then a reflection of her own face and hair. "That's the one," Marie said.

Standing to her side, her father said, "Choose another, Marie."

The shop owner came up and stood behind the display table. "It's lovely, isn't it? And so well made."

"Marie, choose another."

Marie looked up at her father. "Is it too much money?"

Her father stiffened. "No," he said.

Marie looked from him to the shopkeeper's face and noticed some wordless exchange pass between the two, something she couldn't decipher. The shopkeeper looked down at her, smiled, and said, "Perhaps we'll find one better suited for you, young lady."

"But I want this one," Marie insisted.

"Just step this way, child," the man said.

Marie held her ground, looked up at her father, and said, "Papa, I want this one."

Her father grunted, nodded at the shopkeeper, and it was done.

Later, Marie would learn the reason for her father's hesitancy, and she would love him all the more for it.

The carriage suddenly hit a pothole, jarring her into the present. She blinked away the past and allowed the countryside to come into view. The Mazovian Plains were relentlessly flat but brilliantly awash with fields of wildflowers, crops, stands of far-off trees, and an occasional sighting of a creek or river, their flow tugging at the tendrils of weeping willows.

Some six hours later, when they passed through the small city of Sochaczew, she knew two-thirds of the journey was behind them. The carriage slowed as it turned onto a narrow, rougher road that would take them through half a dozen villages until they reached Kiernozia. Soon they were into open country again. Marie looked out at the vast undulating terrain of lacy lavender scorpionweed interwoven with bright swaths of red poppy seed flowers. The sight had held such wonder for her on that day she and her father returned from Warsaw, that glorious doll lying in her lap.

Today, she could only ponder about what she might find at home.

It was still light out hours later when the carriage trundled into Brodno,

9

where Marie had been born. Both of her companions were waking. "Three miles to go," she said, turning away from the window and shifting in her seat.

Upon their arrival in their home village of Kiernozia, a collection of simple whitewashed houses with thatched roofs, steeped in Łączyński family history, Marie felt an odd mix of exhilaration and nervousness.

"I told the driver to stop at the house just before the church," Teodor said, eyes on Amelia.

"That's perfect," Amelia said. "I'm surprised you remembered."

"It's not hard in a tiny village."

"Living next to a church makes churchgoing very convenient for my religious mother, and a nuisance for me. I'm not so religious, but at least I can lie abed until two minutes before the bells start."

Teodor laughed. Marie suspected that Teodor's even features under his tousled brown hair held some interest for Amelia.

When the driver opened the door, the three alighted from the coach. "We'll see one another soon," Marie said, hugging her friend. She drew back now and gave a little tug to the high neckline of Amelia's maroon uniform. "But never again in *these*."

Amelia stiffened, wet her lips, and managed only a half-smile.

Marie immediately regretted her remark. Her mind was elsewhere. No doubt, Amelia had few dresses, and her mother was not likely to allow her to retire her uniform. Marie admitted to herself that even her own mother had said that while the dresses were modest to a fault, the merino wool was soft, durable, and of the highest quality.

"I'll carry your valise to the door," Teodor said.

Amelia flashed a smile. "That's not necessary, but it *will* impress my mother."

"The Piarist fathers have taught him something," Marie joked as she climbed into the coach. She sat down on the bench, her mind turning to the imminent meeting with her own mother, her stomach in flux.

Teodor returned in a matter of minutes and took Amelia's place next to Marie. The carriage began to roll and was soon entering the vast parkland area that encompassed the Łączyński estate.

Marie placed her hand over her brother's. "How long will you stay, Teo?" she asked.

"I can't stay. Oh, for a meal, yes, and a rest for the horses, but the driver is to turn right around, and he's my only way back to school."

"I see. That's disappointing. I'd hoped you'd stay for a day or so. You've always lent me support."

"Why do you feel you need support?"

Marie shrugged.

"You feel I should return to Kiernozia to stay, don't you?"

Marie averted her eyes. "I do wonder, Teodor, how a widow and three daughters can manage an estate that you say yourself has fallen on hard times."

Teodor withdrew his hand and leaned toward Marie. "*Poland* has fallen on hard times, Marysia. Prussia, Austria, and Russia have carved us up like a roast goose. Three times they've done it until there is nothing left. Not even feathers. Poland's welfare must be addressed first. Father saw the truth in that." Teodor's voice trembled slightly, whether from the movement of the carriage over rough road or from emotion. "Father was there fighting against the Final Partition. He took the risk."

"Yes, he did," Marie snapped. "And in taking the risk, Teodor, he died!"

Teodor fell silent.

As the carriage negotiated a turn, Marie glanced out the window to see the poplars that lined the long lane leading to the Łączyński *dworek*, the most significant manor house in Kiernozia. Despite her nervousness, the sight brought a comforting warmth.

They were home, and the unsatisfactory conversation with her brother came to an end. Dusk was falling, but the eleven-hour journey was thankfully over.

In light of what Teodor had told her, Marie couldn't help but assess her home as the carriage moved into the large courtyard. The stone manor house stood proud with its triple-arched entranceway, tall narrow windows on the ground floor and square ones on the first level. However, its need for a whitewashing was underscored by a grayish cast and algae that had spread along the foundation's base and onto the sills of the cellar's rectangular windows. The sad and unkempt appearance was augmented by the twin unpruned weeping willows that stood like sentries on either side of the entranceway. No doubt it looked even worse in bright daylight, she thought. Stepping down from the coach, Marie noticed, too, that the courtyard was overgrown with weeds.

"Marie!" The cry from the doorway pulled Marie from her inspection. Waving excitedly, Honorata, her thirteen-year-old sister, started down the front stairs where several lanterns had been lighted in anticipation of their arrival. The youngest, nine-year-old Katarzyna, slipped out of the house moments later with a sharp yelp and followed suit.

In no time, they had their arms around their elder sister and brother. Teodor picked up Katarzyna and swung her around. "You've grown so big, Kasia," he said as he set her down. "How old are you now? Fifteen?"

"Ha!" Katarzyna squealed. "I'm nine and you know it!"

The four were laughing when another figure appeared at the top of the stone staircase.

Despite her stout appearance, Danusha, their longtime maid, moved with surprising nimbleness as she took to the stairs, one hand holding her skirts.

Smiling, she approached and gave Teodor a little bow, then lifted her hand to tickle what Marie had not even noticed: the sparse hairs sprouting on his chin. Despite the embarrassment that pinkened his complexion, he beamed a wide smile. When he moved his hand to deflect her attention, Danusha abandoned him to give Marie a great bear hug.

"Why, Marie!" she cried. "You've grown into womanhood. Let me have a fair-sized look." She stepped back a pace. "You're a beauty, you are! Oh, I'm not surprised. A little, maybe, that it happened so soon."

"Will we be beauties, too?" Katarzyna asked, as she and Honorata looked on.

"Oh, but of course, Kasia! All the Łączyńska girls will be beauties." With a wink at Teodor, she went on, "And all the Łączyński gentlemen, like Teo here, will be brave and handsome."

At that moment someone coughed softly.

Marie looked up to the open doorway, where her mother stood. Danusha lightly pinched her arm and whispered, "Madame Łączyńska's waiting. You'd best go up, you two. I'll go around the back to the kitchen. We have a late supper nearly ready."

"You go on up, Marie," Teodor said. "I'll get the driver to the stable and bring your valise up to your room."

"Oh, Teo, may we ride in the carriage?" Katarzyna pleaded.

"Why not?" he said. "Come along, Honorata."

Suddenly, Marie found herself alone at the bottom of the stairway. She glanced up to see her mother, silently watching. She took in a deep breath, miffed at her own hesitation, and began the twelve-step climb she had counted nearly every day of her childhood.

As Marie reached the landing, her mother said, "Come into the foyer. I could not imagine why you are so late. Another half hour and the wolves would be out."

"Hello, Mother," Marie said, following. When the countess stopped and pivoted toward her, Marie halted. She meant to embrace her mother, as they had on many occasions, but her mother motioned for her to stay two paces away. She hesitated, wondering what was expected of her.

"Why, you haven't grown much, have you? Well, maybe a whit, but I had hoped you'd be a bit taller." The countess took a step forward. "Now—let me have a good look, Marie. You have blossomed, though, haven't you? There's no denying that." She took her index finger, placed it under Marie's chin, elevating her face. "Pretty as a peach, you are. You won't be in want of a suitor—or a husband. But don't let that go to your head, do you hear?"

"I won't." While her mother had been inspecting her, she had been covertly acting in kind. Into her early forties now, her mother had developed new lines around her eyes and a lower, more somber tone in her voice. The stresses of widowhood, a failing estate, and children to raise were taking their toll.

"Come now, give me a hug, Marie. We'll have a fine meal tonight, a proper celebration for you and your brother. After all, he's to return to Warsaw right away. I hope you've thanked him for making the trip."

"I . . . I will," Marie said as her mother gave her a light embrace.

The countess drew back, holding her daughter at arms' length, her eyes again raking Marie from toe to head. "You'll need some new dresses and slippers. When you were a baby, you survived pneumonia. Do you know what your father said?"

Marie shook her head.

"He told me you were a lucky one, Marie. And it's come true. You will be our fortune."

2

AFTER DANUSHA'S DELICIOUS MEAL OF *bigos*, the countess coerced Marie to play the harpsichord for a while. It was not a talent Marie particularly enjoyed, but one she had improved while at school.

Later, she did her best to entertain Honorata and Katarzyna with convent stories until eleven o'clock, long after their bedtime. As the two were leaving her room, Honorata took Marie's hand, spun around to face her, and asked, "You will be staying, won't you?"

"Now, Honor, where would I go? My schooling is finished."

"You . . . you might get married."

"Not any time soon, dearest. I have no . . . no prospect."

"No?"

"No. Now run along. I've kept you up past your bedtime."

At that moment Katarzyna, who had gone on ahead to her room at the other end of the hall, let loose a spine-chilling scream.

"Kasia!" Marie cried. "What is it? What happened?" She started to move out of her room, but Honorata held her back.

"She'll be fine, Marie. I hear Mother coming up the stairs. She'll handle Kasia. This happens nearly every night."

"What—what happens?"

"When we leave our rooms with our candles, one or two of the bats on the hallway ceiling will dive at some little insect following the candle."

"Bats? We have bats?"

"We do. You'll get used to them."

An hour later, Marie sat on the chair in front of the square window, staring out into the black night. No, she would not get used to bats. Shivering, she turned her thoughts onto another path.

Teodor had returned to his studies at Warsaw with the hired driver directly after supper. During the meal, Marie hoped for a hint that her mother wanted him to return home after schooling to help with the estate. But when Teodor praised Benedykt's position in Napoleon's Polish Legion in Milan, her mother seemed resigned that Teodor would follow in his steps. Over dessert of poppyseed cake, she shared news of Benedykt: "Benny has written that he's been recalled to Paris, where he has been placed on General Louis-Alexandre Berthier's staff."

Marie exchanged looks of wonder with Teodor. They both knew Berthier had been Napoleon's Chief-of-Staff for some years. Marie could see the pleasure in her mother's light blue eyes and felt a surge of pride herself for Benedykt, though her chest tightened at the thought of both brothers risking their lives under Napoleon's command.

At convent school, Marie had learned more than academics. She had learned life lessons from other girls, girls like herself who had brothers. At thirteen, she had been oblivious of the expectations that life and adults had in store. Now, nearing seventeen, her eyes were opened, and she dared not look away.

The devastating 1794 loss at the Battle of Maciejowice presaged the fall of Warsaw and the treaty among Prussia, Austria, and Russia that removed Poland from the map of Europe. Consequently, Polish boys of the *szlachta*—the minor nobility—who lived in Warsaw and the plains of Mazovia were trained for the Prussian military because Prussia had been ceded those territories, including Kiernozia.

Polish girls of the *szlachta*, on the other hand, learned that their fate was still tied to tradition. They were groomed to marry well—and were to know their place. Marie crossed her arms, recalling how her mother had appraised her at the supper table. Oh, it didn't matter that the eyes sparkled with pride. She read in them an intent that unnerved her.

Marie thought of Eliza now. She knew that the nuns invited Eliza to their school to demonstrate more than dance steps, table manners, and proper introductions to men. She was there as a living example of the type of future that girls of their class could expect. At nineteen, Eliza had learned she was to meet a member of the Sobolewski clan, a man ten years older. Marriage was on the table and Eliza was the fish upon the platter. To hear her tell it, she had taken the news of a future planned for her by others with surprising calm. Marie wondered if that was true. For herself, she couldn't imagine doing so.

She looked at her bed and sighed, knowing she was not about to sleep. Her relationship with her mother had changed. What does she have in mind? Am *I* soon to be a fish upon a platter?

Rising, she moved to the little oak desk her father had made for her. The desktop had been polished in anticipation of her return. She sat and scanned the wall behind it, where she had attached her drawings of her father and images of General Tadeusz Kościuszko. The national hero had been captured at the battle where both her father and Poland's independence had perished. Upon his release, Kościuszko spent time in America and then Paris, but seemed disinclined to support Napoleon, who had taken his place as her hero.

During her Christmas visit, she had pinned several drawings of Napoleon to the wall, including two she had penned herself, a half dozen journal articles on his movements, as well as her own poems praising him. Reading her poetry now, she felt her face flush, realizing that her future as a poet was limited. However, her admiration of Napoleon was genuine. She had played it down in the carriage because admitting as much to Teodor would lend approval to his plan to leave home and join Napoleon's Polish legions. Her heart was with the thousands of Poles whose motto was, "God is with Napoleon and Napoleon is with us," but wasn't one brother enough?

Only a year apart, she and Teodor had always shared a bond—until schooling had set them on different paths. It was too late to hope for Benedykt's return, but perhaps Teodor could be persuaded to stay. With his help, they might rescue the estate together.

Marie awoke the next day to the clatter of hooves echoing in the courtyard below. Rubbing the sleep from her eyes, she heard muffled voices. Curiosity piqued, she slipped out of bed and went to the window. Below, a man in a fancy hunting costume dismounted with deliberate care and kissed her mother's hand. They stood chatting for several minutes.

A knock at her door broke her concentration. Before she could respond, Katarzyna burst in. "Oh, finally up, you old slugabed! We've had breakfast already. I wanted to wake you, but Mother said you needed your sleep."

"Ah, ha!" Marie laughed. "So you took your chance when Mother went out to meet that gentleman."

Katarzyna shrugged. "Gentleman?"

"Come to the window and look, Kasia."

"Who is that man?" Marie asked when Katarzyna joined her.

"Oh, him! That's Monseigneur Anastase, that's what Mother calls him. Count Anastase Walewski. Danusha says he's *very* rich. Do you remember him?"

"No—well, maybe, I'm not sure."

"Mother says he lives in a palace."

"How often does he visit?" Marie asked, feigning little interest.

"I don't know. Once or twice a week."

"Is he married?"

"His wife died."

"Indeed." Marie looked again, squinting, wishing for the type of spyglass Napoleon was known to use. "He looks older than Mother."

"He is, but don't mention it," Katarzyna said, turning to look up at Marie. "Honor did and nearly got slapped!"

"I heard that!" Honorata cried as she entered the room. "What are you two up to at the window?"

Marie laughed. "We're looking at Mother and her visitor. Kasia said you thought him old."

Honorata stepped closer to the window. "He is! Just look at those legs. They're like sticks, and don't let that pile of powdered hair fool you. Once, when he bent over some plant in Mother's garden, it slipped off. He's bald as an egg."

The three laughed. "It's a peruke," Marie said.

"A what?" Katarzyna asked.

"A peruke, Kasia. A wig."

As the day passed, her mother made no mention of her caller, and Marie's curiosity escalated.

Two days later, after breakfast, the visitor reappeared in the courtyard, and her mother suggested Marie meet him, employing that flinty expression that gave her little choice. Marie followed her mother out the front entrance and down the twelve steps.

The man bowed before them. "Two loveliest of ladies," he announced in a thin voice.

"Anastase," the countess said, 'this is Marie, my oldest daughter. Marie, this is Monseigneur Anastase Walewski."

After a curtsy, Marie observed the count greet her mother with the French kisses, *la bise*. After her mother followed suit, the count turned his attention to Marie. "So, this is the convent-schooled girl, come home with a basket of good manners and a headful of ideas, I expect." He bent to kiss her now and she froze. At school, she had been taught to turn her head to the left, offering up her right cheek, and much practice of *la bise* had gone on among the girls—often amidst giggling—but she had no kissing experience with men. And he was not in the league of men whom she imagined kissing. She had never envisioned a face as old as his coming at her.

The count managed his kisses with as much aplomb as one might expect in an awkward situation, and when Marie stood paralyzed, he rescued her from complete humiliation by pretending kisses were not expected in return. "What a lovely girl she's become, Eva," he said. "Just lovely."

The count proved his expertise at small talk, covering the weather, the quality of the road from his home to Kiernozia, and the likely engagement of his granddaughter. Marie nodded occasionally as she watched him speak with an air of self-admiration. For riding, he had worn the classic yellow boots of an officer, seeming at odds with the French-influenced dress of a courtier, including a blue frock coat and silk stockings that rose out of the boots. Honorata was correct: the man's legs had no definition at all. He was slight of frame although his tailor had fit him with precision. His gesturing with nearly every sentence called attention to his small, well-manicured hands. The blue coat set off the pale blue of his lively eyes. His features were noble, delicately so, and yet at the same time testimony to his years. Marie guessed he would not see his fifth decade again.

Finally, he whispered something to her mother before suggesting in a normal tone that she walk with him out to her herb garden. Marie was certain she had heard the word "loan" but was distracted when he turned to bid her farewell. Instead of cheek kisses, however, he took up her hand and kissed it. Marie breathed a sigh of relief.

The count smiled and said, "Marie, I now recall the last time I saw you. It was at church and you were holding one of your sisters in your arms. She was but a baby. You had two long braids."

"The baby would have been little Katarzyna," the countess said. "Our Kasia."

"Why, Eva," he said, without turning toward her, "I couldn't have guessed the transformation that would take place in your daughter." He paused, his gaze still fixed on Marie, then brought his boot heels together and said, "*Au revoir*, child."

"*Au revoir*," Marie said, excusing herself as she retreated into the house. *Transformation?* What did he expect? She had not yet turned eight at their first meeting. The thought amused her, but the idea that this man seemed interested in her mother was deeply unsettling. The prospect of her mother marrying again chilled her, as though a ghost had brushed past her.

Honorata called from the dining chamber, but Marie ignored her and headed for the stairs. In her room, she sank into her desk chair, breathless.

She recalled that brief encounter at her father's funeral when she held baby Kasia. She could feel her stomach clenching. The man had spoken while standing next to her father's coffin. She could remember none of what he said, only that he had talked for a very long time.

What did Count Anastase know of her father? Had he served in the volunteer corps that fought so desperately against the Russians? Was he at the Battle of Maciejowice when Poland lost everything in a devastating defeat? What sacrifices had he made, if any, to keep Poland in one piece?

At supper, her questions gnawed at her. After Danusha served the main course of stewed cabbage rolls, she turned to her mother, attempting nonchalance. "Is Monseigneur Anastase an important man?"

"Indeed, my dear," her mother replied, dabbing at her mouth with her napkin. "He was Chamberlain to the King, in the long-ago when we had a king."

"Really?"

"And, like your father, he is a governor of a province."

"A *starosta*? I see. I was wondering if perhaps he was at the Battle of Maciejowice with Father and with our tutor, Monsieur Chopin. But I suspect he was too old."

"Why do you seem to be critical of the count?" Her mother's tone became measured and serious. "In fact, Lord Anastase Walewski was Captain of the First Brigade of National Cavalry at that battle. If he appears a bit self-important to you, there are reasons for it."

"Mother—"

"So, despite his position at our once-upon-a-time Polish Court and his age, Marie, he returned home having done his duty."

Marie bit her lip, realizing she had misjudged him. That night at prayer, she reflected on the many young soldiers who, like her father, did not return home. She finished with prayers for the safety of her brothers Benedykt and Teodor.

3

THREE WEEKS PASSED, WITH THE count visiting twice weekly, engaging in lengthy conversations with the Countess Łączyńska, often in the courtyard, gardens, or the reception room. Marie kept her distance, observing their interactions in an attempt to discern the nature of their relationship.

One afternoon, as Marie passed the reception room, her mother called her in. "Monseigneur Anastase was just inquiring whether you danced, Marie," she said, nodding toward the count.

"Yes, I do. Or at least I make the effort, Monseigneur. The Countess Elżbieta Sobolewska taught us at school. We called her *Madame Eliza*."

"I know her mother, the Countess Grabowska," Marie's mother put in, motioning for her to sit.

"As do I," the count said. "The countess is a supreme hostess and gives the most wonderful balls. However, her son-in-law Walenty Sobolewski," he continued, turning to Marie, his tone darkening, "your friend's husband, signed to the Confederacy of Targowica and that was the beginning of the end for Poland. You might not know about that."

"I do know my history," Marie said, stiffening in her chair. "That was in 1792 and it invited Czarina Catherine to intervene in our politics."

"By Zeus, the nuns have done well by you, then."

"Even before school, Monseigneur, I knew that some magnates wanted the Third of May Constitution revoked because they were afraid of losing power. Monsieur Chopin was very upset about it."

"Oh, was he?" The count appeared intrigued.

"Monsieur Nicolas Chopin was a wonderful teacher, Anastase," the countess added. "It's a shame he didn't stay on. I—I am not in a position to hire another. Honorata and Katarzyna will have to rely on Marie for their history."

"And I'm certain she's most capable," the count said, smiling at Marie.

Marie had hoped the conversation would delve into Eliza's supposed connection to King Stanisław, but instead, it drifted to the count's social activities—his numerous parties, balls, and travels. Bored, Marie excused herself and went to find her sisters.

Later that night, after her sisters had gone to bed, the countess entered Marie's room. "Marie, Monseigneur Walewski has made a suggestion." She approached Marie, who sat at her desk.

"Yes?"

"He wants to arrange a dance at his residence in Walewice."

"Oh? He's invited you, of course, Mother."

"Well, yes, but the dance is for you, Marie."

"For me?" Stunned, Marie twisted in her chair to stare up at her mother. "Why would he do that?"

"Let me tell you, Marie. Monseigneur Anastase is a man-about-town, as you might have guessed. And he sees us struggling here and wants to do this nice thing for us. He was a friend of your father's, too, remember."

"And now, yours," Marie replied, sharper than she intended.

If her mother grasped the implication, she ignored it. "We'll have the most wonderful dress made for you."

"Mother, how can we afford it? Do you mean to say this is to be a ball?"

"Yes, and I'll find a way." Her mother smiled, eyes wide. "Marie, may I tell him you consent? It's to be your debut into society. You won't get another opportunity like this."

Marie shrugged and nodded, her mother's enthusiasm swaying her, but family duty carrying the heavier weight.

Monday, 11 July 1803

Marie stood on a stool in the middle of the shop belonging to French *modiste* Madame Simone, wearing the most beautiful dress she had ever seen. Just a week before, she had travelled with her mother and sisters to Sochaczew, the closest city to boast such a well-regarded dressmaker. They chose the fabric, style, and color for her ball gown. At the fitting today, Marie's mother and sisters encircled her like excited spectators at a festival.

The white gown was made of fine satin, draping to the floor under a gauzy over-dress. The neckline was rectangular, with gold satin banding cinched just beneath her breasts, with a wider banding at the hem. The fitted sleeves were short.

"Your choice of this pearl white, Madame Walewska, is perfect," Madame Simone said. "Its creamy tone complements your daughter's *flawless* alabaster complexion. I've never seen anything like it. A stark white would make her look washed out."

"She looks lovely, like a Greek column," the countess said in French. "However, isn't the neckline too revealing?"

"Oh, no. On the contrary, Madame," the dressmaker pronounced, "I have been most conservative while keeping with the times. I dress many ladies at Court, you know."

"This is Marie's first ball, you see, Madame Simone. She's been away at school, and I hadn't realized how she had blossomed."

"Still, Madame Łączyńska, this is the style." She raised an eyebrow. "So—maybe you wish for me to place a chemisette or ruffle at the neckline?"

While Marie caught the sarcasm, her mother fell into the trap. "Well, perhaps that would—"

"I recommend against it, Madame Łączyńska," the dressmaker snapped. "You don't wish Marie to appear *provincial*, do you?"

The countess sighed. "*Très bien, très bien. . . .*" Color came into her face. "Are the gloves and shawl ready?"

"No, Madame, the gloves, shawl, slippers, and reticule will all be ready the first of next week."

"Oh, Marie," Katarzyna said, "you will be beautiful! Perhaps at the ball you will fall in love."

"Don't talk nonsense, Katarzyna," the countess said.

"Things happen like that only in storybooks, Kasia," Marie put in.

"It's possible," Honorata muttered, delivering the last word.

For the shopping excursions to Sochaczew, Count Walewski had sent his own luxurious coach, replete with driver and two footmen. On the ride home, as Honorata and Katarzyna nodded off, Marie turned to her mother. "Why is Count Walewski doing this for me, Mother?"

"It's your coming-of-age celebration."

"But *why* is he taking it upon himself? Is it to please you?"

"I told you, he is quite the society person in Warsaw and longs for parties here in the countryside. It's a good deed to the family, Marie. He respected your father's sacrifice for Poland."

"So, will he throw balls for Honor and Kasia one day?"

"It's unlikely," her mother whispered. "Don't put nonsense like that in their heads."

"Why should he bother with me, then? And why can't Kasia attend?"

"Because she's only nine, that's why," the countess said, a smile not quite masking her agitation. "Balls are for adults. Did Honorata ask you to teach her two or three of the dances?"

"She did." Marie sat taller, her shoulders pressing into the bench's backrest. Her mother often called her *child*, but her words now implied that both she and Honorata were transitioning into adulthood. Marie savored the moment, pressing her lips together to keep from smiling.

Her mother had sidestepped her question about the count's motivations for hosting the ball. Marie suspected it was a gesture intended to win her mother's favor, as he seemed quite taken with her. Before she could press further, the carriage lurched when it struck a pothole, and Katarzyna stirred, blue eyes going wide. "Are we home yet?"

4

Saturday, 16 July 1803

WITH HALF OF AN HOUR to spare before the arrival of Count Walewski's carriage, Marie stood dressed for the ball in front of her mother's tall mirror that the groom Emeryk had hauled into her bedchamber at her mother's order. Madame Simone had finished everything on time; the slippers matched the gold banding beneath the breasts and at the hem, as did the bandeaux placed above her bangs to hold her coiffure in place. The gloves, shawl, and reticule were of a Pomona green, striking against the white gown. The sandalwood fan unfolded to reveal a motif of tiny pale-yellow primroses. She smiled to herself as she recalled how Eliza had told the class—with demonstrations— how the fan was used to do more than cool oneself. Women used them to shield their mouths when chatting with one another, flirting, or hiding a blush. "It's a prop," she said, "and you should make use of it!"

If only Eliza could attend the ball, Marie thought. But her mother said they couldn't invite anyone because they were not asked to supply a guest list. And Marie knew better than to mention Amelia. Such an event, her mother would counsel, was not meant for the daughter of a village butcher.

Someone knocked lightly at the chamber door. "Marie, are you ready?" It was Honorata. "May I see you? I want to see your dress."

Glad that she had bolted the door, Marie said, "Not now, Honor. I'll be down in time for the carriage."

"Oh, please, Marysia!" Kasia chimed in, rattling the door handle.

"No!" Marie cried. "Now, go away!"

"Are you all right?" Hororata asked. "Shall I have Mother come up?"

"No! —I'm fine, really!"

Her sisters' voices became muffled, and a minute later she heard their retreating footsteps.

She dropped into her desk chair. I should be happy and excited like they are, she thought, her fingers skimming along the desktop. She missed her father. During her three years away, she had learned to set aside her grief. But now, at this significant event in her life, a ball in her honor, she felt empty and unanchored. She wanted him here. What would he think of this occasion? Why, she pondered, must people die when you need them most?

Guilt accompanied her sadness. Each year her memories of her father faded. She fought to keep his face and voice vivid in her mind but feared one day they would be lost. She longed to cry, to feel the release tears would give her.

Her eyes drifted to the drawers of her desk, resting on the bottom one, untouched since the week after his funeral. Her heart accelerating, she leaned over, grasped the handle, and tugged. The deep drawer groaned as if in protest.

There lay the doll she had insisted her father buy that day in Warsaw's Market Square. The glassy blue eyes beneath the real blonde hair stared up at her as if from a casket.

Marie recalled placing it there the same day her mother had told her why her father had resisted buying it for her.

On that day, Countess Łączyńska had been sitting on the bed attempting to comfort Marie, who had been experiencing what the family physician, Doctor Fabianski, called *melancholia*. She lay in bed for days after the funeral, curled up, as if in pain and often bathed in tears. She would soon turn eight years old, and her father would not be there.

After a while, when Marie refused to come to the dining chamber for supper, her mother lost patience. "Very well, Marie. Stay here if you must. You are not serving your father's memory well. I'm going downstairs."

Marie felt her mother rise from the bed, but then movement stopped. Lifting her head from the tear-soaked pillow, Marie turned to see that her mother was staring at the doll, which stood on the bedside table, as if in a place of honor.

The countess pivoted toward the door but turned back to the doll, sighed, and faced Marie. "Your father told me he asked you to choose another doll, but you had made it impossible for him to deny you this one. Do you know *why* he disapproved of it?"

Marie stared through bleary eyes. "No, Mother."

Her mother went on to tell her the doll's image was that of a Russian noblewoman, namely that of Czarina Catherine. Marie was stunned. The doll represented everything her father despised. No wonder he had tried to dissuade her. Her stomach clenched. She was overcome with shame.

Her first inclination then was to destroy the doll. But to do so would destroy the memory of that magical day with her father. With great care, she placed the doll in the drawer, never opening it until now, yet never forgetting it was there.

"Marie!" the countess called from below, jolting her from the past. "The carriage has arrived."

Taking a deep breath, Marie pushed the drawer closed and stood, her gaze taking in the drawing of her father above the desk. "I'll make you proud, Papa," she whispered. "I promise."

"Marie!" the countess called.

As she descended the staircase, her gloved hand cautiously gliding along the railing, everyone looked up, high feminine voices making much of her appearance.

Danusha was adjusting Honorata's sky-blue gown with ivory bands beneath the immature breasts and at the hem. It had been one of her mother's, made over for the thirteen-year-old. "Oh, Marie, you are stepping out of a fairytale."

"She is lovely," the countess said, her own gown of deep blue featuring a short train that would be pinned up for dancing. Her eyes narrowed. "The bangs curled nicely, but the spiraling wisps at your ears need attention. We'll see to it in the coach."

"But it's the style, Mother," Marie countered. "They're meant to be askew."

"Oh, Marie," Honorata whispered, "you are a vision."

Marie smiled and hugged her sister. "And you, as well, Honor. Imagine what a pair we shall make standing like columns against the wall."

Everyone laughed, except for Katarzyna, who had been staring open-mouthed at Marie. "Oh, Marie," she cried now, "you are going to fall in love tonight! You will. I—I know it!"

The others laughed again. "Danusha," the countess said, "take the little fortune teller in hand and make sure she keeps to her bedtime."

Marie barely spoke on the drive, letting her mother tame the wild spirals that were brought forward at her pearl earrings. In less than an hour, the carriage trundled along the gravel lane leading to the count's residence, joining a queue of arriving vehicles. The crisp June air carried the fragrant scent of the blooming linden trees lining each side of the road. "Ah!" the countess exclaimed, drawing in a deep breath, "The linden flowers are in bloom. How delightful! They smell like clover and honey."

"Oh, look!" Honorata leaned toward the window. "I see the palace—it's so big!"

As they approached the Walewski residence, Marie held her curiosity in check until the carriage navigated the semicircular drive fronting the massive limestone façade. The count's estate, Walewice, the largest in the province, was named for him, as was the nearby village, one of a number he owned.

Traditionally, the columned portico of a noble's home, whether of magnate or *szlachta* status, symbolized Polish hospitality. As she was handed down from the coach by a footman in fancy livery, Marie blinked at the grand pedimented portico, suppressing a gasp.

"Come girls," the countess said once they had all alighted from the coach. She lowered her voice. "Now remember, your partners might remove their gloves before a dance, but ladies do not. Gloves are a part of your ensemble." They ascended the steps to the portico and moved into the colonnaded hall, ablaze with a thousand candles and echoing with the sounds of conversation and an orchestra warming up.

Marie took notice of Count Walewski, who was approaching, wearing what she assumed had been his formal attire as Chancellor to the King. Over a white *zupon* the crimson *kontusz* draped beautifully, from the golden epaulettes to the yellow boots. A wide blue ribbon hung from his right shoulder to his left hip, and a gold embroidered sash of Turkish design secured the robe at the waist.

"Ah!" the count exclaimed. "Our guests of honor!" He bowed to each of the Łączyńska ladies and doffed his cap, a white, four-cornered, fur-banded affair. He saved Marie for last. As he stood, he snapped his fingers at a nearby servant in red and white, who hurried forth with a huge bouquet of pink sweetheart roses. The count took the bouquet and offered it to Marie.

Feeling the heat of a blush, Marie thanked him, her eyes rising from the pink of the roses to the pink of his polished pate. He had not worn his peruke.

"Madame Eva, I beg that you lead the Polonez with me? My guests are excited to take to the floor and are waiting for the opening dance."

The countess nodded and as the two walked toward the dance floor in the next chamber, Marie looked to Honorata, who put her fan to her face. "Bald as an egg," she said, giggling. "You see, Marie, I told you!"

Marie cast a sidelong glance at her sister, whose eyes above the fan were crinkled in amusement. She laughed, reminded of Eliza's lesson about the use of fans.

Honorata took Marie's hand and led her into the crowded ballroom. The heat was stifling so that the fan's original purpose was now employed.

The moderate, stately strains of the Polonez, Poland's national dance, filled the air. Count Walewski and Countess Eva Łączyńska led the line of couples, hand in hand, his face radiating satisfaction, hers serene. Marie imagined her mother as she must have appeared, years before, with a beau at her side: graceful, hopeful, and young. On her left, the count moved with precision, his narrow shoulders squared, chin held high. Marie, who had thought the Polonez the least demanding of the dances she had learned at school—finding it boring—now straightened up, trying to see past the feathered ornament adorning the woman in front of her. The dance was transforming before her.

No longer dull, the Polonez seemed to come alive. The couples, resplendent in their uniforms and elaborate gowns, glided in perfect synchrony, taking three walking steps to a measure—the first with a subtle dip—their linked hands held forward, gazes fixed ahead. Couples were smiling, some exchanging quiet words. As the procession unfolded, a second ring of couples began to enclose the first, adding to the visual display. The steady pulse of the rhythm carried the dancers forward, with the muted tapping of the men's boot heels on wood providing a delicate counterpoint to the melody. Choreography shifted as one line of couples gracefully turned, forming bridges for the others to move beneath.

At last, music and motion drew to an end, with the lead couple taking the middle of the floor, the dance complete.

"Welcome, All!" the count announced in his thin, forced voice. "My lovely partner is Madame Eva Łączyńska, widow of the war hero Mateusz Łączyński. Her daughter is just as lovely and is here tonight to celebrate her first ball. He turned his head toward the Łączyńska sisters. "Will the beautiful Mademoiselle Marie step forward?"

Marie froze. She had begged her mother to tell the count not to make a fuss over her, and now he was doing just that. She couldn't move.

"Marie, this ball is for you," the count persisted. "Do allow us just a moment to say hello."

Her fan to her face, Honorata hissed: "Go, now, Marie—go!"

The crowd quieted, expectant. Marie wanted to turn and run, but her mother's slow nod urged her to obey the count. What felt like an honor now felt like a burden. Her breathing quickened. She felt faint.

Through a haze, she heard the count making another plea. Just then, the feathered woman in front of her turned sideways to gawk at her, and Honorata seized the chance to push Marie through the breach and onto the dance floor. She bumped into a gentleman who took her hand and led her through the inner ring of couples, leaving her in the middle of the floor, some ten feet from the count and her mother.

"Ah, here she is, my friends—Mademoiselle Marie Łączyńska! She has just completed her education at the Convent of Our Lady of the Assumption. This is her first ball! May there be many in her lifetime!"

The crowd applauded and a buzz of conversation made the rounds.

Marie's immediate fear was that the count would call her to his side. Without daring to look at him, she forced a smile, curtsied perfectly, and pivoted, passing through the double lines of couples. She reached for Honorata's hand and tried to pull her toward the chamber door. "Come with me."

Honorata resisted. "No, Marysia, what's the matter with you? I want to watch the dancing. —Oh, listen! It's a Mazurka. How wonderful!"

Marie stayed with her sister, holding fast to her hand, and her pulse slowed. She watched as Count Walewski led his mother around the floor.

Honorata spoke from behind her fan. "Did you mean to run away? You told me they taught you all the dances at school, didn't you?"

"I did," Marie admitted, conveniently omitting the fact that all the practice dances had been with other female classmates as partners. She trembled to think of dancing with one of the men in the large hall, men of every age and size who now had been alerted to her presence by the count.

Just then, a slight young man in the blue Collegium Nobilium uniform approached, his sharp blue eyes on Marie. He bowed to her, and then, almost as an afterthought, to Honorata. His gaze returned to Marie. "Forgive me," he said, smiling. "I feel as if you've been introduced since the ball is in your honor, Mademoiselle Marie. I'm Karol."

Marie nodded. "I'm happy to meet you, Karol. This is my sister, Honorata."

Another bow. "A pleasure, Mademoiselle Honorata."

Honorata blushed and managed a curtsy.

The student smiled and turned back to Marie. "Now, if I am not being too bold, would you care to take the next dance with me?"

Marie nodded, knowing she would be expected to dance, and for a partner she could do worse. When the orchestra began a waltz, her heart lifted. They stepped onto the dance floor, and after a brief awkwardness, began to follow the music with fluidity and grace. Relaxing, Marie returned Karol's smile and enjoyed herself.

At the end of the dance, Karol suggested they get punch.

Marie glanced over to where she had left Honorata, but she was no longer there. Lacking an excuse to decline, she agreed.

As they waited in line, Karol said, "You dance very well."

"I can say the same for you."

Karol laughed. "At school, we have only other males to learn with. I can tell you that you're lighter on your feet than they are."

Marie laughed, too, keeping her own dance history to herself. "My brother is a student at the Collegium Nobilium, also. Might you know Teodor Łączyński?"

"I don't."

After receiving punch cups, they turned back to the dance floor. Marie noticed her mother across the way. She was in the hand of Count Walewska as they joined the other dancers in the fast tempo of an Oberek. "Look!" Marie said, her breath catching in surprise. "See how quickly my mother and the count are moving, spinning as if they were young. And the count must be hot with all those heavy robes of his chamberlain's office."

"The count is very limber. Look at that spin! But I must correct you, Mademoiselle Marie. Those are not his chamberlain robes."

"No?"

"No. Those are his official robes as Starosta of Warka. With all the foreign influence within Poland these days, former members of the Sejm and other officials feel they have to occasionally trot out their old traditional robes. His choice surprised me because in Warsaw he's very cosmopolitan and dressed by a French *mercier*. You know—patent leather pumps, silk stockings, ruffles, and the fancy frock coat."

"Really?"

"Yes. There is one advantage to wearing his old *kontusz*."

He was baiting her. "And, what is that?"

"It covers his legs. In his French stockings you can see that he is rather bow-legged." He laughed.

He expects me to laugh, as well, Marie thought. And yet she couldn't.

Karol colored, seeming embarrassed. "Of course, you know what they say about bow-legged men." Karol didn't wait for a reply. "They say a bow-legged man has probably done good service to his country and king through his horsemanship."

"I see." Marie watched as the dance came to an end.

"Well, it looks as if they are staying on the floor. He has yet to change partners. I wonder if he isn't taken by your mother."

Marie drew in a breath. He had just validated her thought. The idea that someone might wish to take her father's place was new, unnerving, and unwelcome. "Do you think so?"

"Who knows? He's had two wives, but I don't count him out."

"You know him personally, I take it?"

Karol turned to Marie. "I'm so sorry, Mademoiselle Marie. I assumed that you knew. I've made *bigos* of our meeting. How stupid of me! The count is my grandfather."

Marie froze. "Your grandfather?" The urge to raise her fan came too late to hide her astonishment.

"Yes," Karol said, eyes widening at her reaction. "I'm sorry. I should have told you at the outset. Everyone says I'm his young twin. Silly, but that's what they say." He turned to watch the dancers as the music came to a close.

Marie studied Karol. It was true. Both were of medium height, lean, and shared similar facial features—quick blue eyes and an aristocratic nose, but the years between them obscured their familial link.

As the orchestra stopped, Karol turned to her. "I'm terribly sorry, Mademoiselle Marie, but I must leave. I'm overdue back at school, but I'm glad Grandfather insisted I stay to meet you. I'm certain we will meet again." He bowed formally. "May I escort you back to your sister?"

Marie blinked back her surprise at his sudden leave-taking. "No, Karol, that will not be necessary."

Karol set his cup down on the serving table. "I'll be off, then." His boots came together and he bowed again. Turning, he strode across a floor crowded with motionless couples anticipating the next dance. Marie was left to wonder if she had made him feel awkward—and whether his grandfather was plotting a future union for Karol and her.

And then it struck her anew: *Grandfather!*

5

"It's not fair," Honorata whispered to Marie. They stood watching the dancers from a recessed area behind the punch table.

"What isn't fair?"

Honorata snapped her fan closed. "That once that student left, you've danced nearly every dance with a different partner."

"You've danced, too."

"Three times only—and I'm certain Mother sent them over. Oh, I'm hopeless."

"Just enjoy yourself, Honor. Your time will come."

"Now, tell me, did you like him?"

"The student? He was nice."

"Really?" Honorata brought her fan to her face. "But did you *like* him?"

"No, not in the way you mean." Marie nodded to her mother and the count out on the floor. "Honor, do you suppose Count Walewski *likes* Mother?"

"What? I—I don't know."

"What if he does?" Marie pressed. "Would that suit you?"

Honorata raised her eyebrows and turned to Marie with a questioning gaze. "It might mean that we could live in his palace and be done with bats. — What about you?"

"I don't know, Honor." Marie played the fan game now. "That student you asked about, Karol—he's the count's grandson."

"Grandson?" Honorata gasped.

"Has Mother mentioned the count's age?"

"No, but you have another admirer. There—across the floor. The handsome soldier with the reddish-brown hair."

"A soldier?"

"Yes, a *real* soldier with medals and everything!"

"What makes you think—"

"He's looking right at you, Marie. He'll come over when this waltz ends. Just watch."

Marie tried to look away but found her gaze drawn to the clean-shaven soldier in a deep navy uniform with gold epaulettes and a wide red sash. "He's staring at us," she said.

"He's staring at *you*, Marie."

"How do you know that?"

Honorata clucked her tongue. "Because you are the beauty of the family, that's why. My nose isn't straight and my hair won't curl. I'd be lucky to find a blind man for a husband. No, you're the golden child. Mother said Father called you that. You told me so yourself."

It was true, but Marie regretted repeating it to Honorata, especially given her sister's self-deprecation. "Believe me, Honor, you will have your admirers."

"The music is winding down," Honorata said. "When he starts across the floor, I'll go out for some air."

"You will not! Honor—Oh! Sweet Jesus, he *is* coming this way." Marie turned to grab her sister's arm, but she was already gone.

Suddenly, the soldier stood before her, bowing and introducing himself. His heart-shaped face and mesmerizing smile made it hard for her to catch his name—did he say *Prince of Italy*? That he didn't look Italian puzzled her. His French was flawless, save for the hint of an accent she couldn't place.

"I am Marie Łączyńska," she said. "Forgive me, I missed your name."

"Just call me Arkady."

Marie nodded, unfamiliar with the name.

Just then, her mother and Count Walewski appeared. "Arkady," the count exclaimed in a stage tone, "You're a naughty houseguest. I would have introduced you, had you waited. That's the way things are done here, you know. —Isn't Mademoiselle Marie lovely?"

The soldier blinked in surprise, a frown fleeting across his face at the interruption. He nodded. "She is, indeed."

"And before you get any ideas, Arkady, allow me to introduce Marie's mother, Madame Łączyńska."

Arkady clicked his heels and bowed. "Enchanted, Madame Łączyńska."

Marie took notice of his auburn hair, cropped at the back and neatly styled forward.

Clearly impressed by his manner, her mother offered him a generous smile.

Marie's smile disguised both her annoyance at the count's intrusion and sympathy for Arkady, whose confident posture seemed to wilt under the count's inquiry.

The count's chest lifted as if he was about to deliver another pronouncement, but Marie interjected, "If you will excuse us, Monseigneur Walewski, I've promised this dance to Arkady." Nodding at the count and her mother, she took the soldier's hand, and led him away, momentarily catching a glimpse of the count's astonished expression.

At the edge of the dance floor, Marie looked up at Arkady. "It's a waltz," she said.

"For which I am most grateful. I can manage a waltz, but it's already started. How do we join in?"

"I think we look for an opening and blend in. In a waltz, each partner watches out for the other. If a collision seems likely, you tap the other person on the shoulder."

"Perfect! And thank you for looking out for me, Mademoiselle Marie." Arkady nodded toward Count Walewski.

Marie laughed. "Sometimes you need more than a tap."

Arkady chuckled, blue eyes sparkling. "You're quick. —Shall we dance?"

By the end of the waltz, Marie felt relaxed, and Arkady appeared more confident. When the strains of a Polish dance began, however, he said, "I'm afraid I must withdraw from the field on this one."

"It's not a hard dance, Arkady. It's a *Kujawiak*. It's named for a region to the north, Kujawy."

"Just the same, I—"

"I'm told it's becoming popular all over. You'll have to learn it sooner or later, or people will consider you boorish."

Arkady laughed. "Will they?"

"Of course! It's simple and calm with some spinning I'll teach you, but no sudden tempo changes."

"Very well, Mademoiselle, I yield!"

"Good!" Marie took his hand, surprised at her own boldness in teaching a foreign soldier—especially one whose ribbons and medals suggested weighty accomplishments.

After the Kujawiak, Arkady said, "Thank you, Mademoiselle Marie. The count showed me his terrace this afternoon with its lovely view of his back acreage. Would you care to see it?"

Marie's heart caught. "It's very dark out."

"But there is a moon, Mademoiselle."

"Well, I should—"

"You're safe with me. Others will be out taking in the fresh air, as well."

He'd read her hesitancy. Unwilling to appear fearful—or provincial, Marie nodded.

Arkady took her hand and they moved through the crowd toward the terrace doors.

The sultry night air was cooler by comparison to that of the ballroom. The terrace had twin staircases at each end leading down, past female mythological statues glowing white in the moonlight, to a body of water banked by shrubbery and shadowy trees.

Only one other couple stood on the far end of the terrace, speaking in low tones. Romantic tones, Marie thought.

"See how the moon is reflected on the water," Arkady said, leaning on the stone balustrade. "Is that a tributary of the Vistula?"

"I think it's a pond. It's still. The count mentioned having one on his property. If it were a tributary, it would be from the River Bzura, which feeds into the Vistula."

"A pond! I'll wager you're correct. You know your geography. Did you learn that at your convent school?"

Marie laughed. "Yes, but our family French tutor ensured we learn Poland's landscape, especially here in the central region."

"He must be why your French is so perfect."

Marie shrugged, casting him a sidelong look. "You're not French, are you?"

"Is my French really so bad?" he teased.

"Oh no, I didn't mean to imply that."

Laughing, Arkady turned his gaze toward the moonlit water.

Marie had meant to ferret out his nationality, hesitating to ask him outright because Eliza had advised her against discussing such matters in social settings. Instead, she asked, "How well do you know Count Walewski?"

"Not at all, Mademoiselle. You see, I was traveling from the west toward Warsaw when my carriage broke down nearby with a shattered wheel. The count chanced to pass by and took mercy on me, insisting I stay a few days while the carriage is being repaired."

"How fortunate."

"Indeed!" His eyes narrowed, carrying a forward intensity she found unnerving.

"When do you leave?" she asked, suddenly self-conscious of her own boldness.

"I plan to leave tomorrow, provided the carriage is fixed. The roads are easier on Sundays. However, the count has suggested I stay a bit longer. He wants to show me his parkland and his villages."

How like him, Marie thought. "Does he own many?"

"Some forty, he says."

"So," Marie countered, "about thirty, I'd wager." She stifled a smile.

Arkady's eyes widened in astonishment, and when he caught her expression, he let loose the laugh of a tenor, melodious and infectious. "I see the nuns teach subtraction."

Marie laughed. "Only in certain situations." She felt proud to entertain this handsome soldier, recalling the kind of humor that got her in trouble at school. "And so—will you?"

"Will I?"

"Delay your journey to Warsaw." She doubted that Warsaw was his final destination. His native tongue was not Polish—but she was certain she had heard a similar accent before but couldn't remember the situation.

"I'll decide tomorrow."

As they chatted, the music within the ballroom flowed and ebbed. Arkady asked about her family, and she provided concise descriptions, avoiding mention of Benedykt and his military service for the French. While she was not free to speak in the presence of strangers about Poles gone over to Napoleon's side, she did tell him of her father's patriotism and death. Arkady took her hand in both of his and expressed his condolences. She passed lightly over the nature of his death and made no mention of her fondness for Napoleon Bonaparte.

When Arkady seemed out of questions, she asked, "Do you have brothers or sisters?"

He stiffened slightly, looking out at the water. "I do. A sister."

"What's her name?"

"Natalia. She's nine years older. See there, another couple is down near the water. Would you care to go down?"

Marie shook her head. Another *couple*. It was the first time she had been referred to in those words. "I should go in, Arkady."

"Take my arm, then."

They entered the ballroom in time for Count Walewski to announce the final dance—a waltz.

"We must dance this one, Marie," Arkady said. "May I call you that?" Without waiting for an answer, he added, "How fortuitous. We begin and end with a waltz."

For the first time, Marie gave herself over to the music, forgetting to count steps and to worry over onlookers' opinions. In Arkady's arms, she felt confident and poised. Their movements were fluid and faultless. The faces of the other dancers became blurred. Eliza had told her that in the spell of a perfect waltz she would feel nothing else. She would find herself "transfixed in time."

As the dance concluded, Marie felt as if awakening from a trance. "I—I must find my mother and sister," she stammered. Just two hours earlier, Arkady had been a stranger, so the sudden closeness she felt caught her off guard.

Wordlessly, Arkady offered his arm, and they walked into the colonnaded entrance hall, where her mother and Honorata stood near Count Walewski, who was bidding goodbye to his guests.

"Where have you been, Marie?" her mother asked, her lilting tone not quite masking a sharper edge.

"We went out on the terrace for a breath of air," Marie said, noticing her sister's smug smile.

"It was my fault," Arkady said. "I'm afraid I kept her in conversation with a barrage of questions."

"I see," the countess said, her smile tight.

"Ah! Here is the lost one!" the count exclaimed, breaking into the group, positioning himself between Marie and Arkady. "We thought the guest of honor had walked home." He turned to Marie, winked, and asked her opinion about the orchestra and refreshments. As she assured him everything was perfect, she noticed Arkady lean toward her mother and whisper something that made her eyes widen.

When the count finally accepted Marie's spirited assessment of the ball's success, he announced that he would escort them to the carriage.

"Then, this is goodbye," Arkady said. He kissed the hands of the Łączyńska women, lingering over Marie's hand, his vivid blue eyes locked onto hers—until the count disengaged them by taking Marie's other hand and directing her to fall in step with her mother and sister.

Outside, Marie pleased her mother by offering additional heartfelt praise to the count for the evening. Despite enduring his insufferable cheek kisses, made all the more repellent by the sourness of his brandied breath, she knew this night would linger in her memory a very long time. A footman assisted her into the coach, and as they settled in, she imagined Arkady's name would grace a few pages of the diary she had begun at school. With time, both the evening and Arkady's charm would fade from memory, like the final strains of the last waltz. But the experience, the perfect moment in time, would remain preserved for her to read and revisit.

"Well," Honorata exclaimed, once the carriage had moved away from the palace lights, "what did you think of Arkady, Marysia? Tell us!"

"Hush, Honorata," the countess said.

"I want to know, Mother. She liked him better than that student. Didn't you, Marie? Will you write to him?"

"No, Honor, I won't write to him."

"Why? Why not?"

"Stop it, Honorata," the countess warned.

The coach was dark so that Marie could barely see her mother and sister across from her.

Honorata started to speak but suddenly went silent. Marie suspected her mother had pinched her. It was her way, sometimes.

"Mother?" Marie asked.

"Yes?" The countess's voice came as if disembodied.

"What did Arkady say to you?"

A long silence ensued. Marie wondered whether she had fallen asleep.

"Mother?" Marie pressed.

Her mother sighed. "The young soldier asked if he could come to Kiernozia tomorrow."

Marie exhaled sharply. Her heart raced. "He—he did?"

No response.

"What did you say?" Marie asked.

Another silence.

"Mother, what did you say?"

"I don't recall, exactly. He took me by surprise."

Marie looked toward the dark window and said in a quiet, halting voice, "You—you didn't forbid him, then?"

"No, Marie, I did not."

6

Sunday, 17 July 1803

IN THE MORNING, MARIE SAT at her desk, adjusting her upswept hairstyle in a small mirror when Katarzyna burst into the bedchamber. "Marysia, we're going to church in style. Now I'll get to ride in the fancy coach, too!"

"What do you mean, Kasia?"

"The count is here to take us to church. He quite surprised Mother."

"I imagine he did."

"It'll surprise everyone at our little church, even Father Albin."

"Kasia—did he bring anyone with him?"

"No—should he have?"

Marie hid her disappointment. "I just wondered."

As they processed into the church, the presence of Count Walewski with the widowed Countess Łączyńska on his arm caused a stir among the villagers. Marie noticed Amelia and her mother. Amelia waved, her face registering surprise at the escort, while her wide-eyed mother stared, fingers at her lips.

The count had worn his French attire, topped with a closely cropped peruke with a red ribbon holding its queue. He sat next to the countess in the first pew of Kiernozia's little church, one that had been saved for the Łączyński family since Mateusz Łączyński was named Starosta of Gostyń. His death as a patriot in battle ensured the family's honor for years to come.

At the far end of the pew, Marie leaned forward during the service to steal glances at her mother and the count.

She noticed him whispering to her mother now and then, to which the countess responded with a nod or single word.

After a restless night, Marie's feelings had crystallized: she disliked the idea of her mother marrying this older man, despite his wealth, even though it might rescue their estate from poverty. He could never replace her father. How dare he even think so! Oh, it was more than the pretentious clothing, bald head, or predilection to boast and pontificate. She imagined him commanding troops from atop his horse at the Battle of Maciejowice, while her father died attempting to carry a wounded soldier to safety. She felt guilty for being unfair, yet it stung that the count had come through unscathed. Her stomach clenching, she leaned forward again to take another look.

Katarzyna, sitting next to her, noticed. "What are you staring at, Marie?" she whispered.

"Never mind—it's my business," Marie hissed. Turning her gaze to the back of the priest, who chanted as he raised the chalice at the Offertory, the heat of anger and helplessness flushed through her, mingling with guilt for knowing she was wrong. Still, she reasoned that if the count was pursuing their mother seriously, it affected her and her siblings, too.

Outside, after the recessional, Marie was waiting for the count and her mother to finish chatting with the priest when someone touched her elbow. She turned to find her friend Amelia.

"Well," Amelia said, her green eyes round as coins, "you have made an entrance for yourself, have you not?"

Marie laughed. "The count insisted on driving us."

"I'm referring to last night."

"The ball? You mean word has gotten around already?"

Amelia shrugged. "Several in the parish work for the count, so the talk doesn't have a chance to get stale. —So, what was it like? To finally dance with men instead of school mates at convent school?"

"Oh! It was thrilling, Amelia. I was beyond thankful for those classes."

"Marie!" the Countess Łączyńska called.

"I have to go, Amelia. I think Mother wants me to say hello to the priest."

"Oh!" Amelia cried, tilting her chin down and frowning.

"I'll write to you with all the details."

"Promise?"

"Yes, and don't think our adventures together have ended." Marie reached out and embraced her friend. "There will be more."

On the return trip, Marie's mother suggested to the count that he stay for the afternoon.

"Ah, I'm afraid I can stay only a short while. My houseguest is leaving this afternoon and I should see him off." The count's eyes fixed on Marie as if with some purpose.

"You mean the young soldier?" her mother inquired.

"Yes, I thought he might stay longer, a week or so, but I suppose it is too provincial here for him."

Marie, seated on the opposite bench, her sisters on either side, forced a smile even as she felt a tightening of her chest. Arkady would not come calling. Sensing that he was watching her again, she looked toward the window and out at the passing countryside. The count was correct, Marie thought. *Central Poland is provincial. And so am I.*

It was all she could do to keep her tears at bay. She consoled herself with the knowledge that the ride was short and that the precocious Kasia was in a chattering mood.

Once the church party had alighted from the coach at the Łączyński portico, the driver directed the carriage toward the stable, where he would await the count's return to Walewice.

No sooner had it pulled away than a huge jet-black horse bearing a rider wearing a top hat came galloping through the wide wrought iron gates, slowing only slightly before approaching the stunned group, at which point the horseman pulled tightly on the reins. The huge stallion reared up, then settled and came to a halt, snorting and proudly tossing his head as the rider swung one leg over the animal and dropped to the ground.

Marie blinked. She thought she was seeing things, or wishing them into existence.

Arkady doffed his hat and bowed before her mother. "Madame Łączyńska, pardon my abrupt arrival." He smiled, blue eyes coruscating in the sunlight. "You have my sincerest appreciation."

In a tone more dutiful than supportive, Count Walewski welcomed Arkady and introduced him to Katarzyna before turning to Honorata and Marie. "And you met this lovely pair last night."

"I did, indeed!" Arkady said with a forward confidence.

Marie watched him bow, stunned all at once by three things: his arrival, his clothing, all French tailoring instead of a uniform, and his greeting to her mother. Had she extended an invitation to him? Is that what he meant by his *appreciation*?

"Am I to understand," the count asked Arkady, "that you are not leaving today?"

Arkady bowed toward the count and brought his boot heels together. "No, sir, I could not pass up your invitation to stay a while."

The count's stance stiffened. He tilted his head but did not reply.

"Let's go in now," her mother said. "The house is cooler than here in the sun. Danusha is orchestrating a meal that should be on the table in an hour."

"Countess Łączyńska," Arkady said, "May I take my horse to your stable?"

"Of course," the countess said before turning to Marie. "Show him the way, will you, Marie?"

"Yes, Mother." Heart quickening, she took a deep breath and moved toward Arkady. What she had thought was a single romantic encounter to be recorded in her diary and forgotten might indeed be something more than that, or so she dared to think.

"You seemed surprised, Marie," Arkady said as they walked. He led the heavy-bodied black horse on his left. Marie walked on his right.

"I thought you would be on your way to Warsaw."

"So did Count Walewski. I changed my mind only this morning. I could use the rest." Arkady sighed.

"Don't you have business in Warsaw?"

"Nothing that can't be put off."

The mystery continues, Marie thought. Where is his home? Is he avoiding talk of his homeland? "Your uniform—"

"Ah, yes. I wanted people to see I am more than a man in a costume."

"A uniform is more than that. It speaks volumes. For you. For your country."

"Too much, perhaps."

"What do you mean?"

"Never mind. I just wanted to show off my new clothes."

"Ah, here is our groom," Marie said as they came to the front of the stable. Emeryk's eyes widened at the sight of the horse.

"It belongs to Count Walewski," Arkady warned Emeryk, "so take good care of him. He's a Silesian. His name is Mars."

"Yes, Milord." Emeryk said. "I've not seen the count ride this champion before."

Outside, Arkady turned to Marie. "Between you and me, I think he's a bit spirited for the count these days. Marie, must we go straight back to the house? Your mother said we had an hour."

"We can walk a bit. —Last night, did Mother invite you to visit?"

"You might say so."

Very cryptic, Marie thought. "It's this way to Mother's garden, if you care to have a look."

"I'd like that."

As they walked through the herb garden, Marie noticed it was poorly tended, overrun with weeds. The toll of the staff reduction was visible; she resolved to revitalize it, hopefully with her sisters' help.

They continued through the beds of chickpeas, celery, carrots, onions, and garlic, chatting—at Arkady's urging—about Marie's favorite dishes and the herbs and vegetables that flavored them. "The onions and garlic are necessary for *bigos*," Marie said, glancing up at Arkady, who looked puzzled.

"It's a Hunter's Stew," she said.

"Oh!" His face lit up. Marie knew at once he hadn't spent much time in Poland. "It's quite delicious," Marie continued. "My sisters and I will spend a day hunting for the perfect mushrooms for the stew. It's Benedykt's favorite. He always pleads for second helpings. I doubt he's found *bigos* in Paris."

"Benedykt? —The student?"

"No, that's Teodor." Marie's stomach tightened. She had avoided telling him about Benedykt, who, like so many other students, had left an occupied Poland to enlist with Napoleon. One had to be careful, and she had been stupidly careless.

"So, you have another brother."

"Benedykt is the oldest. He's twenty-four."

"And he's in Paris?"

"Yes," Marie said. She wished she could retract her answers, but the damage was done.

"Paris?" Arkady asked, tilting his head. "What is a young Pole doing in Paris?"

"Probably falling in love," Marie said on impulse. "They say it's the city of love, you know."

"It's also a city for those who follow Napoleon. He attended school here in Poland, didn't he?"

"Yes," Marie answered after a pause. His tone was conversational, but Marie sensed his probing nature. Poles who enlisted with Napoleon were the pride of a Poland occupied by three countries, but families kept silent about it. "You know," she said, adopting her own casual tone, "he never writes, so we're clueless as to his activities."

They came to the road leading back to the stable. "Arkady, we should return to the house."

"Yes, of course." He suddenly pivoted to face her. At first, she thought he meant to continue his questioning about Benedykt, but she was wrong. "Sometimes your sisters call you Marysia. May I, too?"

Marie looked into his lapis blue eyes, transfixed. "Yes," she heard herself say.

They walked in silence for a while.

As they approached the stable, Arkady spoke: "Have I said something wrong, Marysia?"

She stopped, wheeling about. "Why would you ask that?"

"You were thinking of blue diamonds."

"Me? Daydream? No—well, perhaps." How strange that he knew that Polish expression, she thought, heat rising in her face.

Arkady smiled, his teeth white and perfect. His hand reached up now, and she flinched at the unexpected move. The back of his fingers brushed against her cheek. They had touched before, on the dance floor and when she put her arm through his as he played escort, but this was something different, something electric. Marie was at a loss.

"Marysia," he whispered, his hand falling away, "you are so beautiful."

Marie's heart pounded. It wasn't the compliment. In the past year she had learned her entrance into a room could cause a stir. No, it was this soldier who had by chance found himself in Walewice on the night of a ball. It was this Arkady who set her pulse racing. Grasping for a response, she asked, "Do *you* have a diminutive?"

"Ha!" Arkady gave a little laugh. "I didn't think that I had one, but my Polish friends call me Arek. And since you are Polish and much more beautiful than they are, you may do so, as well."

"Arek it is," Marie said, laughing.

"May I come see you this week?"

"This week?" Marie felt faint all over again. "What day, Arkady?"

"Tomorrow! And Tuesday—damn! Every day this week, if I'm welcome. Forgive my language, Marysia."

"The nuns would be shocked, I'm afraid," she said, giggling, certain that he wasn't serious. "But you're leaving for Warsaw!"

"I won't leave."

"What do you mean? And after this week?"

"I won't leave until you accept me."

"Accept you?" Marie felt dizzy. "Arkady, this is—"

"Arek!"

"Arek, then. We've only just met."

"But we are—are attached. You feel it, I know you do. I won't leave without you."

His words ran like a bolt through her. Arkady seemed so fervent and sure of himself that Marie questioned her own feelings. He had touched on something she could not explain, something that she did indeed feel. But it frightened her, this feeling.

Arkady turned abruptly. "There's the stable. Let's check on Mars." He took her hand and pulled her in the direction of the stable door.

Marie tried to resist, saying, "We shouldn't. The meal will be ready, Arek."

But he held fast. "We won't be long. Come." Arkady pulled open the door and entered, drawing Marie in with him.

"No," Marie said, "we should go to the house."

Once inside the cooler, musky interior, they paused, eyes adjusting to the dimness. Mars stood in a stall at the rear.

Arkady turned, pulling Marie against him. "Oh, Marie," he whispered, "Marie—"

Suddenly, unexpected sounds—a scraping noise followed by a low grunt—pierced the silence, startling them.

Emeryk's head and shoulders emerged from a nearby stall, muck and shadows clinging to him. He blinked in surprise, his gaze flitting between them, his expression a mix of confusion and embarrassment.

"Marie!" someone called from without.

"That's Kasia!" Marie exclaimed, pulling free and fleeing the stable, Arkady following.

Katarzyna stepped out of the courtyard into the middle of the lane leading up to the house. "Mother said to call you in. The meal is ready!"

Even at the distance of thirty or forty feet, Marie could read the curiosity on her sister's face as she looked from her to Arkady and back. "We're coming in directly, Kasia," she called. "Go back now.'

Marie waited for her sister to disappear into the courtyard, then turned to Arkady. "We must go in." As she started to walk, he reached for her hand and stepped close to her. A tremor coursed through her body. He held her hand in both of his.

"Say I'll be welcome tomorrow. Be warned, I'll come, regardless, but tell me, Marysia."

"I—I . . . yes, you may."

Arkady leaned into her now and gave her the lightest of kisses, on the forehead first, then the cheek, then the lips.

Marie would remember those kisses, but little of the foods that were served or the conversations at the meal. Arkady sat at her side, and his agreeable chatter in his distinctive French charmed her sisters, who sat across from them, eyes riveted. At the foot and head of the long oak table sat her mother and Count Walewski, exchanging looks that hinted at a mysterious tension. Had they argued? Perhaps the chances of their union were lessened—she could hope so.

When the count's gaze fell upon Arkady and her, it held the sternness of a schoolmaster addressing unruly students. Her mother's attention was softer, almost approving. More was being exchanged here than bowls of carrots and cucumbers in cream.

She sensed another silent communication throughout the meal, one with Arkady. She felt his eyes on her, and although he had made his feelings for her clear at the stable, she felt unnerved and avoided his gaze.

Kasia had predicted she would fall in love at the ball. Had she done just that? Where could it lead? Arkady had asked her myriad questions about her and her family, yet he revealed little about himself. Something in the way he spoke today jarred her memory, calling to mind a classmate, Jelena, of Serbian descent. Her accented French was remarkably similar to Arkady's. Marie had read that Serbia was in the midst of a struggle for independence from the Ottoman Empire. If he is travelling on military business, she reasoned, that could explain his reluctance to disclose much of his background.

Before rising from the table, Count Walewski surprised everyone with his abrupt announcement that he and Arkady would leave for Walewice directly. "My compliments, Madame Łączyński, for a delicious repast."

Her mother nodded, though her eyes questioned the suddenness.

Marie cast a sidelong look at Arkady, whose dark expression went beyond surprise.

"Madame Eva," the count said, "would you send word to your groom to bring Arkady's horse around?"

"Yes, of course."

"May I go tell Emeryk, Mother?" Katarzyna asked.

"You may. You are excused."

The count stood, looking at a cheerless Arkady.

Marie clenched and unclenched her hands beneath the table. The man galled her. Oh, he might have been Chancellor to the King, but how could he play lord of the manor in a house not his? What inspired such audacity? Did he believe he had a right to assume her father's role?

Arkady stood and Marie followed moments later. She nodded toward the doorway, indicating she would show him out. Recovering a semblance of good humor, Arkady bowed toward her mother and smiled. "Thank you for your hospitality, Madame Łączyńska. The meal was delicious."

Neither Arkady nor Marie spoke until they came to the front door. "I'm sorry for the count's behavior," Marie said, turning to him. "He acted as if he were the head of our household."

"It's fine, Marie. I am his guest for now." Arkady opened the door. "I have an eye for his motives, but it doesn't matter."

"Motives?"

"Never mind. I'll call at noon tomorrow." Arkady took her hand, bent, and kissed it. Lifting his head, his blue eyes locked with hers. Her heart quickened, captive to the intensity of his stare. The moment hung fire.

Gradually, repetitive sounds entered Marie's consciousness, sounds she came to recognize as the rhythmic clip-clop of Arkady's horse entering the circular drive below.

"Tomorrow, then!" Arkady exclaimed and bolted down the stairs.

Without thinking, Marie followed. By the time she reached the bottom, he was already mounted on the massive Silesian stallion. He called to the retreating Emeryk. "The count will want his carriage now."

Emeryk picked up his pace and disappeared.

Arkady glanced at Marie and smiled, but the sound of footfalls on the stone steps behind her drew his gaze away, and the smile died.

Marie spun about. Count Walewski stood on a lower step, not ten feet from her. Turning again, she saw Arkady direct the horse away from the house, calling, "*Au revoir*, Marysia!"

Beginning at a trot, the Silesian transitioned into a three-beat canter, and the horse and rider receded from view. In a whispered voice, Marie repeated, "Until we meet again," her words rising and falling like a haunting melody against the thundering gallop of hooves. He means to come back, she thought, thrilled.

Suddenly, a sharp cry from her mother stopped her cold. "Anastase!"

Marie whipped around to see her mother at the top of the stairs, her face dark, her arms akimbo.

"Anastase, don't!"

The count ignored her, coming to stand in front of Marie. He cleared his throat. "My dear child," he said, "come, let's take a walk. There are things you must know."

He took her by the arm just above the elbow. Marie glanced up at the doorway—her mother had vanished. They walked along the lane toward the road. She lifted her arm so that the count had to release his hold. "I'm fine, Lord Walewski," she said. "What is it you want to say?"

"Arkady is a bit of a mystery." He cleared his throat again. "You find the handsome soldier enchanting, yes? A romantic, yes?"

Marie did not respond.

"Have you lost your heart to him, Marie?"

"No," she said. It was a lie.

"That's to the good, Marie. Just what has he told you about himself?"

Marie squared her shoulders. "He has a sister several years older. Natalia, I think."

"What about his home country?"

"I believe he's Serbian."

The count blinked in disbelief. "Serbian?"

Marie flushed with embarrassment. "The truth is, I wasn't concentrating when he introduced himself and the music and commotion at the ball was loud. I thought I heard him say, '*Prince of Italy*,' but I thought that was impossible."

"Ah! That was one of his father's titles, and it might have been passed down to him, along with the title '*Count of Rimnik*'."

"Rimnik?"

"It's in Wallachia. His father was a general who had won an amazing victory there against the Turks."

Marie stopped, her stomach clenching, and pivoted to face the count. This was recent history, a famous battle, not much more than ten years before. She knew who that general was—and on whose side he fought. His very name triggered her hatred. He died just a month before she started at convent school. Upon learning of his death, they had all, nuns and students alike, celebrated.

Marie looked up at Count Walewski. "You're wrong! He could not be related to that man—that monster!"

The count tilted his head, as if with sympathy. "He is, Marysia."

"Don't call me that! I won't have it!"

The count's head pulled back. "I'm—I'm sorry."

Marie drew in breath, surprised at his use of her diminutive—and at her own outburst. Still, she wasn't about to apologize. She drew herself up, certain that the count was in error. "Monseigneur Walewski, are you trying to tell me that Arkady's father is . . . is—"

"Generalissimo Aleksandr Suvorov, yes, Marie."

The image of the doll at the bottom of her desk drawer flashed in her mind. She pressed her hand to her mouth, feeling faint. "So," she gasped, "the uniform Arkady wore at the ball was a Russian uniform?"

"It was indeed. He himself is a lieutenant general, even at his young age."

"His father led the Russians at the Battle of Maciejowice. My father died there, Monseigneur Walewski. And then came the Praga massacre, where 12,000 citizens died trying to escape across the bridge into Warsaw."

The count spread his arms at his side, hands open, as if to helplessly agree. "You know your history."

"Yes! Because it is *my* history, mine and my father's!"

The count nodded. "Arkady's full name is Arkady Alexandrovich Suvorov. The titles that passed to him from his father include 'Count of Rimnik,' 'Prince of Italy,' and—Czarina Catherine named his father 'Prince of Russia' before he died."

Marie felt tears welling. She turned away in disgust, but thoughts of Arkady's earnestness came with doubts. She wheeled around again. "Is what you say true, Monseigneur Walewski?"

The count shrugged. "It is, Mademoiselle Marie. He did not hide his identity from me. But I must say, he had no part in the Russian campaign of nine years ago; in fact, he lamented what happened. In all of Europe, he must be one of the most eligible men. The family has status, power, and immense wealth. He is a man on the upsweep of history with a bright future."

"What?" Marie felt a pounding at her temples. "You reveal the true Arkady to me and then dare to recommend him?"

The count shrugged, his expression opaque.

Marie recalled Arkady's words about the count's motives. What had he meant? What is the count's game? she pondered. Drawing a breath, she squared her shoulders. "I—I have heard enough, Monseigneur Walewski. You are to tell the soldier that he is no longer welcome here."

The count cleared his throat, but before he could reply, Marie turned and ran. Racing up the front steps two at a time, she entered the house and slowed. Passing the reception room, Marie caught a glimpse of her mother. She hurried past.

"Marie!" her mother called.

Marie took to the stairs as if she had not heard.

"Marie, wait!"

Marie ignored her. On the first-floor landing, she headed for her room. Before closing the door, she paused to listen. Below, the count had followed her into the house and was conversing with her mother in hushed tones, clearly in disagreement.

Entering her bedchamber, Marie went directly to her bed and threw herself onto it.

Why had the count chosen to make the revelation when he did?

Her heart caught. And why had her mother warned him against making it?

7

Monday, 18 July 1803

WHEN MARIE AWOKE, SHE FOUND herself on her side, curled up and perspiring. Birds were singing. It was early morning, five o'clock, she guessed. She had slept for no longer than three hours. She thought about rising, but every muscle in her body seemed heavy and hurting. Her head ached.

Marie turned onto her back and stared at the ceiling, her mind wandering. Two nights before, she had come home from Walewice Palace exhilarated by the attention she had received at the ball, especially by the attention of one handsome soldier, one with a mystery accent. She held no illusions that anything would come of it—until Arkady suddenly appeared, telling her he was prepared to alter his travel plans, assuring her with both words and cobalt blue eyes that he felt an attachment to her—and that he knew she felt the same.

And it was true. Her heart had opened, only to be broken by Count Walewski, who unmasked Arkady as a loathsome enemy. As she replayed Arkady's conversation in her mind, she came to realize the accent was indeed Russian. Why hadn't she heard it?

Time passed slowly. When Katarzyna came to the door, she refused to go down to breakfast.

She did not expect Arkady to come. No doubt, the count had told him that he was a mysterious soldier no more and that he would be an intruder at the Łączyński manor house.

Pride would keep him away, Marie believed. A Suvorov would not deal well with rejection. By now, he was probably in sight of the walls of Warsaw.

At half past eleven, Marie stirred, sitting up and pulling herself to the side of the bed. She felt no better and sat for a long time, vacillating between dressing and going downstairs or falling back into the softness of the bed—and the oblivion of sleep.

Suddenly, she heard the muffled, thudding hoofbeats of a horse entering the courtyard below. Her eyes went to the clock on her desk. Twelve o'clock.

He wouldn't dare!

Marie's breaths started coming fast. Had he come? Had he so much nerve?

She stood and hurried to the window. By the time she was able to look down, a horse stood riderless and tied to the hitching post.

Marie caught her breath. It was the black Silesian.

She pressed her face to the window. She could see most of the steps leading up to the entryway, but from the angle of her window she couldn't see the door. He must be standing there, her mother even now telling him he was not invited, that he would never be welcome.

Minutes passed. He did not return to the horse. Someone had invited him in!

She stood, stunned, aware of her own heartbeat. The reality that he was within the manor house was just settling in when she heard quick footsteps on the stairs. She rushed to her door and bolted it mere seconds before there came an insistent rapping.

"Marie," Katarzyna called. "Open the door. You have a visitor!"

Marie put her mouth to the doorframe. "I will not see him," she hissed. "Tell him that."

"But you must."

"How dare you, Kasia, to invite him into our home!"

"I didn't!"

"Who did?"

"Mother, that's who!"

"Mother!" Thunderstruck, Marie took a minute to slow her breaths. "Nonetheless, Kasia, tell him I'm ill, very ill."

"Are you sure?"

"I am." It was true. She did indeed feel ill.

Marie moved to her desk and eyed the mementoes of her father on the wall, along with clippings about Napoleon and sketches she had done of him. How these beloved items stood at odds with everything Arkady Suvorov and his family represented!

In less than a half an hour, the horse below whinnied happily as if greeting his rider. Marie remained sitting, daring not to go to the window out of fear

Arkady might look up and see her. In minutes came the muted hoofbeats of the horse moving away from the house, its increasing gait transitioning into a canter as it moved toward the long, poplar-lined lane leading to the main road.

Marie imagined a frustrated and angry Arkady lashing the beautiful Silesian as he galloped back to Walewice. And yet, she knew she was being unfair. She could better accept this unhappy end if she thought he harbored a dark side. Oh, he might be warlike on the battlefield, but at her core, she felt that Arkady Suvorov's intentions were as sincere as sunlight.

But he is not for me, Marie thought, recalling how her father had often met disappointment with the words, *Fate is a hard tutor.*

She was left to herself for the remainder of the day. Honorata brought her a tray of food in the late afternoon. "Why, you do look ill," her sister said.

Marie took the milk and plate, not because she was hungry but because she knew she had to eat something, and not to do so would cause a stir and bring her mother upstairs. She was surprised that her mother had yet to check on her.

"Do you think he's gone for good?" Marie asked.

Honorata shrugged. "Is that what you want?"

"Yes, yes, it is."

Honorata turned to leave but stopped at the door to say two words: "I wonder."

"Wait, Honor. Why hasn't Mother come up to see me?"

"She says you need time to think."

"Really? She said that?"

"She did."

Late in the day, Marie sat by the window when Katarzyna burst in. "You have a letter!" she cried. "It's from Paris!"

"Really? Bring it here, Kasia!"

Katarzyna stepped forward, holding it at arm's length.

"Is it from Benedykt?" Marie asked, eager for news of Napoleon.

Katarzyna shook her head.

"Then it's from Eliza! Kasia, give it to me. I'm hoping she's returning to Warsaw and will visit us here."

"Only if you will read it to me."

"Ha! I don't think your French is good enough yet, do you?"

"Then you must tell me what it says."

"Fine, now hand it over."

Katarzyna obliged, stepping back as Marie broke the seal and unfolded the letter.

"Well?" Katarzyna pressed. "Is she coming?"

Marie looked up and smiled. "No."

"Then why are you smiling?"

Marie let loose a yelp. "Oh, Kasia, it's even better. She's invited me to visit them in Paris! Can you imagine?"

"Really?"

"Really! Isn't that exciting?"

Katarzyna grimaced. "For you! How long will you be away, Marie?"

"A few weeks."

"You won't want to come back to Kiernozia. I know you won't."

"Don't be silly, Kasia. This is home!"

"Will Mother allow it?"

"Why wouldn't she?" Marie asked, forcing a smile, for the question came like a sudden storm cloud. "It's just for a visit."

Before Katarzyna left the room, Marie made her promise not to mention the invitation to anyone.

A few weeks away from Kiernozia would add time and distance to the debacle with Arkady. Her heart would mend. Marie was thankful that what novelists called a *budding romance* had not gone further.

And yet, she sat now, her mood darkening like the falling dusk outside. Her sister had touched the matter with a needle. *Would* her mother give her blessing? Marie had yet to turn seventeen. To make such a trip, she would need more than a blessing; she would need money and travel clothes. Eliza had written that she would write to the countess for permission. Marie could only pray that she was as persuasive on paper as in person.

On Tuesday at noon, to Marie's astonishment, Arkady returned, and the day played out like Monday. Despite Honorata's urging, she refused to meet him. "Is the man dense?" she shouted at the locked door. "Has the cannon fire taken his hearing? I will never see him!"

Arkady lingered downstairs, nonetheless, clearly entertained for more than an hour. Had he forged connections within the household? It seemed likely—his charms were undeniable. She could not deny the attraction she felt for him.

Wednesday followed suit. This time it was Katarzyna who pressed her to go down and meet her *handsome caller*. Marie felt equal parts anger and jealousy toward her mother and sisters, resenting the way they seemed drawn to Arkady's presence.

In the late afternoon, Marie unlocked the door for her mother, who brought her a tray bearing milk and a bowl of *bigos*.

The countess eyed her nightdress. "You're still lying abed, I see," she said, setting the tray on the desk. "Marie, put on your dressing gown and sit here. I'll sit by the window."

Marie complied, positioning the chair so that she faced her mother. Had she received the letter from Eliza? Might this little tête-à-tête be about that?

"This can't go on," the countess said, settling into the upholstered chair, her hands interlocked in her lap. "I've given you enough time to yourself—perhaps too much. You'll make yourself sick."

"I *am* sick, Mother."

"You're afraid to face things, Marie. You've been sheltered in convent school for three years."

Marie stiffened.

"I want to speak to you about something, Marie."

"What?"

Her mother drew in breath. "It's about Arkady."

Disbelief robbed Marie of words. A chilling presentiment took hold.

"He is a serious young man and from a prominent family."

"Do you mean to act as his go-between? Really?"

"Arkady—"

"Arkady Suvorov, Mother. *Suvorov!*"

"I know. I know all that."

"About his father? About the battle in which Father was killed? Killed by an army led by a Suvorov!"

"Yes, yes, I do know. You find your voice when it pleases you, don't you? Please listen. Please, Marysia. We are a noble family and that sets us apart. Do you hear?"

Marie leaned against the chair's hard back, her hands tightening on the hand rails.

The countess cleared her throat. "I understand your feelings for your father and your hatred of the men responsible. But, Marie, we were a family while your father was on earth, and we remain a family without him."

"Mother, I—"

The countess put her hand up. "No, you will listen. The interests of a noble family come first, before the interests of a single individual. Each individual bears a responsibility to do what is beneficial to the family. With that in mind, I begged your father not to follow General Kościuszko. Before nations come families."

Her mother had tried to dissuade her father from joining the battle to save Poland? The revelation sent shivers down her spine.

"And so now," the countess resumed, "we are left impoverished. I've tried to hold things together, but we owe money to everyone. We're about to lose not just the village, but this manor house, too. We are in desperate straits. Are you listening, daughter? Do you understand?"

"Yes."

"To hold on to our estate and our stature, my girls must make good matches. Across Europe, noble brides marry into families who once were enemies. Bloodlines combine. It can be a good thing, Marie. Arkady is well born, and he is as serious about you as anyone I've ever seen bitten by love. A union with his family can save us from ruin."

"He's talking about marriage?"

"The subject is implicit, you might say, but he is a serious young man."

Fighting off tears, Marie twisted about in her chair and stared blankly at the drawings and clippings on the wall.

"Your wall of heroes won't help us. You're thinking of your father, as do I. Don't you think he would want you to hold together what he has left behind?"

Marie shifted back to her mother. "Why must it fall upon me? I'm not yet seventeen. Benedykt is twenty-four and Teodor is older, too. They are the men in the family!"

"They are determined to fight for a bigger prize, our country, as was your father. How can I fault them for that? We women must fight for hearth and home. I'll tell you something I'd never say to your sisters."

"What?" Marie asked.

"Your father called you our golden child. You are the brightest—and the most beautiful."

"And the most valuable, Mother?"

The countess tilted her head, blinked away a look of surprise, and gave a little nod.

"You would have me taken to live in Russia?"

"It would be a sacrifice."

"Mine, you mean."

"As you say."

"You knew from the first, didn't you—that he was Russian?"

Her mother pressed her lips together.

"I won't do it." Marie stood. "His father is responsible for Father's death, as well as the Praga massacre. I could not live under their roof."

The countess released a long breath. She stood. "You are a stubborn girl. This is your final word?"

"It is."

"Very well. I'll inform the young soldier. He sincerely thought the two of you had established a bond. I thought so, too."

Marie shifted her line of vision to look past her mother to the window and the bright afternoon sky. She gave no reply. He was not mistaken, she thought. Another few days and she might have been won over, despite his lineage. It was Count Walewski's timely disclosure that allowed her to close her heart to Arkady.

"Perhaps it's for the best," the countess said, moving toward the door.

Marie felt disoriented. Her mother was yielding too easily.

The countess paused at the door, turned around, her expression seeming to soften. "You're right, Marie. A foreign marriage might not do. A local one is preferable, I think." With that, she left, closing the door behind her.

The surrender felt ominous. Marie stood there, shaking slightly, one hand held to her throat. A local one? What did her mother mean?

And what of Eliza's letter?

Arkady was not one to give up. He appeared again on Thursday and Friday, while Marie stayed in her room.

On Sunday, assured by her mother that Arkady had left for Warsaw, with Russia his final destination, Marie—still weak—was coaxed down to accompany her mother and sisters to Mass, accompanied by the elegantly attired Count Walewski in his splendid carriage with its driver and two footmen.

At Mass, Marie closed her eyes to the priest's actions at the altar, directing her inner sight instead to the Paris invitation.

Outside, Amelia pulled her aside. "Marysia, you look awful."

Marie forced a smile. "I've not been well."

Amelia gasped. "Is it the soldier Honor told me about? It is, isn't it?"

"Not anymore. He's gone, as was my wish."

"Really?" Amelia took hold of Marie's arm. "What is it then?" Her voice dropped to a whisper: "Is it your time?"

"It's not. Eliza has sent an invitation to visit her in Paris."

Amelia's jaw dropped slightly, and her green eyes widened. "She did? Oh, Marie, I'm *so* jealous!"

"It's just that—" Marie was interrupted by her mother's call for her to board the Walewski coach. "Amelia, do come visit soon, yes?"

8

Monday, 25 July 1803

IN THE LATE MORNING, MARIE heard the soft hoofbeats of a horse in the courtyard below. She rushed to her window, heart hammering. What if Arkady had not left for Warsaw? What if circumstances, and her own confounding emotions, taken together, could still engineer a marriage with the Russian?

Marie recognized the Silesian that Arkady had used, but in the saddle today was Count Walewski, resplendent in his blue French frock coat. That she was immediately disappointed brought home to her that her heart had reacted before her head.

The count struggled in getting his one leg over the animal and dismounted with some difficulty, his face flushed. He was greeted by her mother, who escorted him inside. He stayed for two hours, time that Marie kept to her room, her thoughts reverting to Paris and how delightful the trip would be. Her mother had yet to mention a letter from Eliza. Should she bring it up? She decided against doing so, hoping that Eliza would prove persuasive enough.

The count returned about the same time every day that week, utilizing a much smaller horse, a mare, convincing Marie that he had been trying to prove something by riding the horse Arkady had so easily managed. A pattern emerged; he would visit with the countess for an hour or so before Marie—only Marie—was called down to join them in the reception room or music chamber. Then, after fifteen minutes, the countess would excuse herself in order to conduct some errand. She would be gone some time.

On Saturday, Marie's mother did not so much as sit down before she left Marie and the count alone in the reception room. Something at Marie's core tightened. She could only wonder where her sisters were. Had they been deliberately kept away? Her first reaction was to beg her leave and flee to her room. But what excuse could she invent?

"Good morning, Mademoiselle Marie," he said, bowing slightly.

"Good morning, Monseigneur Walewski," she replied.

"Come, Marie," he said, "let's sit in those chairs by the window. They look most comfortable." His frock coat today was of an apricot hue.

He moved sprightly, allowing no time for her to answer. He expected obedience.

Marie followed, situating herself in the high-backed upholstered chair across from him, her arms tightly crossed.

"Marie, I asked your mother to allow us a bit of time together."

Marie's jaw clenched. "Oh?"

"Yes. You see, I felt guilty about revealing Arkady's identity. I don't enjoy being the bearer of bad news."

Marie nodded, suppressing her irritation.

"I thought you needed to know his history before you . . . you—"

"Lost myself?"

He shrugged. "As you say."

"You misjudge me, Monseigneur Walewski."

"That was not my intent, Marie." His faded blue eyes blinked rapidly. "I was concerned you would develop feelings for the young Suvorov and thus be hurt when his identity was revealed. Believe me, I had only the best of—"

"Mother thought I should consider him," Marie interrupted, her voice sharp. "She believes a marriage with Arkady would benefit the family."

The count's lips flattened into a tight smile. "She's been burdened with many worries since your father died."

"I know. And I mean to help, but not from afar and certainly not in the home of the enemy."

He leaned forward, the blue eyes brightening. "You're right. You can help right here, I'm certain."

Marie couldn't speak. His intimate tone and direct gaze heightened the anxiety that had dogged her these last days. She felt a prickling at the nape of her neck. Count Walewski most decidedly did *not* have his sights set on her mother.

His thin smile returned, suggesting he was about to reveal some secret. "A proper Polish marriage could be fortuitous for everyone concerned."

Marie found her voice. "To a count, perhaps? Maybe a local *starosta*?" The spontaneous words lacked the sarcasm she intended.

The fool smiled. Had he missed her bitterness? No, he was choosing to overlook it.

"You're a clever young lady, Marie. You're anticipating my suggestion. I will not voice it as a question. Not today, not now. I can provide for you and see that your mother does not work herself to the bone in an attempt to hold on to your father's legacy. Oh, I'm quite a bit older—I know that."

Marie sprang to her feet, towering over him. She looked down at his gray peruke and lined face and said, "I've danced with Karol, your *grandson*, Monseigneur Walewski. Your grandson is older than me! You're a silly old man to think I would marry you."

The count's eyes went wide, and his head pulled back, retreating into his fleshy neck. He grasped the arms of the chair, preparing to hoist himself into a standing position.

Marie was not about to wait. She turned and fled the room.

"Marysia," he called after her.

That he dared to use her diminutive only quickened her pace.

Once in her bedchamber, she leaned against the bolted door, breathless with rage. The man's nerve knew no bounds. Had he lost his sanity? What was he, even now, telling her mother? Did she know his intention? The likely answer frightened her.

She sat. Half an hour passed, and she felt calmer. No sounds issued from below. She walked to the window and peered down. The Silesian remained tethered to the post, his tail flicking flies off his haunches. The count was still here!

Marie sank into the chair by the window, feeling weak. Her mother would come up, she was certain. But what would they say? Whose side would she take? The count had befriended the family, advising her widowed mother. Did he stand as the only barrier against poverty?

How she wished Eliza were here to provide advice, guidance, and empathy. But the Countess Sobolewska was in Paris.

Paris! I've been invited. I will go to her! —But how?

Certain that her mother would come up to her bedchamber after Count Anastase's departure, Marie fidgeted, shifting from sitting to standing to pacing.

Half an hour passed. She listened at the door. The house had gone silent. She considered forgoing supper but had no desire to call further attention to herself. Neither did she wish to put off their inevitable meeting. She slipped into a pale pink dress that, like much of her wardrobe, had become a bit too small. After plaiting her blonde hair into two braids—signifying her unmarried status—she left her room.

At the top of the stairs, dizziness washed over her. She gripped the banister to steady herself, her anxiety surging. How would her mother react to the count's overture? Marie drew in breath, steeled herself, and descended the stairs.

Entering the dining chamber, she found everyone with their heads bent for prayer. The countess looked up and fixed her gaze on Marie. "You nearly missed Prayer before Meals. Take your seat at once. You may lead us."

Marie hurried around the table, took her seat next to Honorata, and lowered her head for *Modlitwa przedjed jedzeniem*. After, Danusha entered carrying a large tureen of her savory Hungarian goulash.

Even the tantalizing aroma and spicy taste of one of Danusha's prize dishes, one Marie hadn't enjoyed for a year or more, didn't bring calm. Honorata and Katarzyna chatted in lively fashion across the table, until they realized they were the sole contributors, at which point they fell silent. After the meal, they both helped Danusha clear away the dishes, thus earning an early release.

The countess sat at the head of the table, eyes averted from Marie.

Alone with her mother now, Marie fingered the rim of her crystal water goblet, at last summoning the nerve to speak first. "You knew, didn't you?"

Her mother looked up, her expression inscrutable. "I suspected as much the day he happened to see you upon your return. Count Walewski is not difficult to read."

"And his arranging the ball confirmed your suspicion?"

"It did, Marie. And it stirred up questions in your mind, too. Questions I didn't answer in a—"

"Honest way?" Marie interjected

Her mother gave a slow nod.

"You gave him permission?"

The countess's eyes widened and she forced a little shrug.

"But then you supported *Arkady's* advances."

"I did."

"Why?"

"Because I saw the spark between you two. He was obviously enamored with you. Don't look at me like that. I'm as aware of his family name as you."

"A family of killers!"

The countess sighed. "But I thought it could work, Marie. He charmed you. I could see that. And he is so much closer in age."

Unable to challenge her attraction to Arkady, Marie seized on the age factor with the count. "Mother, do you know that when I arrived home from school, I thought the count was interested in *you*. And I thought then he was *too old* for you."

The countess looked away. "You . . . you need to marry well, Marie."

"To Count Walewski? To him! To a—"

The countess swiftly turned back, forefinger raised. "Be careful, Marie, what you say of him."

"Why? I've already said it *to* him. He won't give me a second look now, you can be sure." Marie took a breath. "He didn't tell you what I said?"

"He did."

"And?"

"He was not overly concerned."

"What?" The complacency she felt bled away at once, and for moments she was rendered breathless. She thought she would be ill. "So—you mean he'll be back again to—"

"No, he won't," her mother snapped, shaking her head.

"Good! Then he understood me." Marie exhaled. "I'm glad."

"He has duties in the Warka District, where he is the starosta, and that's a good many miles away."

"And then?" Marie asked tenuously, suddenly fearful of the answer.

The countess produced a thin smile. "He returns to Walewice on Saturday and will drive us to Mass on Sunday."

Marie realized she had a dangerously tight grasp on the bowl of the stemmed crystal water goblet and freed it at once. "Do you mean he wasn't angry—or even discouraged?"

The countess shrugged. "Sometimes, men appreciate a challenge."

Marie's thoughts spiraled. Did her mother not understand? Did she mean to side with him?

The countess attempted to change the subject, but the conversation faltered. Eventually, Marie pleaded a headache and retreated to her room.

Locking the door, she paced, stopping after a time to stare out the window. Paris wouldn't leave her mind. Only that morning, Katarzyna had played sentry while Marie crept into their mother's bedchamber to sift through recent correspondence. It was there—the letter from Eliza—and the seal was broken. Within minutes, she read and replaced it. Her mother knew of the invitation and yet had said nothing.

Something else had come of the detective work that left Marie conflicted and restive. She found the letter amidst dozens of notices of money owed.

9

Monday, 1 August 1803

"Count Walewski!" Amelia shrieked. "You don't mean it, Marie! Why, he must be fifty! And he's got legs like those French sticks of bread."

"He's sixty-eight," Marie replied in a flat voice, knowing its effect.

Amelia fell backwards into Marie's upholstered chair, speechless.

Marie stood over her friend, thankful for her visit. "He's been married twice already and has six grown children."

"Six?" It was all Amelia could manage.

"Oh, one is not from a marriage."

"What?" Amelia tipped her head to the side, her face tightening, blond brows drawn together. "How would *you* know these things?"

"Danusha told me. She once worked at the Walewice Palace, so she *knows*."

"Really? Marie, you can't marry an old man. —What does your mother say? "

"She's not about to put an obstacle in his way. I think she's creating castles in Spain, as they say. Now everything we speak of here today is between us, yes? I mean it, Amelie." Marie stressed her friend's diminutive in a meaningful way.

Amelia leaned back, hands in her lap. She looked up at Marie and said, "Always, and always we will be friends, Marysia."

"I believe so, too." Marie let out a great sigh. "Well, our estate is struggling. My mother is unable to pay for things. We've lost servants. Things around here are falling to pieces. We even have bats in the house."

"Oh—and the count is rich!"

"Exactly."

"But marriage! You . . . you don't want to marry him, do you?"

Marie took the desk chair, adjusted it to face her friend, and sat. "No."

"And your mother is in favor of marriage?"

Marie flinched at the question. "It seems so."

"Who is there to take your side?"

"You, I hope, Amelie."

Amelia shrugged. "What good am I?"

"And there's Danusha. She says she sees the writing on the wall. She wants to help."

"But she's no better than me. She's a servant. . . .. What writing?"

Marie laughed. "It's just one of her sayings."

"What about your sisters?"

"Oh, Honor seems to be sympathetic, but if the count were to throw her a ball, well, I'm not so certain."

"And Katarzyna?"

"Ha, Kasia! She's all aflutter because I'll be living in a palace and have fine clothes and carriages. Of course, she's too young to know what goes on between a married man and woman. Why, I'm not sure Honor knows what goes on."

Amelia rolled her eyes. "And neither would we if it were not for Madame Eliza's telling us."

Marie chuckled at the memory of some of the girls' reactions. "Indeed. —I am hoping that Teodor will plead my case. I've written to him."

"And your other brother?"

"I don't know. Benedykt is so much older. He writes to me of his exploits in Paris. We write of politics—freedom for Poland—but little else. Wait, he did mention some actress he had met."

"A Paris actress!"

Marie smiled, gave a knowing tilt of the head, and continued, "I've also written to Eliza there in Paris to tell her about my predicament. I trust her to give me good advice."

"I thought you were invited to Paris."

"I was, but—it's complicated."

Oh, Marie, you must go!"

"I need the time away from here, as well as her advice. I need to know my future."

At that moment, the countess called for Marie from below.

Amelia stood. "I should leave."

"Wait, I have the letter to Eliza here." Standing, Marie turned to retrieve a sealed letter from her desk, and held it out to Amelia. "Please take it to Father Albin and ask him to see that it gets posted. Not a word to him about anything else, you hear?"

Amelia hesitated, her expression for the moment blank. "But why—"

The countess called again.

Without a word, Marie shifted her gaze toward the door and Amelia understood the need for secrecy. She accepted the letter with a nod.

At the chamber door, Marie whispered, "Hide that in your skirts, Amelie."

Amelia obeyed. She looked down the hallway, then up at the ceiling. She turned to Marie now, her face paling. "Bats?"

Wednesday, 3 August 1803

Marie sat at her desk in the early afternoon when Katarzyna knocked and entered, carrying two unlit candleholders. Her mother followed, balancing a metallic object. "You have a present, Marie," she announced. "Clear your desk a bit. "Katarzyna, stand aside and wait a minute."

After Marie complied, her mother laid before her a footed desk set holding two inkwells, a rocker blotter in its place between the two. The metallic stand and pieces were all filigreed and polished. At the center of the grillwork behind the three pieces was a backing bearing a coat of arms she had seen before.

"All right," the countess said to Katarzyna, "come place one of those on each side." Katarzyna did as asked, moving quickly. The metal and filigree of the candleholders matched the other items. "The candles are beeswax of the highest quality," the countess said.

Marie leaned back against her chair and looked up at her mother. "They're from him, aren't they?"

The countess tsked and turned to Katarzyna, saying, "Go downstairs now, child, and close the door behind you."

Katarzyna pulled a face and moved to the door before barking out, "They're from the count!" With lightning speed, she passed into the hall, pulling the door shut with a bang. Kasia has spirit, Marie remarked to herself. If she is allowed to attend school, the nuns will no doubt find her another Łączyńska problem child, whereas Honorata will be a model student and fade into the woodwork.

Her mother inhaled sharply, then sat on the bed to the side of the desk and managed a tight smile. "He left them with me before his trip. The set is French cast-brass, Marie. Isn't it lovely?"

Marie thought of saying she had no intention of accepting it. However, her father had often told her she had to pick her battles, and this was not the one she wanted to have this day. "Is he here?"

"No, he doesn't want to pressure you. He wants to give you time."

"I do need time, Mother." Here was her opening. "A few weeks ago," she blurted, "Countess Sobolewska invited me to visit her and her husband in Paris." Marie took a breath, her eyes on her mother. "I'd so like to go. The countess said they would take care of everything. I would stay only a week or two and then return."

"Yes, that would be delightful for you, but it is not possible. You know we are teetering on the edge of poverty. I cannot afford such a luxury, and I won't take their charity."

"I have a way to at least help with my journey to Paris. Teodor has written to me that he is leaving college to enlist in Napoleon's Army. He'll be coming here to say goodbye. I could go with him to Paris. He will get me there safely."

The countess's back straightened. "Oh, really? He's just a year older than you. And once the Prussian authorities in Warsaw catch wind that he's leaving college to join up with Napoleon, he'll have a target on his back. You would slow him down, Marie. Besides, there will be no carriage. He'll take a horse and ride like the wind."

Lips pressed tight in disappointment, Marie turned away from her mother to stare at the desk set, eyes falling on the Walewski crest, a festooned helmet. "Is this my future?" she muttered.

The countess ignored her comment and started across the room. "You may take your *time*, but you will have to do so here at Kiernozia."

Marie looked up. "But—"

Without turning, the countess raised her hand to silence her daughter. "I'll extend your gratitude to Count Walewski," she said, reaching the door.

"Mother," Marie called, her heart racing, "the Countess Sobolewska said she wrote to you about the invitation. Did you receive her letter?"

The countess stopped all movement at the open door, keeping her back to Marie.

Marie held her breath. They had reached a moment of truth. Was her mother going to lie to her?

The countess cleared her throat, and yet held her silence a few more beats. At last, she said, "I did receive it. She and her husband have been informed of our straitened circumstances. It's not something I would have people know—but there it is. The trip is impossible, Marie. I'm sorry. Now, come down for supper."

Her mother's palpable reaction was two-fold: embarrassment for having kept the letter secret; and humiliation at having to disclose the family's monetary crisis.

Despite the subterfuge, her mother had been honest in the end, and yet Marie found it difficult to empathize with her. There would be no Paris.

Sunday, 7 August 1803
Marie stood in the family pew at the far end, watching Father Albin's movements through the Mass, trying to match his prayers to those in her Roman Missal, but concentration came hard.

Having returned in time for Sunday Mass, as her mother had forecast, Count Walewski sat at the other end of the pew. Earlier, Marie had gone through the motions of expressing her gratitude for the desk set. At great length, he provided details on the Walewski crest, its extravagant artistry and current worth. This was his plan to win her over, she thought, that she would be little more than the desk set, a possession. She broke out in a cold sweat.

Suddenly, she realized the congregation had taken their seats. She was standing alone, feeling naked, as if everyone's eyes were on her. Longing to run far away, she looked down the pew, her only exit. She would have to pass in front of Honor, Katarzyna, her mother, and *him*. The count turned and glanced up at her, a supercilious smile playing on his thin lips, his peruke slightly askew.

Marie grew dizzy, sensing a great black wave approaching, closer and closer, rising, the wooden flooring beneath her falling away. Then—nothing.

Slowly, she came awake to someone taking her hand. Then, her mother's worried voice: "*Jezus i Maryja*! You frightened us, Marie!"

A panic took hold of Marie—until she recognized her surroundings. She had been placed on the blue couch in the reception room. "What happened?" she asked, her anxiety fading as she remembered. "I fainted?" Even as she asked the question, the memory came back to her in full.

"Oh, my dear," her mother whispered. "Father Albin had just come to the Offertory, and—and you fainted dead away. We spirited you out through the side door at once, but not without causing quite a stir, I can tell you. Quite a stir!"

Marie regarded her mother's face, trying to decode the emotion behind it. Was it empathy? Embarrassment? Or perhaps a bit of pride at the attention?

"We got you to the carriage and home here in little time. The count's footmen carried you in. Oh, Anastase is most concerned. I'll send him word that you've been revived. . . .. Are you able to take the stairs?"

"Yes, I think so."

The countess placed the back of her hand on Marie's forehead. "Why, child, you're burning up!"

10

Thursday, 11 August 1803

MARIE COULD HEAR SOMEONE CALLING to her from far away, her name echoing, as if from a cave. "Marie, Marie!" came the call again, and slowly the voice grew louder as she struggled to pull herself closer to it.

Marie opened her eyes. Kasia was peering down at her.

"Oh, Marysia," the nine-year-old pleaded, "aren't you well yet? It's been days, and now I've come to tell you the news—"

"How many? —How many days?"

"This is Thursday. You came home Sunday." Katarzyna counted on her fingers. "So, that's four."

"Yes," Marie said, embarrassed that her little sister solved it first. She shook her head in an effort to brush away the cloudiness.

"You must hear the news, Marie . . . please!"

Marie pulled herself into a sitting position, adjusted the pillow against the vertical bars of the iron bed frame, and leaned back. Her nightdress felt damp with perspiration.

"Teodor is coming home."

"When?"

"At the week's end."

"Really? You're certain?"

"Mother's heard from him. It's to say goodbye. He's off to take up with General Napoleon. Now, you must get well. I'm tired of being told to be quiet."

Marie laughed. "I'll try, Kasia. I promise."

Marie was left alone with the regret that she would not be travelling to Paris with Teodor.

Saturday, 13 August 1803

Marie rallied so that by Saturday mid-afternoon when she opened her bedchamber door to Honorata, she was fully dressed in a yellow gown that had been one of her mother's.

"He's here, Marie!" Honorata exclaimed.

"Oh, I've heard all the excitement."

"Then come down. Danusha is preparing a feast!"

"I plan to, Honor, but do me a favor. When you go down, tell him I would like to speak to him alone. Ask him to come upstairs. Will you do that?"

Honorata flashed a brief frown and tilted her head slightly. "What? What is it?" she pressed, leaning in close and wetting her lips.

"It's just that I'd like to speak to him alone first. So, please, tell him that."

Honorata sighed. "Yes, yes, I will."

Drawing her sister's face closer, Marie kissed her on the cheek. "Thank you, Honor."

After exchanging kisses at her bedchamber doorway, Marie embraced Teodor tightly. "It's so good to see you," she said.

Teodor held her for a long minute. "Why, you're trembling, Marie. What's the matter?"

Marie pulled away, wiping at her eye. "I've missed you, that's all. Can't a girl miss her big brother?" She smiled and held him at arm's length. "Why, you're not in uniform. You look like a farmer!"

"I'm no longer a student, Marie. Did you think I'd already have a French uniform? All in good time, that. I dress like this to avoid trouble with Prussian officials."

"Your clothing reminds me of those days years ago when we tended the garden together."

"I remember. Afterward, Mother would check your hands and nails to see that you washed well."

"Yes, while you escaped to—where?"

"I don't remember."

"When do you leave, Teo?"

"Tomorrow, early."

"I'm jealous."

"Mother said that you've been unwell."

Marie managed a smile. "In body and mind, Teo."

"Tell me."

Marie took his hand and drew him into the room. "Come, take the comfortable chair."

As Teodor sat, Marie paced in front of him, updating him on the ball given in her honor, Arkady Suvorov, the Paris invitation, and the not-so-veiled proposal by Count Walewski.

"You've not been idle, have you?" Teodor said, chuckling. "I'm going to have a stiff neck gaping up at you. Sit down, will you?"

Marie halted and leaned down close to her brother. "Do you think this is funny? Do you?"

Teodor blinked, reconsidering. "No, Marie, really I don't. Forgive me."

Marie sighed, pulled the desk chair closer, and sat knee to knee with him. "Oh, what am I going to do, Teodor?"

"I'm still trying to imagine Mother suggesting a union with a Suvorov."

"Well, she did. May Papa rest in peace."

"The count didn't come around much after this part of the nation fell to Prussia."

"He's made up for it, I can tell you. —Teodor, did Mother mention him to you?"

Teodor's eyes widened a moment before his gaze dropped, and he stared down at his empty hands. "She did."

"She has hopes, doesn't she?"

"Hopes?" Teodor looked up, shrugged. "She has bill collectors."

"What am I to do about him? What?"

"Is he such an ogre?"

"You haven't seen him? He's not down there now?"

"No."

Marie exhaled. "Small blessing. However you recall him, he's gotten no younger."

Teodor seemed to take her statement for a joke but quickly recovered. "Mother said he's performing his duty as staosta in the Warka District."

"Ha! If he were here, he'd be boasting about his position there and his status as Chancellor to the King before the government toppled."

"A bit of self-pride? That's not necessarily a bad thing, Marie," Teodor teased.

"Oh, I'm afraid that you're going to like him. He makes people like him."

Teodor looked past her. "Shall we go downstairs?"

"In a moment, Teo. I need your help. This is serious."

Teodor shrugged. "I do understand, Marysia. But I'm off to Paris. I—I don't know what I can do."

"You can talk to Mother!"

Teodor sighed. "Yes, I can do that. And I'll make the attempt, but you know she has a will of iron once she's decided."

Marie crossed her arms, feeling cold. He was right. What could he possibly do? "If only . . ."

"If only what?"

"If only I were a boy. *I* could be off to Paris, too, off to fight with the great man. I could decide for myself."

"Don't wish that, Marie. It's not your fate. Things will turn out well for you, you'll see."

Marie forced a smile. "Do you think so? Promise me this, at least."

"What?"

"Talk to Benedykt when you get to Paris. Tell him what Mother has in mind. Maybe he'll have a way to rescue me."

"I will, but I see a chance for you closer to home. A hope perhaps."

"What? Tell me!"

"Mother said the count leaves right after *Dożynki* to take the waters at Bad Gastein."

"So? She knows that his harvest festival at Walewice will be full of fun and feasting, while our own *Dożynki* here will amount to nothing. We have no workers to bring in what there is of the crops. All the more reason to see me married to the count."

"Let me finish my thought, Marie! It's then, after he takes the waters that his custom is to continue on through the Brenner Pass before the heavy snows—and on to Italy, Rome, in fact."

"Rome?"

"Yes, he visits a palace of his ancestors there who had come to Poland hundreds of years ago."

"So—he won't be back until—until—"

"Spring. Do I see the hint of a smile at the corners of your mouth? I'm thinking that perhaps he'll forget you! All of this worry will come to nothing."

"Oh, do you think so?" Marie paused for a moment, then shook her head. "Ah, but you don't know him."

"He could change his mind. Just don't make a commitment before he leaves." Teodor stood. "That's my advice. Now, let's go down."

Marie followed suit, and as they came out into the hallway where excited voices wafted up from below, Teodor leaned over and whispered in Marie's ear. "You know, you'll be in my thoughts. And just remember, Marysia, that the former Chancellor to the King will be travelling roads where avalanches are very common." He laughed and drew his head back. "They say the young may die, but the old will die."

Marie looked up to catch one of his green eyes open and one winking. She couldn't help but laugh.

At midnight, a sleepless Marie sat at her window gazing out into a sky heavy with clouds, searching for stars.

If only I were a boy, she had told her brother. Had she been born male, she could fight for her country, her Poland. Her father had been able to attend the Knights' School, a military school organized by Prince Poniatowski's uncle, King Stanisław. He proved himself many times over, until he fell in battle.

Even though the Cadets' Corps, as it was sometimes called, was closed when the nation fell to its three neighbors, its goals of instilling honor, a sense of self-worth, and patriotism became the core of legend. And both Benedykt and Teodor had the advantage of attending the Collegium Nobilium, which was designed to prepare the sons of magnates and the sons of the minor nobility, the *szlachta*, to protect and run the country. Now, both brothers were aligned with General Napoleon and in the thick of the effort to win back Poland's independence.

And daughters? Marie brooded.

Daughters were relegated to convent schools and, more often than not, arranged marriages.

Marie stared out the window. The clouds had not lifted.

From the forest came the howling of wolves.

Saturday, 17 September 1803

The countess knocked and opened the door to Marie's bedchamber, leaning in. "Anastase leaves tomorrow. I won't allow you to miss this visit, Marie."

"I won't Mother. I'm getting dressed."

"Good. Hurry now. Wear one of your new dresses, and part your hair in the middle, twisting it at the back. Would you like for me to come back up to assist?"

"No, I'll be fine."

"Very well." Her mother smiled and closed the door.

Marie went to stand in front of the tall, gilt-framed mirror that had been delivered for her the week before. Whether it had been the count's idea or her mother's, she didn't know, but she knew who had paid for it. She examined herself in the glass, smiling. How she had looked forward to this occasion.

She turned now and took from the wardrobe one of several new gowns her mother had Madame Simone create for her. Honorata and Katarzyna had received one each. The waist to the gown she chose sat—in the current style— just under her breasts. It was of a light blue silk with short, puffy sleeves and a skirt that fell straight to the floor. The rectangular cut of the bodice was the least revealing of the new gowns.

Her hair took a little time. Marie followed her mother's direction but added what had become quite a fashion in Warsaw: wisps and ringlets hanging on the forehead, at the ears, and at the nape of the neck. Her mother would think it a disheveled look, but so be it.

Marie hummed as she dressed. Just two days before, the world had seemed bleak as the dead of winter. The celebration of *Dożynki* had passed without any mention of the count's annual journey. She began to fear he wouldn't go this year because of her. But then, her mother confirmed his plans to travel to Bad Gastein and then to Italy. Tonight was his goodbye supper.

Marie sat to lace the dark blue slippers meant to complement the gown, thinking how the supper was in reality a gratitude supper. The count had paid for more than the gowns. Amelia had visited with the surprising news that the Kiernozia harvest festival had come off well; somehow, forty reapers had been hired and paid. Someone had stepped in to save the estate, Amelia explained, as well as provide the funds for the *Dożynki* food and music.

"Where is everyone?" Marie asked, coming to the bottom of the stairs.

"In the reception room," Danusha said, moving toward the kitchen. She paused, eyes wide. "You're stunning, Marie!"

"If only that were not the case, Danusha."

"What? —What did you say?"

Marie rolled her eyes toward the reception room.

Danusha caught on immediately. "The count's been here for some time. Your sisters are quiet and very serious for the moment. It's their new dresses, I expect." The servant leaned in and lowered her voice. "Seems like there's no subject he doesn't have something to say about."

Marie giggled.

"Supper will be in half an hour," Danusha said, hurrying toward the kitchen.

Marie drew in a long breath and moved to the reception room.

"And now the little family is complete!" Count Walewski sang out as Marie entered. "Little Marie is so—so beautiful!" He sprang up and bowed.

Her sisters—Honorata in peach and Katarzyna in Pomona green—voiced their compliments, too. The countess's eyes narrowed as her gaze moved up from Marie's slippers to her hair. A shadow of disapproval crossed her face before she managed a slow nod.

"You look lovely, Mother," Marie said, noting her new dark blue gown and the very hairstyle she had prescribed earlier for an errant daughter. Her mother was still a beautiful woman.

Attired in a cranberry-colored frock coat with gold embellishments, the count approached Marie now, the silver buckles on his patent leather pumps catching the light. He initiated *la bise*. Marie returned the kisses. She had prepared herself.

Whether by chance or design, the only likely seat for her was on the couch, and that is where the guest of honor now led her.

Knowing that this man's pursuit of her was about to go into a lengthy lull allowed for the evening to pass with a degree of pleasure.

11

Wednesday, 7 December 1803

DANUSHA ENTERED THE DINING CHAMBER carrying her dessert specialty—a fragrant poppyseed cake. The faces of Honorata and Katarzyna lit up. "My favorite!" Katarzyna squealed. "It's for you, Marie," Honorata added.

Marie caught her mother's eye. The countess gave a little laugh. "Did you think we forgot, Marie? Believe me, when you bring a child into the world, you'll remember the day. We'll have a much bigger celebration in August for your name day, but the day of your birth is special too. Gratulacje, Marie!"

"Thank you, Mother."

"Gratulacje, Marysia!" her sisters chimed.

"Mother," Marie said as Danusha finished cutting the cake, "may Danusha join us here? It seems only fair."

Caught off guard, her mother quickly nodded. "Yes, Danusha, bring a chair up to the side, next to Marie."

Marie's gaze went to the empty chair at the foot of the table. Even nine years after the death of her father, her mother still considered it her husband's place, leaving it unoccupied. Hot tears pooled in her eyes at her father's memory, but her attention was soon diverted by a great clamor of horses and voices in the courtyard.

Everyone looked up in confusion. The countess rose and hurried to the window. Marie and her sisters knew not to move.

"What could it be?" Danusha whispered.

"I can hardly see through the blowing snow," the countess announced.

"Wait, there are six sleighs, all decorated, horses and all. Holy God!" she exclaimed. "It's a *kulig*! What can they be doing here?"

"A *kulig*!" Katarzyna cried, her eyes ablaze.

The countess turned from the window, her face pale. Her eyes swept the table. "Someone must know about this sleigh party."

No one moved or spoke for a long moment. Then came the booming noise of the door knocker.

Danusha started to rise, but a gesture from the countess halted her. "I'll see to this. Everyone stay seated."

Katarzyna was the first to disobey once the countess had left the room. She darted across the room and scrambled onto the window seat. "It *is* a *kulig*! Oh, it is, it is! Come look, everyone. The sleighs and horses are beautiful!"

Honorata looked to Marie for guidance. When Marie shook her head and remained seated, Honorata nonetheless jumped up and joined Katarzyna. The two soon filled the room with oohs and ahs.

Danusha clucked her tongue. "Should your mother find the two of you there, you'll be sorry, my girls."

"Oh, come see, Danusha," Honorata tempted, any sense of guilt gone. "Have a good look and then watch the door for Mother. You come see, too, Marie!"

The celebrants outside broke into a song now, and Danusha needed no more convincing.

Marie sat with her back to the others, a sinking feeling at the pit of her stomach. She knew she was in trouble. She had been invited to partake in the *kulig*, but she refused, telling no one about the invitation. How could she have known that they would come to Kiernozia?

Minutes ticked by.

"The mistress is coming!" Danusha hissed, reclaiming her seat.

Honorata and Katarzyna turned from the windows, panic on their faces, and managed to seat themselves seconds before the countess entered, her gaze locking onto Marie. "Come here at once, Marie!"

The chamber went silent as a convent.

Heart thumping, Marie slowly stood and approached her mother.

The countess drew in a deep breath. "You were invited to this sleigh party that sits outside?"

"Yes, Mother."

"And you refused?"

Swallowing hard, she said, "Yes, Mother."

"You refused, even knowing that the invitation came from Count Walewski's three sisters?"

"I—I wrote a respectful reply. I sent it with Emeryk to Walewice, so I know they received it."

"You declined without consulting me. I don't understand you, Marie. They tell me they have not initiated a *kulig* in years, and they did so this year at the express wish of the count—in honor of you! Did you know that, child?"

Marie kept silent. She felt faint.

"*Why* did you refuse?"

Marie avoided naming the count as the primary reason, instead voicing a secondary one. "Mother, you've told me you've been on *kuligs*, so you know when the train of sleighs stop at a house along the way, the host is to act surprised and offer a great spread of food and wine. There's to be music and dancing too. We have Danusha but other help would be needed. Musicians would have to be hired. So—"

"What, Marie? —Oh! It's the cost, then. Is that it?"

"Yes."

"I would have found a way to afford it, rather than face this kind of embarrassment. You've humiliated me, Marie."

"I'm sorry, Mother. I didn't mean to."

"Now," the countess said, "you're going to march out there and face the count's sisters."

"They're—they're here?" Marie reached for the dimpled area at the base of her neck. *God save me.*

"I left them in the reception room. Come along."

Marie froze. "But *kuligs* are for the young, Mother, and they must be—"

"They're here to fetch you. The young people are out in the sleighs. Now, come along. Go on—lead the way."

Mortified, Marie cast a look at her wide-eyed sisters and stepped into the hallway, heart hammering.

There was no avoiding this confrontation. What am I to say to these women? she worried. Should I apologize? Is that enough?

"Don't drag your feet, Marie," the countess said, nudging her forward.

"Hello," Marie ventured as she entered the reception room where the three stood.

Two were at least in their sixties; the third was decidedly younger and prettier.

"Why, I meant for you all to be seated," the countess said, flushing. "Forgive me."

"We're still a bit wet with snow, and we won't stay long," one of the older sisters said. "We're here to ask Marie in person to accompany the young people on the *kulig*."

The countess introduced Marie to the trio. The gray-haired speaker was Jadwiga. Teodora, also gray beneath her bonnet, seemed less stern, but just as plain of face. Marie guessed that the third sister, Teresa, was still in her forties. Her hat and coat, like her eyes, were of a vibrant blue. She, alone, smiled.

"Now then, Marie," Jadwiga said, "Anastase sent word from Rome that we were to organize this *kulig* for your benefit. We simply could not accept your refusal."

"We've gone to a great deal of bother," Teodora added.

"Begging your pardon," Marie interjected, "but I thought I made myself clear in my letter."

"You were rather vague, young lady," Jadwiga said. "Something about being ill-prepared to play hostess. Now, if times are too austere for your family, that's not a good reason." The woman's eyes swept the room as if the furnishings could speak for the well-being of the estate. "Our brother said he will pay for everything."

"In any event," Teodora said, glancing at the countess "we have not included your estate as one of our stops, so that eliminates any responsibility for you."

Marie felt her mother stiffen at her side. She put it down to shame at being exposed as poverty stricken, as well as anger at her.

Picking up on her sister's disparaging inference, Teresa spoke for the first time. "Forgive us if we misinterpreted, Madame Łączyńska. It's just that we do try to please Anastase."

"Indeed, we do," Teodora snapped. "Why, you don't know Anastase. When his wishes are not—"

"We best stay on topic, Teodora," Jadwiga interrupted, casting a flinty look at her sister, who, Marie surmised, had already said too much. "Now, will you come with us, Marie?" We have two families who have prepared their manor homes for our *surprise* arrival. There will be food and dancing."

Marie tried to think of any excuse to avoid going with them.

"This is your birthday, isn't it?" Teresa asked, her smile indicating confidence in the answer.

The question took Marie's breath from her. There was no refusing now. She nodded.

"Our brother knew," Teresa said, "and he insisted we prepare the *kulig* for today. My sisters will be returning home, but I will be your chaperone for tonight—happily so."

"You should give your answer, Marie," her mother said. Marie felt the weight of her mother's expectations but couldn't find her voice. Then an idea struck. "Will you go, too, Mother?"

"No, my duty is here, Marie. And you just told me a bit ago it was for young people."

Marie heard a noise coming from the hallway and with it, another idea. She drew herself up as if seeking a compromise with the enemy, and said, "If I am to come along, I would like my sisters to accompany me. We've always celebrated our birthdays together." She heard her mother draw in a sudden breath.

Teodora spoke first. "Your sisters?"

Marie smiled. "Yes, please."

"I don't know whether there's room for *three* more," Jadwiga said. She affected a smile.

"Oh, we won't take up much space," Marie countered.

"How old are they?"

"Honorata is thirteen. She danced quite well at the count's ball. Katarzyna is nine."

"Awfully young," Jadwiga snapped. She looked to her sisters for some indication of how to address the issue.

Teodora offered a hesitant smile and shook her head.

"Oh, Jadzia," Teresa said, her tone light. "I'm certain they'll fit in nicely. Remember the gift we brought for the household? That will free up room in one of the sleighs."

Reluctantly, Jadwiga smiled tightly. "Very well, Marie, if your mother permits. You'll have to dress quickly. We're running late."

Marie looked to her mother, who smiled and nodded. Behind her, the faces of Honorata and Katarzyna were lit with wonder.

"Hurry now, Marie," the countess ordered. "Take the two eavesdroppers here and get ready. Wear your prettiest gowns and warmest coats."

Marie approached her sisters, thrilled by the adventure of a *kulig* and heartened that the two older Walewska sisters would not be joining them. Behind her, she heard Jadwiga instruct Teresa to go out and tell the footmen to bring in their brother's Christmas gift.

12

THE SKY BRIGHTENED IN THE east as the long night of revelry came to an end. Five sleighs of exhausted merrymakers halted on the main road in front of the Łączyński estate, while the sixth pulled into the courtyard. Marie and her sisters thanked Teresa Walewska as they climbed down from the sleigh into a foot of snow.

"It's been a delight!" Teresa called as they started up the staircase. "We'll see you soon!"

As Marie and Honorata picked their way up the snow-laden steps, Katarzyna raced ahead. The moment the door opened, Katarzyna cried, "Where is it, Mother? Where is the present?"

"In the kitchen, Kasia."

"Oh! What is it? A platter of sweets?"

"Go look," the countess replied, and Katarzyna dashed toward the dining chamber. "Come in, Marie and Honorata. Katarzyna didn't take time to remove wet boots, but you two should. Did you enjoy yourselves?"

"Oh, we surely did!" Honorata exclaimed. "I danced and danced. More than at the count's ball."

"And you Marie?"

"Oh," Honorata interjected, "she danced just as much, and she even won a contest and had to suffer a kiss from a handsome young man."

Marie laughed. "We did have a good time, Mother," she said, sensing her mother was placing significant emphasis on her answer.

Boots and cloaks squared away, Honorata asked, "What is the gift?"

"Well, come see," the countess said.

They followed the trail of puddles from Katarzyna's boots. "My stockings are getting wet," Honorata complained.

In the kitchen, Katarzyna squealed, "Oh, it's wonderful, Mother! We must name him!" She knelt beside a large, round tin tub.

When Marie and Honorata approached, they saw that the tub was filled with water. "It's a fish!" Honorata exclaimed. "A huge fish!"

Marie stared at the captive fish. They hadn't had a Christmas carp this large since her father's death. Occasionally they did without. A heat rose to her face as she realized the gift was yet another one of Count Walewski's claims over her. Dizziness washed over her as she watched the fish swim in circles.

"It's for Christmas Eve," the countess said, coming up behind them. "And it will likely be even fatter by then."

"Oh, may I feed him?" Katarzyna pleaded. "He shall be my pet!"

"You may," the countess said. "But it could be a lady fish."

"Really?" Katarzyna asked. "Just the same, I'm going to call it *Claude*."

"How will Danusha cook it?" Marie asked, feigning interest in the subject.

Gasping, Katarzyna turned away from the tub, her blue eyes wide. "Cook it?"

"That will be up to her," the countess said. "Perhaps she'll make her gray sauce. Or the plum and cherry recipe."

"Oh, I prefer the one with the cherries, Mother," Honorata said.

"Oh," Katarzyna whined, "must we cook it?"

Marie closed her bedchamber door and leaned against it, lost in thought. She didn't notice the candle in the chamberstick tilting until hot wax dripped onto her hand. Minutes had passed. She went to the desk and lighted the pair of chambersticks that Count Walewski had given her. Slowly, she undressed and pulled on her nightdress.

Daylight broke as Marie settled into the cushioned chair by the window, arms crossed. She replayed the night in her mind. She and her sisters had been welcomed by several other young people in a sleigh drawn by three horses. Oblivious to the cold, they cut through the snow-laden road at top speed, lending their voices to those of the passengers of the other sleighs in singing carols, accompanied by harmonica and horns. Honorata and Katarzyna happily joined the chorus, but Marie held back—until the infectious Czech carol "Zima, Zima, Zima," pulled her in. How her father had loved that tune! Looking back, she realized she had fully enjoyed the invigorating snow, songs and camaraderie of the *kulig*. Count Walewski was, for a time, forgotten.

The sleigh queue made two leisurely stops, each nearly two hours long—first at Brodno and then at Rybno. The *szlachta* families feigned surprise, but suddenly, after welcoming speeches, tables laden with delicacies appeared, as well as musicians to set the party-goers to dancing. Neither Marie nor Honorata lacked dancing partners, and Katarzyna danced for the first time, to the easy cadence of the Polonez.

At both manor houses, Marie felt herself under scrutiny by the adults, and when none of her dance partners asked for a second dance, it became clear that they had been warned off. Count Walewski's true intention in arranging the *kulig* was no secret. This was a drama of courtship. The thought made her ill with humiliation, increasing her dread of the future.

Laughter—Katarzyna's—floating up to the first floor brought her back to the present. *The carp!* The gift would be the centerpiece on Christmas Eve. The tradition reminded her of her father, and yet she smiled, imagining Katarzyna doting on her pet fish in the days leading up to the celebration.

While the night's events left her torn with competing emotions, both of her sisters had experienced a perfect night—orchestrated by the count.

Something in her stomach tightened. *If he—and everyone—has his way, I am the one to be laid out on a platter like a Christmas carp.*

13

Noon, 24 December 1803
Wigilia (Christmas Eve)

MARIE BUSIED HERSELF PREPARING THE *Wigilia* table, placing knots of hay—symbolizing the manger—among the gold-edged dishes reserved for special occasions. She paused at the foot of the table. Christmas Eve was the only day it was fully laid out, in case a guest or a stranger in need should stop by. Or a missing person. Marie ran a finger around the gold rim of the plate, recalling how her father joked with her in his effort to persuade her to eat her mashed turnips. Once, when her mother looked away, he sprinkled sugar on them and winked. It might have been on this very plate, she thought.

The countess left the sideboard and came over to inspect the table. "Why, it's beautiful, Marie." She picked up one of the plates and held it to her breast, tears welling in her eyes.

"What—what is it, Mother?" She wanted to reach out, but held back. She asked again, more gently.

The countess set the plate down and wiped her eyes. "That woman," she muttered, her voice low and sharp.

Marie blinked in surprise. "What woman?"

"Madame Jadwiga Walewska, that's who, Marie. She saw my dishes when her footmen delivered the fish that night, the night of—"

"Yes, I know the night. Did she insult them?"

"No—she wanted to buy the entire set. Why, it belonged to my mother and hers before that!"

Marie caught her breath. "She thought you would sell an heirloom? As if you would even consider it. How absurd!"

"Don't be too certain!" her mother snapped—and left the room.

Marie stood staring after her, heart hammering. Had they been brought so low?

Marie dressed slowly for supper. She had lost the opportunity to ask her mother about Count Walewski's whereabouts. The night before, she had a troubling dream that he took her father's place at the table, and she awoke perspiring and chilled. She tried to reassure herself that he was in Italy by now, but what if he had not made it through the Brenner Pass before the snows closed it down? Might he return home?

At dusk, Marie left her bedchamber. Below, her mother and sisters were waiting for her in the front hall. "Isn't Danusha coming with us?" she asked, taking her wool cloak from the hall tree.

"She has enough to do preparing her *Wigilia* specialties," her mother said.

"I want to be the one to discover the first star," Katarzyna said as they passed through the front entrance and down the stone steps.

"But I shall be the lucky one," Honorata teased.

"You did it last year, Honor," Katarzyna said, her tone serious.

"What does it matter?" Marie questioned. "Once it's done, we can get out of the cold and break our fast."

The gray of the sky was deepening as the four stargazers came to ground level and moved out into the courtyard, each establishing a different vantage point from which to watch the skies.

Some minutes passed before the sky had darkened enough for the traditional quest. Marie caught a twinkling in the east, high over the roof of the manor house. She took a few steps, tapped her youngest sister's shoulder, and nodded in the direction of the blinking.

Katarzyna was quick to take the hint. "There!" she cried. "There! It's the Star of Bethlehem, and I found it first!"

"The eyes of the young are always the sharpest," the countess said, turning for the house. "Now we can begin our *Wigilia* feast."

As the three fell into line, Katarzyna cast a sheepish look at Marie, who put a finger to her mouth. Leaning into Katarzyna, Marie whispered, "I saw only a twinkling, Kasia. You saw the star." Then louder: "Kasia is our Copernicus today!"

The countess and Honorata agreed as they stepped over the threshold. "Oh, the house smells so wonderful," the countess said. "The aromas of gingerbread and almond cookies are in the air."

When they entered the dining chamber, Marie saw at once—from behind—that the high-backed chair at the foot of the table *was* occupied. From where she stood, it was a man wearing a blue velvet frock coat, ruffles at the sleeves and feet clad in buckled pumps. She froze, certain that the previous night's foreboding was unfolding before her.

A quick minute of confusion reigned as everyone noticed the visitor.

Her sisters ran ahead to discover the man's identity, stopping and staring, mouths agape.

The person in the chair turned toward the two.

"Benedykt?" Honorata asked in a low, tenuous tone.

"The same," he answered, standing, "now come give me a proper hug." As he and Honorata embraced, Marie whispered to herself, "Sweet Jesus, thank you."

Katarzyna, who knew her much older brother only from occasional visits, held back and had to be coaxed into a hug.

Those greetings done, Benedykt asked, "And Marie? Where is my Marie?"

The countess, surprised by none of this, said, "Behind you," and nudged Marie forward.

"Oh, Benny," Marie cried, falling into his welcoming arms. Equal parts joy and relief surged within her. She craned her neck to look up at him. "I've grown, Benny, but you're taller than ever."

Benedykt laughed. "And you are prettier than ever. All my sisters are lovely!"

Katarzyna found her voice: "Where is your uniform?" she blurted.

"In France, Kasia," he said, "I can't wear a French uniform in a Prussian-occupied country."

The countess clapped her hands. "All right, let's take our places and share the *oplatek*. Danusha has put together a feast for us."

Everyone obeyed in short order. All the many colorful and fragrant platters and serving bowls were laid out beautifully, the gold-edged plates at each diner's place waiting to be filled. The holy wafer came to her now. Breaking off a piece, she placed it on her tongue and glanced down the table as if to reassure herself that it was indeed occupied by Benedykt. *Might he be my salvation?*

Suddenly, Benedykt cried out in his deep voice, *"Quel plat! Magnifique!"* His eyes were on Danusha, who had come through from the kitchen, carrying a huge platter laden with the carp Katarzyna had christened "Claude."

Even with the head and tail removed, the huge fish took up the length of the platter, smothered in Danusha's savory gingerbread sauce. As the oohs and ahhs went around the table, Marie's gaze fastened on Katarzyna, who sat across from her, tears forming in her eyes.

Only two days before, when Marie had come upon her feeding Claude from her fingers, Kasia looked up and whispered in the most heartbreaking tone: "Oh Marysia, how am I ever going to bear it?"

"You shall, Kasia," she said. "You shall."

Marie watched now as Katarzyna allowed the platter to bypass her without the spillage of a single tear.

After supper, the family gathered in the reception room for prayers, carols, and Benedykt's tales of Italy and Paris. Marie gave a show of enthusiasm, but her heart wasn't in the festivities.

When Benedykt slipped away after an hour, Marie followed him to the landing of the front staircase, where he was lighting a pipe. "I'd like to talk with you, Benny," she said.

"You'll catch a chill out here, Marie. Go back inside."

"We must talk—privately."

"Fine, but go back in. I'll come up to your room afterward."

Benedykt kept his promise after everyone had gone to bed. He stood in the doorway with a bemused look. "I was just now nearly bitten by a diving bat."

Marie stepped back as he entered. She laughed. "Welcome to Kiernozia. They don't really bite, Benny. You probably disturbed an insect that was following the light. But, maybe you can do something about the bats while you're here."

"I'll be here only a short time, Marie. Mother will have it attended to."

"Do you think so?" Marie pointed to her upholstered chair. "Sit down, Benny. You don't see that the estate is crumbling all around us since you've been gone?"

"I'm told, dear sister," Benedykt said, settling into the chair, "that you resent your brothers the right to take up arms for Bonaparte. You rather we were here mucking out the stables."

Someone had twisted her words. Her chin lifted, Marie moved toward her brother. "Who told you that? Mother?"

"No—Teodor."

Marie sat down heavily in her desk chair. "Oh, it's not that. It's just that . . ." Marie trailed off, unsure how to explain.

"You don't believe in Napoleon any longer, is that it? But I see clippings there on the wall I've sent you, as well as some nice sketches of him. Are you the artist?"

"Yes. And, of course, I believe in him. Why, he is our only chance for freedom." Marie leaned forward and took her brother's hand. "But with both of you gone now, Mother expects so much."

"Does she? —Do you mind if I smoke, Marie?"

She shook her head and sat back a little, withdrawing her hand. She watched him pull out a clay pipe and tobacco pouch from inside of his coat. After silently packing it, Benedykt stood up, opened a window slightly, lit the pipe, and sat back down. Smiling, he said, "I've found ladies prefer a little fresh air to pipe smoke."

"Like your actress friend?"

"Ha! —You're quick. Now, Napoleon, on the other hand, prefers snuff." When Marie did not respond, he said, "All right, then, let's return to the matter at hand. What does Mother expect?"

Marie drew up against the chair's back. "I think you know, Benedykt. If

Teodor didn't tell you, Mother did. She is allowing Count Walewski to court me."

His head angled downward, eyelids lifted, the midnight blue eyes mocking her. "And you don't like it?"

"Benny, I'm just seventeen this month. He is sixty-eight, with grandchildren older than me."

"I see." Benedykt puffed on his pipe and blew the smoke off to the side.

"What if your actress friend was sixty-eight?"

Benedykt laughed. "That's another matter."

"I had an invitation to Paris from my friend Countess Eliza Sobolewska. I had hoped to stay a few weeks, that's all. I wanted to see you—and your actress friend."

"A trip to Paris and back has its dangers, Marie. Dangers and costs."

"Eliza offered to pay for the whole trip, everything."

"That's nice, very nice. But Mother sees other dangers in Paris."

"What dangers?"

Benedykt paused, sighed. "Oh, she imagines the city overrun with young soldiers who would find you very beautiful . . . and innocent."

"So, she thinks I will find a husband there?"

"Or worse."

"What? —Oh! She's afraid I'll be swept off my feet by some suave Frenchman? Well, believe me, Eliza would be sure to protect me and send me safely back."

"Oh, the Sobolewskis are very fine people, but Mother would not have you inconvenience them. I think it's a matter of pride, too."

"Wait a minute, Benedykt! You *know* them? You've *met* them?"

Her brother's eyelids went to half-mast and his cheeks at the top of his beard colored. He cleared his throat, took a puff of his pipe, and deliberated. "Yes, Marie," he said upon exhaling. "Mother asked me to call on them."

Marie felt blood rising into her face. "Why?"

"To explain to them why we had to refuse, that we could not take such charity, and—"

"What? —And *what*?" Marie felt a stiffness in her neck and jaw.

"That you had duties here at home."

Marie gasped. Words failed her. No wonder all these months had passed without a word from Eliza.

Benedykt took her hand now in an awkward overture. "Listen to me,

Marysia. We all have . . . obligations. Teodor and I are bound to Napoleon's Grande Armée."

"With Paris actresses on the side?" Marie shot back. "You two get to frolic in Paris while I'm chained to an old man. Well, I won't do it, do you hear? I won't!"

"You have no choice, Marie."

"Who says so? You?"

"Women in good families must marry well."

"Fine, but I have time. I'll choose who I marry, on my own terms."

"History doesn't wait. It's flying at us. There's little time."

"I won't do it, Benedykt. I won't marry him!"

"War is coming, Marie. Teodor and I will stand with Napoleon for a free Europe, a free Poland. We know the risks. And the estate, Marie, the estate. Mother showed me the papers today. It's heavily mortgaged: the lands, farm, village, home, everything! Even if Teodor and I came home, we could not save it. But *you* can, Marie. There isn't time for you to make a leisurely decision about whom you might *like* to wed."

Marie was struck dumb.

"Marysia, stop for a moment and look at the opportunity you might have."

"Opportunity?"

"Yes! Listen to me. You can be the most important woman in the province. People will look up to you, respect you. And the relentless work and worry won't send Mother to an early grave. You will make the right choice, Marie."

"Choice?"

Benedykt sighed. "Listen, Marie, and stop your pouting. The count is an old man. You'll outlive him, and then you can make all the choices you want. You'll be liberated, and you'll have a palace and servants. Oh—and if you're worried about . . ."

"About *what*?"

"You know. At his age, I doubt that he will impose himself on you."

Marie took this in and her core went icy cold. She felt as if she had been struck. Her brother's allusion to what goes on in the bedroom brought her face-to-face with reality. She watched dumbly as Benedykt put away his pipe and tobacco pouch and stood, adjusting his coat.

"I leave very early in the morning, Marie, but I will come up and make a proper goodbye." He moved toward the door.

Marie drew herself up. "Don't," she said, her voice sharp.

He turned back, surprised. "Happy Christmas, then," he said.

Marie looked down at her folded hands resting in her lap. When she glanced up, he was gone. She had saved them both from an awkward morning goodbye.

She stared vacantly at the open window for a time, then stood, went through the motions of undressing, pulled on her nightdress, and threw herself onto the bed.

Marie was unable to focus for a long while. Benedykt supported the match with the old count. Eliza had not written; she must have bowed to the wishes of her mother, as delivered in person by Benedykt. And despite their closeness, Teodor was no doubt so excited to begin his life in the service of the Little Corporal that he had forgotten her. She could scarcely blame him, she admitted to herself. If she were a boy, she would be little different. While a lifestyle of parties, *kuligs*, clothing, and carriages might turn the heads of Honor and Kasia, she would happily serve in the Grand Armée with her brothers.

Marie felt alone, hopeless.

How she longed to talk to her father, disclose her fears, listen to what he might expect of her. She recalled how he would pick her up and swing her around while she laughed uncontrollably; how at breakfast, when she would not finish the last of her *kasza* for her mother, he would coax her into doing so with a laugh and a bit of the cereal on her nose. And always, her memory replayed the magnificent trip just the two of them had made to Warsaw. Sweet memories, but tragically bitter, too, in the irredeemable yearnings they awakened.

The room grew cold, colder. She knew she should put some wood on the grate and close the window, and yet she couldn't even stir herself to get under the quilt.

She closed her eyes. At seventeen, she thought, her life was over.

"Mother, Mother! Come upstairs, hurry! It's Marie!"

The cry seemed to come from a great distance, like a voice echoing through a hollow chamber. Marie stirred, vaguely aware of Katarzyna's excited tone. It's a dream, she thought, drifting back into sleep.

Suddenly, someone grasped her hand, rubbing it gently. She attempted to open her eyes but her eyelids seemed weighted.

"Marie, Marie," someone whispered close to her ear. "You're so cold, my child. So cold." Her mother's voice.

Where am I? Marie wondered, as voices murmured around her. Several hands were now pulling her, turning her, rolling her back and forth. She groaned, enveloped by pain.

"Pull the quilt over her," someone said. A bit of memory slipped into place. She lay in her bed. She'd meant to crawl under the covers, but hadn't.

She managed to open her eyes a bit, but the intrusion of light brought the lids down again. *Daylight? How is it possible?*

"Marie," someone said, a hand pressing to her forehead. "My God, she's burning up. Marie, can you hear me?"

Yes, she tried to say, but the pain, a sharp and relentless ache, held her captive. She tried to draw in breath enough to speak, but every attempt felt like blades stabbing at her chest. She began to shake violently. Panic flared up and she tried to lift herself from the bed.

Someone sat at her side, embracing her. Her mother's voice was soothing in her ear. "Lie still, Marysia. Lie still. I've sent Emeryk for Doctor Fabianski. Just lie still."

Marie's labored breathing and pain intensified as the day wore on. By the time the doctor arrived, a fatigue had settled over her. Still, she couldn't sleep and had developed a painful cough. Every muscle hurt. She continued to shake uncontrollably, and yet a feverish heat burned through her skin. The doctor's words and those of her mother sounded distant and muffled.

The doctor's large hand moved from her forehead to her cheek to her wrist. "See that she drinks a good deal of water," he said.

Marie felt a weight settle on her. Opening her eyes, she saw the top of the doctor's head come into focus, his ear attuned to her chest. A long minute passed before he stood up.

Marie couldn't keep her eyes open. The room was silent for a short while. Then she heard the doctor speak in a low tone: "It's the winter fever, Madame Łączyńska. But, from what you've told me about her extended depression, I suspect it was melancholia, and a bout of that could have brought it on."

Marie heard her mother's sharp intake of breath, and her conversation with Doctor Fabianski fell to whispers.

Fear jolted through Marie like sudden lightning. She remembered Magda Borowicz, a year younger at school, who had suffered from the fever the year before. She was moved from the dormitory to one of the nun's chambers, where she languished for weeks, her body failing by the day, until her lips and fingernails turned dark blue. It took two months for the winter fever to claim her.

Her mother's voice broke through her thoughts. "Thank you Doctor Fabianski," she said. "I'll see you out. Happy Christmas."

Marie turned her head into the pillow. *Oh yes, Christmas.*

Marie slept through most of Christmas Day. Occasionally, she was urged into wakefulness by her mother's litany of annoying health questions. That her sisters were kept away as a caution for their well-being came as a relief. She wanted no company, nor chatter about the world beyond her bed. She was thirsty and did accede to constant offers of water, but it did little to ease the fever. Despite the fire in the hearth, the room felt icy. The few shivering steps to the chamber pot were a trial she attempted only when absolutely necessary, and when finished, she hurried back to the cocoon of covers and safety of sleep.

14

MARIE'S CONDITION DID NOT IMPROVE. Her fever persisted, and what was a dry cough became phlegmy. Her chest pain increased, and she would wake up wheezing and gasping for breath, fear filling her in place of air. Fatigue, something she had never experienced before, rendered it difficult to move, to speak, to think. She was only vaguely aware of being made to eat and use the chamber pot.

The clouds of sleep offered the only real comfort. Her mother was often at the side of the bed, applying cool compresses to bring down the fever and its companion chills.

The days and weeks slipped by uncounted.

Today, Doctor Fabianski stood nearby talking to her mother. His visits seemed sporadic. "The shaking is not to worry about, Madame Łączyńska. It's a sign that she's fighting off the fever. However, if the fever leaves her and the shaking continues, send for me at once. I attended a similar case of the winter fever last year."

Marie heard her mother whisper something.

"No, it did not end well, Madame Łączyńska," the doctor replied, "but Marie is young and strong. We can hope."

He spoke what Marie had known in her heart the whole time: her life was in danger. Beneath the covers, she felt her heart pounding.

Her thoughts went to Magda Borowicz now, as they often did. The image of her classmate's still body on a stretcher being carried from the convent school haunted her dreams.

I will get well. I will!

1 March 1804

Winter began to loosen its icy grip on Kiernozia, and slowly, the fever loosened its hold on Marie. But fatigue remained a constant weight.

One morning, after a visit from the doctor, her mother came in with a note of cheer in her voice. "Doctor Fabianski says you will be up and about soon," she said. Marie forced a smile. For herself, hope remained elusive.

Count Anastase Walewski had not sent a word in all these weeks. She dared not question her mother, who avoided any mention of the man. Maybe he had forgotten her. Maybe he had realized the marriage would be nothing more than an exercise in his vanity.

Another thought: maybe in Italy his head had been turned another way. Or— maybe his health had in some way come to the fore. Maybe . . . he was dead. She turned the thought over, luxuriating in it—before her faith awoke her sense of guilt.

In the end, she knew that her mother and the estate were at his mercy. She feared that the count would come back, and she feared that he would not come back.

In a dream the week before, she had answered the door to find Arkady. He fell to his knees, took her hand, his upturned Russian blue eyes imploring her. He was an enemy Russian and of the hated Suvorov clan, but in the dream, all that was forgotten, the electricity that had once passed between them reignited. His charm, good nature, and passion for her were everything.

Now—with a future uncertain, she found herself questioning her past decision.

What if he *were* to call again?

15 March 1804

Marie awoke early, hungry for the first time in weeks. Her appetite was returning.

But somebody was in the room. She sensed it.

She opened her eyes. A shadowy figure sat across from her. She knew instinctively it was neither her mother, nor sisters. She thought at first it was Benedykt although she would have preferred Teodor, whom she longed to see.

She picked her head up off the pillow and stared through the morning gloom. For the briefest of moments, she thought of Arkady, and her heart caught. *Could it be?*

The chair legs scraped against the floorboards as the figure stood, the black silhouette against the brightening window like a *wycinanki*, a papercutting. Marie could make out the outline of a fancy frock coat and the brightness of buckled pumps.

The figure approached her, heels clicking against the floorboards.

"Oh Marie," came the croaky, familiar voice. "You've had me worried to death."

He bent over, his fingers brushing at her cheek.

Marie looked up into the weathered face of Count Anastase Walewski, her arms instinctively clutching her chest. Her stomach lurched, the world tilting away from her. It was done—she had met her fate.

PART TWO

"She had canaries to choose from and she chose a sparrow."
~Polish Proverb

15

17 June 1804

On a sunlit, summer day, Marie Łączyńska and Anastase Walewski were married in the Kiernozia village church.

From the front pew, Marie watched Father Albin conclude the Nuptials Mass, relieved she hadn't fainted. She counted twenty-four beeswax candles on and around the altar, all still alight. Some of the old women in the church surely believed the ancient tale that if a candle went out, one of the newly married couple would die young. Ironic, she thought, her humor dry—only one was young.

Anastase stood beside her, with her mother and sisters in the pew behind. Neither Benedykt nor Teodor were in attendance. Teodor had sent their regrets, citing duties, but Eliza Sobolewska and her husband hadn't even bothered with that courtesy. The omission sent a dagger to her heart.

Marie suspected that her lack of enthusiasm had led to the decision for a short, one-day wedding: the ceremony at the Kiernozia village church and the reception at the Walewski Palace. Her mother and the count's sisters had deemed the usual two or three days of festivities too extravagant. For that, she was grateful.

The priest motioned for the married couple to step into the aisle. As they turned to face the congregation, Marie glanced at Anastase's three sisters across the aisle—well-dressed, grave. Behind them sat his six children, grandchildren, and a host of relatives and friends. On the bride's side, behind her immediate family were her friend Amelia and her family, then Danusha and hers. The pews behind them were filled. Sunday weddings always drew a crowd of villagers, who not only met their weekly obligation, but also enjoyed the drama of a marriage ceremony. This one, Marie knew, would prove worthy of comments.

Ever eager to impress, Anastase had arrayed himself in his former Chancellor's uniform: a crimson *kontusz* with golden epaulettes worn over a white zupon and tied with a golden Turkish sash featuring embroidered horses. His yellow leather boots were freshly polished.

The organ began its soft prelude, breaking the awkward silence. Marie tensed, anticipating the rise in volume and tempo that would signal the march to begin. Madame Simone had created a diaphanous gown of soft yellow Swiss muslin for her, while Honorata braided her hair into a single coil, placing it atop her head. Crowning that was the customary wedding wreath of rue, made especially colorful by Kasia who intertwined the evergreen of the rue with red poppies.

It was said that if a bride did not shed tears, she would cry throughout her marriage. Marie looked out at the sea of faces, expectant expressions on a good many. *Let me cry,* she prayed, *Sweet Jesus, let me cry.*

No tears came.

The organ swelled into the lush and loud strains of the march, setting the floorboards beneath Marie's slippers vibrating. Marie pulled the most tragic face she could manage, simultaneously dabbing at her eyes as if to wipe away the wet. The count took her hand and guided her forward. She felt as if he were treating her like a mechanical doll.

Their joined hands lifted, the pair processed down the aisle as though leading the Polonez, Marie wiping at invisible tears, the clink of Anastase's steel-heeled boots punctuating every step.

When they reached the narthex, they stood side by side to greet the departing congregation, who offered congratulations as they filed past. Marie, faint from fasting since midnight, managed to smile through her exhaustion, wondering how many envied her—and how many pitied her.

When the last guest had passed, Anastase led her outside. A cheer erupted, and handfuls of grain pelted them. The count, ever spry, hurried Marie through the well-wishers to his waiting carriages.

The plan was for him to deliver Marie to her home, where she would breakfast with her family and begin the daylong preparations for the wedding supper and festivities at the Walewski Palace.

As the count was about to help her into the coach where his three sisters sat, she stopped him. "Forgive me, Anastase, but I must do something else now. You go on ahead and I'll see you at the supper."

"What is it, Marie?" he asked, eyes narrowing. "What must you do?"

Marie nodded toward the churchyard.

Anastase's expression softened. He seemed to understand. "We'll wait for you."

"No, please don't. Do go on," she urged.

He gave her a long look and sighed. "Very well. The coach with your family will wait."

Marie turned to glance at her mother, who stood near the second carriage, and hurried away, coming to stand in front of the Łączyński mausoleum, heart pounding. She longed to kneel down, but the thought of soiling her dress held her back.

"It's done," she whispered. "Do you approve, Papa?"

Minutes passed. Her father's funeral flooded her memory—how, at eight years old, she'd said her last goodbye. She still kept the handkerchief she had used that day, tucked in a box on her desk.

"You gave your life for us and for Poland," Marie murmured. She pressed her palm hard against the cold stone. "And so, this is my destiny, and I ask for your blessing, as brides do. I love you, Papa. Watch over Benedykt and Teodor. Keep them safe."

Tears, absent in the church, now streamed down Marie's cheeks, unchecked.

"Mother said she has just the necklace for your dress," Honorata said.

Marie and her sisters had gathered in the kitchen to witness Danusha's unveiling of the *kolacz*, the wheel-shaped wedding bread.

"Did she?"

"She didn't tell you?"

"No," Marie replied, her eyes on Danusha, stationed like a sentry near the large brick oven.

Danusha staged a little cough. "I thought you girls were here to learn about the making of the wedding bread."

"Can we steal a peek?" Kasia begged.

"No!" Danusha snapped. "The temperature must stay even for the bread to cook right. The top of the bread is braided and if anything goes amiss, it will crack."

"How do you know if the temperature is just right?" Honorata asked. "Or how long it takes?"

"Well, Honor, aren't you the one with the questions?" Danusha lowered her head toward Honorata, her blue eyes challenging. "I just do. I've made the *kolacz* for nearly every wedding in this village and several others." She shifted her gaze to Katarzyna. "You know, Kasia, if the braided top cracks in the cooking, the marriage will not be a good one."

Katarzyna's jaw dropped. "Really?"

Danusha caught Marie's eye now, and Marie—always good at reading faces—was certain she saw regret in Danusha's downturned mouth and loss of power in her response to Kasia: "Well, so they say."

"You must bake my *kolacz* then," Katarzyna said.

"Ha!" Danusha laughed. "Let's see about your sister's wedding bread first. —I believe it's time." She spun around, opened the oven, and, using a flat beechwood peel, withdrew the round loaf, placing it on the kitchen workbench. "Now, come gather around, girls."

"Why, it's lovely," Honorata said, pointing at the motif of leaves and two birds.

"They're love birds!" Kasia trilled. "Oh, it's perfect, Danusha. —What's inside?"

"The finest wheat, eggs, and a good measure of sugar. That's why it's really more like a cake than a bread."

Danusha's gaze came around to Marie, who struggled to conjure up an eager expression and the right compliment.

At that moment, the countess called for Marie from the floor above. Marie smiled at Danusha. "Kasia's right, Danusha," she said. "It's perfect."

A sparkle came into the servant's eyes.

As Marie turned to go, Katarzyna blurted, "Maybe it's her pearl necklace you're to wear, Marysia!"

"Oh, not pearls, Kasia," Danusha hissed. "Never pearls!"

"Why not?" Kasia asked.

Marie halted and turned toward Danusha.

"That's just the way of it, it is," Danusha said. "Pearls on a bride will bring a lifetime of misery. My mother often said so as if she was quoting the Bible. Now, you all should leave the kitchen. I have several more of these to bake so that all the guests at the reception will have a piece. Now—be gone!"

Marie made her exit, slowly climbing the stairs. So many cautions to worry about, she thought: tears, wedding bread, and now pearls. Why were there so many obstacles to marriage? *Anastase Walewski is enough of an obstacle.*

In her mother's room, Marie was relieved to find a gift not of pearls but an amber pendant. Marie loved amber. At school she had learned that the early Greeks valued it highly.

Her curiosity was aroused when she took a closer look. "Why, there's something dark in it, Mother."

"Come to the window and see it in the light."

Following her mother, Marie held the pendant to the daylight.

"Do you see it?" her mother pressed

"I do, Mother. It's a . . . a—"

"A bee, Marie. A bumblebee that lived and buzzed perhaps a hundred lifetimes ago!"

Marie drew in breath. The bee was held trapped in the amber as if in movement, as if it had just paused for a moment in its daily flight from flower to flower. Even the stripes of the bumblebee were apparent. It was a rare thing, indeed. "Oh, Mother, it is too precious."

"It was my first piece of jewelry as a married woman. I haven't worn it since your father . . . well, now it is yours."

"I shall treasure it always."

It was only later, as Marie stood at her mirror, fully prepared for the reception, that she remembered her tutor, Monsieur Nicolas Chopin speaking of amber's supposed ability to calm the mind. Was her mother's gift made with the intention that the gemstone would sooth her? It was an unnerving thought.

How am I to survive this night?

16

MARIE AND HER NEW HUSBAND sat at the center of a long dining table in the Great Hall, facing several guest tables. She had forced a smile when her mother and Anastase's sister, Jadwiga, ceremoniously presented the couple with bread and salt—symbols of both abundance and trials ahead. Now, Anastase stood and gave a long, meandering speech, intended for his wife but often veering off course.

When he finished, the room fell quiet and Marie was coaxed to stand. She managed a faint, tremulous "Thank you, Anastase."

"Speech," someone called out, inciting other calls.

Marie felt her face run red. Shaking her head, she sat again.

The count gestured for silence. "She is a young beauty," he said. "Forgive her— After all, my friends, remember that a noisy cow gives little milk."

A few women gasped, and the hall stilled, the count's ill-chosen proverb hanging in the air. Realizing his faux pas, the count managed a stage cough and said it was time to toast his bride. "Ah, my beautiful Marie Walewska," he announced, his eyes on Marie, "be it rich or poor, quick or slow, may you know nothing but happiness from this day forward."

He paused, looking toward the crowd. "So you see, a Pole is wise only after the harm's been done."

"There is truth in that!" someone called out amidst an upswell of laughter. The count smiled, pleased with himself. "And now, the toast!"

Marie stood again, holding a glass of clear liquid, one matching Anastase's. The superstition was well known: one held water, and one, vodka; the person who swallowed the vodka would be the true sovereign in the family.

She rang her glass against her husband's and swallowed down the contents. While she maintained the notion that she had a considerable acting ability, she couldn't pretend the liquid didn't set fire to her mouth, throat, and belly. It was impossible to avoid the giveaway of a grimace and a hand to her throat.

The crowd laughed uproariously.

"To beauty goes the power," Anastase bellowed, throwing in a dramatic shrug and a mischievous grin.

The couple smashed their glasses against the wall behind them, triggering cheers and applause. They sat and Marie surveyed the company. Most were the guests of the Walewski family, with a few important magnates mixed in. Marie's side was represented by her mother and sisters, though she had insisted that her friend Amelia be invited even though she was not of the *szlachta*. It had been her first confrontation with Jadwiga, Anastase's sister who ran the household. It was a small victory, one tempered by the knowledge that she will now live with his three sisters, and an assortment of other Walewski relatives.

The crowd called, "*Gorzko, gorzko!*—" Bitter, bitter"—a traditional chant demanding newlyweds to kiss, balancing out the sharpness of the meal and liquor. The cry would rise a dozen times throughout supper. The customary purplish Hungarian wine—tapped from two kegs and delivered by servants in the Walewski red and white livery—was anything but bitter. The count leaned in and kissed Marie, his wine-sweetened lips dry.

Count Walewski stood, raised his crystal wine glass, and propelled it in a wide, ostentatious arc that included Marie and all the guests. A flurry of purple droplets rained down on the white tablecloth, several landing dangerously close to Marie's light-yellow wedding dress. Seeming not to notice, he went on in turgid fashion to toast the dethroned King Stanisław and express his wish for Napoleon to rescue Poland from foreign powers.

At last, the wedding feast began.

The wedding couple was served kasza, porridge steeped in milk, to symbolize the sweetness of their married life. Platters of baked chicken were placed on all the tables now, along with sauerkraut, beet soup with noodles, and peas that represented fertility. Finally, the *kolacz*: the many wheels of Danusha's wedding bread were brought out and enjoyed. If the top of the bread had suffered even the slightest crack in the cooking, no one said anything. The compliments were many and loud enough for Danusha, who worked behind the scenes with the serving staff, to hear. *Wiśniówka,* cherry liqueur in stemmed crystal glasses, accompanied the dessert.

With the meal finished, the guests moved to the ballroom, where a Gypsy wedding band was playing. The band was chosen by the count for its exceptional violin and dulcimer playing, if not its inclusion of women musicians, and its reputation was enough to win over the doubting Jadwiga.

The wedding couple opened the dancing by leading the many pairs of dancers in the Polonez, their linked hands held forward. To Marie's relief, the stately dance allowed for a serious expression, rather than a smile.

Other dances followed—waltzes, Mazurkas, Obereks, and one born there in central Poland, the Kujawiak. Everyone wanted to dance with the bride, it seemed, and so the count had to give her over to a number of other partners. For a while, the often-intricate steps, excellent music, and cheerfulness of her partners infused a lightness in Marie, but each time the music came to an end, so too did the fantasy. As midnight loomed, the strangeness of her position came home to her when one of her partners from last year's ball claimed the final waltz: Karol Walewski. Anastase's grandchild appeared unruffled that she had just become his step-grandmother, but she was well aware that others, through looks or whispers—disdainful or mocking—had indeed noticed. No one, Marie was certain, could glance at the married couple and not note the gap of years between them.

At midnight, the music shifted to a romantic interlude of violins, signaling the start of the capping ceremony. The count left Marie standing in the middle of the ballroom, her cheeks catching fire.

The music ceased, a lively commotion and buzz of anticipation replacing it. As prescribed, some six or seven of the married women encircled Marie. Roza, a plump young lady, stepped forward and removed Marie's rue and poppy wreath.

Roza now unwound the single blonde braid that Honor had intricately coiled atop Marie's head. Another woman approached, carrying sheep shears. Marie's heart ached as the braid was cut away, symbolizing the transition from girlhood to womanhood.

"Who has the cap?" Roza called.

Silence settled over the ballroom. Finally, someone stepped out of the crowd and hesitantly approached the ring of women. Palms up, she was holding something as if it were an offering to the gods. It was the *czepek*, the wedding cap.

The gift bearer was Amelia. Marie's breath caught in her throat. Her friend had kept her part in this ceremony secret. Amelia's reassuring smile at Marie lightened the moment as she handed over the cap and made her retreat.

Roza lifted the brimless cap, a creation of white lace and embroidered pastel flowers, and pinned it to Marie's head, marking her new identity. It would be worn at Easter, Christmas, special festivals, and, one day, at her burial.

The audience clapped in approval. Servants appeared with trays of small glasses of vodka for the circle of women, who downed the vodka and held their empty glasses up to Marie, who drank last. "A girl no more!" Roza called out, crashing her glass against the fireplace. The others, Marie included, followed suit, and the many glasses shattered in quick-fire style.

The music resumed as the women joined hands and moved in a circle around Marie at an increasingly fast pace. With each revolution, they sang:

> Everyone, take a good look
> She was in a wreath and comes in a cap.

After a dozen full turns, they stopped, as did the music, except for the strains of a sad, lone flute. Marie ran short of breath as if a weight were pressing on her chest. Her temples thrummed. How she longed to run from this place! Her body stiffened as if preparing to flee, but a glance at her mother held back the urge.

"And now," Roza called out in her husky voice, "comes the bedding down!"

With high-pitched catcalls and laughter, the married women whisked Marie upstairs to the large bedchamber that was to be hers and Anastase's. Marie's heart beat fast with trepidation. The room dazzled her; a glow of candlelight, rich tapestries, heavy drapes, and massive dark furniture scented with beeswax polish. The centerpiece, a colossal mahogany bed, sat between two tall windows. Its sheer size made it seem like a boat, the purple velvet drapes hanging from the carved tester above, its sails.

Marie realized now there were eight women as she was introduced to each. Agnieszka, stood at a tall table pouring vodka into glasses. Two toasts were made— "A girl no more!"—the second one sharper than the first. Marie's refusals were ignored and she was made to drink. The third round inspired individual toasts. "May all your ups and downs come only in this chamber," Agnieszka said, her blue eyes alight with mischief. Another chimed in: "A woman cries before the wedding, a man after." A third added, nodding toward the bed: "May the strength of three be in your journey."

Roza regained control. "It is time to test the bed, ladies. Do you hear? It's playtime! Come, Joasia, we'll have the honors."

Marie watched in astonishment as the two, by far the stoutest of the lot, climbed aboard the bed. They began bouncing on the thick mattress, deeply denting the rose bedspread while laughing and calling out lewd jokes. "Move over," another—Krysia—ordered and climbed onto the bed, jumping out of sync with the others. Marie braced herself for the crash.

But the bed frame held firm.

Agnieszka provided another round of vodka and Marie was coerced to drink yet again. When the three on the bed noticed that they were missing this last round, they stopped cold, just as Krysia jumped in sync with the other two, and the trio came down hard, collapsing onto the mattress in a tangle of arms, legs, and laughter.

The bed still held, but on its right side the bedspread lifted like a woman's skirt and a great puff of feathers blew out.

Dizzy with drink, Marie watched the scene unfold as if in a dream. She found herself laughing with the others.

Suddenly a heavy knocking came at the locked door, silencing the women and shutting down Marie's reluctant laughter. Dread returned. She glanced from one to the next, reading their wide eyes and expressions.

"It's the men," Roza said as the three climbed down from the bed and hurried over to the table for their final drink. "They've come to deliver the count."

The three raised their tardy toasts to Marie.

Joasia smirked. "If only the count was a young man."

"Shush, Joasia," Roza said. "And if your grandmother had a moustache, she'd be your grandfather."

"The bedding down is nearly complete," Krysia said. "Now, no laziness this night, Marie!"

A tremor ran through Marie's body.

The heavy knocking came again. A chorus of deep voices, drunken voices, grew louder. "Time has come!" one called.

"Open the door, Krysia," Roza ordered.

Marie stood frozen with fear as Krysia went to the door.

Once unlocked, the double doors crashed open and a dozen young men tumbled in, like a slow-moving herd. Above them, they carried the Count Anastase Walewski like a war hero—or a corpse. He sat upon an ancestral shield she had seen hanging in the reception room.

His wig askew, his gaze—though clouded with drink, focused on the women before him. A slow smile spread across his face as he recognized Marie. "Ah," he slurred, "I've been here before, but they do say the third time is pure magic!"

Marie's hand instinctively went to the pendant at her neck. She felt trapped, like that once-lively bumblebee in amber. The sharp, high-pitched laughter of the women and the raucous roar of the men faded into the distance. Before she knew it, she had crumpled onto the purple Persian rug, the world spinning wildly around her.

PART THREE

"Wherever you go, you can never leave yourself behind."
~Polish Proverb

17

Bad Gastein, Austria
Saturday, 13 October 1804

MARIE SIFTED THROUGH HER TRUNK and selected a long-sleeved green frock, appropriate for a hotel dining hall. She changed quickly, for the sharp and biting alpine air could permeate stone walls and human flesh. She had resisted taking the thermal waters with Anastase, despite his insistence. It was a small enough victory, considering she had not wanted to come on this trip at all.

They had spent the summer at the palace in Walewice, as was customary for landowners. The harvest celebrations marked the change of season, but Marie found little joy in the rigid life overseen by the overbearing Jadwiga. Despite missing her own mother and sisters, she rarely visited her family estate at Kiernozia. Her *sacrifice*, as her mother called it, allowed her brothers to continue their service to Napoleon, as well as ensure each sister a fine education and good marriage prospects. The estate, too, was flourishing, easing her mother's burdens.

Marie had hoped to avoid Anastase's annual tour that included Bad Gastein by feigning a recurrence of what Doctor Fabianski had called *melancholia*. The subterfuge failed, however, when he insisted on staying home to be at her side. She realized she could either endure another soul-stifling season at the palace or embark on a journey that offered new experiences.

"Do you intend to go to Rome from there?" she asked.

"Yes, of course, my dear, and I can guarantee an audience with the pope. Can you imagine?"

Marie managed a smile. She would prefer an audience with Napoleon Bonaparte, but choked out, "I'll go."

"You'll not regret it. The warm weather will be a tonic for the malaise you're suffering."

At Walewice, Marie shared Teresa's lady's maid but declined Anastase's offer of bringing her own maid on the tour. She viewed it as unnecessary and intrusive. Their travel coach was manned by a driver and two Walewski servants. While the cities afforded them opulent lodgings, they carried bedding and kitchen supplies for posthouses where they stayed in modest hospices run by monks. In this way, they passed through Kraków, Vienna, eventually reaching the spa town of Bad Gastein, nestled below Salzburg.

Now in their suite at the Hotel Gastein—an imposing former nobleman's castle perched high on a mountain—Marie settled into a comfortable chair near a window, pulling on a fichu to keep off the chill. Upon arrival, they were told of a mix-up in reservations and a single room had been booked, with no accommodation for servants. After a heated conversation between Anastase and the *maître d'hôtel,* they secured these rooms, having displaced another guest in the process. The count's name and former position as Chancellor had done the trick.

Situated at the highest peak of the Alps east of the Brenner Pass, Bad Gastein impressed with its stunning waterfalls and healing thermal caves. Marie had to admit to Anastase that the landscape of deep valleys, gorges, and snow-capped mountain peaks was breathtaking. Yet, as she gazed out the window, she felt an icy loneliness settle in her chest. However magnificent, the landscape made her feel small and abandoned.

Movement, far below, caught her eye: a coach negotiating the narrow road into town, hikers returning before dark, and tourists making their way to or from the nearby baths.

Marie was lost in thought when Anastase entered, followed by Michał and Jakub, the two Walewski lackeys. Michał carried the count's valise to the bedchamber while Jakub waited at the door. Anastase had changed at the baths into a dark blue frock coat, white trousers, silk stockings, and buckled pumps—his apparel for dinner. He had not worn his peruke and his head shone like glass. He nodded at the servants, his way of dismissing them.

"Did the manager secure a room for them?" Marie asked after the men left.

"I didn't think to ask. His plan was to put them up with some of his staff." Anastase walked to the window near Marie's chair. "Have you seen this view, my dear?"

"I have."

"I wish you had come to the baths," he said, his tone earnest. "They're supposed to be therapeutic, and I always feel renewed afterward. There's something invigorating about the hot springs here that we can't replicate at home."

Well acquainted with the town, Anastase had shown her the caves the day before, intent on enticing her to join him. They were fascinating, Marie admitted, but she had no inclination to take the waters herself. He grew vexed by her refusal, threatening to cut two days from their stay. She instinctively crossed her arms over her middle. Of late, she found herself more susceptible to the cold. She didn't protest, for the thought of Italy's warmer climate was a definite lure. In the end, she suspected that Anastase would not follow through on his threat to leave early, and so she resolved it was time to reveal her secret.

Suddenly, Anastase spun away from the window, his faded blue eyes searching, a smile forming.

A weight lodged in her chest. She knew that expression, the glitter in the eyes, the sly smile he no doubt thought seductive. Would he at least wait until after supper? As he moved toward her, she silently cursed her brother, as she had done on a certain night back in June. How Benedykt had assured her that the count's advanced age would keep him from imposing himself. How wrong he had been. And as for an early emancipation, well, she doubted that, too. He was as healthy as an ox.

For months, she had mastered the art of excuses. But now, her mind blank, she stood up with a start and said, "I must dress for supper."

She told him in the hotel dining hall, after the *soupe aux champignons*.

His head jerked back. "A baby?" he stammered. "Are you sure?"

Marie nodded.

"No wonder you wanted no part of the baths," he said, his voice softening.

She gave a little shrug.

As the waiter stooped to clear the soup bowls, Anastase looked up and addressed him, saying, "We're to have a child."

Marie thought he sounded as if he was trying to convince himself.

The waiter's slow smile did not fully mask his shock at being addressed in such a casual way. He looked from Anastase to Marie, and back again, the smile ever so slightly twisting. "Well . . . well, my congratulations to you both." He bowed and disappeared with the bowls.

Anastase reached across the table and placed his hand on Marie's. "By all means, we should cut our stay short. Marie, do you wish to return home rather than travel to Italy?"

Marie had anticipated the question. "No, Anastase. Like you, I long for the warm climate."

"Really? A second surprise!" His eyes widened. "I thought you'd prefer being at home, near your mother?"

"There will be enough time for that after Rome."

"After supper I'll talk to the *maître d'hôtel* about our departure. Oh, wait until my sisters hear the news!"

Marie fought off a chill as the waiter arrived with the goose entrée.

Marie went to bed relieved that the news was out and that Anastase seemed enthusiastic about the prospect of a child. She knew she couldn't have kept the secret much longer. Even the current fashion of dresses cinched just below the bosom would soon be of little help. Upon discovering her condition, she had found her own emotions in turmoil. She had no wish to bear a child in a loveless marriage, yet as the weeks stretched into months, a protective instinct toward the baby gradually took root. In recent days, those feelings deepened, forming a bond with the child she was carrying.

18

Rome, Italy
Friday, 2 November 1804

MARIE AND ANASTASE ARRIVED IN Rome at dusk, checking into their capacious apartment at the Hotel del Sole al Pantheon in the Piazza della Rotonda, its windows overlooking the grand Roman temple. The city buzzed with news that Napoleon Bonaparte would be crowned Emperor of France on 02 December—a revelation that thrilled Marie, eclipsing any excitement upon their arrival in the ancient City of Seven Hills. They retired early so they could rest for the morning's visit to Anastase's Italian cousin, but the exciting news from France kept Marie awake until late.

In the morning, as they dressed for the visit, Anastase boasted about the palace's impressive gallery, detailing the many portraits of family members and paintings by masters like Van Dyck and Botticelli. "Why, the gallery is longer than the Hall of Mirrors in Versailles," he said as he pulled on his green frock coat, his chest puffed like a parrot's.

"Why aren't we staying there, Anastase? Surely your cousin has room."

The count gave a little grunt. "The Polish branch of the Colonna family separated from the Italian long ago. I'm a fallen-away distant cousin, you might say. Besides, I value the independence of a hotel. I would not wish to be beholden to the princess and have to account for my comings and goings."

"I see," Marie said, certain that things were left unsaid.

A generation older than Count Walewski, Princess Caterina, the lone resident of the Colonna Palace, sat at the far end of the painting gallery. Marie and Anastase walked toward her, their footsteps echoing. As they approached his cousin, she came into focus as a thin, elderly woman dressed in an oversized black gown. When they stopped before her, the princess looked them over with dark, scrutinizing eyes. "Ah, Anastase, I thought you might pass on your visit this year, given your recent marriage," she said, turning her gaze on Marie. "So, this is the young wife, is it? Your third, yes? Or have I missed one?"

Surprising herself with her retention of basic classroom Italian, Marie understood the princess's barb. Anastase stiffened beside her but said nothing, bowing instead. Marie curtsied, acutely aware of why her husband had suggested she wear her most conservative dress, dark blue and lacking any embroidered design.

Anastase smiled through the introduction, first in French, then Italian.

The princess's thin smile barely shifted as she gestured for them to sit in a pair of gold-embossed chairs placed some five feet away from hers.

They sat. Anastase and his cousin engaged in an Italian exchange swifter than Marie could manage. She caught snippets about the travel through the Brenner Pass, the death of a niece, and sights to be found during Holy Week.

Suddenly, Anastase's tone took a confidential turn and the word *bambino* caught Marie by surprise.

The princess's hooded eyes swept over Marie. *"Per quanto?"* she asked.

"Five months," Marie interjected in Italian before Anastase could reply.

The princess's eyebrow arched in a knowing gesture, her lips curling into an enigmatic smile before she turned her gaze to Anastase and resumed their conversation.

Ten minutes later, she dismissed them, ringing for a servant.

The interview was over.

As they rose to leave, Princess Caterina spoke to Anastase again, as if remembering something. He answered in a quick exchange, but Marie thought she caught a name she recognized.

In the carriage, Marie asked what the princess had said.

"Nothing important, Marie," Anastase replied. "She told me that Madame Henriette de Vauban is here for Easter week, and she's staying at our hotel."

"Really?"

"Indeed. She's an old friend—quite the *doyenne* of Warsaw society. I'll introduce her to you once we take up winter residence at the townhome. She's often on the arm of Prince Józef Poniatowski and will stand in as hostess at his copper-roofed palace when the prince entertains."

"I see," Marie said. Eliza had told her that Madame de Vauban emigrated from France during the revolution and that her role went beyond playing hostess. She was the prince's mistress and lived with him. Not only was she a decade older than the prince, Eliza confided, but her husband also lived at the copper-roofed palace.

The next morning, Marie awakened to find Anastase back from a morning walk. "Why didn't you wake me?" she asked.

"I looked in and you were sleeping like an angel. You need your rest, especially now."

"The weather?"

"Perfect—sunny and warm. Oh, I bumped into Madame de Vauban in the lobby."

"Will I get to meet her?"

"No, unfortunately, her time has been spoken for, even here in Rome. Imagine that. However, she introduced me to a French woman, who said she would be delighted to take you in hand come Wednesday when I'm occupied with business."

Marie pulled herself up in bed. "Take me in hand? Really, Anastase, I'm not a child. I hardly require a governess."

"Oh, I think you'll find her interesting. Henriette says she's a woman of letters and quite opinionated."

"What's her name?"

"Madame de Staël. She's a woman of fifty or so."

"Germaine de Staël?" Marie questioned, fully awake now.

"Yes, I believe so. Do you know of her?"

"She wrote a novel titled *Delphine*. Quite a few of us read it in convent school."

"Fine! Then you won't mind being placed in her company?"

Afraid to appear too giddy, Marie shook her head. "Is she pretty?"

Anastase shrugged and turned to leave. "Now, do get dressed; we're to explore the Pantheon today."

Marie felt relieved that Anastase did not ask what the book was about. *Delphine* had struck a chord among the students because it was about a woman's place in the world, a world of the aristocracy. She and the other girls were awakened to the reality that they were embarking on futures that were going to be narrowly defined by the men around them. Trapped by circumstances, the character Delphine is driven to despair and suicide. Had Marie revealed the storyline, she was certain Anastase would have no sympathy for the character's tragic end.

19

Wednesday, 7 November 1804

DIZZY WITH EXCITEMENT, MARIE LEFT the hotel room, having convinced Anastase that she didn't need a servant to attend her. "Very well," he had said, relenting, "she said you would know her by her red turban. And I trust you to stay in Madame de Staël's company."

Marie hoped to do just that. Eliza had told her that the author was widely celebrated, not only for her novel *Delphine*, but for the literary and political salon she hosted in Paris, one that attracted prominent figures from letters and politics.

Marie descended the two flights with a deliberate slowness, gripping the banister, taking in the ebb and flow of fashionable men and women below, relishing her freedom. She wore a dress of deep blue, cinched under the bosom with pink ribboning. That she was a woman on her own in such an extraordinary city, even for a short while, made her pulse race.

Stepping onto the hotel's patio, Marie quickly spotted the turbaned woman at a far table near the parapet that separated the hotel from the piazza. She drew in a breath and moved toward her.

As Marie approached, the woman stood, her striking scarlet taffeta dress daringly off-the-shoulder, showcasing an ample bosom.

"The clock is striking ten and here you are, Countess Walewska," Madame de Staël said, laughing lightly. "Oh, I know you Poles don't use your titles in direct address because of some amendment your Seym passed decades ago. What shall I call you, then?"

Marie's face ran hot. She curtsied. "Marie," she said, her voice soft. "Madame de Staël."

"Marie, yes! Let me see you. Now, just stand there for a moment." Her French was swift. "The count went on and on, praising you—how lucky he was for you to marry him. I didn't think that you'd live up to his compliments, but I see I was wrong. You are certainly beautiful, my dear. No wonder Generalissimo Suvorov's son fell madly in love with you. What was his name?"

"Arkady," Marie managed to say. "My husband told you that?"

She nodded. "As a way of boasting, I must say. So—I've kept you standing long enough and in your condition. Yes, he told me that, too." She laughed. "He talks like an old gossip. No offense, my dear. Now, do let the waiter seat you. Take this chair next to mine so that we both will face the piazza." Madame de Staël waved her hand and a waiter held the chair for Marie. He asked if she wished to order.

"I'm having a lovely Rhine wine myself, Marie," Madame de Staël said, taking her seat. "Will that do for you?"

Marie shook her head. Wine in the morning struck her as odd although she thought it no odder than what the writer chose for a daytime dress. "No, I'll have tea," she replied, rewarding the young waiter with a smile.

"Then bring some scones, will you?" Madame de Staël interjected before the waiter could retreat. "And jam!"

"Look across the way to the Pantheon, Marie. What a sight it is. Why, it's the only ancient temple still standing as it was, even though it's been transformed into a Catholic Basilica. I *adore* this city. And you must instruct the count that to truly experience Rome, you must view it from each of its seven hills. Oh, time and nature have demoted the hills from the mighty mountains they once were, but they remain impressive."

Madame de Staël took a lace-edged kerchief from her beaded red reticule and held it to her nose. "It's scented with vanilla—French, of course. You'll need to keep something like this, as well, for those times when you're near one of those wretched swamps around the city that give off *mala aria*. Roman fever or bad air—whatever you call it, it can kill."

Madame de Staël resumed her verbal tour of Rome for half of an hour, allowing only nods or single syllables from an enrapt Marie, who followed her flow of French almost seamlessly.

Madame de Staël was speaking about the Roman Forum when something in the piazza caught her attention. Her large hazel eyes widened. "There—look, Marie, across by the fountain. It's my children and their tutor. He's looking this way!" She waved him over.

The tutor approached the parapet, followed by a young boy and younger girl. Marie was introduced to Monsieur August Schlegel and his charges: Albert, fourteen—nearly fifteen, the boy insisted—and Albertine, seven.

Across the parapet, Monsieur Schlegel—with blurted interjections from the precocious Albertine—relayed their morning tour activities thus far. He was a handsome man, perhaps in his late thirties.

Conversation between Madame de Staël and the tutor was light and easy, so much so that Marie wondered at the informality. After some minutes, Schlegel and his charges moved on.

"Ah, dear man," Madame de Staël said, smiling fondly. "I don't know what I would do without him. He's a philosopher, you know. They pop up in Germany like blades of grass. A poet, too. He has plans to translate the Shakespeare plays into German."

"Really?"

"Indeed. But why, you ask, is someone with his mind and talent tutoring my two rapscallions? Simple—he's poor as an orphan, and I need a tutor. Lucky for me! And, well, he's taken a liking to me. I don't know why. I'm no great beauty. You, Marie, on the other hand—"

"So, you have two children," Marie interjected as a way to avoid countering her statement. Madame de Staël was certainly striking in appearance and eccentric in dress, but, while she had lovely hazel eyes, alert and bright, she could not be called beautiful.

"I have three. My eldest, Auguste, is away at school."

Marie nodded. "You're a wonderful writer, Madame de Staël! All the girls at convent school have read *Delphine* and cried over her fate."

"What—and the nuns allowed it?"

"Oh no, the novel is quite forbidden. A single copy made its way from under one girl's mattress to the next."

Madame de Staël threw her head back in uninhibited laughter, her full bosom undulating with the motion. "Too progressive for the nuns' taste, no doubt!" She laughed so loudly that it startled the patrons at a nearby table. Taking several moments to calm herself, she asked, "Do you know why it's forbidden, Marie? It's because I allow you, my reader, to feel. To *feel!* Did you girls feel for Delphine? The fear? The pity?"

"Oh, yes, Madame! Much pity! Both fear and pity! Our tears bonded us all."

"It's good to hear, Marie." The authoress looked away briefly, then returned her gaze to Marie. "I want more than tears, Marie. I want my readers to act."

"To act? How?"

"That would depend on them, don't you agree? And on you!"

Madame de Staël laughed again. "Oh, I have my detractors, you know, those who accuse me of sentimentality."

"We didn't think so, I can tell you. —Madame de Staël, you lived in Paris. . . .. I do so long to visit."

"Ah yes, Paris! I was eleven when my father was named Director-General of Finance and we moved from Switzerland to France."

Marie held back a gasp. "Under King Louis?"

"Yes, Father was in favor, dismissed, and recalled so many times I've lost count. He was the first director to publish the nation's finances, and thus found favor with the people more than with Louis. But when the coffers went empty, Father's popularity lessened. He was a favorite of Marie Antoinette, and I'm certain that she was responsible on at least one occasion for his recall."

"Were you in Paris during the . . . the—"

"*La guillotine?*"

Marie nodded.

"Fortunately, Louis had dismissed my father one last time and my parents left, but I stayed—a bit too long. Discussions in my pre-revolutionary salons focused on the kind of reform that might have averted the violence. Even my father supported reform . . . before the ugly times." Madame de Staël sighed. "I'll spare you the details. After all, Marie, I engineered our little meeting to talk about *you.*"

"You did?"

"You see, once your husband expounded on his marriage to you, I immediately felt a great empathy for you."

"You did?" Marie felt herself coloring with embarrassment.

"I also found myself in an arranged marriage."

Marie felt an uncomfortable tightening at her center.

"Oh, I had a sizable dowry and a few suitors," Madame de Staël continued "but I married at twenty to Monsieur de Staël, who'd been negotiating for my hand since I was twelve." She laughed. "It was a political alliance. He was tenacious, one must admit. I imagine the count was persistent, as well. By coincidence, he had been Chamberlain to the King of Sweden just as your husband had been Chamberlain to your King Stanisław, something your husband underscored."

Marie smiled.

"Our situations, yours and mine, Marie, are not completely in alignment, however. Eric is eighteen years older than I." Without taking a breath, she said, "How much older is Count Walewski?"

"Than I?" Marie asked. "I was seventeen and a half when we married. Anastase was sixty-eight."

"I thought as much," she said, tsking. "And his previous marriage? His wife died, I assume?"

"He was married twice, Madame de Staël. Both wives died."

"I see," Madame de Staël said, her tone flat. "Children?"

"Six, and a growing list of grandchildren. And a seventh now who might not be welcomed by his siblings." Suddenly, a floodgate within Marie broke and the words flowed out. "My father died fighting for Poland, and the responsibility fell upon me. I married the count to save the family estate and secure the well-being of my family."

"Men should know such bravery, Marie, the kind that's quiet and resolute. They can march to the front lines, knowing they may not return—but that sacrifice ends when the war ends. For women, though, the battlefield never ends. We women go to the front every time we bear a child. And in an arranged marriage, we enter with no real understanding of our husband's intentions—nor the duration of the union."

Marie offered a tight smile.

"No words in reply? I must teach you the art of conversation. I had the advantage of attending my mother's salons at a tender age and then creating my own in Paris. In France, everyone converses, no matter their station. It's a skill I've honed and one that will serve you well. We shall be friends, you and I. Would you like that?"

"Yes, Madame de Staël," Marie said, wondering whether she was suggesting further meetings. Or correspondence, perhaps.

"Good! I will say that your husband possesses the art to an extent." Madame de Staël laughed. "Why, his discourses are . . . shall we say, relentless."

Marie floundered for some comment. She wanted both to laugh and defend her husband. She took a different tack: "Does your husband know the art, Madame de Staël?"

"Of conversation?" She scoffed. "He neither knows nor appreciates it. His art lies at the gambling tables. I value three things in a man: empathy, ambition, and love of glory. My husband lacks all three, and while Anastase may have held ambition and glory as important, his time has passed. His age betrays him. As for empathy, well, it was just one morning's encounter over a tea tray, but I could detect none. He sees you as his possession."

Unable to counter the observation, Marie averted her gaze. While she knew it was true, it stung to have a stranger point it out.

Madame de Staël didn't press the issue. "Men have always had such freedom. Or they assume it. Eric, I came to find out, thought nothing of having a tryst here and there. But he soon learned just whom he married. Ha!"

Marie sat tongue-tied.

"You and I are alike, too, in that I found myself with child the year after our wedding."

"You mean Auguste. Anastase would like a boy, as well."

"Oh no, it was a girl. I had a little girl before Auguste and the two children you met. She died in infancy."

"Oh, Madame de Staël, I am so sorry."

Madame de Staël gave a dismissive wave of her hand. "Gustavine was her name."

"A lovely name."

"Yes, Gustavine. *She* was his, my husband's."

Her statement came like a bolt. Did she really mean the other three were not her husband's?

Madame de Staël caught her expression. The corners of her lips turned up in what Marie read as a smirk. She winked. Instead of speaking, she waved the waiter over for more wine and tea.

Once the drinks were delivered, Madame de Staël turned to Marie. "We will write to one another, you know. And it's time you call me Germaine. I insist that your letter salutations shall read Germaine, and that is how you will address me here in Rome when not in company. Your husband said you are staying in Rome through Holy Week, yes?"

"That's his plan."

"His plan? I see. Well, do you think you can find time to meet with me every Wednesday? Your husband can be left to his own devices one day a week, I should think." Then came the rich, throaty laughter. "Maybe he can amuse the *maître d'hôtel.*"

Marie almost laughed herself. A refreshing breeze filled the air, carrying the scent of vanilla. "I would like to join you, Madame de Staël. I mean *Germaine*. I shall ask Anastase when I—"

"No, no! You must *tell* him," Madame de Staël interrupted, smiling playfully. "But there's another subject I must bring up. The count tells me you have a kind of hero worship for one Napoleon Bonaparte."

"Oh, yes, Germaine. He is Poland's savior, I'm convinced. At least I pray that he is. All of Europe is counting on him." Marie drew in breath. "Have you met him? Oh, you must have!"

"Indeed, I have. And now, child, I must, at some length and with much passion, disabuse you of your notion of Monsieur Napoleon Bonaparte."

20

Monday, 22 April 1805

THE WALEWSKI CARRIAGE DEPARTED ROME a week and a day after Easter Sunday, proceeding south, along the Appian Way. Marie sat holding the palm branches against her enlarged middle, fronds that she had received from one of the Italian cardinals on Palm Sunday. This was a novelty and a blessing. In little Kiernozia, the village priest—like most in Poland—had no access to palm branches, using instead branches of pussy willows.

"I'm disappointed we didn't meet with Pope Pius, Marie," Anastase grumbled. "I was able to secure an audience with him on each of my last two visits."

"Well, we might excuse him this time, Anastase. His duty carried him to Paris and the crowning."

"Yes, of course, but that was early December! People expected the pope back in Rome long before Easter. Instead, he's not due until the middle of next month, and we must get *you* back home." The carriage lurched and rumbled through a bad patch of road. "Are you comfortable, my dear?"

"I'm fine."

"The pope wasn't truly needed," Anastase said, unwilling to let the subject drop. "It's been reported that Napoleon took the crown out of Pius's hands and placed it on his own head. Of all the audacity. . .." In a short while, the count's head fell forward, and he dozed off.

Marie was relieved to have some time to think. Anastase had been chattering since their early morning departure.

Truth told, she cared little about having an audience with Pius VII. She would have found him interesting merely in his connection to the emperor. Marie's appraisal of Napoleon Bonaparte had not waned despite Madame de Staël's skewering of the general on that first Wednesday. She had been shocked at how intensely the woman disliked him. They despised each other, it seemed, enough to motivate the emperor to exile her from Paris. "Too progressive, I was," Madame de Staël blurted. "He felt threatened by me, if you can believe that." She scoffed. "You wouldn't think a woman could threaten him. But it was my salon and my conversation among the political figures that frequented it that unnerved him. For years, I warned people that he would not settle for being First Consul, that he had his sights set on a more enduring regime, namely a hereditary monarchy."

Marie had listened, sitting stoically stiff while Madame de Staël railed on for an hour that day, citing Napoleon's faults and misdeeds, granting little acknowledgement to his victories. Despite her father's position in King Louis' government, she had supported the revolution—but not the Terror that followed. She hoped for the creation of a parliamentary monarchy. "Philosophers should triumph," she said, "not generals—or even *little corporals*, for that matter."

Marie stood firm in her belief that Napoleon would bring peace and equality to Europe, and when Madame de Staël realized that she was having little influence on Marie's opinion of the man, she vowed not to return to the subject again during their Wednesday excursions. "You are like my younger self," Madame de Staël said, "and I have more to impart than talk of that man."

In no time, Wednesdays had become the highlight of the week, and when one was done, Marie began counting the days until the next. As the two explored St. Peter's, The Capitol, The Forum, St. John Lateran's Church, the Villa Mellini gardens, and a dozen other sites, Madame de Staël expounded on more than architecture, sculptures, and paintings. It was her view that after the revolution, the stature of women declined. "You see, Marie," she said, "during the monarchy women were abused and derided, but under such a republic as we have now, women of a certain intelligence are *hated*. Women like me, women capable of ideas and conversation, find success in the salon, but seldom in our romantic ventures. Nonetheless, I encourage you to develop your spirit. Fate has placed us in the spheres of men, powerful men. It is the way of the world. Our gifts—yours and mine—are the abilities to understand, to give, and to exert enthusiasm. And to characterize love, even if we don't experience it."

Although sometimes Marie struggled to understand the authoress, she found her fascinating. She was impossibly progressive for one thing. Napoleon had hit the mark in that regard. Only the first of the four children was sired by her husband. Her two boys were fathered by one lover and the girl by another. One lover was a Bishop in the Catholic Church, Charles Talleyrand, who was, Madame de Staël insisted with an air of amusement, a man pressured by his family into the priesthood, a man completely lacking in religious conviction. Her tone changed to one of disdain when she added that he was now Foreign Minister and one of Napoleon's closest advisors.

The tutor Schlegel, as companion and lover, came later, and it was there in Rome that he was displaced by a Portuguese nobleman, Don Pedrode Souza e Holstein, twenty-four years old. Madame de Staël spoke so freely of her lovers that Marie wondered if it was not by design. But why? To shock her? It had done that.

The mystery stayed with her. Once, while they were touring a Roman columbarium, Madame de Staël had abruptly turned to her and said, "If I had been born as beautiful as you, Marie, I would have been more selective with my charms." That, too, was a mystery Marie plumbed as the carriage rattled on toward Poland.

Amidst a springtime downpour, as the carriage drew close to Kiernozia, Marie felt the child move in her womb. She pressed her hand to her middle, and for a moment felt happy. She looked to Anastase at her side, dozing. Madame de Staël's parting words, memorized now, came back to her: "Arranged marriages, my child, call for one to be *en garde*. Happiness will come later, will come at intervals, may never come."

Marie shivered.

"We're home!" Count Walewski said. "At last."

Marie looked out the carriage window. The rains had stopped. They were on the entrance road, entering now the huge circle drive fronting Walewice

Palace. The massive four columns supporting the portico came into view, the two-storied wings of wide, high windows spreading to the right and left, the arched half-windows cut into the steep roof of evergreen shingles above. She had yet to call—or *feel*—that this fortress-like building was her home. As the carriage ground to a halt, she could see a flurry of quiet, orderly activity as Walewski grooms and servants came from several directions.

By the time Anastase handed her from the coach, the three Walewska sisters had appeared near the door. She steeled her back at the sight. She took Anastase's arm, and they moved toward the door, past a line of male and female uniformed servants.

"You stayed long after Easter," Jadwiga said, her face pinched. "We have been fully prepared for a week."

The count, used to her sour ways, gave a dismissive wave of his free hand. "We held out hopes that the pope would return from France."

"And he didn't?" Teodora voiced the obvious.

Only Teresa, younger half-sister to the other two, smiled. "Well, everything is set for your arrival. Welcome home!"

Marie nodded to her and managed a smile as she and Anastase passed into the house. Her body, so cumbersome now, ached from the long travel days and often uncomfortable overnight stays. In the vestibule, she looked up and was suddenly reminded of the exceedingly long and twisting staircase leading to the first floor.

Anastase must have seen her wince. "We'll have my men carry you, Marie," he said, turning to give an order.

"No!" Marie said, more forcefully than she intended. She took a breath, adding, "I can do it."

She moved slowly up the stairs, her left hand on the polished mahogany banister, Anastase on her right. She would show herself capable. She recalled Germaine's words about enthusiasm. She would embrace this return, even if it felt like a battle.

21

Thursday, 13 June 1805

SIX WEEKS AFTER THEIR ARRIVAL at Walewice, Marie's water broke early in the morning, moments after she had risen. She had slept alone in the room she shared with the count, the room in which they spent their wedding night. Since their return, he had taken to sleeping in a nearby bedchamber to avoid disturbing her sleep.

Barefoot, Marie stepped through the wetness, pulled the bell cord, and collapsed onto the side of the bed.

The maid most often assigned to Marie appeared within minutes. She stepped close to the bed. "What is it, Madame Walewska? —Oh!" Her eyes widened as her gaze moved from Marie to the floor and back again.

"The baby is coming, Hania. Tell the count to send for the doctor. Hurry!"

"Yes, Madame," she said, turning to leave.

"And don't say anything to—" Before she could say *Madame Jadwiga*, Jadwiga Walewska herself stepped in, pushing the door open with a swift motion, her quick, birdlike eyes taking in the scene.

"It's time then, is it?" Her sister-in-law put her hand out and stopped Hania. "Don't bother the count, Hania. Go directly to the head groom and tell him to collect Midwife Anusia from the village. Go!"

The girl shot a timid look at Marie and fled.

Marie shifted on the bed in an attempt to sit. "But I—"

"Never mind," Jadwiga cut in. "Lie still. Doctor Fabianski is too far away. And I don't trust him. He should never have allowed you to stay in Italy for so long. Just look at you! I was twice as large when I gave birth."

Marie glanced down at her abdomen. The doctor had not given any advice about extending their stay; it was Anastase, who had his heart set on an interview with the pope, that made the decision. However, Jadwiga's comment about her size ignited her own fears. Would this be a healthy delivery?

Jadwiga turned to leave. "I'll send a girl to clean that up," she added over her shoulder, distaste in her tone.

At midmorning, Anastase looked in. He was dressed in his riding clothes, having just returned from an outing. No one had told him anything, so Marie alerted him to the situation, whispering her preference for Doctor Fabianski. Flustered but concerned, her husband agreed to send for the doctor. However, after he left, his voice and that of Jadwiga's could be heard coming from the hall. Marie knew at once the doctor would not be coming.

Soon after, Midwife Anusia arrived and gave Marie a brief examination that did nothing to bolster her confidence. "How often are the pains coming, Milady?" the rotund woman asked.

"Every ten minutes or so."

"I see. It will be a while yet. Lie quietly, Milady." Then, almost as an afterthought, she asked, "When did you last feel the child move?"

"Just a minute ago."

"Good," Anusia said, pulling an upholstered chair closer from the other side of the room. She settled into it and watched quietly.

Hania and another maid entered, setting down basins, towels, and sheets, on a table before quickly curtsying and leaving.

Marie lay back and closed her eyes. The room seemed to warm, and she shifted in discomfort, her breathing growing heavier. Morning lapsed into afternoon—two hours? Three? She couldn't tell. She ran her hands through her damp hair, wishing for it all to end. Sweat beaded on her skin. The pains were coming more frequently and more intensely now.

Opening her eyes, she saw that Anusia had nodded off in the chair.

"Anusia," Marie called, surprised at how weak her voice sounded. "Anusia!"

The midwife jolted awake. "Milady?"

"The pains are coming every four or five minutes now, maybe sooner. I'm sweating."

"Not to worry, Milady. We still have a bit of time."

By the time dusk began to fall, the room felt stifling. Sweat soaked her nightdress, and the pain became unbearable.

Anusia finally sprang into action, calling Hania in from the hallway and instructing her to go to the other side of the bed.

Panic surged through Marie. Her heart raced. She gripped Anusia's arm.

"The pain gets worse, it does," the midwife murmured, gently releasing Marie's hold. "It won't be long now."

Marie suppressed a scream. "No—no, it's the baby, I don't feel him moving! Oh—!"

"Hush now, Milady. The contractions are taking over. It's the contractions. The child is fine." She ordered Hania to fetch three pillows.

Marie bit her tongue. *How could she know that? What if my baby is dead?*

Anusia and Hania spoke in low, rapid tones that Marie could not decipher. Something was wrong.

"We're going ease you into a partially sitting position," Anusia announced. "Try to move with us, Milady, as we draw you forward."

"What?" Marie cried. "Why?"

"Just do it," Anusia snapped. "The pain will lessen, and the birth will come more easily."

Marie fought off panic and nodded. She had no choice but to trust the woman.

With no little effort, it was done. Marie lay at a slant, the three pillows lodged behind her. However, instead of the pain ebbing, the move coincided with a contraction. Marie could not contain her scream.

"The time is close, Milady. You need something to hold onto as you push."

Hania suggested one of the count's walking sticks.

"It must be something secured," Anusia said, reaching for the bell cord. "Here!" She looped it around a bedpost and tied it, handing the tasseled end to Marie. "Hold tight with both hands when you push, Milady, do you hear?"

Time slowed. The contractions gripped her body, forcing her to cry out in agony. Anusia tugged at Marie's nightshift, pulled her legs apart, and brought the knees up. Marie closed her eyes, praying for her baby. She felt the contractions, but not the baby.

"You are to push now!" Anusia commanded.

Marie held tightly to the bell cord and pushed, each contraction coming sharper that the last.

"Again," Anusia urged. "Push, Milady, again."

As the pain reached its zenith, Marie could no longer summon a cry. She held to the cord, knuckles white as chalk.

"It's coming!" Anusia's voice broke through the haze of pain. "Push!"

Marie obeyed, feeling as if she were engulfed in white-hot flames.

"The head is coming!" Anusia hissed. "Lean forward a little and push again."

Marie could hear Hania whispering prayers.

"The shoulders, now," the woman said, her voice calmer but insistent. "Push, Milady. Just one more push."

Moments later, at last, Marie felt the baby leaving her body.

Anusia spoke the words Marie had been waiting to hear: "It's here—the baby is here!"

The pain ebbed. Marie leaned back, listening to the midwife give some order to Hania, who cut the baby's cord. Suddenly the baby was lifted away by Anusia and taken to the preparation table.

As Hania went about the business of aiding in the final stage of labor, Marie's focus was riveted elsewhere—on Anusia's back. Something was wrong, terribly wrong. No sound issued from the infant.

My baby!

Her voice returned. "My baby!"

"It's a boy," Anusia said, her voice dry and distant.

"He's—is he—" Marie's voice cracked. "Let me have him!"

"Wait, Milady!"

Marie went cold. Long, long seconds passed.

Suddenly, the midwife raised the child in the air. Marie blinked. It couldn't be . . . But it was—the baby.

He was so small, smaller than she'd expected. But it was his silence that made her heart freeze. His silence!

Before Marie could draw breath to scream, Anusia slapped the baby—once, with a sharp crack. Marie flinched.

Another slap!

And then, weak but unmistakable, came the tiniest cry—a faint, trembling sound, like the chirp of a bird.

Marie lay in bed, her newborn son sleeping in the crook of her arm. The pain was gone but not the fear. Would this child survive? Her husband assured her as much, as did the midwife before making her goodbye. And yet, Marie had dark images coursing through her mind that she couldn't stave off, images of a small coffin, a funeral, a burial plot in the churchyard beneath an iron gray sky. She dozed off, her mind inventing promises that might facilitate a contract with God.

———•⚜•———

Marie awoke suddenly. A small audience surrounded the bed. Anastase stood at its foot, his sisters Teodora and Teresa on either side of him. Hania stood on the left side of the bed, while Jadwiga stood a little farther down.

Anastase cleared his throat. "Marie dearest," he said, "the wet nurse has arrived."

"What? We've not discussed this, Anastase." Marie felt a heat rise into her face. "I'm perfectly able to nurse my child. I already have!"

"You need to heal and grow strong yourself," Jadwiga interjected. "You've married into our family, child. You must adapt to our ways."

"It's the Walewski way, my dear," her husband added, with a shrug.

"Where is she?" Marie demanded, shifting in the bed to take hold of her son. She would not release him.

Jadwiga was quicker, however, swooping down like an eagle and lifting the baby from the bed.

Marie dared not resist. The baby was too small and delicate.

"Why, he weighs almost nothing," Jadwiga remarked. "So very puny."

"Anastase," Marie pleaded, her voice breaking, "where is this woman, this wet nurse?"

"She's in the nursery, Marie," Teresa said. "We trust her, dear. Her name is Nadia." Teresa was the one sister who treated her with respect, but she stood with the others on this issue.

"No!" Marie cried. "Bring her here. I want my son with me!"

Her words made no difference. Jadwiga turned to leave with the baby. Her sisters followed.

Marie pulled herself up against the headboard. "Anastase, don't let them do this. You can't allow it!"

Her husband sighed deeply, shifting from foot to foot. "My sister is right. You must adapt to our ways." He bent to kiss her forehead, and, turning to leave, he said to Hania, "Stay by her."

Once alone with Hania, Marie said, "This place is so big, Hania. Tell me, where is the nursery?"

"It's at the far end of the other wing and a floor above."

"In the *attic*?"

Hania nodded. "It adjoins the governess's room. That's where the groom brought the wet nurse's trunk. Out of breath with the weight of it, he was. She's come to stay for a while, Madame."

PART FOUR

"A wife, a razor, and a horse are things that should not be lent."
~Polish Proverb

22

Warsaw
Sunday, 9 November 1806

MARIE SAT IN THE RECEPTION room of the Walewski Warsaw townhome knitting a cap for little Antoni. She was in particularly high spirits, as she had recently received news that the French had routed the Prussians from Berlin, following two successful battles in mid-October at Jena and Auerstedt. These victories were the latest in a series of triumphs for Napoleon, who had already defeated Russian and Austrian armies, forcing Russia to retreat and Austria to surrender.

Though the French and Spanish navies had suffered a disastrous defeat at Trafalgar the previous year at the hands of the British, Napoleon had shifted his focus to land-based campaigns. Now, with Austria and the Prussians on the run, and Berlin secured, Napoleon and his Grande Armée of 180,000 were preparing to move east to engage the retreating Russian forces. Marie knew that before that could happen, Napoleon had to consolidate his control over Eastern Europe. Napoleon Bonaparte was headed to Warsaw. She was thrilled.

Marie's attention was taken from her knitting when the Walewski butler entered, announcing, "The Madame Eliza Sobolewska."

Marie rose to greet her friend, exchanging cheek kisses. She gestured to the chair opposite hers.

Eliza offered a nervous smile and settled into the upholstered chair. "I'm so glad you responded to my note, Marie, and that you've forgiven me for not insisting you come to Paris. I should have pushed harder."

The months of silence between them still stung. Marie bit her lip, holding back the hurt. "It would not have made a difference, Eliza. Both my mother and Benedykt were set against it."

"I did write when I heard of your plans," Eliza said. "You must allow me that."

"You did? About what?"

"Yes, about your marriage plans. I was . . . concerned."

Marie tilted her head. "Eliza, I received no such letter."

Eliza's face paled. "My God, do you mean it was lost? I suppose it was. It happens often enough."

She believed her friend. "Lost or hidden," Marie murmured.

"Hidden? By whom?"

"Eliza, what did you write?"

"It hardly matters now that I find you so settled." Eliza sighed. Her eyes darted toward the hall, and her voice dropped. "But I wrote to discourage you from going through with the marriage. You don't think your mother hid—"

"Why did you write that?" Marie cut in.

Eliza stiffened. "I warned you that marrying the count might lead to regret, that you'd eventually be tempted by a younger man."

"Is that all?"

"No, I mentioned that I could introduce you to at least two young men more suitable."

Marie crossed her arms. "Men who could lift us from poverty?"

Eliza nodded. "I waited for your reply."

Marie was stunned and at a loss for words. Her life might have taken a very different turn. She was convinced her mother had intercepted the letter.

Eliza quickly added, "That's in the past now, Marysia. Perhaps you wouldn't have cared for either of them. And now, you're a mother. How wonderful. What is the baby's name?"

Marie collected her thoughts. "Antoni Colonna Walewski. I had little to do with his naming or baptism."

Eliza blinked in surprise. "Oh? —How is he?"

"He was very small and weak at birth, but he's growing, little by little."

"How old is he now? May I see him?"

"Sixteen months. He's not here, Eliza." Marie pressed her lips together. The subject tugged at her heart. "Antoni is at Walewice. I don't see him often, but tomorrow we will return there for a few days."

"Is he still—frail?"

"No, it's his overbearing aunts who oversee his upbringing and keep him from me. They have their way of doing things. A governess has been hired, even though he still has a wet nurse. I suppose they'll soon be interviewing tutors. And Anastase goes along with it." Marie paused, holding back tears. "Eliza, when I am able to hold him, I feel like I'm holding another woman's child."

"Oh," Eliza said softly, "I'm sorry, Marie."

"It's a cross I have to bear—one I never expected," Marie whispered.

Eliza cleared her throat and changed the subject. "Have you heard the latest news about Napoleon?"

"His victories in Prussia? Yes! It's wonderful! I'll get to meet Marshal Davout at Walewice because Anastase has offered the palace as headquarters for his staff. His Guard Brigade is occupying Łowicz."

"That's very exciting!"

"It is, Eliza." Marie paused for a few moments, then said. "Teodor wrote that Napoleon's push across the continent is very unpopular with the French people. Is that true?"

"I'm afraid so. I witnessed it there in Paris—the endless wars, the casualties—it's wearing on them."

"It's no wonder. And yet, he follows his own drumbeat. How I would like to meet him, Eliza!"

"Meet Napoleon Bonaparte?"

"Yes! You know I believed the day would come when he rescued Poland. And now it's happening! If only for my father's memory, I want to plead our case in person."

"Oh, I think your fascination with him is more than that," Eliza said, smiling. "But even though thousands of our men march with him, your brothers, too, he has issued new demands of Warsaw."

"I hadn't heard. —What demands?"

"Forty thousand more soldiers, as well as food, horses, everything that might be needed for his Grande Armée's campaign against Russia."

"Oh, Eliza, what else could we expect from him if he's to give us our independence?"

"Ah, you have supreme hope, like nearly everyone here in the capital these days."

"Don't you? Don't you have hope, Eliza? Or do you doubt it?"

"Let me finish with his demands. He wants to see Polish society restructured. Poland would be re-established—yes, but as a Polish state under French protection."

Marie's breath caught. She paused, mulling over the news. "And how have our leaders here reacted?"

"Most still support Napoleon. They think this could be the first step toward complete independence."

"And others?"

"Like me, they question. Would we become a puppet nation? And, when he comes to final terms with Prussia and Russia, how adamant will he be regarding having our lost lands returned *to us?*"

"Austria already gave up Polish lands upon their defeat."

"That's true."

"Eliza, we must believe in Napoleon. We have no other card to play."

"You're right there. The capital is secretly readying for his arrival now. With the Prussians all but beaten, central Poland and Warsaw will soon be free. General Koehler's days as military governor of Warsaw are numbered."

"Praise God! —Tell me, with all your time in Paris, have you met him—Napoleon?"

"Ha! I don't want to knock him off that pedestal on which you have him perched."

"Oh, Madame de Staël tried to knock him off it, but in vain." Marie laughed.

"Germaine de Staël? You met her? Oh my! Tell me everything."

"Another time. You must tell me about *him*."

"Yes, I met him in passing at social events, all very formal. Sometimes, I merely observed him from afar. They call him 'The Little Corporal,' but he's really of average height. He has gray-blue eyes that can paralyze a person. I've seen it occur. His relationship with Josephine is waning, so they say, because she has failed to provide him with children."

"Other women?"

"Yes, but none seriously, and not when he's on campaign. He's cynical about women. My husband says Napoleon thinks it's the power that attracts them, like an aphrodisiac."

Marie recalled Madame de Staël's assertion that *Fate places women in the spheres of powerful men.* She had encouraged Marie to develop her intellect, explaining that women capable of ideas and conversation could hold their own with powerful men. However, she warned that those very traits might limit their success in love.

"At any rate, he's on his way," Eliza continued. "Preparations are underway."

Marie snapped to attention. "Already? Oh, but I'll be in Walewice!" She leaned back in her chair, clutching her chest. "I'm liable to miss his arrival!"

Eliza shook her head. "Not if you stay only a few days."

"Good!"

"Marie, you'll be twenty soon, yes?"

"The seventh of next month. Why?"

"You seem so different—aside from your hero worship, that is," Eliza said, with a laugh. "It's the way you carry yourself, the way you dress, the way you speak. You've changed in the months we've been apart."

Marie felt the heat of a blush.

Eliza giggled. "Although you can still turn red as a strawberry like the provincial maiden you once were."

The two friends laughed.

Later, as Marie lay in bed, she thought about Eliza's words. I *have* changed, she realized. Marriage and motherhood had shaped her, for better or worse. Travel had influenced her, too—Vienna, Rome, Italy. Madame de Staël had made her impression, and so had her sisters-in-law.

23

MARIE FOUND THE TWO-DAY CARRIAGE ride to Walewice tiring and marked by rain. Upon arrival, the Walewskis found that Marshal Louis-Nicolas Davout and his staff had already settled into the palace. Although the building had ample space, her husband insisted that they would be more comfortable staying in the estate manager's house near the main road.

The following afternoon, Marie visited little Antoni in the attic nursery. To avoid her sisters-in-law, she used the servants' stairwell. Berta, Antoni's governess, was a large, no-nonsense woman who couldn't quite conceal her irritation at the intrusion.

Antoni's health was improving. He was walking with growing confidence and starting to speak a few words. During their time alone, Marie tried to teach him to say *matka*, but the effort was met with disappointment. Her frustration deepened when Berta returned and Antoni toddled toward her, happily saying, "*Baba.*"

In the evening, Marie chastised herself for allowing her thoughts to drift toward Napoleon's impending grand arrival in Warsaw, instead of fully embracing her time with her son. The next day, she felt more centered, and Antoni began to warm to her attention, making a good effort this time at calling her

Matka. The thought that one day she might reclaim Antoni from the influence of her husband's domineering sisters brought her a quiet sense of reassurance.

By the time Marie awoke on the third day, Anastase had already gone up to the palace to offer assistance to Marshal Davout. Like Napoleon, Davout was still in his thirties, leading Marie to wonder how readily her husband's advice would be received. With the days' long rain finally stopping, Marie prepared to walk up to the palace. She stepped outside onto the tiny platform in an ivory dress, blue cloak, and bonnet, only to find the road had turned to mud.

"Oh no," she whispered, assuming she would have to wait for Anastase. Just as she turned to make her retreat, she noticed a cavalry officer approaching on foot, his scabbard gleaming faintly in the weak sunlight.

The young man stopped across from her, removed his helmet, and bowed. "May I be of service?" he asked in fluent French.

Before Marie could find her voice, he walked toward her, his boots splashing through the mire. "Allow me, Madame Walewska, I'll carry you to the palace."

"You know me?"

"Come along," he urged, "before we get the next downpour."

Before Marie knew it, she was lifted into his arms and carried up the road, where he set her down on the flagstones in front of the palace. Though she knew she should feel affronted, she did not.

The officer bowed. "Forgive me, Madame Walewska. I am Lieutenant Charles de Flahaut. I was sent by your husband to escort you."

"To rescue me, you mean. My husband sent you? You should have said so."

"I apologize, Madame." Another bow.

Marie smiled and gave a dismissive wave. She looked toward the portico, where Anastase was pacing, his yellow leather boots spotless. For a moment, she imagined him carrying her up the muddy road instead of the dashing lieutenant. She covered her mouth, stifling a laugh.

At supper that evening, Marie and Anastase joined Marshal Davout at his table, a welcome change from the previous two nights when they had dined with the Walewska sisters. Marie found the marshal charming and chatty, learning that he was married to a woman whose brother was Napoleon's brother-in-law. Keeping to the subject of marriage, she turned to the officer who had rescued her earlier. "And you, Lieutenant de Flahaut, are you married?"

"Please call me Charles, Madame Walewska," he answered. "No, I am not."

It was an innocent exchange, but she sensed Anastase becoming tense. He spoke little the rest of the meal.

When they retired, her husband confirmed her suspicion of jealousy when he related the gossipy news that Charles de Flahaut was the illegitimate son of Charles Talleyrand.

"Do you mean Bishop Talleyrand?" Marie gasped. "Napoleon's Grand Chamberlain and Minister of Foreign Affairs?"

"The very same," Anastase replied, with a smirk.

"And his mother?"

"An authoress, as the story goes. Madame de Sousa."

Marie felt a sudden jolt. Madame de Sousa had written *Adèle de Sénange*, a novel that had been part of her convent schooling. At the time, it had seemed almost comically dark, particularly because the heroine, Adèle, marries an aristocrat nearly seventy. But now, the story's unsettling relevance was impossible to ignore.

Marie lay awake, her thoughts turning to Talleyrand and his son, each with the name Charles. Might her introduction to Napoleon come through them?

On the day they left for Warsaw, Marie insisted they stop at the Kiernozia village church so she could pray for her father at the family mausoleum. Anastase reluctantly agreed.

24

IN THE DAYS AFTER THEIR return to the capital, Marie found that the air buzzed with news, activity, and excitement. The French were coming. Homes were prepared for Napoleon's marshals and other officers, and even the simplest households, whose owners knew little French beyond *"Vive l'Empereur,"* offered their hospitality. Eliza enlisted Marie to help with a group of women preparing local hospitals with bedding and bandages, anticipating the influx of wounded. After three days, they were redirected to assist in readying the Royal Castle for Napoleon's stay. It was a daunting task because it had sat vacant and dusty since King Stanisław's forced abdication by his one-time mistress, Russia's Catherine, eleven years before, after Poland's final partition.

Eliza moved through the castle's grand chambers, dusting marble tabletops, pedestals, and statues, while Marie followed, polishing with a soft cloth and occasionally treating stains with a poultice of clay and water. As the rooms came alive again, Marie worked with greater energy, struck with the thought that the castle would soon host Napoleon.

Eventually, they entered the Conference Room, where portraits of Pope Pius VI, King Stanisław, and four of his contemporary European monarchs adorned the walls. Marie paused to stare at the image of a serene King Stanisław, then turned to Eliza. "They say his final wish was not to be the last King of Poland. Maybe his wish will come to pass."

"I hope you're not suggesting we might see your French hero crowned king."

"No, Eliza," Marie replied. "It's more likely to be Stanisław's nephew, Prince Józef Poniatowski He's popular and carries the Poniatowski name."

"Pepi looks the part, too," Eliza said, employing the informal name people called him by. "But who knows? Napoleon made his brother King of Naples earlier this year. Maybe he has another brother—or maybe he'll crown himself, like he did in Paris."

"Maybe he will," Marie taunted.

"Ha! I imagine you would like that!"

As the French grew ever closer, Eliza's prediction regarding the Prussians played out. General Koehler, the Prussian military commander of Warsaw and his forces withdrew from the capital, their retreat met with mockery by the local population and even heckling of schoolboys. They crossed the Vistula, joining the Prussian Army that had been routed days before by the French. Once across, they burnt the Vistula Bridge linking Warsaw to its suburb of Praga and the East.

27 November 1806

Loud shouts echoed through Warsaw. "The French are coming!" Cheers rang out in front of the Walewski townhome and all along the narrow Bednarska Street, their cries echoing across the rooftops from other streets. Marie soon learned that a French reconnaissance patrol had entered from the west at Wola, a suburb of the capital. They were met with a tumultuous welcome.

The next afternoon, as Marie and Eliza stepped out of the townhome, it wasn't the cold air that made the fine blond hairs on Marie's arms rise, but the sheer exhilaration of the moment. Warsaw's citizens had turned out in force, lining the streets and hanging from balconies, shouting their welcomes: "Witam! Witam!" to the incoming troops. Perched on a white stallion, French Marshal Joachim de Murat led the cavalcade, his ostentatious uniform—crowned by a shako with a tri-colored plume of white, red, and blue—the epitome of military grandeur. Behind him rode his adjutants, followed by endless columns of foot soldiers in blue and red. Prince Józef Poniatowski, who had welcomed de Murat at the Wola city gates, rode beside him.

"Now there's a man," Eliza remarked, "who might contest Poniatowski for the Polish throne."

"What?" Marie questioned. "Why do you say such a thing?"

"Look at how he sits bolt upright on that magnificent animal. See how he drinks in the adulation of the crowd. He bears himself like a Caesar. And he is Napoleon's brother-in-law."

Marie didn't respond, but the thought nettled her for the rest of the afternoon. To her mind, only a Pole should sit on the throne.

29 November 1806

Marie had forgotten the comment by the next day when another parade passed by, this one with Marshal Davout on a black stallion, leading his troops, having newly arrived from Walewice. When he noticed Marie, he gave a tight smile and nodded. An officer beside him leaned forward and waved.

"Who is *that*?" Eliza demanded. "The one that waved! Not your older brother?"

Marie giggled. "It's Lieutenant Charles de Flahaut. I met him at Walewice."

"So, his wave was for you."

Marie shrugged.

"He seems handsome enough and the uniform makes for a pretty patina," Eliza said. "Truth now, tell me, were not taken by him?"

Marie laughed. "Not in the way you imply, Eliza." Once she informed her friend the details of their muddy meeting, they both laughed.

"Oh, this Charles may not hold your interest, but I warned you once that temptation would come." Eliza's eyes narrowed. "Just the same, tell me about this Lieutenant Charles de Flahaut."

"He's interesting to me because he is the son of Charles Talleyrand, a favorite of Napoleon. Knowing him might give me *entr*ée to a visit with the man himself."

"Quite the schemer, aren't you, Marysia? Who would have thought?"

"Ha! You might be interested to know that his mother is Madame de Sousa."

"What? —His mother! Why, I read *Adèle de Sénange* twice."

Marie nodded. She wanted to close this conversation before mention could be made of *Adèle's* age in relation to her husband's. "It's cold," she snapped. "We should go in."

"Wait!" Eliza said. "You met one authoress in Rome and the son of another in Walewice. How odd. You know, not everyone enjoyed that story. Some of the girls were horrified or even sickened by the match that had been made for Adèle, but I thought it quite entertaining." Eliza turned now, as if to ask Marie her opinion, but Marie pivoted and moved toward the townhome.

A day later, Anastase announced at supper that they would attend a reception for Marshal Joachim de Murat at the Royal Castle. "Prince Poniatowski said de Murat wants to see Polish beauties." He put his fork down, his small blue eyes narrowing. "I think he might wish to show *himself* off."

"At the castle? Marie asked, alarmed. "He's not staying there, is he? It's being made ready for the emperor."

"So it is. The marshal was to stay at the Hotel Raczynski, but it seems his suite had a smoking chimney." Anastase laughed. "Poor man! He thinks well of himself, you know."

"Where is he staying, Anastase?"

"With our friends, the Potockis."

"Really?"

Anastase harrumphed. "She and her husband have gone to the limit. It seems they've given over their entire ground floor to the Frenchman."

As Marie dressed for the ball, her excitement was tempered by political concerns. While Warsaw's citizens heartily welcomed the French army, Polish nobles—both magnates and *szlachta*—were divided. Some, like the general citizenry, viewed Napoleon as a savior; others, like Eliza, feared his intentions. *What will Napoleon think when he finds the nobility divided?* Marie asked herself. She feared that it would hinder his motivation to win Poland's independence.

Was discord always to be the Polish way? If, in her father's time, certain magnates had not, out of selfish motives, invited Catherine to *protect* Poland from the democratic Third of May Constitution, Poland would not have fallen. The wily czarina knew a golden opportunity when she saw it.

Marie was handed up into the coach by Anastase, her hopes for the evening high. She wore an exquisite light-yellow gown, but he sat in silence, his usual pride in her appearance absent. He seemed sullen during the short ride to the Royal Castle. His earlier reluctance to attend the reception for Prince de Murat had come as a surprise because he was loath to miss any social event. Marie had had to persuade him.

Marie recalled that Anastase had been strangely moody since returning from some meeting the day before. When questioned, he refused to talk about it and left the room. Something had happened.

Upon their arrival at the castle, they entered the Senators' Gate, where they gave over their winter cloaks. A servant offered to show them the way, but Anastase frowned and waved him away.

"I could show *him* cubbyholes and crannies here in this building he'd never find his way out of," he muttered as he guided Marie to the white marble circular stairs. Crystal sconces lighted their way to the first floor and the Great Apartment, its windows facing the River Vistula. They arrived at the Marble Room where portraits of past kings lined the walls. They moved into the National Hall, expecting that the prince would be receiving guests there. They were greeted by Aleksander and Anna Potocki, who informed them—with exchanged glances—that the reception was being held in the Throne Room.

Anastase blinked in surprise, bowed, and conducted Marie toward the room that had not been put to use since the partitioning of the nation some eleven years before. It was warm and crowded. His face dark as thunder, Anastase nodded toward the front of the room. Prince Joachim de Murat stood holding court a mere two steps from the dais supporting the gilt throne, upholstered in red. With grand gestures and a confident, dulcet voice, he was boasting of his recent victories.

Anastase grunted. "Why, he needs to take only two steps to seize the throne," he muttered.

Marie silently agreed.

They joined the slow-moving reception line, and by the time they came to the front, Anastase, draped in his heavy Lord Chamberlain's uniform, was perspiring.

Prince Józef Poniatowski introduced them to Prince de Murat, who gave a perfunctory nod to Anastase, his attention quickly shifting to Marie. "Delighted," he said. "The dancing will be a highlight, I'm told. I hope your husband will allow me a turn with you."

Anastase offered an unsmiling nod to the prince. Afraid that jealousy could put the evening in jeopardy, Marie maintained a serious expression as her husband led her away.

In the Great Assembly Hall, lighted by sculpted candelabra and massive chandeliers of gold and crystal, Marie took in the opulence. The marble columns, mythological statues, and gilt furniture seemed to evoke the grandeur of the past. The crowd was thick, voices animated. Tonight, the room swirled with sound and color as nobles, military men, and women—all in brilliant finery—socialized in high spirits as though the continent were not embroiled in war.

Anastase began to expatiate on the ceiling painting featuring Chaos stepping from the void. Marie well knew the myth but allowed him to go on because doing so seemed to cheer him. It seemed the castle reminded him of better years.

He was still talking, their eyes on the ceiling, when a deliberate little cough interrupted her thoughts. She lowered her gaze to see Lieutenant Charles de Flahaut bowing before her.

"It's a pleasure to see you again, Madame Walewska," he said. "May I introduce Prince Charles de Tallyrand?"

The name brought Anastase to attention.

Turning toward Talleyrand, Charles introduced Marie and Anastase, adding, "Monseigneur Walewski was Royal Chamberlain to King Stanisław."

"Was he, indeed?" the prince asked, his eyes widening.

Marie sensed her husband's shoulders lift. She hoped his wounded pride from the introduction to de Murat would be mollified by the attention of Napoleon Bonaparte's Foreign Minister.

"We met once before," Anastase put in.

"Yes?"

"Indeed! It was in Versailles, some twenty years ago now, I think, before Madame Guillotine, of course. I accompanied King Stanisław on state business."

"Ah, yes!" Talleyrand said. "I do recall now. It's so good to see you all these years later."

Anastase's lifted his chin and grinned.

Marie, however, saw through the social lie and was grateful for it.

"You know, Monseigneur Walewski," Talleyrand continued, "I've always denounced the partitions. The strength of the Commonwealth of Poland and Lithuania was a necessity to the peace of the continent."

"Yes, it was," Anastase said. "The Commonwealth stood as a strong buffer state between the West and Russia."

"Perhaps, Monseigneur Talleyrand," Marie said, inserting herself, "you can be influential in convincing Napoleon of the advantages of our independence?"

Talleyrand turned slightly to face Marie, his jaw dropping a bit. "You consider such things, Madame Walewska?"

"I do. —Shouldn't I?"

"What? —Yes, I suppose so." He paused for a moment, seemingly embarrassed. "I can tell you that I have spoken to the emperor on the matter dozens of times."

"To what end, Monseigneur Talleyrand?"

"He is encouraging, Madame Walewska."

"How encouraging, Monseigneur Talleyrand?"

Talleyrand winced. Before he could reply, however, the orchestra struck up, playing the opening tune, the Polonez. The crowd applauded.

Prince de Murat and Henriette de Vauban, mistress of Prince Poniatowski, led the stately first dance. Well into her forties, the countess dared to wear an emerald green gown with a startlingly low décolleté.

When Anastase remained silent, Marie suspected he was piqued by her entry into the conversation between him and Talleyrand. Charles de Flahaut took advantage of the moment. "If Monseigneur will permit and if Madame obliges, may I have this dance? I'm afraid it's the singular one at which I'm proficient. The cadence is slow and who cannot manage a dip now and then?"

"You have my permission," Anastase said.

Marie would have much preferred pressing the issue of Napoleon's mindset with Talleyrand, but she acquiesced and gave Charles her hand. The two took their place at the end of the procession. As they fell in with the music, Marie whispered: "Was your invitation a desire to dance, Lieutenant, or did you wish to conclude my awkward moment with Monseigneur Talleyrand?"

As they came upon the top of the room and followed a gentle turn, Charles had only to turn his head slightly to affect a wink. "It was a bit of both, Madame Walewska—but I think the wish to dance with you won out."

Later, Marie found herself in the company of Count Potocka and Prince Talleyrand. She saw an opportunity and meant to seize it.

"Prince Talleyrand," she said, "were you not with the emperor in Posnań?"

"I was, Madame Walewska," he answered. "The emperor insisted I come ahead to Warsaw."

"To 'test the waters,' as they say?" Marie flashed her best smile.

"Excuse me, Madame?"

"Are you not here to gauge the emperor's reception, particularly among those less trusting of him?" Marie lowered her voice. "Is he concerned, as I've heard?"

"Heard?"

"And read," she added pointedly.

"Are you searching for state secrets, Madame?" Talleyrand seemed genuinely befuddled. "You're quite young for such interests."

"Ah, Monseigneur Talleyrand," Count Potocki interjected, "my wife is much the same, often talking politics."

"Is this the Polish way of wives and mothers?" Talleyrand asked.

"It can be," Marie said, her voice full of sugar, "when a country has been carved up like a prize duck, leaving its daughters unanchored and heartbroken."

"You see, Monsiegneur," Lord Potocki said, "this lovely young woman lost her father to the Russians at Maciejowice."

"The Battle of Maciejowice?" Talleyrand asked, his expression softening.

"I was eight," Marie said flatly.

Talleyrand bowed his head. "My deepest condolences, Madame. I've often told the emperor that Poland's removal from the map of Europe was deplorable. I've urged him to restore your country's independence."

"Thank you for that," Marie said. "And the emperor's reaction?"

Lord Potocki drew in a sharp breath.

"Ah, Madame Walewska, you are relentless." Talleyrand laughed. "If you swear not to talk to newspapermen, Madame, I'll be truthful. The emperor is vague in his intentions."

The answer stung.

"Monseigneur Talleyrand, I'll be direct, as well. Assuming you are correct about the emperor's intentions, I'd very much like to have an interview with him. Can you help facilitate my wish?"

Talleyrand's eyes widened, and he stared at her some moments before collecting himself. "Madame Walewska, you are the last woman I would set before the emperor. You'd stand a better chance in a lion's den."

"What do you mean?"

"I've introduced women to Napoleon before. In fact, he says I have girls falling out of my pockets. But not you, Madame. Not you."

Marie felt a twinge of understanding—he was likely trying to protect her—but the answer hurt, nonetheless. If the emperor's defense minister was determined to block her, what hope did she have of meeting Napoleon Bonaparte?

An awkward silence followed.

"You're disappointed," Talleyrand said. "I'm sorry for that. But perhaps I can cheer you with some news that the papers have not had time to print. Do you know Józef Wybicki?"

"Of course, he wrote the patriotic song, 'Dąbrowski's Mazurka'."

"He did indeed. Well, the emperor sent Wybicki ahead so that he could assess the mood of your countrymen regarding the welcome he'll receive. The man requires a, shall we say, *significant* welcome. Wybicki was also given authorization to set up a provisional government, something only a Polish patriot could do. To that end, he convened a meeting today that lasted all morning. Lord Potocki was there. Lacking Polish blood, I couldn't attend, but he told me your husband was present."

Marie glanced at Lord Potocki, who merely gave a hesitant nod.

"So, within a day or two," Tallyrand continued, "you will know who will be fulfilling what role in the new government."

Anastase appeared now, wine glass in hand. Marie turned toward him. "So that's where you were all morning," she said.

Anastase's eyes widened and Marie thought he paled slightly.

"The Foreign Minister has just been telling me about the meeting with Józef Wybicki, so you needn't keep it to yourself. He says the papers will have it all tomorrow."

"That—that," Anastase stammered. "I—I was just coming to say that I've ordered the carriage. I'm feeling unwell. We must make our goodbyes, Marie."

In the coach, Marie fought to hold her temper. "You had not ordered the carriage, had you, Anastase? You didn't order it until we came down. I saw you. *Are* you unwell?"

"No."

"Why then did you say so?"

"I wanted to go home."

"It has to do with the Wybicki meeting, doesn't it?"

Anastase didn't respond.

"What went on there? The Foreign Minister says it will all come out in the papers, so do tell me."

Anastase stiffened, his shoulders hard against the bench's leather backrest. "Decisions were made, Marie, as to the provisional government."

"And? Who is to lead it?"

"Prince Poniatowski is to lead the war effort."

"Yes, that makes sense."

"Senator Ksawery Działyński will be next in command. Other leaders include Stanisław Małachowski, Aleksander Potocki, and Wybicki, who will head the Interior. All good choices."

"And your role, Anastase? You're saving the best for last, I suspect."

"I am not, my dear. I am not."

"Do you mean to say you'll have no role to play?"

Anastase shrugged.

"None? You'll have no access to the emperor? But you were Chamberlain to the King! Surely there's a place for a chamberlain, even without a king."

"Ludwik Gutakowski was given that post."

"You are out in the cold, then?"

"I'm old, Marysia. These men are more capable."

"The men you mention are all old, but for the prince."

"That may be true, dearest, but Napoleon and his marshals are all young.

It is a new generation that will help us regain our independence. I began to realize that during our visit to Walewice."

They fell silent for the rest of the way. Marie came to terms with the dual disappointment of the evening. Two doors to Napoleon closed. She was determined to find others.

But how many doors of promise for Anastase? She wondered. He will be seventy-two next year. His exclusion from the provisional government had wounded him deeply. She felt it in his silence and quiet sighs. He seemed to hunch forward as the carriage rumbled over the city cobblestones. King Stanisław himself had often sought his opinions and advice. He might exaggerate his influence, but the main features of his narratives often proved true.

Anastase had lived up to their bargain of marriage, a fact Marie often overlooked in light of the sacrifices she had made. She often wondered what might have been, had fate been kinder. Regret was always near at hand, but tonight, she felt his loss, his sadness.

When they arrived at the townhome, Marie reached for his arm, detaining him in the vestibule after their cloaks had been taken. She kissed him on the cheek. "You're tired, dearest," she said. "Come, let's go up to bed. You need your rest. As this new government takes shape, you will be needed again."

Marie did not know if he believed it, or whether she believed it herself, but he breathed deeply, his pale blue eyes conveying gratitude.

25

Warsaw
7 December 1806

MARIE TURNED TWENTY WITHOUT ANY fanfare. She continued her hospital work, organizing nursing groups and preparing public spaces to care for the expected influx of wounded. As the days passed, she began to wonder if Napoleon meant to bypass Warsaw. If he did, how could she meet him? In any case, she prepared her speech.

The next day, Marie returned from her hospital shift to find that Anastase had granted her request to bring Antoni from Walewice to stay through Christmas. She was thrilled. Her delight was tempered a few days later when he arrived in the company of the governess and the two older aunts, Jadwiga and Teodora. At a year and a half, Antoni seemed more attached to Berta and the two aunts than to her, stinging Marie's heart.

Marie held to her schedule at the hospital, arriving home each day in the early evening, thankful that the Walewska sisters' habit was to retire shortly after supper. She was then able to persuade Berta with sweets from the kitchen and small gifts to allow Marie two precious hours with her son.

When word reached Warsaw that Emperor Napoleon and his Grande Armée would finally enter the city on the eighteenth, Anastase left the house planning to help in the preparations. Marie thought Talleyrand's caution that the welcome be significant was unneeded because the excitement in the city was palpable. Anastase was rebuffed by the welcoming Citizens Council when he tried to offer the group suggestions. He arrived home, muttering to Marie, "They're all upstarts, Marie, young upstarts."

On the designated night for the emperor's arrival, two massive triumphal arches decorated with flowers from private conservatories stood in the city center. They were lighted at dusk even though Napoleon had yet to arrive. They carried the message:

Long live Napoleon, the Savior of Poland!

The two popular theaters, the Francuski and the National had opened their doors to the public for the occasion, but Marie and Eliza chose to walk to the outer courtyard of the Royal Castle and await the emperor's arrival there. Dozens of bonfires blazed as the two folded into the huge crowd.

The evening wore on without the object of the city's desire showing himself. At midnight, with hopes diminishing, word spread that the terrible winter rains had made the main road to Warsaw all but impassable with flooding and deep mud. The emperor would not be coming tonight. The disappointed crowd began to disperse.

Marie and Eliza were nearly the last to leave, silent as characters in a dumbshow.

Eliza called at the Walewski townhome at mid-morning the next day.

"You won't believe this!" she cried as Marie entered the reception room. "You won't!"

"It's Napoleon, isn't it? Is he hurt?"

"No, no! But he's here. When his carriage couldn't navigate the mud, he ditched it for a horse. He and his bodyguard arrived at the Royal Castle after two in the morning."

Sighing audibly, Marie said, "We should've waited and not given up hope!"

"How could we have known? And it was very late. My husband said the emperor had to awaken the castle warden, whereupon he had them scare up a supper. After eating, he went straight to bed."

"So today will be a celebration. We will see him today! —What? Eliza, why has your face clouded over? What is it?"

"The city is in for a disappointment. You, too, Marysia."

"What? Tell me!"

"He has refused to even meet with the Citizens Council. His business now is war. He plans to review his troops for the next few days. The Russian armies are awaiting the French north of Warsaw, near Pułtusk. They are supported by a surviving Prussian battalion or two."

"God's teeth! Oh, I have no doubt the French will prevail. After all, the emperor has had a string of victories. Besides, he has the Polish hussars with him, too, his Imperial Guard. My brothers are likely there, too. —But, Eliza, this delay is *so* disappointing."

Four days later, Napoleon left for the front. The celebratory mood in the city shifted into one more serious. Battles were imminent. Marie continued her work with the women of Warsaw as they prepared for the expected casualties. In the evenings, the time spent with little Antoni came with its rewards. Marie was winning him over.

Christmas Eve and Christmas Day were unlike any Marie had ever known. They followed the old customs and sang the old hymns, without verve. Minds and hearts were elsewhere. The papers brought news that an engagement with the enemy occurred in the northeast at Bieżuń. The surviving Prussian forces of the Jena and Auerstädt battles were outnumbered and swept away, giving up five hundred prisoners. Marie found it odd that no mention was made of losses on the French side.

Friday, 26 December 1806
Marie awoke with guilt, realizing her complaints about missing Napoleon were trivial compared to the hardships and sacrifices of soldiers. How small her concerns seemed now. Had I chanced to meet Napoleon, she asked herself, what good could have come from it?

She could hear Jadwiga out in the hallway now barking orders to Berta about taking more care in packing up Antoni's belongings. Anastase insisted the boy leave for Walewice as planned, citing how the city's air in the winter was bad for children. He had a point, but she knew, more than anything else, he was bowing to the wishes of his sisters.

She dressed quickly, resigning herself not to shed tears until the carriage pulled away. Afterward, she would occupy herself at the hospital.

Three days later, Marie found the papers filled with details of the anticipated battle near Pułtusk. Napoleon delivered significant losses upon the Russians, despite their superiority in numbers and artillery. Amidst alternating rain and snow, they managed to retreat in orderly fashion. The incessant freezes and thaws hampered the French and their artillery from following. Cannons became lodged in mud and a few soldiers were lost in the bogs. The French were hungry, cold, and disagreeable. Napoleon lost contact with the retreating Russians, concluding his only choice was to go into winter quarters. He was to return to Warsaw. Unhappily, no doubt.

New Year's Day 1807
When Marie entered the dining room for breakfast, Anastase was already seated, a pensive expression on his face. "What is it?" she asked.

"I've been out already and the news is all over town. The emperor will return today."

"Today?" she asked, her heart catching. "You seem so serious, Anastase. Why is that?"

"Who's to know what mood he'll be in when he arrives? I hear he's been blaming Poland for our inclement weather and bad roads. And they say the actual number of French killed at Pułtusk was five or six thousand, with fifteen hundred wounded. No wonder they kept silent about the dead and wounded. They say underestimating is a habit with the emperor."

The number shocked Marie, but in light of the numbers filling the hospitals, it did not surprise her.

A maid came in to announce that Madame Eliza Sobolewska had arrived and was waiting in the reception room.

As Marie hurried from the room, Anastase called, "Your breakfast, Marie. Don't be long."

Her cloak still buttoned at the throat and the veil on her dark hat pinned back, Eliza shook her head when Marie entered and suggested they sit. "He's coming today, Marysia. Today!"

"I know, Anastase told me."

"Get your cloak."

"What? —Why?"

"We must act, that's why. My husband has had word that his carriage will change horses at Błonie."

"Yes, so?"

"So! It's the last relay station before the capital! Half the city is streaming north to meet and welcome him."

"Eliza," Marie said, her throat closing on her, "are you suggesting—"

"I am. Get your cloak and a warm hat."

"But—how?"

"What is the matter with you? You were the one fired up to meet him."

"And you were the one doubting his intentions."

"Ha! I'm a woman of two minds. Now, I have a driver waiting in the street. Hurry—there's not a minute to lose."

It wasn't the muddy and pitted road that slowed the one-horse, open-front carriage. It was the long line of vehicles headed to Błonie. At the snaillike rate it was moving, Marie doubted they would cover the twenty miles in time. This was a foolish undertaking, she thought. In their hurried departure, she had not told her husband, deliberately so. He would have forbidden her, she was certain.

The carriage vibrated as it trundled along for what seemed like hours.

"Błonie ahead!" the young driver, Szymon, called back.

Another ten minutes and they were in sight of the relay station, but had become enmeshed in a line of stalled vehicles. The small town was packed with citizens who had come to catch sight of the great man.

"We'll alight from the coach here, Szymon," Eliza ordered.

Szymon jumped down to help his passengers step down. "There's a mighty fancy coach up ahead," he said. "Its horses are being hitched now. I think we've made it in time but not by much. Should I come with you?"

"No! You must stay with the carriage," Eliza ordered. "We'll find you, Szymon."

"But the station is mobbed," Marie complained.

"I see it. We can *push* through. Come!" Eliza said, latching on to Marie's hand and drawing her into the dense crowd.

"Make way for a countess!" Eliza called out, to Marie's horror. Her friend continued acting like a brusque lady's maid running interference for her better. "Make way for the Countess of Walewice, wife of the king's chamberlain!"

The stunt was repeated again and again, and it worked for a good while as the two moved in tandem—until they came upon a human wall. No one there seemed to listen or care.

Eliza tapped a female citizen of some size on her shoulder. "Step aside, if you will," she said. Too stridently, Marie thought.

The woman turned to face Eliza, her face grim, eyes narrowing. She looked from Eliza to Marie, seeming to take in that they had no male attendant. "And I am Louise, Queen of Prussia!" she snarled. "You shall not pass!"

If the woman's quip took Eliza by surprise, she didn't show it. The woman had turned sideways to address them, and Eliza attempted to push through the narrow gap that movement allowed. With a sudden jolt, Marie was pulled with her, but before Eliza could slip past, the woman screamed, "No, you don't!" and shoved Eliza so that she fell to the ground, letting go of Marie's hand.

Chaos erupted all about them. The woman's male companion drew her away, and they disappeared into the multitude. Marie managed to help Eliza to her feet. Flinching in pain, Eliza said, "I've turned my ankle, Marie. I can't walk. Listen, you go on. You go on. Find the man."

"But—but, you—"

"Never mind me. I'll find someone to help me back to the carriage. Give me your hat."

"What? —Why?"

"So, the man can see you. It's been your desire for how long, now?"

When Marie hesitated, Eliza reached up and took the hat and deftly removed several hair combs, allowing Marie's blonde tresses to tumble to her shoulders and halfway down her back.

Completely stunned, Marie had no time to speak, for Eliza took hold of her hips, turned her in the direction of the relay station, and pushed.

Marie drew in breath and began to move through the dense sea of Polish patriots with less aggressiveness than Eliza had done. "*Przepraszam*," she kept repeating, again and again. The apology induced people in front of her to turn and look at her. Amazingly, the crowd parted, allowing her to progress to where a line of French soldiers stood, cordoning off the excited onlookers from the royal carriage. She found herself face to face with a soldier, his gold epaulettes and several medals indicative that this was an officer of some standing.

"Monsieur, s'il vous plaît!" Marie said, summoning a pleading—almost pathetic—tone. The switch to French caught his attention, his forehead furrowing in curiosity.

It was enough of an opportunity for her to lift her chin and explain in fluent French that she must see the emperor, if only for a few minutes, and that her mission was of supreme importance.

The officer lowered his head, staring at Marie in wonder, blue eyes narrowing. "And why should a beautiful young girl like you wish to throw herself at the emperor?" He crossed his arms, an action that both underscored his smugness and made his body a barrier to any forward movement.

"You misunderstand me, Monsieur. You do. I'm not a girl! My hat was taken from me. I am a married woman."

The officer cocked his head and gave a tight smile, as if he was both suspicious and amused.

Marie spoke in French now with urgency and at a speed of which she didn't know she was capable. She spoke at length of her father, his sacrifice at the hands of the Russians, the dismemberment of Poland, and her need to inform the emperor of the deep faith the Polish people had that he would deliver them from bondage. "I continue in my father's mission," she said, realizing she had taken too long—and yet thinking that she had not made an impact. "What was in his blood is in mine. Please allow me to see the emperor. *Please!*" She felt hot tears welling in her eyes. "I'll hold him back for only seconds."

"Mademoiselle," the officer said, "your French is superb, as is your enthusiasm."

Thinking he had forgotten that she was married, Marie was about to correct him, saying "Madame," but he had turned toward the royal coach. "The postilion is mounted!" he announced.

Marie's heart lurched in her chest. If the rider who guided the team of horses was mounted on the lead horse, so too was the driver. The coach was about to pull out. Her effort had come to nothing.

At that moment, the officer bowed before her. "Grand Marshal Géraud Duroc of the Palace, at your service. He grasped her wrist and drew her forward. "*Attendez!*" he called in a deep voice. "*Attendez!*"

Was he calling *wait* to the postilion or to the emperor? Or both? Marie grew dizzy with the thought that the Emperor of France was being detained for her.

"Follow me, Mademoiselle," the marshal said.

In just moments, she found herself looking up at the coach window, into the face she had drawn any number of times. He looked slightly older in person. And tired. Fear seized her. She felt a clenching in her stomach.

Napoleon Bonaparte sat back against the bench, head tilted back, his arm on the window sill, fingers tapping his impatience. Without turning his head, he lifted his hand in a cursory, final wave. He had no smile for the crowd, however. It was clear that he was not happy that weather had allowed the Russians' escape, forcing him to seek winter quarters at Warsaw.

"Your Majesty, this young mademoiselle wishes to address you," the marshal announced. "She's bravely faced this horde to do so."

Marie stood dumb as Napoleon turned his head, tilting it downward. He cast a long look at her.

Now came a smile that transformed his visage. He seemed suddenly handsome, younger, and his gaze drew her in as if she were the only person present. He doffed his hat, the signature bicorne of black felt. "What could a beauty like you have to say? Regrettably, Mademoiselle, I've been delayed here long enough."

He nodded to the officer, who quickly stepped up into the coach and sat on the bench opposite the emperor. Marie realized that she had been rescued from the throng by a very important aide-de-camp.

The emperor's attention came back to her. "You are very beautiful, Mademoiselle."

Marie drew in a deep breath. There was no time to correct him, only moments to relay her message. And yet—the speech she had prepared for months flew out of her head. Her moment was slipping away. She swallowed hard, sensing defeat.

Napoleon turned away.

However, in moments he was lifting a small wreath of white winter roses through the window, toward her. "Take it," he said, his penetrating eyes, deep-set under dark brows and a broad forehead, holding her motionless. "Take it," he repeated, dropping it into her hands. "I have a dozen more beside me." He rewarded her with another wide smile before calling to the postilion: *"Aller!"*

The carriage wheels began to turn, grinding in the gravel street.

Marie managed to pull just the first line from her prepared speech. "Welcome to Poland!" she called, forgetting his title. What came to her now came on the fly. "You will save us! My brothers fight with you. If only I were a man, I would join your Guard!"

"The Imperial Guard?" he asked, smiling as if amused. Amidst the roar of the crowd crying out their goodbyes, she thought she heard him call back in a strained voice, "Will I see you in Warsaw, Mademoiselle?"

She stood immobile, tongue tied.

As the coach moved down the street, Napoleon thrust his hand out the window and waved his bicorne until the coach was gone from sight.

Marie found Eliza waiting in their carriage, seemingly recovered and excited to hear Marie's account.

For just a fleeting moment on the return trip to Warsaw, Marie luxuriated in the thought that the wave of the bicorne was not for the worshipping multitude, that it was for her. She clutched the wreath of roses to her breast.

26

Saturday, 3 January 1807

Having sent word to the kitchen that she would await her husband's arrival before taking supper, Marie sat staring at the empty gilt-edged bone-white china plates, fingers tapping on her silverware. Anastase had been out all day. He was seldom tardy for supper. She couldn't help but feel that something was afoot.

An hour later, Anastase entered, apologizing as he took his seat at the head of the table. Marie, sitting at his right, raised an eyebrow in silent question.

"The reception for Napoleon is set," he announced, snapping his fingers for an attendant to signal the kitchen to serve supper.

"Has it?" Marie asked. It was not unexpected news, but it set her nerves on edge.

"Indeed! It's Wednesday, the day after the Feast of the Epiphany, so it will lead off the *karnawał* season."

"You seem buoyant about it, Anastase."

"And why shouldn't I be? Prince Pontiatowski put together the guest list with a bit of help from the emperor himself, and he assured me that we are on it. The invitation should arrive tomorrow."

Marie hesitated, searching for delicate wording. "I just thought since you were slighted by both the welcoming council and the provisional government, that you might feel uncertain about attending."

"Nonsense. None of that matters. The emperor, who—God willing—will restore our independence is returning to Warsaw." Anastase beamed as soup was brought to the table."

Marie withdrew into silence, her thoughts distracted as she slowly spooned the white borscht. She had no wish to attend the reception, no wish to meet Napoleon again. After the initial Błonie meeting, which she now referred to as an *incident*, Marie felt more and more foolish for her behavior then, fumbling through her words in front of the emperor, hatless with her hair falling all about her.

What if he remembered her? Or one of his officers did? Others would find out. People would say she had thrown herself at the emperor. She would be disgraced. Her gaze flickered to Anastase, who was enjoying his fried cod, oblivious to her inner turmoil. How would he react? She had lost composure and dignity. What would anger him most? Her breach of societal decorum, or his raw jealousy of her, an anger she had witnessed often enough? While her husband preened himself, luxuriating in showing off his young wife at theatricals, suppers, and balls, he was easily inflamed with anger when she dared a ten-minute conversation or second dance with the same man. Red-faced, he would insist, words escaping between clenched teeth, that they depart at once, and his foul mood would often last a day or two.

When the entrée was served, she allowed the servant to take her unfinished soup. She cut into her fish for the sake of appearance. She had no appetite.

She had been wrong to go to Błonie. She had been wrong not to tell him. But she couldn't bring herself to tell him now.

Anastase continued to eat, talking of the reception and its preparations.

Before Marie knew it, the meal was finished, and a maid was speaking to her. "Your *sernik*, Madame?" she asked.

Marie had not touched the cheesecake. "No, thank you," she said in a deliberately sheepish way. The maid took it away, just as she had done the unfinished soup and fish dishes. There would be talk in the Walewski kitchen.

Marie had no sooner retired to the small reception room and taken a chair across from her husband than her nerve spiked. "I have no wish to be presented to the emperor, Anastase," she said in a rush.

"What? What are you saying, Marie?" Anastase asked, taken aback. He repeated the question, as he often did when he needed time to digest something that startled him.

Marie kept silent.

"You've talked about meeting Napoleon since your days at Kiernozia. This is your chance."

Our chance, he means.

"Anastase, you've introduced me to many of the elite here in the capital, but I don't feel confident enough to attend such a reception with so many high-ranking citizens." It was a lie she hoped he would believe.

"Confident? Nonsense—you're my wife!"

"Of course, *you* must go," Marie said. "I insist. It's your duty."

"And it's your duty to stand by me." He took hold of the chair and pushed himself up, stamping his foot. "You are my wife! You will go, Marie!"

Marie recoiled. She had not expected histrionics.

He paced, then suddenly turned to her with a solution. "I'll employ Madame de Vauban to shore up your confidence. She can advise you on what to wear, how to address the many titled guests, and maintain your poise."

Marie's lie had brought an unexpected result, and she couldn't contrive how to extricate herself.

Anastase made his way toward the door and turned in what seemed a theatrical afterthought. "By the way, dearest," he said, leveling his small, pale blue eyes in her direction, "I've sent our groom to Walewice to retrieve my mother's sapphire and diamond necklace. Keep that in mind as you go through your wardrobe prior to Henriette's arrival."

The city lay blanketed in snow on the evening of Prince Poniatowski's reception for Emperor Napoleon Bonaparte. Marie looked out the coach window to see lines of vehicles snaking toward the Royal Castle from several directions, all converging for the nine o'clock invitation. She had suggested they walk since they lived exceedingly close, on Bednarska Street, but the count wouldn't hear of it, citing sodden shoes. "And how would that look to all the *haut monde* in their fancy carriages, Marie," Anastase asked, "our trudging through drifts of snow?"

After a long wait, the carriage finally reached the castle courtyard. Marie smoothed the folds of her pale blue gown and fingered the sapphire and diamond necklace. It was the first time she had been allowed to wear it, and she felt a flutter of excitement at its touch.

The necklace had arrived the day before, one of a good number of family jewels in a locked box. Accompanying them were two unexpected houseguests: Jadwiga and Teodora Walewska returned to Warsaw for the occasion, leaving the more sanguine Teresa in Walewice, along with Antoni, his governess, and a new tutor. That Marie had played no part in choosing who would play roles in her son's upbringing was deeply frustrating and hurtful.

Now, the sisters-in-law sat on the bench opposite, eyeing her with subtle interest. Marie took her hand away from the necklace. They seemed less serious, less dour, than usual. Perhaps, she thought, they were even experiencing a hidden thrill that they were about to attend the reception for Emperor Napoleon Bonaparte.

Anastase had kept his word. He had sent for Madame Henriette de Vauban to coach Marie with her preparations. The countess was cheerful and confident, though her presence made Marie more uneasy. But she was helpful in the choice of silver slippers and a blue velvet gown. "Ah!" Madame de Vauban cooed, "the blue of the gown matches your eyes as do the sapphires." Marie was uncertain about the revealing neckline and said so. "Ah, my dear," the woman replied, "the stunning necklace requires an appropriate foil so it can direct the eye, if you know what I mean." She winked and went on to warn Marie not to be too forward in her approach to Napoleon. "At my salon yesterday, I heard several wives say that upon meeting the emperor, they were inclined to lay their hopes at his feet for Poland's immediate independence. I warned them not to be so brash and so foolish. It would be most inappropriate at a presentation. He would think them *déclassé*."

Marie suspected that this was a warning meant for her and prompted by her husband. *If only Madame de Vauban knew she had already met the emperor.*

What does it matter? Nonetheless, she intended to stay a full chamber's distance from Napoleon. If this were a *bal maskowy*, she fantasized, she would be assured of anonymity behind a *karnawał* mask."

They shed their cloaks and ascended the white marble staircase, two by two, Anastase and Marie first, Jadwiga and Teodora following. On the first level, they passed through the various chambers, each jammed with people in their finest, buzzing like the combs of a hive.

They came into the Great Assembly Hall, where the Potockis stood near the far wall, waving them over. The emperor had yet to make his appearance.

"Our houseguests, Marshal de Murat and Lieutenant de Flahaut, will arrive with the emperor," Anna said. She had worn a black velvet gown, sewn with gold threading and pearls and set off with a narrow Van Dyck ruff.

The dress stood out from the others worn that night: gowns cinched just below the bosom and draping in straight lines to the floor.

"Your gown is lovely, so original," Marie said.

Compliments were exchanged all around, with special attention given to the Walewski necklace.

It was eleven o'clock before they heard a commotion near the tall mahogany doors leading from the National Hall. "Make way! Make way!" someone was calling out.

At that moment the two words people were waiting for reverberated through the Great Assembly Hall: "The Emperor!"

A charge of electricity ran through the chamber, and then a hush fell.

Emperor Napoleon Bonaparte fairly stomped into the room, halting in a circle of his worshippers, boot heels resounding, like a fighter fully confident he would prevail. His gaze beneath the black bicorne, with its single tri-colored cockade, did not dip but stayed above the crowd. Marie had read that he always wore the favored hat tilted, with its two peaks at the sides, rather than positioning it front to back, as was the intended design. In addition to making him easily recognized, the hat also added to his height. The grey double-breasted greatcoat draped so that it covered everything except for the shoes of his black top boots. The simplicity of his dress stood in stark contrast to the flamboyant colors, plumes, and gold embroidery of his marshals' and ministers' costuming. Marie suspected that was his intention. No one would mistake him for another marshal.

Nonetheless, his presence was extraordinary. He did not bow to the assembly, but stood there, shoulders squared, as if to allow everyone to take in his appearance, seeming to revel in his role as the hero of the hour. He removed the bicorne, turned back to the crowd, and smiled. His dark hair above a broad, pale forehead mirrored Marie's expectations based on her first meeting, but the strong jawline and the smile, radiating boldness and authority, were affects she had not noticed at Błonie.

A long moment of awe passed among his supplicants, with protocol forgotten. Gasps and murmurs rippled through the crowd. Marie felt an acute awkwardness for the guests, though Napoleon seemed to bask in the attention.

Then, tardily, the men bowed and the women curtsied.

Marie was struck by the thought that deposed King Stanisław had stood in this very chamber among his citizens. Her mother had described him as mild and meek, implying that had he been more dynamic, Poland might have endured. A wistful sadness seemed to swell in her chest. If only the last king of Poland had possessed the commanding presence of the Little Corporal.

The emperor was bookended by Prince de Murat on his right and Lieutenant de Flahaut on his left. Another officer stood right behind de Murat. Marie took in a quick breath. Her heart caught. It was Napoleon's *aide-de-camp*, the officer who had facilitated her meeting with Napoleon at Błonie. She leaned over to Anna. "Do you know who is standing near Marshal de Murat?"

Anna stood on tiptoe to get a look. "Oh, that's Grand Marshal Géraud Duroc. He's been to our house. Why do you ask?"

Marie managed a smile. "Oh, I'm just curious about who's in the emperor's circle."

In truth, she was worried that her impulsive and foolish behavior at Błonie would become known by Warsaw society—and Anastase. While the emperor might not recognize her this night, gowned and made up as she was, Marshal Duroc might! It seemed more likely that he would recall the woman he had plucked from the crowd and brought before the emperor. She couldn't confide this concern in Anna. Only Eliza would understand, and she was not present.

"Are you quite all right, Marie?" Anna asked. "You've gone pale."

"Yes, yes," I'm fine," Marie answered, her eyes on the emperor who, hat in hand, started to make the rounds. The floor cleared almost as if for dancing, attendees breaking into groups. Prince Poniatowski led Napoleon around, introducing him to a few selected guests. Talleyrand and Duroc remained near the entrance.

Napoleon awarded cursory nods to those clusters he passed without stopping. Feeling panic rise up, Marie looked for a way to avoid being seen. Her group of four had come to the front, but were tightly hemmed in on the other three sides. The floor was empty in front of them, but escaping that way would only bring attention to her.

She held her breath and kept her gaze at the floor as the prince and emperor were about to pass, praying the prince would not introduce Napoleon to her husband.

The emperor was close by now, and telling someone, "Your Polish mud has saved the Russians—for the winter at least."

And then the two were in front of them.

Marie put her head down and curtsied several beats before Anna followed suit and their husbands bowed. She stayed in place several moments until she thought they must have passed on. She stood and lifted her head only to be looking into the eyes of Napoleon as his gaze moved from her to Anna. But it returned, lingering a few seconds as he inspected her, his broad forehead creasing. Was he recalling their meeting at Błonie?

He suddenly blurted something in his quick French, and the prince moved him on.

Had he recognized her? Only now was she able to confirm the color of his eyes as gray-blue, just as Madame de Staël had told her, and just as piercing as she described.

"Did you hear that?" Anna whispered.

"What?"

"How could you not? He said it as he looked at *you*. '*Ah, Il y a de jolies femmes à Varsovie.*' Now that's something to put in your diary, Marie. Do you keep one?"

Marie did not respond, her fear of discovery such that she had not processed the compliment.

Anastase grunted. "Indeed, there are pretty women in Warsaw! —I thought the prince would introduce him to me." His face had gone red. "I met him in Paris, in my capacity as Chamberlain to the King."

Glancing across the way, Marie sighted Marshal Duroc, whose gaze seemed locked on her. *Sweet Jesus!* Did he remember that day?

Seconds passed before she caught her breath and looked away. She saw that Napoleon was drawn into an extended conversation with a beautiful dark-haired woman gowned in red satin.

Anna spoke now. "What baffles me is that there is to be no supper or dancing."

"It is strange," Anastase said.

Lord Potocki spoke: "The Russians' escape has left the emperor in a bad mood from what I'm told. But now he's at least able to comment on the pretty women here in Warsaw, so that's an improvement. Not to worry, Anna and Marie, there will be many balls and gatherings during *karnawał*. Why, Talleyrand is to have a ball on the seventeenth. And you, Anastase, will have your moment with the emperor, I'm certain."

"Oh, look, he's leaving." Anna said.

Marie looked up at the entrance. The prince and Napoleon had returned to the entrance where Duroc and Talleyrand stood. When the emperor faced the assemblage, Duroc sidled up to him and whispered something. Napoleon lifted his head and surveyed the chamber from left to right as if he were on the field with his eyeglass. Then he gave a salute, placed his bicorne on his head, pivoted, and made his exit.

Had Napoleon's gaze fallen for just the slightest few seconds on her group, on her? Marie felt faint. She was certain that Duroc had recognized her earlier. Had he revealed her presence to the emperor? *Why?* she chided herself. Why would she be of any interest to two of the most important men on the continent?

"I suspect he's returning to his apartment," Lord Potocki said.

The reception had come to an end. Marie's gaze went to the group at the far right. The woman in red had vanished. Might Napoleon have made an assignation with her?

Marie's sisters-in-law were crossing the floor toward them. For once, their expressions seemed self-satisfied, almost happy. She knew, however, that in the carriage her husband would repeat his complaint about being slighted by the emperor.

Marie squared her shoulders, pushing aside the fear of her Błonie escapade being discovered, and donned a merry expression worthy of a *karnawał* mask.

27

In the following days, Marie kept thoughts of Talleyrand's upcoming ball at bay. She had no wish to go. Attending, she thought, would tempt fate.

Three days before the ball, she and Eliza fell into conversation after a day's volunteering at the hospital.

"I wish you had come to the reception," Marie said.

"I wish I had, but I was ill for a couple of days. Still, you had the Countess Anna Potocka to keep you company."

"Yes, but only you know the secret of Błonie."

"That is precisely the reason I wanted to speak with you, Marie."

"What? Really?" Marie felt her heart speed up.

"Well, it seems you made quite the impression. Anna told me what the emperor said as he passed."

"Oh, that! He might just as easily have been complimenting both Anna and me."

"Now, you know that's not the case. It's what made me think your secret was out. —You don't think he recognized you?"

"No, you're jumping to conclusions," Marie said, summoning a confidence she didn't feel. "He was seen making comments a number of times as the prince led him around the room. I saw him speaking *tête-à-tête* with a dark-haired beauty who disappeared about the same time as the emperor's exit."

"Now, you're jumping to conclusions."

"Just the same, I'll be forgotten once I'm out of sight."

"You're not going to Talleyrand's ball?"

"No."

"I don't understand you, Marie. We dared life and limb to meet the emperor at Błonie so that you could intercede on Poland's behalf. Why the sudden change?"

"Listen, Eliza, Anna Potocka told me that she had to deflect the attention of Prince de Murat, despite the fact that they had generously granted him the use of their entire ground floor."

"Really?"

"Yes, it seems the generals come here with hopes of having conquests in places other than on the battlefield."

"And you think—"

"That my forward behavior at Błonie could easily create the wrong impression—yes!"

"Ah, I see."

"In fact, at the reception for Prince de Murat, Talleyrand seemed to brag that he had girls falling out of his pockets into Napoleon's arms."

"Seriously?"

"Yes, and as for any good my patriotism might elicit, Madame de Vauban made me understand that I am just one of many women who mean to speak up and that the emperor would not appreciate a woman's suggestions about the future of Poland!"

"Do you believe that?"

"I don't know, but I need you to keep our secret, Eliza. Anastase has no idea we ran off to Błonie that day."

Eliza's jaw dropped. "You never told him of our adventure?"

"Adventure? It was a fools' errand. He was asleep when I arrived home, and I have my own bedchamber now. Eliza, my husband is a jealous man. Let's not stir up a hornets' nest."

At supper, Anastase regaled her with Talleyrand's plans for his ball—who would attend and what would be served. "And, do you know," he concluded, "the emperor has his own orchestra follow him from place to place, and some famous *chef d'orchestre* is set to arrive by sledge in time for the ball. How extraordinary!"

Unwilling to invite conflict, Marie kept to herself the decision not to attend. She would bide her time.

Later, in the music room, she thought about her options. Staying out of the public eye was the best path forward. She needed to avoid Marshals Duroc and Talleyrand, and especially Napoleon himself. She decided to return to Walewice, and to her son. The decision to withdraw from Warsaw society brought a sense of relief.

Marie climbed into bed that night, closed her eyes, and released a long sigh, her palm to her heart.

In the morning, she descended the stairs, prepared to tell her husband of her intention to go to Walewice and that she would not attend Talleyrand's ball. She smelled the aromas of the breakfast buffet, but had no appetite.

Before she came to the ground floor, she became aware of a second male voice coming from the dining room. Stopping, she strained to identify it, unsuccessfully. She continued down the stairs and came to stand in the doorway of the dining room.

"Ah, here is Marie now," Anastase said, rising. "We have a guest, Marie."

Marie blinked.

Prince Józef Poniatowski stood, bowed, and greeted her warmly. "Madame Walewska, how lovely to see you."

Marie could scarcely think. She dropped into a curtsey. "Sire," she said.

Anastase gestured for her to take her place at his right. A servant assisted her as she settled in, directly across from the man who would be king, were it not for the dismemberment of Poland. She cleared her throat, but could not manage a thoughtful observation of any kind.

Once she was seated, the prince leaned forward. "I've come to personally invite you to Talleyrand's ball for the emperor." Looking from one to the other, he continued, "Of course, I trust the former Chamberlain to the King and his beautiful wife have already received the invitation, but we wanted to make certain that you would be in attendance."

"We?" Marie asked.

Her question brought a quizzical reaction from the prince and a subtle grunt from her husband.

The prince quickly recovered. "Monseigneur Talleyrand and I, Madame Walewska." Then, turning to Anastase, he said, "I reminded the emperor that he had met you years ago in France."

"And he remembered?" Anastase asked.

"He did!"

The answer came a beat late. The prince was lying in order to appeal to her husband's vanity.

"Oh, I knew he must." Anastase said, his pale blue eyes sparkling. "Of course, we will attend, Sire."

The prince cleared his throat. "Undoubtedly, the emperor will be happy to see you again, Monseigneur Walewski." He nodded across the table. "And you, as well, Madame Walewska."

Marie couldn't move, couldn't think of a reply. The prince had said that as if he knew something. And his facial expression suggested an intimacy that only she caught. Why, she thought, he might as well have winked.

"I'll not be attending the ball, Sire. Of course, my husband will attend."

Marie sensed her husband turn toward her, felt his gaze upon her.

The prince lowered his head and stared. "Oh, but you must, Madame Walewska, you must!"

"I have made plans to go to Walewice, Sire. I have been separated from my son for too long." Marie turned to her husband. "Anastase, you knew I was making plans."

"But—but, so soon? When?"

"Tomorrow, dearest. The coach has been ordered."

"Madame Walewska," the prince said in a tone both authoritative and pleading, "you are one of Warsaw's young flowers. I do ask that you reconsider."

"There is an entire garden here in the capital, Sire. I won't be missed."

"Marie," Anastase said, "surely you could postpone your visit just a few days."

"Oh, but I so wish to see our child, Anastase." Marie stood. "I beg your leave, Sire." She curtsied toward the prince and nodded toward Anastase, who seemed stunned by her certainty and fumbled for something to say.

The prince stood as Marie turned to make her exit, Anastase following suit. She took several steps toward the staircase, then halted, backing up against the wall. She listened.

"Your wife is a beauty, Monseigneur Walewski."

"Yes, indeed." Her husband's voice sounded odd, uncertain. Her exit had startled him.

"It's an important event. I do wish she would agree to attend."

"Marie misses our son."

"Do you think you can persuade her?" the prince asked, his tone urgent.

"I will attend, naturally. Sire, Marie is from the provinces and she feels a bit out of her depth mixing with Warsaw cognoscenti. And the notion of meeting his Royal Highness—"

"But, Monseigneur Walewski—she has already met him."

Marie forced her fist to her mouth in order to keep an audible gasp from escaping.

"Met him?" Anastase said. "Met *whom*?"

"Napoleon, Monseigneur. She's spoken with him."

"Oh, Sire, you are mistaken. At the palace reception, the emperor nodded to us in passing, but there were no introductions, no conversations, I can assure you."

The room went silent. Marie listened as the pause in their conversation seemed to go on and on. The prince had to know about her awkward and foolish appearance at Błonie. Marshal Duroc would have provided every detail. Her heart felt as if it would beat through her chest as she waited for the truth to spill out. She held a hand at her throat, knowing her husband would be furious to hear how she had made a fool of herself.

The prince harrumphed. "Hmm. . . it just came to me, Monseigneur Walewski, that there is a young lady who resembles your wife. Perhaps your wife was mistaken for her. Do you know the Countess Zofia Branicka?"

"Yes, of course, I know her. There is a likeness," her husband admitted, a bit grudgingly, "I grant you that."

The prince did not miss a beat. "I'm sure it was Madame Branicka and not Marie. My mistake. Oh, and she's not nearly as beautiful as your Marie."

"Indeed."

"Now, my dear Lord Walewski, I must confide in you that the emperor is tired of listening to Polish officials pleading for our God-given independence. We've tried his patience. He's more interested in how many fighting men and officers we're able to muster for him when he resumes the trail of the Russians. He says quite emphatically that any other decision regarding Poland will come at the end of the campaign."

"I've heard this, Sire. It must be frustrating for you."

"But," the prince said, "a beautiful lady might be able to bend even the most imperial ear without ruffling its owner."

"I see."

"A true beauty might go where even angels fear to tread."

"True, true," her husband said.

The prince harrumphed again. "Countess Branicka is no longer in the capital, so she will not attend the Talleyrand Ball. Now, it would be *very* unfortunate if you are unable to persuade your wife."

Marie heard their chairs scraping on the floor. The prince was about to leave. She knew she should immediately make for the stairs.

And yet she held back.

"Must you leave, Sire?" the count said.

"I have other calls to make this morning," the prince said.

"We are so pleased that you have visited us."

Marie could hear the prince draw breath. "May I count on you *both* to attend, Monseigneur Walewski?"

Marie's breath caught.

"You may, indeed," Sire.

Marie rushed for the stairs, those last words ringing in her ears.

Shortly after the prince left, Anastase tapped at Marie's bedchamber door.

"I'm lying down, Anastase," Marie lied. She was standing, eyes riveted on the unlocked door. "I'll see you at the afternoon meal."

Anastase fell silent, but did not retreat.

Her husband never entered without her permission, but she held her breath just the same, afraid that he would enter anyway.

"Very well, my dear," he replied. His steps fell away.

She did lie down now, fully clothed, the scene at the table replaying in her mind. That the prince knew about the scene she had created at Błonie and played the gentleman by creating a fabricated story about Countess Branicka seemed unbelievable to her. She was thankful for it—but how could that story hold water for long before Anastase and all of Warsaw found out?

How can I possibly go to the ball? she worried, anxiety increasing. It was as though Prince Poniatowski had imposed a duty on her in exchange for his kindness. People would expect her to play her part, to be more than just a woman at a ball. Did the prince truly believe a woman like her could wield political influence over the emperor?

The thought snapped Marie to attention, and she pulled herself up, her back braced against the headboard. Was the prince thinking that at Błonie she had wanted to show herself as available to Napoleon, whose *aide-de-camp* was known for supplying the emperor with girls for his entertainment—and pleasure? Did the prince think that she hadn't told her husband of the Błonie venture because her intentions were impure?

Marie felt her face flush hot. Was she setting herself up for scandal? Or was there truth in the prince's words—that a woman might be instrumental in placing Poland uppermost in the emperor's mind? Had he meant an *innocent* woman?

By the time she descended the stairs for the afternoon meal, she had yet to make a decision about the ball.

28

Saturday, 17 January 1807

"We're going to be late, Marie," Anastase called from outside her door. When she didn't respond, he tried the doorknob. This time she had bolted the door. Hania moved toward the door, but Marie stopped her with a shake of the head.

"Are you nearly ready, dearest?" Anastase asked.

She knew that tone. The words contrasted with his impatient mood. He had been in a bad mood since the fourteenth when Emperor Napoleon called for a provisional government, naming it the Governing Commission. The decision met with general displeasure because the Commission was deprived of real legislative powers and had to report any initiatives to the French Minister, Secretary of State, Hugo Maret. Anastase's bad mood, she suspected, was more the result of his not being named one of the seven commissioners.

"Nearly so, Anastase," Marie called back, masking her anxiety. "I'll be down momentarily."

He grumbled something and moved away.

Marie gazed at her reflection in the mirror, filled with dread for the night ahead. She had abandoned her plans to go to Walewice, yielding to both her husband's insistence that she attend Talleyrand's ball—and fate. Now, she regretted that decision. Even at this late hour, she searched for some excuse to avoid the event.

"Are you all right, Madame?" Hania asked. "You've gone a bit pale."

"What—yes, I'm fine, Hania," Marie replied, her gaze still fixed on her reflection.

Despite her husband's request that she wear her most beautiful gown and jewels, she had chosen a simpler white satin dress. It was high-waisted, with a bustline higher than that of the blue gown she had worn to the palace. She rejected the sapphire and diamond necklace, opting instead for a double-stranded pearl necklace. Completing the look, she slipped on long silk white gloves.

Hania helped her arrange a wreath of laurel leaves atop her upswept blonde tresses.

"Marie!" the count called from downstairs.

Hania's eyes went wide.

"Never mind, Hania. Bring me the blue cloak with the fur lining."

By the time she descended the staircase to a red-faced Anastase, she had fully buttoned up the cloak so that he couldn't see the simplicity of her ensemble.

"The carriage has been out front holding up traffic for nearly an hour," the count said through clenched teeth. "You know how narrow Bednarska Street is, Marie. Let's go."

The distance to Talleyrand's borrowed palace was short, but the streets were lined with slow-moving carriages and crowds hoping to catch a glimpse of Napoleon. When they reached Miodowa Street, they found it all aglow with barrels of lighted tar for the *karnawał* season. Lively dance music greeted them as they stepped down from the coach.

The count turned to Marie. "The dancing has already started," he said, frowning. "You know, that means the emperor has already made his entrance. You've made us late, Marie."

Marie stiffened, pushing back her shoulders. "And so, we shall make our entrance now, husband."

Anastase's forehead wrinkled in surprise, but she didn't wait for a comment and strode into the palace courtyard, passing through a double line of the emperor's Guard of Honor, Anastase trailing.

Inside, at the cloak room, Anastase took notice of Marie's ensemble, his jaw dropping. "Marie, what came over you to wear such a hapless gown for this event? And my mother's necklace? I wanted you to sparkle."

"I thought it most appropriate," she answered, moving toward the first of several linked reception rooms. Beneath the façade of self-confidence, she was trembling.

Eliza suddenly appeared and gave a quick curtsey to the count. "You're so late, Marie. I began to think you weren't coming. Everyone's here. Everyone! Come along, now that you've arrived."

Eliza quickly escorted them to the ballroom, where the dancing had just paused. As they crossed the dance floor, Anastase excused himself to speak to someone.

Marie took her friend's hand and held her in place. "Oh, what am I to do, Eliza? If I'm recognized and our escapade to Błonie is found out, Anastase will be furious." She kept to herself the deeper fear that Napoleon would approach her.

"Don't worry, the emperor and Marshal Duroc have already paid their respects to the Potockis. Let's hide you there."

Marie agreed. It seemed a hope, at least. The two hastened across the floor.

The Potockis welcomed Marie, who worked at wedging her way between and behind them, her eyes scanning the crowd across the room. She saw both Napoleon and Duroc, but almost immediately the orchestra struck up a waltz, and the dancers obscured her view.

Lord Potocki brought Marie a flute of champagne and she allowed herself to relax a little. She took a sip and then another, lifting her eyes above the rim of the glass to take in the room.

Marie caught brief glimpses of her husband directly across the floor as the dancers glided around the crowded floor. Then came a gap in the dancers, allowing her to see who stood next to him. Her heart caught. It was Prince Józef Poniatowski, who had kept her secret about her trip to Błonie. She prayed that he wouldn't let mention of it slip, cursing herself for coming. She wished she could leave.

With great enthusiasm, Napoleon's *chef d'orchestre*, Kappellmeister Paer, tapped his podium and introduced himself to the crowd, saying he was initiating a short intermission while the orchestra prepared for a *contredanse*.

A buzz went around the hall, not all of it enthusiastic because many of the Polish attendees had never attempted the dance.

The room went surprisingly still as the orchestra made their adjustments.

"Look!" Anna blurted.

Marie looked up. A soldier was walking across the empty dance floor, his gaze set on their group. She didn't recognize him. He was handsome but very young.

The dark-haired youth stepped right up to Lord Potocki, clicked his heels, bowed toward Potocki, and then toward the three women. He was blushing. "Forgive me," he stammered. "I am Louis de Périgord, aide de camp to Marshal Louis-Alexandre Berthier."

Marie sucked in breath. Berthier was Napoleon's Chief-of-Staff. Benedykt served under him.

The aide's gaze went to the ladies.

"Yes?" Lord Potocki asked. A sharpness in his tone regained the aide's attention.

"I'm sorry, Monseigneur?"

"You wish to dance with one of our party, is that it?" Potocki asked.

"What? —no, no, not at all!"

"What, then?"

"I'm to ask—which lady is Marie?"

Marie felt a clenching in her middle.

"Marie, are you hiding there behind Eliza?" Potocki asked. "Step forward, will you?"

Marie obeyed, slowly.

The aide gave a bow. "Mademoiselle—" he started.

"Madame," Marie contradicted. "Madame Walewska."

"Forgive me." He gave a little nervous cough and took in breath. "I have been instructed to find you, Madame, and invite you to be the emperor's partner in the *contredanse* that is about to start."

The room seemed to spin, round and round. Marie thought she would pass out. "I cannot," she said. "I'm sorry, but I must refuse."

"Refuse the emperor?" Potocki questioned, his head jerking back.

"You can't refuse the emperor," Anna said, her voice firm. "Tell the soldier you accept."

"But it's a *contredanse*," Marie said.

"So?" Anna asked. "Eliza just told me she had taught the *contredanse* at convent school. It's related to a quadrille, she said. In any case, you know it, Marie."

Deflated, Marie cast an unhappy glance at a sheep-faced Eliza.

"You can't allow this young soldier to fail at his task, Marie," Potocki said. He bent down and whispered in her ear: "Tell him you accept, Marie. There's more to fail here than a pimply aide-de-camp."

Marie knew at once he had Poland's independence in mind. Everyone was to be on their best behavior. Certainly, that a refusal to dance could cause a political wave was an exaggeration, but such a warning coming from the very serious Count Aleksander Potocki was not without credit.

Marie was just about to respond to the aide when Anastase stepped into the little group, and Potocki quickly informed him of the situation.

Anastase turned toward Marie and took both of her hands in his. "It's the emperor, Marie. You must dance with him. You dare not refuse."

Marie saw no way out. Once she nodded in agreement, the aide-de-camp announced the details. "The men comprising the foursome with the emperor are Marshal Berthier and the emperor's brothers-in-law Marshal de Murat and Duke Camillo Borghese." The aide's eyes flitted from Anna Potocka to Eliza Sobolewska. "Ladies, I have also been asked to request your participation in the dance."

Unlike Marie, both Eliza and Anna were delighted with the opportunity. The next thing she knew, she was standing in the middle of the floor next to the aide-de-camp, Napoleon's place-saver. She burned with embarrassment. There would be rumors, gossip. And Anastase had sent her off to the floor with a smile. A smile! That he was *pleased* that the emperor had chosen her was astonishing. It occurred to her that perhaps he thought she was finally living up to the name of Walewski, living up to it and burnishing it to a brilliant luster.

It was a mean thought, Marie knew. She put it out of her mind as the distinguished men of the quadrille—all but Napoleon—appeared. Marshal Duroc was pleasant enough but gave no indication he recalled their meeting at Błonie. The fourth woman was introduced as Madame Zofia Branicka, the woman the prince had mentioned. While she was blonde and lovely, Marie couldn't see how anyone would mistake one for the other.

Louis, the place-saver, stood with Marie in one corner of the square when the *contredanse* began. One blink of her eyes and it was Emperor Napoleon Bonaparte standing across from her, lifting her hand to his lips, his eyes simultaneously searing into her. "So serious?" he purred. "I expected a different greeting."

Marie felt her lower lip twitch as she attempted a smile.

The emperor ran his eyes from her slippers up to her shoulders in the most scrutinizing way. "You do know," he said, "white on white is a terrible blunder." The purr in his voice belied the sharpness.

The comment stunned Marie. He was referring to the white gown against her particularly white complexion. The French *modiste* Madame Simone had called it *alabaster*. A heat came into her face. She chose not to answer the insult.

Taking in his appearance, she noted that he had shed his greatcoat for what must have been the latest style in French court wear, rather than military dress. The coattails, waistcoat, and breeches were of an amethyst velvet and embroidered in gold design, the needlework exquisite in its detail. The only simple part of his dress were the white gloves that he removed and tucked into his waistcoat pocket.

"We are the head couple. The pair across the way will follow our lead, sometimes interacting with us," he continued, assuming, it seemed, Marie was unfamiliar with the dance. "The other two couples rest and in due time, we rest and they imitate us. Come along, now. The first figure is *le pantalon*. This is quick, Marie. It's no minuet! Ha, ha!"

Napoleon led Marie through a number of steps, and it took no matter of time to realize that even the most fashionable attire could mask how badly the Emperor of France danced. His steps were off, as were his turns. That he evidently could not feel the beat of the music would have thrown her off as well, had she not been one of the most natural dancers at school. Marshal Berthier and Anna Potocka shared a number of steps with them, and when Eliza stepped forward for a ladies' turn, Marie couldn't look at her out of fear the two would start laughing.

The other two couples managed nicely once Napoleon and she had returned to their corner. By the time they were into the second figure, he was confusing movements from the three remaining figures and making the clumsiest possible steps.

With all of Poland society watching, the *contredanse* passed at what seemed a glacierlike pace. While Marie found the experience humiliating, surprisingly, the emperor acted as if it were great sport, as if it were a joke on him and on everyone. Marie did find some satisfaction in thinking that people would leave the ball thinking about his atrocious dancing, rather than the identity of his dancing partner. If she was lucky, they would sympathize with her.

At the conclusion of the dance, Napoleon bowed toward Marie, donned his gloves again, and turned to address Anna: "Madame Potocka, you could see from a distance. Would you say I'm a good dancer?"

Marie felt two things at that moment: great relief that he had not asked *her* that question, and great fear for how Anna would answer him.

Anna Potocka's age and experience was telling. "Sir," she answered, "for a great man you dance perfectly."

Marie breathed a sigh of relief—and took a lesson in diplomacy.

Napoleon suddenly pivoted back to her and took her hand in both of his. "You seem so melancholy," he said. He stared at her for what seemed a long while, the gray-blue transfixing. "I must be away," he said at last. "I have fences to build and fences to mend this night." He glanced down and seemed suddenly to realize that he still held her hand captive. Releasing it, he said, *"Au revoir, Mademoiselle."*

He was gone before she could correct him.

Marie watched as he circulated through the room, sometimes proselytizing, sometimes merely chatting, but she soon noticed that his gaze kept drifting back to her.

Eliza noticed, too. "He's watching you, Marie. What did he say to you at first?"

"Why, he insulted me by saying wearing white on white is a blunder."

"Not surprising. In Paris we often heard of his oddly rude comments. He would inquire whether an uncommonly fat woman liked to dance, or why a newly divorced woman's husband had left her. Once he sarcastically suggested to a homely woman that her husband must often display his jealousy. So, do not take it to heart."

Anastase turned to her now, whispering, "The emperor keeps turning to see if you're still here. You've made an impression."

Marie felt ill. "Perhaps we should leave, Anastase."

"What? I think not."

Later, Anna took Marie aside. "I saw how long he held your hand."

"Yes—so?"

"Well, it means something, you know."

Another half hour of Napoleon's less-than-subtle glances in Marie's direction brought unwanted attention from various quarters.

At Marie's persistent urging, Anastase finally agreed to leave for home.

Anastase started humming once they were settled in the coach.

"You seem to be in a good mood," Marie said, wondering if it was the liquor even though she had not seen him drink more than a glass or two.

The humming ceased. "What did he say to you, Marie?"

"He—he made a comment about my gown."

"Did he? But it's so plain. I'm certain he was merely being polite."

And I'm certain he was not. She would not give her husband the benefit of repeating the emperor's insult. He would merely gloat.

"I fell into quite a conversation with Marshals Talleyrand and Duroc."

"Really?"

"Military officers can be like old ladies," Anastase pronounced.

"Oh?" So, he *knew*!

"Quite the gossipers."

Marie could not find words.

"You know, my dear, you should have told me about your Błonie escapade." The humming resumed.

At home, Marie hurried to her bedchamber and locked the door. Quickly changing into her nightdress, she climbed beneath the covers, but her mind was a long way from sleep.

Napoleon seemed to expect a certain behavior from her. Just what did he expect? What? The French Court before and after the Rising was awash with flirtations, so she read. Eliza and her husband had spent time in Paris and said as much. Did the emperor intend only a flirtation? No doubt he had been told she was from the country and he thought he would amuse himself. And yet—and yet, he had the audacity to insult her. Was that part of the amusement? Marie had no wish to find out. She resolved to leave the city at once and return to Walewice, as she had planned to do. Warsaw had become dangerous ground for her. She would leave the next day.

Would Anastase allow her to do so? Anastase! Her secret trip to Błonie had been found out, but he had made only the slightest of comments about it. How had she so misjudged him? What had diluted that jealous temper of his?

A knock came at the door now.

Marie caught her breath. "I'm—I'm very tired tonight, Anastase," she called.

The knock came again, a softer knock than her husband's. "It's Hania, Madame."

"Hania? I've already undressed. I don't need you tonight."

Hania's voice seemed to come between the narrow gap in the doorframe. "Madame," she whispered, "I have a note."

"A note? From whom?"

"A young officer at the side door."

Marie went to the door. Unlocking it, she took the note, a piece of notepaper folded and sealed rather untidily with red wax. "Thank you, Hania. You may retire now."

Hania nodded and took a step back, her green eyes round in wonder.

Marie closed the door, placed a lighted chamberstick near a cushioned chair and sat. She took a nail file, undid the seal, and opened the note.

It read:

Madame Walewska,
I had eyes only for you. You alone! I desire no one but you. Please reply promptly in order to cool my impatience.
Napoleon.

Marie thought she would be ill. Her heart beat erratically. She glanced up at the door. The light from the sconce in the hall allowed for the shadows of two feet to play beneath the door. Marie jumped from her chair, hurried to the door and pulled it open. "Hania!"

"The officer said I should wait."

"You said he was young?"

"Oh, yes, handsome, too."

"Hania, go and tell him not to wait for a response. There will be none. Do you hear?"

"Madame it's a very fancy carriage in the street."

"I'm certain it is. Now, do as I say, Hania. Then bolt the door."

Marie went back to bed but couldn't sleep. How dare even an emperor write so boldly? Especially, since it was clear someone had informed him of her marital status.

She lay awake preparing a speech should Anastase attempt to keep her from returning to Walewice. She rose early and began to pack the things that she would take with her.

29

MARIE DID NOT GO DOWN to breakfast. She finished her toilette at midmorning and was dressed in a dark green dress when a knock came at the door. She opened it to find Madame de Vauban, a bouquet of roses in her hand.

"What—what's this? Marie stammered.

"Invite me in and I'll explain."

Marie stood aside allowing Madame de Vauban to enter, and then closed the door, leaning back against it.

"Oh, don't look so shocked. Your husband sent a note asking me to make a return visit."

"And the flowers?"

"Oh, they're not from Anastase."

"Oh?"

"They're not from me, either. Ha!" Madame de Vauban laid the flowers on Marie's dressing table and removed her fox-trimmed purple cloak and tossed it onto the bed, her gaze running over a number of dresses and stacks of folded clothing lying there. She made no comment as she smoothed the lines of her revealing lime-green dress. She turned to Marie. "Downstairs I ran into Marshal Géraud Duroc, who is visiting with your husband. He asked me to bring the flowers to you. There's a note attached to the single white rose in the middle of the red."

"Marshal Duroc?"

Madame de Vauban's eyes narrowed. "You've caught someone's attention, haven't you?"

"I—I have, to my consternation."

"And it's not Duroc, is it?"

Marie shook her head. "I suspect you know whose it is, don't you? It seems everyone must." Marie went to her bedside table and retrieved the note from the previous night. She handed the missive to her guest, motioning for her to sit on the dressing table bench.

Madame de Vauban showed little surprise upon reading it. She looked up, dark eyes intent. "Bold and direct, isn't it, like the man himself? And have you replied?"

Marie stood at the end of the bed, one arm encircling a bedpost as if for support. "I have not."

"I see." Madame de Vauban nodded toward the trunk that stood upright near the window. "You're going somewhere, Marie?"

"I had planned to return to our Walewice residence but lost energy halfway through packing. I don't think Anastase will stand for it. Oh, I'm in a terrible predicament, Madame de Vauban."

"*Henriette*, please call me Henriette, my dear."

Marie nodded. "Can you advise me—Henriette?"

"Let's see what's in the note that came today, shall we?" Madame de Vauban lifted the white rose from the bouquet and removed the attached note. "My, my, roses in winter. The man knows someone with a productive conservatory." She stood and delivered the bouquet to Marie, who sat on the bed.

Marie felt a tightening at her shoulders, a thrumming at her temple. She clumsily broke the seal with her fingers, sending tiny red shards of wax to the floor. She unfolded the note and silently read it.

Madame,

I am hurt. At Błonie, you seemed smitten, or am I mistaken? Can your heart have changed course so rapidly? But perhaps not irrevocably? So many questions. Allow me a bit of hope. Allow me a response. Madame, you owe me two!

N.

"Two notes in two days! You have indeed caught his attention." Madame de Vauban took the letter from Marie and read it. "Ah, so he signed this one with only his first initial."

"Is there some significance in that?" Marie asked.

Madame de Vauban shrugged. "Perhaps it's meant to be more personal, or perhaps he was merely in a rush. It might mean nothing at all."

"But the message does."

"Oh, yes, it does." Madame de Vauban's voice dipped low. "And there's something else you'll need to consider."

"What?"

"When your husband went to collect the marshal's overcoat, Géraud told me that an invitation will be coming later in the day for a small supper and concert at the Royal Castle."

Marie gasped. "Sweet Jesus—I don't want to go, but Anastase will insist on it."

Madame de Vauban inclined her head toward Marie. "The marshal whispered that it's to be a *small* supper."

"You mean—that Anastase is not included?"

Madame de Vauban nodded. "There's to be a dozen or so guests, but only one from the Walewski household. You."

Marie sat in stunned silence for several minutes. "But," she said at last, recalling Henriette's duty at the castle, "you will be hostess, yes?"

"No, the prince has asked Madame Tyszkiewicz, his sister."

"Oh." Marie rose and went to the window and stared out. Suddenly, she pivoted to face her guest. "Henriette, I've heard Prince Poniatowski say that beautiful women are able to influence men of importance."

"Well, as a Frenchwoman, I find Poland either a land of innocence or subtlety. But in France, our recent history bears witness to the prince's statement. Louis's mistresses Madame de Pompadour and Madame du Barry each served as the king's advisor." She giggled. "Not simultaneously, however."

"Their calling is not my calling, Henriette. And didn't du Barry go to the guillotine?"

Henriette waved her hand. "Oh, that was much later, during the Uprising. She was actually bravely assisting *émigrés* escape the revolution."

"And if I go to this supper, how am I to tell Anastase that he is not invited? What will he think?"

"Leave that to me, Marie."

"For that matter, what will people say?"

"If you can speak for Poland, as the prince believes, what does it matter?"

"I failed once in making my plea for Poland. My nerves deserted me. I would not fail again. And I would gladly give over what wealth I have or even my life. But, Henriette, my intention at B*ł*onie was innocent and noble. I am a wife and a mother . . . you do understand me."

"I understand. You have scruples."

Marie didn't respond. She couldn't discern the tone of Henriette's observation. Was it a straightforward comment, or one meant to mock her? What attitude toward scruples might this Frenchwoman of a certain age harbor? It struck Marie now that this woman who, along with her husband, lived as Prince Poniatowski's mistress in the same residence, an unusual triangle to which Polish society seemed to have turned a blind eye. Marie realized now that Madame de Vauban's visits—albeit initiated at the request of Anastase—conveniently aided the implementation of the prince's intentions.

"Marie, when the emperor says that he desires you, you must not misunderstand. It is common for the French to use layers of meanings. What does ring clear, though, is his appreciation of you. You should be proud. Any number of women would be."

Marie scoffed at the idea. "Then one of them might please the emperor more. I would welcome it. I'm frozen in fear, Henriette!"

"Accept the dinner invitation, Marie. You're an adult now. Things needn't go too far. I know you can defend yourself." Henriette pulled on her cloak. "You've grown up in the provinces and here in Warsaw society you feel at sixes and sevens. I don't think you have a true sense of your self-worth, or *amour propre*, as we say in France. You are the most beautiful woman in this city. Forget Walewice. I must be off. One last bit of advice: guard yourself against his eyes. They are beguiling. They are his weapon. Now, as for Anastase, I'll talk to him before leaving. I've known him for years, and I can assure you that his *amour-propre* is not lacking. It's inflated, in fact. So, he *will* allow you to go. I'm confident he will be flattered that his wife has been so honored."

Later, when Marie went downstairs, she found that her husband had gone out. She ate dinner alone.

Anastase reappeared in time for supper. "Hello, my dear," he said as she seated herself on his right. A maid entered with a tureen of mushroom soup and ladled it into his bowl.

Marie glanced down at her empty bowl and discovered that it held a formal envelope, her name alone scratched on it in a handwriting she had come to recognize. *Madame Marie Walewska, Countess of Walewice*

Marie immediately looked to her husband.

Anastase lifted a spoonful of soup to his lips but managed an enigmatic smile before placing it in his mouth.

Marie withdrew the invitation as the maid approached and slipped it into her skirt pocket.

The meal continued with no mention of it. But she was certain he had seen it and guessed as to its contents.

30

Monday, 19 January 1807

As per the invitation, a carriage from the Royal Castle arrived at eight in the evening, with Marshal Duroc as her escort.

Marie met him in the reception room. She wore a pale-yellow taffeta gown.

"You look lovely," he said.

"Thank you, Marshal Duroc. I'm ready."

He gave a sidelong glance toward the hallway that she was quick to interpret.

"My husband is not at home." Marie offered no further details because she had none. Anastase must have known about her invitation and his exclusion, and yet he hadn't mentioned it. It was a mystery.

Duroc nodded, offering no comment.

———— ⁓ ————

Marshal Duroc escorted Marie up one flight to the Green Room in the King's Apartment and introduced her to Countess Marie Teresa Tyszkiewicz, Prince Poniatowski's sister, who today was playing the role of the emperor's hostess.

"You are as lovely as I've heard, Madame Walewska," the countess said, leading with the exchange of kisses. "This was my King Stanisław's small conference room. Today you see that it is set for the after-supper piano concert. Now, come this way."

Madame Tyszkiewicz led them to the next connecting room, the Yellow Room. "I'm so happy to see this chamber used as a small dining room again. Uncle Stanisław held his famous Thursday Night Dinners here. Every important person of arts and letters, not to mention historians, have supped here. —Until it all came tumbling down," she said with a sigh, dabbing at her eyes. "Now, please excuse me."

Marshal Duroc bent slightly toward Marie. "Countess Tyszkiewicz was married off at eighteen by Stanisław to a Lithuanian count. It seems she found marriage stifling, and so she left him years later. These days you'll often find her in the company of the emperor's Minister of Foreign Affairs."

"Talleyrand?"

The marshal nodded. "Appropriate, don't you think?" He winked.

Marie afforded his little joke a smile. Anastase was correct: military men were inclined to gossip.

Marie was pleased to find her friends Aleksander and Anna Potocki present. Anna hurried over to her. "I'm so glad you could come, Marie. How lovely! If the marshal will release you for a bit, I'll take you around."

"Enjoy yourself, Marie," Duroc said, bowing.

When they passed Louis de Périgord, the *aide de camp* who had searched her out to dance with Napoleon, he gave Marie a wide smile, drew his heels together, and bowed. Marie afforded him a smile despite the sour memory of the dance with the emperor.

Anna introduced Marie to a small group of men whose names she recognized as members of the new Governing Commission, including Józef Wybicki and Anna's husband. She became immediately suspicious that the evening's purpose involved politics.

"*We* seem to be the minority," Marie said, drawing Anna away after a bit of polite conversation.

Anna gave a little laugh. "It seems so. Well, besides us, there is the hostess. That's three."

Marie was left to wonder whether Anna was playing a part in this.

Napoleon had not yet arrived by the time the seating took place at a table set for twelve. Madame Tyszkiewicz guided Marie to her seat between Louis de Périgord on her left and Marshal Henri Bertrand on her right. Of different generations, both were engaging conversationalists, and she leaned into their chatter as a distraction from her growing sense of unease.

Marshal Duroc approached the table, a worried look on his face. He leaned over Bertrand and suggested he move a seat away so that he could sit next to Marie. When the marshal pretended not to hear, Duroc moved around Marie and suggested that Périgord change his seat.

It was at this moment that the emperor was announced, and Duroc settled for the empty chair next to Périgord.

Madame Tyszkiewicz led Napoleon to the single gold-painted chair at the head of the table. The emperor wore a double-breasted tailcoat of scarlet velvet and white breeches, both embroidered in gold. He whispered something to the hostess and stepped away to take the chair directly opposite Marie, displacing one of his marshals. Madame Tyszkiewicz quickly sprang into action, sending the marshal to the seat of honor. The two men at Marie's sides—Périgord and Bertrand—rose, along with the other guests, to salute the emperor, after which they sat, oblivious to the French emperor as they continued to vie for her attention.

A parade of servants began. The hostess had arranged for a Polish winter table that included boiled potatoes with herring in sour cream, noodles with poppy seed, pickled beets, and stuffed dumplings. A variety of wines accompanied the courses.

The emperor spoke of his intentions for a spring offensive and seemed to enjoy replying to a number of questions from several guests. His short and precise answers were delivered in a friendly tone and with a winning smile. Marie could feel his eyes upon her. Twice when she dared to look across the table, she found his salt-white smile trained on her. She dared not return his gaze. The peril was real because for the first time she was forced to admit to herself that he was able not only to project attraction, but that he was just as gifted to *inspire* attraction. *I must tread carefully.* She was thankful for the annoying attention given by her two side companions because it provided an excuse not to look across the table.

When a cinnamon-scented compote of apples, apricots, raisins, and cherries was served, she did happen to glance up and notice that the emperor put his hand on his heart while his gaze seemed to send some signal to Marshal Duroc. The marshal leaned forward so that Marie could see him, and said, "Madame Walewska, I thought perhaps you would be wearing the flowers you were sent today."

It became immediately clear to Marie why the marshal had so wished to sit next to her: the emperor was to send him signals such as she had just witnessed.

Marie turned toward Duroc, her face heating up. "Marshal Duroc, one doesn't wear flowers to a dinner party, here in Warsaw, at least. I gave one to each of our maids, and they were delighted, knowing the source. As for the single white one, I pressed it in a book of fairy tales so that my son would have it one day." She looked up at the emperor now and gave him a smile that she hoped was as brilliant as her lie.

Napoleon's brow came down and his eyes narrowed. He pursed his lips into a flat line. He was not pleased.

Périgord and Bertrand reverted to their chatter, but minutes later, the table went suddenly quiet. Marie looked up to see that the emperor had left his place.

She turned to see he was leaning over the hostess's shoulder, whispering something. After a moment or two he glanced up, seemed to take in the whole of the table, pivoted, and left the room.

Countess Tyszkiewicz announced that in fifteen minutes the concert was to be held in the Green Room.

In short order, the dozen guests—minus one—settled themselves in cushioned chairs for the piano concert. No excuse was made for the emperor's absence. Marie could not help but feel he left in anger—anger at her. Grateful that she could be silent and not have to respond to a barrage of comments and questions, Marie nevertheless found it difficult to truly enjoy the composition, so absorbed was she in the exit the emperor had made.

One piece by Haydn came to an end, and before the pianist could announce the second piece, Madame Tyszkiewicz approached Marie, leaning over, a fan to her face. "Madame Walewska," she said in a soft, nasal voice, "it seems you have a visitor awaiting you in the King's Chapel."

"What?" Marie whispered, although she had clearly heard the message. Fear ran through her like a cold sword.

Madame Tyszkiewicz repeated the message word for word.

Marie stood, aware of the many eyes on her.

"Follow me," Madame Tyszkiewicz said.

Marie obeyed, though she wanted to turn and run.

Passing through several rooms, they came to the closed chapel doors. Madame Tyszkiewicz turned to Marie. "I'll leave you here."

She faced the gilded doors now, taking in a huge breath. It's a chapel, she told herself, God's house. What harm could befall her here? Before a negative answer could form, Marie reached out, took hold of the handles on the double doors, and pulled them back with a strength she didn't know she had.

The room was dimly lighted by votive candles. She entered, moving toward the front, where a dark-haired figure sat in the shadows.

As she approached him, she realized that even seated, he seemed taller than the emperor. He was hatless, but the collar and epaulettes were those of a soldier, an officer. Another one of his *aides de camp*?

The figure stood as she approached, and he turned toward her.

Her already racing heart beat faster. She looked up into the familiar face. Words failed her.

He stepped toward her, smiling.

"Benedykt!"

Her brother laughed. "You seem surprised."

"I'm—I'm overcome. The last I heard you were with Prince Jerome's army near the Baltic."

"Are you going to hug me, or not?"

"Yes, yes, of course." Marie took a step toward him and they embraced. Marie then gave him a little push and held him at arm's length. "What are you doing in Warsaw—and how did you know I was here tonight? Oh, you must have seen Anastase!"

"Shall we sit?" Benedykt shifted two chairs so that they faced each other.

Marie's mind swam. "I have so many questions. How is Teodor? Is he here, too?"

"No, he's still in the Baltic, but he could be transferred soon."

"Here?"

Benedykt shrugged. "You've made a splash, it seems."

"Ha! I was foolish and stupid, and now I'm in an impossible situation."

"And why is that, Marie?"

Marie drew her shoulders back, took a long breath and relayed the story that started at Błonie and led to the present moment, underscoring the despondency she felt. "At times, Benedykt, I've felt almost as melancholic as that winter after I sent Arkady away."

"You weren't meant for Arkady, Marie. You were destined for something more."

"If you mean becoming Countess Walewska of Walewice, you're wrong. I've not been happy these two years." Marie surprised herself with the declaration.

"Listen to me, Marie. I was never too free with my compliments for you. It was the way of brothers, I suppose. You don't have any idea how beautiful you are, do you? How attractive you are to men?"

"So I've been told."

"But you don't believe it? You should. It's brought you here to the Royal Castle."

"What are you saying?"

"I'm saying you worshipped Napoleon Bonaparte for years, and now you hold him in the palm of your hand."

"Unhappily so. I didn't worship him in a romantic way. I don't know what you've been told, but do you know generals come into conquered lands with plans to conquer the women, too? I do! And then they march off to war or return to wives. You don't look shocked. Perhaps it's true of *lieutenants*, as well?" Marie's eyes went to the various ribbons and medals on his elaborate coat. Her gaze stayed there for a long moment then moved up to her brother's face.

Benedykt smiled. "Colonel," he said.

Marie had to catch her breath. "Colonel!"

He nodded.

"Mother wrote just yesterday. She didn't say a word."

"She doesn't know."

Marie's jaw dropped a bit. "That recent! Oh, congratulations! You've followed him for ten years, yes? I'm so happy for you. But you must keep yourself safe once fighting starts again in the spring."

"I will."

"Father would be so proud."

"Marysia," he said, waving a dismissive hand, "listen to me."

"Yes? You're so serious."

"I am. Marie, you have a destiny."

"What do you mean?"

Benedykt reached into the inner pocket of his military jacket and withdrew a folded and sealed note.

Marie became lightheaded. This isn't happening, she told herself. It isn't!

But her name was written on it, and by now she knew that scribbling. Suddenly, everything about the night's goings-on made sense. The emperor's disappearance after supper, her brother's timely appearance, and now his duty to deliver another missive, another plea.

"I—I can't believe this!" Marie stood, took several paces, and wheeled around to her brother, her eyes on his uniform. "From First Lieutenant to Colonel in—how long?

"That doesn't matter."

"Oh, yes, it does. How many ranks did you bypass?"

"Three."

"Three ranks! And all for that," she said, nodding toward the note. "A comparable reward to thirty pieces of silver, wouldn't you say?"

His face clouding, Benedykt stood and stepped near her.

"How did he find you, Benedykt?"

"I don't know, Marie. Someone told him you have brothers fighting."

"Sweet Jesus," Marie said, drawing in a sharp breath. "It was I—I told him."

"I couldn't believe it myself. Marshal Duroc had me brought here. I met the emperor yesterday. He's very serious about you."

"For no reason."

Benedykt's expression softened. "Come, sit down. You look faint."

"I am faint." Marie sat, her back tense. She watched her brother settle into his chair, the note still in his hand.

Benedykt noticed her gaze. "He wants to see you alone."

"I won't see him alone. You know as well as I that—"

"Listen to me, Marie. You need to humor him, that's all I'm saying. And in doing so, you can be the voice of all of us. You can do it for Poland. You can aid in getting our country back."

187

"You once told me I should make a sacrifice for our family, yes? For Mother and for the estate? I did and the results of doing my familial duty now stand in the way of *this* that you are suggesting."

"That you are married."

"And a mother! It's not been a happy union, Benedykt, not one I chose. I should have chosen someone whom I could love, no matter his family name."

"Arkady? Arkady Suvorov, whose father, Generalissimo Aleksandr Suvorov led the Russians at Maciejowice, where *our* father died. You could have compromised yourself?"

"Arkady loved me. I might have a happy life now instead—"

"Do you think so? It just took a letter directed to the right person for me to get a sense of your Arkady. Are you listening, Marie? When he begged you to go off with him, offering everything he had in life, tell me—did he mention marriage?"

"It's what he meant, Benedykt!"

"Really, Marie? I've allowed you to keep your pure notions of Arkady Suvorov all this time. I see that was a mistake."

"What do you mean? He spoke in good faith. I was cruel in my rejection."

"He is Russian," Benedykt said, his tone softening. "You knew that, of course. But you didn't know that he was already married."

"What?"

Benedykt nodded. "At the time he was pursuing you, he had been married since 1800. He had three children."

"Is this true?" Marie felt a trembling sensation in her chin.

"Why would I lie? In any case, you decided you could not marry into the family of Father's killer."

Marie turned her head away. "Was I so deceived? Am I so gullible?"

Benedykt took the letter, placed it in Marie's cupped hands, and allowed his hand to stay on hers for several moments. "The past is gone," he whispered. "*This is the present.*"

"Was the reunion a happy one, Madame Walewska?" Marshal Duroc asked as he assisted Marie into the coach.

Marie turned her gaze away as he climbed in and sat across from her.

"He did give you something, Madame Walewska?"

Marie pulled her cloak tighter. "He did."

From above, the driver called, "Come, my boys!" The carriage began to move, the horses' hooves clattering over the cobblestone courtyard of the Royal Castle.

"You have your doubts about him, Madame Walewska? The emperor?"

Marie looked at the marshal but remained silent.

Several minutes passed before the marshal shifted tactics. "I find it incumbent upon me to mention a conversation I had just today with Constant Wairy."

"Who?"

"Constant Wairy is the emperor's *valet de chambre*."

"Oh."

"He's extremely observant and something of a diarist." When Marie didn't respond, he continued. "He said the emperor has been agitated of late—restless, irritable, and slow to dress. Constant sealed the letters sent to you, Madame Walewska, and he's aware that they have not been well received."

"I accepted tonight's supper invitation."

"Yes, you did. Now—" Marshal Duroc cleared his throat. "Monsieur Wairy said that the emperor thought the notes' receiver is either too proud, or . . ."

The coach stopped in front of the Walewski townhome.

"Or?"

Marshal Duroc cleared his throat again. "Or—that she is a *coquette*."

Marie drew her shoulders back against the bench rest. "A prideful woman or a coquette? As if there could be no other explanation?"

Marshal Duroc shrugged. "It could be merely Constant's viewpoint."

A footman pulled open the door and stood waiting for Marie.

Marie gathered up her cloak, but before she could move, the marshal reached across, detaining her. "Monsieur Wairy also said the emperor considers himself irresistible to women and that his *amour-propre* has been damaged."

That expression again—self-esteem! Marie shivered, turned and stepped down from the coach.

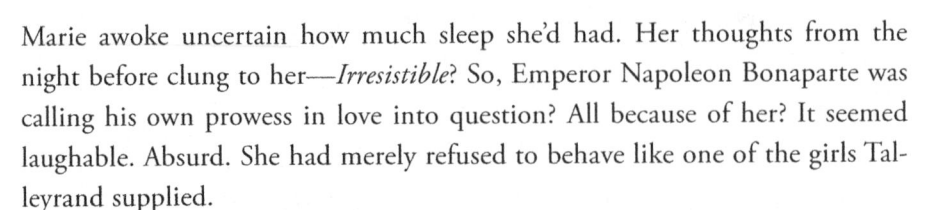

Marie awoke uncertain how much sleep she'd had. Her thoughts from the night before clung to her—*Irresistible*? So, Emperor Napoleon Bonaparte was calling his own prowess in love into question? All because of her? It seemed laughable. Absurd. She had merely refused to behave like one of the girls Talleyrand supplied.

Her thoughts shifted to her brother Benedykt. He had played his part the night before, just as he had done in encouraging her to marry Anastase. The thought was jarring. Did he truly believe she could influence Napoleon's mindset regarding Poland's fate? Or was his own ambition at play?

A knock came at the door.

"Come in," Marie called, expecting Hania.

The door opened to reveal Henriette de Vauban and a younger woman, likely in her thirties. "Hello, you slugabed. I know it's early, but I couldn't wait to hear about last night." The two entered.

Marie responded with a dark look.

"Oh, I see. Well, you can tell us about it while you dress. This beautiful lady is Emily Cichocka. Why, she would be my first choice for lady-in-waiting were it not for her tendency to marry and then jettison husbands." Henriette laughed.

"Only two," Emily snapped, laughing, her tawny complexion and almond-shaped black eyes likely indicative of Tatar ancestry.

"But, Emily," Henriette put in, "you've already captured a third heart, one of a *young* soldier."

Henriette and Emily laughed like girls as they settled themselves on the chaise lounge. "Marie, tell us how the evening unfolded. Oh, I understand there's a third letter. Have you read it yet?"

"I have not."

"Lovely, then we are on time."

Marie rose and went to the wardrobe to select a dress, wondering what Henriette meant.

"First, I should say that we ran into Constant Wairy out front," Henriette continued. "Monsieur Wairy is—"

"The emperor's *valet de chambre*, I know," Marie interjected, turning to face Henriette.

"Ah, good," Henriette said. "Well, it seems he was here on a mission from Prince Józef to deliver a letter to your husband."

Marie crossed her arms. "A letter?"

"Yes. He also told us the emperor left in anger last evening, without staying for the concert."

"He was angry at *me*," Marie said, turning back to the wardrobe and quickly selecting a green dress.

"At you? No, you're mistaken! He was incensed at the way the soldiers on either side of you vied for your attention."

"Is that true?" Marie moved toward the bed.

"It is," Emily chimed in. "But he let them know afterward."

"How?" Marie asked.

Emily continued. "The young one, an *aide de camp*, I gather, was—"

"Louis de Périgord?" Marie asked.

"Yes, that's right," Henriette said, taking charge of the story. "Today the emperor sent him off to join his forces in East Prussia. The other, Marshal Henri Bertrand, whom I know, was ordered to join Prince Jerome's army on the Baltic. Neither will bother you again."

"Sweet Jesus," Marie hissed, dropping back on the bed, the dress clasped to her chest. Could it be true that her presence had caused these soldiers to be reassigned into war zones?

The two visitors attempted polite conversation as though they had no intention of leaving. From time to time, they would exchange cryptic expressions. Finally, Marie stood and rang for Hania.

With her maid's help, she dressed behind a privacy screen, ignoring the whispering of her guests. They fell silent when Marie emerged, sat at her dressing table, and had Hania aid with her makeup and hair.

Her toilette finished, Marie dismissed Hania and sat at the foot of the bed, facing her two guests.

"Well?" Henriette asked. "Where is it?"

"What?"

"Don't play coy with your friends, Marie. Where is the letter you say you have yet to read?"

"It's true. I haven't."

"You didn't destroy it, did you?" Henriette asked.

"Or worse—return it!" Emily cried.

"I have it in my jewelry case," Marie said.

"A good place for it, *after* you read it," Henriette said. "And now is the time."

"Oh, yes, do read it," Emily said. "I hate suspense."

Marie felt outnumbered. Clearly, Henriette had brought Emily for support. But to what end?

Marie retrieved the letter and went to stand before her audience, feeling a bit like a student at the podium in Latin class. She broke the seal and read aloud.

My dearest Madame Walewska,

Sometimes an emperor faces difficulties harder than on the battlefield. I'm comfortable there, but place me in a room with the most beautiful woman with sapphire eyes and I am lost. I wave the white flag. Do I even have a hope of success? Meeting in company has proved a disaster, as it was at the dinner. Will you come to the castle to see only me? Marshal Géraud Duroc will see to every detail. I could refuse you nothing. Why, your country would be so much dearer to me, should you have mercy on this poor heart.

From this day, I shall call you, My Marie.

N.

Marie's hands were shaking by the time she finished. She looked up. Her audience of two was awaiting her reaction. She took in a deep breath, felt for the bed behind her, and sat.

"You have a conquest, Marie," Henriette said, her face bright.

"Indeed!" Emily concurred.

"But—I can't . . ."

"You would refuse the greatest man on the continent?" Emily asked. "Oh, Marie, you can't."

Henriette's bright expression had gone dark, serious. "Listen to me, Marie. The talk at the Royal Castle is that the Prussian and Russian armies might still lure Napoleon away from his winter quarters. If that occurs, how will he protect us from our old enemies?"

"He can't do it from afar," Emily put in.

"Add to that the fact that he is tired of hearing the prince and the members of the Governing Commission beg for independence," Henriette said. "His stock answer is that he will decide at the end of the campaign."

"What the emperor writes toward the end of the letter," Emily said, "is all-important: that Poland would be dearer to him should you consent."

Marie swallowed hard. "He is asking for a secret meeting."

Emily's face darkened and she blurted: "Yes, of course, he is—"

"Listen to me, Marie," Henriette said, interrupting her friend and taking a softer approach, "I've lived some years at the French Court. I can tell you that women *can* be influential. It's true. Especially beautiful women, like you. Poland could be returned to its former glory through Napoleon. And you could have a part to play in that, Marie Walewska."

"At a price, Henriette. A very high price for surrender."

"You're worried about your reputation," Emily said.

"Yes, of course. And I have a conscience.""

"Do you think Polish society would be so cruel, so unforgiving?" Henriette asked. "Look at Madame Grabowska, your friend Eliza's mother. Is she shunned because she was the former king's longtime mistress—or wife in a morganatic marriage, should that be true—and bore him children? No. Even now, she is referred to as the wife of General Grabowski."

She took a breath and leaned back against the chaise lounge. "And—consider me," she continued, "most of Warsaw knows the prince's interest in me, and yet I live *with my husband* at Pepi's palace *and* maintain my life as Madame de Vauban. Society protects its own, Marie. It will close around you like a Roman shield wall."

A minute of silence passed as Marie sorted through these assertions.

"As for your conscience," Emily said, her tone careful and steady, "would you be able to live with yourself if Napoleon became hostile—not to you, but to Poland's cause?"

Marie turned her gaze from Emily to Henriette. "Why is it that Prince Poniatowski invests faith in me?"

Emily answered instead, blurting, "He does—and not only him!"

Henriette shot Emily a cautionary frown.

Marie studied Henriette. "What does she mean?"

Henriette let out a deep breath. "She means that the other members of the Governing Commission have weighed in on the subject."

"The subject! *I* am the subject?"

"You are," Emily said.

Marie exhaled, glancing from one to the other. "And the consensus?"

Henriette hesitated, looking briefly at the ceiling before meeting Marie's gaze. "That you should be encouraged to obey the emperor. That you should be grateful for the role you're being asked to play in the destiny of your country."

"Go to him," Emily said, her voice low and insistent. "Tell him of your love of Poland. Tell him you seek only his friendship and respect. All will be up to you. Nothing needs to happen, Marie. —Now, say that you will go."

Nothing needs to happen. It was a wisp of hope thrown out into the void like the filament of a spider. Marie grasped onto it. "Very well. I'll go."

"Good!" her two companions chorused.

"But, my husband? Anastase?"

"He will be occupied tonight, Marie," Henriette said.

"What?"

"He's been invited to the home of Józef Wybicki," Henriette replied.

"What? How do you know that?"

"The invitation was in the letter Monsieur Wairy delivered downstairs."

"We dallied in the vestibule just off the reception room while we removed our cloaks," Emily said in a rush. "And we just happened to hear Monseigneur Walewski read the invitation aloud and say that he would attend. He seemed quite pleased."

"It's a formal meeting of the Governing Commission," Henriette added, her tone edged with irritation as if Emily had stolen her thunder.

Marie sighed to herself. Of course, he was pleased. Nothing would keep him from attending. Any thought that Anastase would forbid her to leave the townhome was put to rest. That there were things at play beneath the surface left her breathless.

31

At ten in the evening, Marie stood in the front hall of the townhome, fully cloaked in black bombazine silk, with a matching wide-brimmed bonnet.

"You must put an end to those tears, Marie," Henriette said. "You look as if you're going to a funeral—but you're not."

Marie was tempted to respond with a sharp retort, but she knew it would be futile. Henriette and Emily had spent the entire day with her, clearly worried that she might weaken in her resolve.

Henriette reached up to Marie's bonnet and drew down the dark veil. "Remember, no tears once you arrive at the Royal Palace."

Emily opened the door. "Remember also," she said, "that you hold the high card. You *are* the high card."

Marie's heart pounded as she stepped onto the threshold.

"The imperial coach is just down the street to your left," Henriette directed. "Godspeed, Marie."

Marie hesitated. Moments went by. A hand on her back gave her a gentle push forward, jarring her into motion. She approached the carriage.

In the shadows, a footman extended his hand, and she stepped up into the carriage.

Inside, she found herself seated across from Marshal Duroc. Relieved to see a familiar face, she attempted a smile.

"Good evening, Madame Walewska," he said.

Marie nodded, struggling to keep her composure. The marshal attempted small talk during the short drive, but her frayed nerves left her unable to reply.

Upon arriving at the Royal Castle courtyard, Duroc led her around to a hidden entrance along the riverside of the building. After rapping twice with the brass knocker, he turned toward her. "You're frightened, Madame Walewska. But know that you are making history. I must take my leave now."

Sudden fear took hold of Marie. *Who am I to create history?* She reached out to stop him, but he was already disappearing around the corner of the castle. She longed to run away, but in that moment, her attention was drawn to the vibrations of the heavy oak door swinging open behind her.

Pivoting, she was startled to find herself facing the top of a white turban, wide as a plate. A dark-complected mameluke in full Turkish costume was bowing before her. Rising, he said, "Welcome, Madame Walewska," in near-perfect French. "I am Roustam, the emperor's bodyguard."

Marie blinked back her surprise. She knew of mamelukes—former Ottoman slave horsemen incorporated into Napoleon's Imperial Guard—but had never seen one up close.

"Follow me, Madame."

A short walk brought them to the circular marble Great Stairs. One floor brought them into the King's Apartment, passing then into the next chamber.

"Be seated, Madame. This is the King's Study. The emperor is waiting." Roustam said, bowing and leaving her alone.

Marie sat on a French settee, its fabric depicting a pastoral scene. A nearby pot of lavender sent a sweet, evergreen scent into the air, but it did nothing to ease her anxiety. The two chandeliers had not been lighted. The dim lighting came from several sconces and two candelabra. She looked across the room to a gold door. She guessed that it led to the King's Dressing Room with the King's Bedchamber beyond that. She wondered how many women over the centuries had been smuggled into the castle's secret entrance and up the stairs in the dead of night.

A shiver ran through her. *Nothing needs to happen.*

She heard a different door open, and before she could react, a figure was before her in a blur of movement, kneeling at her feet. He wore a dark blue frock coat, white waistcoat and breeches.

He stared up at her. "Did Roustam not offer to take your cloak and hat, dear Marie?"

She froze, struck dumb, scarcely able to believe that the man kneeling before her was the Emperor of France.

"How can I see you with your face covered?" Napoleon asked, a teasing smile on his lips. "Why, someone could be playing me a mean trick by sending a changeling." He lifted the veil from her face. "Ah, it is no changeling! It is Marie, my Marie."

He stood and extended his hand, helping her to her feet. She noticed he was at least two inches taller than she, something she hadn't noticed when they danced the *contredanse*. She recalled Madame de Staël 's comment in Rome that Napoleon was of average height for a man, thinking now that her writer-friend had been correct.

"It appears you came dressed for a funeral," Napoleon said, chuckling as he assisted her in the removal of her cloak and bonnet, placing them on a chair nearby.

Marie did not respond. Recalling his comment about her white gown, she held her breath, waiting for him to deliver his opinion of what she was wearing under the cloak. She had shunned the revealing gowns Madame Vauban put forward, choosing instead a muted blue gown with a conservative neckline.

The gray-blue eyes took in her choice, from the embroidered hem to the neckline. To her relief, he did not comment. "Now, sit, dearest," he said. When he returned to sit next to her on the settee, Marie immediately regretted not choosing the chair, which would have kept him at arm's length.

"You are lovely tonight," Napoleon said, "but I saw that your eyes were a bit puffy and red when I removed your veil. Are you unhappy? Has someone made you unhappy?" His eyes held hers. "Is it me, Marie? You were so different at Błonie. Do you hate me now?"

That he would ask such personal questions—added to the fact that this meeting *was* unwanted—brought fresh tears to her eyes, and they spilled down her cheeks and onto her gown.

"There, there," Napoleon whispered, taking a handkerchief from his waistcoat pocket and pushing it into her hand. "I'm no good with tears, Marie. They tug at my heartstrings."

Marie wiped her cheeks with the monogrammed silk square, dabbed at her eyes, then let her hands fall into her lap.

"You haven't answered my question, Marie. Do you hate me now?"

She shook her head, took in a breath, and released a rush of words. "No, Your Majesty. I have only admiration for you and the belief that one day you will rejoin the three pieces of my country that have been stolen by our neighbors. I went to Błonie so that I could tell you how dependent we are upon you and the Grande Armée. I wanted to be the first. I acted on impulse without even informing Anastase, my husband. At convent school, we all followed you and the Grande Armée. I had a little altar to you with your picture and news items. I prayed at it every day for you and for Po—"

"Was it a good likeness, Marie?"

"It was, Majesty."

"And how do I compare in the flesh?"

Sweet Jesus! Marie paused, unprepared for such a question. Some moments passed before she managed to say, "Favorably, Majesty."

"What difference do you find?"

Marie was afraid of this very response. She studied his face. His nose was not perfect. It was slightly curved but not as crooked as some artists portrayed it. She would not tell him that, however. Her heart beat fast. "I find you a little taller than . . ." Here she stopped herself from saying *rumors that you are short.*

"Than?"

"Than what I imagined from the pictures and drawings I've seen."

"Marie, you keep twisting that ring on your finger. Are you nervous?"

"Oh," Marie said, looking down at her hands. They were clammy and the ring moved easily. She covered the ring with the other hand. "Perhaps," she mumbled.

"Now, I ask myself, why would you keep your trip to Błonie secret from your husband, the former chamberlain?"

"I had not asked his leave to go, Majesty."

"Does he keep you like a bird in a cage, Marie?"

"No, Majesty."

"How did this marriage to an elderly man come about, Marie? How old is he?"

"Seventy-two."

Napoleon grimaced. "And you?"

"Twenty."

"How long have you been married?"

"Two years, Majesty."

"Ah, so you were eighteen."

Marie nodded. "Seventeen and a half."

"Hmm . . . I won't press you further, but it cannot be a happy union."

"We have a child," Marie said, avoiding his eyes.

"Whom you produced as a duty to this provincial count, I would venture. What influenced you to marry this, this dotard?"

Marie turned to face Napoleon. "That is offensive, Majesty."

"You defend him, Marie. Admirable. But, tell me, was it his status? His money? His palace, which I hear from Duroc is quite impressive?"

The questions came like shots fired from a pistol. Marie looked away, wordless, emotions swirling.

"Marie?" Napoleon pressed.

"My—my mother."

"So! A mother with a triptych design—status, money, *and* residence. A matriarch with determination possesses power beyond that of a queen!"

Marie fought the urge to again accuse him of being offensive. Instead, she said, "When my father died fighting the Russians, our estate fell on hard times. The count came to our aid."

"What is the situation with the estate now?"

"Mother says it is self-sufficient."

"I see—so, you were bartered away, no less."

Marie felt the tears forming again. "We would have lost the estate and my younger sisters would not be able to go to school in Warsaw."

"Your mother expected it of you, then, an arranged marriage?"

"My elder brother convinced me that it was the only way to save the estate, as well as my mother's health."

"And you could not do battle with both your mother and Benedykt."

Marie shook her head. A heat rose into her face. Napoleon Bonaparte knew her brother by name! Of course, he did. Benedykt had not appeared at the Royal Castle by chance. A tide of colliding emotions took hold, humiliation chief among them, as well as dread of what might be in store. *I should not have come.*

"What is it, Marie?"

"What? Nothing, really."

His right arm slipped around her shoulders, drawing her closer.

Marie pulled away, shifting to the end of the settee and dislodging his arm.

"Marie, do I disgust you? Won't you spare a little love for your emperor? Why have you come, if not to please me?"

"The members of the Governing Commission—"

Napoleon shot to his feet, his face reddening, his white waistcoat expanding. "The Commission!" he cried, bending slightly toward her. "I am so tired of that gang of gadflies. They hound me from morning till night. I do what I can to avoid them."

Marie stared in disbelief, her mind racing to make sense of his explosive outburst.

Something in her expression seemed to affect him. He suddenly straightened, took in breath, and calmed. "I interrupted you. I'm sorry for that. Please go on." He sat again.

Marie swallowed hard and spoke with her eyes averted. "It seems that some members believe that a woman might find favor with you and therefore be the one to lay our plight before you."

Napoleon let out a hoot of laughter. "Well, someone in the group has his head on properly. They are not all dolts."

She kept her eyes on the far wall. "Majesty, they are patriots."

"Yes, forgive me. Of course, they are patriots. And cheers for those who thought a woman would best win my attention. A woman of supreme beauty, no less." He moved closer. "Won't you look at me, my Marie?"

She turned her head to him. Those eyes that paralyzed her at Błonie now took and held her gaze.

"I'll address the concerns of the Governing Commission before you leave here. What time is Duroc returning for you?"

"At two, Majesty."

"No, no. You must call me Napole, do you hear?"

Marie couldn't imagine doing so. But his lips lifted into a smile, and a sparkle came into the eyes that quashed the thought of dissent. She surrendered. "Yes, Majesty."

"Yes, *Napole*!"

"Yes, Napole." Marie thought for a moment, grasping for something to say. "Tell me, do you have a diminutive that your troops address you by?"

"My men call me *Le Petite Caporal* on occasion, but it's out of affection, mind you, not height. The damn English, however, take cruel satisfaction in portraying me as short in stature." He paused. "I've also been told the epithet stems from my humble beginnings as a low-ranking officer who swiftly rose through the ranks."

"To become emperor," Marie said.

Napoleon nodded, his shoulders lifting. "Still, there is another diminutive. . ." His face seemed to light up and he laughed.

Marie could not help but smile. "What is it?"

"I should not tell you this, but my parents called me *Nabulio* when I was young."

"Nabulio?" Marie repeated, intrigued.

He nodded, the laughter continuing, soft laughter, as if he were remembering past days. "You're to tell no one, do you hear? It means 'little meddler'."

"You got into mischief?"

"Indeed, I was quite mischievous. But I was also deeply curious about people. I asked questions. I enjoyed gossiping. I still do. I daresay I know hidden things about people right here in your capital. —You've made me say too much. I beg you not to repeat this to anyone."

Marie laughed. To think that this man she had set on a pedestal—one whom she had idealized as a hero and savior of Europe—indulged in gossip was both surprising and endearing. It made Emperor Napoleon Bonaparte seem more human, even charming. And she couldn't deny that his *confiding* in her pulled at her heart.

"It's good to see you smile and laugh, Marie." Napoleon leaned slightly toward her, suddenly serious. "I've told you a secret. Now, before I reveal my intention for your beloved country, you must tell me something."

"Yes?" Marie hugged her arms to her middle.

"You've told me why you married Count Walewski. Now, I ask you to tell me why you continue to stay with him. Tell me that."

Marie was taken aback. "Marriage is a contract," she said, shocked by the question. "It's not to be broken."

"Contracts are broken all the time, my dear."

Marie avoided mention of his own marital status. "It was a choice, one made before God."

"Ah, yes," he said. "And you will have other choices in life, Marie. Better choices, I pray. Perhaps sooner than later. Now, there! You see—I'm a little meddler!" He laughed.

Napoleon stood and faced Marie, serious again.

"Now, allow me to give you a history lesson before I discuss the future of Poland." He began a lengthy account of his dream to unite all of Europe, eventually coming to the status of the current wars with the very countries that had divided up Poland in 1795. Taking an occasional pinch of snuff from his little gold box, he paced back and forth, going into detail about his recent successes over Prussia, as well as expressing his dismay over the winter delay in his conflict with Russia.

"And Austria?" Marie asked.

Napoleon stopped and pivoted toward Marie. "Austria?"

Marie wet her lips. "You made peace with Austria after the Battle of Austerlitz not much more than a year ago, Napole. A peace that continues?"

Napoleon raised his dark eyebrows. "It does. I can see that you *have* followed me, Marie. I'm impressed."

"So, Napole, at that time, Austria gave up Tirol to Bavaria, Venice to you, and various other properties I can't recall." Marie noticed that his jaw dropped slightly. "But, it seems," she pressed, "that the treaty did nothing to return to Poland the lands Austria had stolen. That is in the past and Poles are quick to forgive. However, is it your thought that independence for Poland *today* would upset Austria and risk that peace?" She had watched his expression darken as she spoke, certain he was now more irritated than impressed. Only later, when she was alone, would she wonder what wellspring of daring she had tapped for her to speak so boldly.

Napoleon huffed in displeasure. "Is this *your* question—or have you been schooled by Prince Poniatowski or one of the other members of the Governing Commission?"

Marie drew her shoulders back against the settee. "The question is mine, Napole."

For some moments, Napoleon's gaze lingered on her, and as he scrutinized her, the lines of his face eased and his eyes softened. "I apologize, Marie. Your face is as sincere as it is beautiful. I believe you. I want to see Poland independent, but my plans for Poland will come only after I fully settle things with Prussia and Russia."

At that moment a knock came at the door. Napoleon jerked his head in that direction. "Already? Is it possible?"

For Marie, it came at an inopportune time. She wished for more time to plead the cause for immediate independence. However, she feared that Napoleon might dismiss Duroc. She could not chance being left without means of escape. She made a move to rise from the settee, but the emperor was once again on his knees, holding her in place. He took hold of one of her hands. "My heart is yours, Marie. May I count on your affection?"

"I—I should go."

"Wait." His grip tightened. "I've spent too much time on politics and war tonight. You shouldn't have allowed me to rattle on so. Time has slipped away. Will you come again tomorrow? Will you, my dearest?"

"Your friendship is what I wish, Majes—Napole. And your respect."

"You have my love, Marie." Napoleon stood, and still holding her hand, aided her in rising. His eyes held hers for some moments before drawing her to him and kissing her cheeks. He drew his head back slightly now, aborting her return kisses—and kissed her on the lips.

Marie withdrew her hand, pressing it against his waistcoat, holding him at a distance. "I must leave." Pivoting, she retrieved her cloak and slipped it on, her back to him. "Majesty," she said, deliberately using the title, "please allow me to leave, without tarnishing this memory." She adjusted her bonnet, tears welling up again by the time she turned back to him.

"Oh, Marie, have I ruined the evening?" Napoleon pleaded, his face reddening, his posture slumping. "Don't leave without saying you will return, that I haven't ruined everything."

He took a step toward her, but she shook her head. It was enough to hold him at bay.

Another knock, slightly more insistent.

Their eyes locked. Napoleon's face hardened. He advanced now, took Marie's hand and led her to the door. Turning to her he said, "I'll not open it until you promise to come back tomorrow."

Marie met his gaze in her attempt to hold her ground.

Napoleon stiffened, his back seeming to add height. "I will not," he said in a low-pitched voice.

Marie imagined this was the stance and confidence that he showed on the battlefield. It did frighten her.

A long moment passed.

Marie nodded.

Napoleon's face relaxed, and a tight, relieved smile appeared as he stood aside and opened the door.

Marie brushed past him and into the care of the mameluke, who escorted her to the secret riverside entrance where Marshal Duroc waited.

32

Tuesday, 20 January 1807

Like clockwork, Madame Henriette de Vauban appeared at Marie's bedchamber door at precisely midmorning, knocking once before entering. Marie, seated at her dressing table and brushing her hair, glanced up through the mirror and managed a tight smile to disguise her annoyance. At least Emily was not with her. Yesterday's encounter had left her feeling outnumbered and outfoxed. She knew that beneath Henriette's mask of friendship lay an intricate web of influence tied to Prince Poniatowski, members of the Governing Commission, and, either directly or indirectly, to Emperor Napoleon Bonaparte himself.

Twisting on the bench, she watched Henriette advance toward her, carrying a hinged brown leather box.

"What, no flowers today, Henriette?" Marie asked, her tone light but edged with wryness.

"Oh, you *do* have flowers, Marie. Your maid is arranging them." Henriette placed the box in Marie's lap. "This came with them."

Marie glanced down at the box, embossed with gold letters spelling *Meissen*. She tilted her head, curious.

"Oh, you are from the provinces, dear, aren't you?" Henriette trilled. "It's a renowned royal jewelry and porcelain firm in Meissen, near Dresden."

Marie hesitated, tempted to reject the gift outright, but her curiosity prevailed. She unfastened the latch and opened the box. Inside, nestled among fresh laurel leaves, rested a brooch—meticulously fashioned in the shape of a bouquet, with diamonds glittering on every sprig.

The sight filled Marie with a mix of awe and dread. Was Napoleon attempting to buy her favor with such opulence? Did he think to *purchase* her with jewelry?

Marie's anger surged, causing a bitter taste to rise in her throat. Impulsively, she pushed the box from her lap, sending it crashing to the floor where the cover snapped off, spilling the contents.

"Marie!" Henriette exclaimed. "Oh, look what you've done!"

"I won't have it!" Marie shouted. "I will not accept it!"

Henriette knelt and carefully collected the brooch and scattered leaves, replacing them in the damaged box. Her face ran red as fire as she stood and tried to reaffix the lid, unsuccessfully. "Perhaps the hinges can be fixed," she offered.

"No!" Marie spat. "Have one of the maids downstairs tie it up with string. You will then return it to the emperor without a message and certainly without an apology."

Henriette stared at Marie, shocked by her forceful stance.

Marie stood and squared her shoulders, triumphant that Henriette had no counterargument. "Come along, I'll go down with you, but I warn you not to try to dissuade me from sending it back. You will deliver it, won't you?"

Henriette blinked, then gave a slow nod.

At the foot of the staircase, Marie sent Henriette to the kitchen with the broken box, and entered the dining chamber.

Anastase was not alone at the table. Sitting on her husband's left was a woman with her back to the doorway. Recognizing the familiar upswept hair and posture, Marie hurried toward the table's end.

"Mother! — What a shock!" she blurted.

Countess Eva Łączyńska turned, smiling. "What kind of a greeting is that? I came for a visit. Come here and spare your mother a kiss."

Still reeling from the morning's events, Marie deferred, exchanging kisses with her mother.

Her mother's eyes narrowed as she studied her daughter. "Marie, you look, I don't know, distracted."

"I'm fine." Marie drew herself up. "I was merely taken by surprise. What are you doing in Warsaw?"

"Must I announce a visit to my daughter? Since your marriage I've been able to count your visits to Kiernozia on one hand."

Marie aborted the impulse to use the baby as an excuse. Her mother would see through that at once. The truth—her lingering resentment over the pressure placed on her to marry Anastase—would remain unspoken. "I know, Mother," she said instead, "I shall have to do better once we are back at Walewice. Don't you agree, Anastase?"

The count rose from his chair. "Indeed. In the meantime, Madame Eva is welcome here for as long as she wishes. Now, I have some business to attend to, so I'll leave you two to catch up on things."

Something in his comment rang false. Marie watched him leave the room, suspecting that he had been waiting for the right opportunity to do so. She glanced down at her mother. "You look quite well, mother. How are the girls?"

"Katarzyna is as precocious as ever. She is quite a handful, but Honorata is excelling at school."

"Oh, so you'll be visiting her there."

"Well, perhaps, but I'm here to see you."

Someone entered now from the hall that led to the reception room. Marie pivoted toward the doorway, where her brother stood in his full colonel's uniform.

"Benedykt!"

"In the flesh, Marysia." He gave a little laugh. "You look like you've seen a ghost."

"No, not a ghost." Marie said, her hand moving to her throat.

"Benedykt came to Kiernozia to collect me," her mother interjected.

"Oh, I see." Marie became certain now that something considering the Napoleon question was afoot and her family was involved. She felt ill.

Henriette entered from the kitchen. "Oh, look, Marie. The string was unneeded. Your clever cook mended the hinge. It's like new—or nearly so." She set the Meissen leather box on the table in front of Marie.

Marie had no need to introduce Henriette to her mother since they were already acquaintances, but in introducing her to Benedykt, she noticed some little ray of recognition flicker in her brother's eyes, strengthening her suspicion that a conspiracy was underway.

"Now, just what is that?" Marie's mother asked, her eyes on the box. "Meissen?"

"It's a royal jewelry workshop near Dresden, Eva," Henriette said.

"I know," she said with a hint of sarcasm. "It's a gift, then, for you, Marie?"

"It's being returned," Marie said, more sharply than she intended. She turned to her guest. "Madame de Vauban, perhaps you should take it and go now."

"Oh, not yet," Marie's mother cried. "I must see it. —May I?" She reached for the box.

Marie quickly moved it out of her mother's reach. The countess looked up at her, the cool, intent expression on her face one Marie recognized from childhood, one that had often rendered her helpless.

Her mother directed her gaze to Henriette. "Madame de Vauban, would you be so good as to leave me alone with my daughter?"

Henriette looked from her to Marie and back again. Marie's dark, cautionary gaze did not dissuade her. She turned to leave.

"You, too, Benedykt," the countess said.

Benedykt squared his shoulders, brought his boot heels together, and bowed his head.

When Henriette passed him by, he nodded to her and followed, crossing over to the reception room. *These two are not strangers*, Marie thought.

Her mother stood, went to both chamber entrances and closed the doors.

Marie could feel a flush rising into her face. She was being treated like a child again, and it infuriated her.

"Now, Marie," her mother said, returning to the table, "we will both sit and you will do your mother the courtesy of showing her the gift you are so insistent on returning."

"So, you know who it's from?" Marie asked, once they were seated.

Her mother worked at smoothing the lines of her violet dress. Eyes on the box, she said, "I have an idea."

"Is this why Benedykt has brought you here?"

"Kindly allow me to see it, Marie."

Marie slid the box toward her. The countess opened it and gasped. "*Jezus i Maryja!* They're diamonds, Marie, and in the shape of a bouquet!" She gently withdrew the brooch from the laurel leaves. "It must be priceless."

Marie did not respond.

"And look, beneath the laurel leaves here—there's a note." Taking it up, she added, "It's sealed. You haven't read it."

"I have not."

"Before you return it, you must at least read his message."

"It's not the first. I have no desire to read it."

"Shall I read it to you, Marie?"

Marie knew it was useless to decline. "If you must."

Her mother skillfully broke the seal and opened the note. She cleared her throat and read:

I awakened today, my Marie, thinking of you. You said you would return and I look forward to it. Do not disappoint me, dearest. Do not. Others here in your beloved land have disappointed me, but I trust you won't. You will come to a dinner that Count Działyński is hosting. Ask Madame de Vauban for the details. Marshal Duroc will come for you an hour before.

I long to see you wearing the brooch. If someone asks about it, tell them it's a family piece. It will be a secret sign between us. Now, when you see my hand reach for my heart, you will reach up to your bouquet. Don't forget, my Marie.

N.

The countess folded the note, sat back in her chair with a sigh, and let her hands rest limply in her lap.

Marie turned her gaze away from her mother, trying to decode her body language. She resolved not to be the first to speak. Minutes passed.

What must she be thinking? Marie wondered. Benedykt had brought her from Kiernozia in winter weather. He had used his influence. Just what had he told her? What does she think of Napoleon's gift? Of his infatuation? Of her daughter?

The countess straightened in her chair. "This is preposterous, Marie," she said. "When Benedykt told me about this situation you've gotten yourself into, well, I couldn't quite believe it. But this note . . . you say there have been others. Like this?"

Marie nodded.

The countess turned her head toward Marie, her eyes narrowing. "And you met him in private?"

"Once."

"And what—"

"Nothing happened, Mother. Nothing. And I did not orchestrate this *situation*, as you call it."

"But you did go to Błonie, yes?"

"Yes, that's true. But I went only to stress how Poland needed him."

"And?"

"When I actually stood before him, I was dumbstruck and managed to say very little of my prepared speech."

"And yet he took notice of *you*?"

"He did."

The countess unfolded the note and studied it, her lips silently moving.

"The emperor says," she began, "that he's been disappointed by Poles and that he expects not to be disappointed by you. Benedykt tells me that those disappointing him are the members of the Governing Commission and perhaps Prince Józef himself."

Marie shrugged.

Benedykt told me the prince maintains that if the emperor does not grant us independence now—before he pursues the enemy across the steppes of Europe—we might never regain our nation. Who's to say how his bold venture to unite all of Europe will pan out? He hasn't lost many battles, but he is not invincible. Our independence is the issue of the moment, you understand?"

Marie closed her eyes as she listened. She felt bile rising at the back of her throat. Her mother was not in her camp.

"Look at me, Marie."

Marie complied.

"Now," the countess resumed, "as unlikely as this turn of events may seem to you and me, it has arisen. It has, Marie." She took the note, replaced it in the Meissen box with the laurel leaves and diamond brooch, closed it and passed it to Marie. She drew in a long breath and said, "You cannot return this, Marie. You dare not."

Throughout this interchange, Marie had thought about telling her mother how she had learned that Napoleon and his generals advanced into country after country, with conquests other than battles in mind. She feared that their family name, her reputation, and her very soul hung in the balance.

Marie was held paralyzed, however, under the almost supernatural spell of her mother's intent blue stare, much as she had been on occasion as a child.

Marie said nothing. The supper was a foregone conclusion.

33

Upon their entering the Działyński reception room, Marshal Géraud Duroc introduced Marie to the host and hostess, Count Ksawery Działyński and his wife, Justyna.

Marie guessed the rather plain-faced count's age as fifty, his wife at least a decade younger. His dark jacket featured a high, gold embroidered military collar, with a white ruff at his neck. His attempt to mimic the French emperor's hairstyle—brushing his silvered black hair forward struck Marie as deliberate and slightly pathetic.

"Oh, my dear," the countess said, "we are so very happy you could attend our little soirée!" Her green eyes sparkled with excitement. "What a night this is! The emperor arrived a little while ago," she whispered. "Now, we must chat before you leave tonight."

As the two hosts excused themselves to welcome others, the count's eyes moved over Marie's emerald gown as if inspecting the livery of one of his servants.

Marie shook off her unease and surveyed the room. Most members of the Governing Commission and their wives were present, including Walenty Sobolewski, Eliza's husband. Prince Poniatowski, Minister of War, was there, too, Madame de Vauban at his side. A crowd of fifteen or twenty other nobles mingled, adding to the buzz.

Marie caught Eliza's eye. Her friend smiled broadly, broke away from a small group and approached her. After the greeting formalities, Marshal Duroc withdrew, saying he was leaving Marie in good hands.

Marie watched him make a straight line for Napoleon and his circle of men at the far end of the room.

"I've not seen you since the Talleyrand ball," Eliza said. "Mountains have moved since then."

Marie shifted her gaze to her friend. "What do you mean?"

"You're the talk of Warsaw, Marie. Just look around."

Marie glanced around the room. Eliza was right. Eyes were on her. Some guests watched her covertly, others rather boldly. Marie became lightheaded and turned back to her friend.

"Oh, don't be embarrassed, Marysia. You are the chosen one."

"I'm not embarrassed, Eliza. I'm *humiliated*. I shouldn't have come."

"Well, don't look now, but Marshal Duroc just said something to the emperor, and he's coming this way."

Marie allowed a few moments to pass, then pivoted to take in the emperor, who was striding in their direction. Hatless, he was attired in blue coattails, white waistcoat and breeches. He raised his head, his gaze meeting hers, his expression hardening.

At that moment, Ksawery Działyński went up to Napoleon, forcing him to stop and be introduced to the last Governing Commission member to arrive, Ludwig Gutakowski, an interruption that seemed to irritate the emperor further.

As Napoleon's attention came back to Marie, it dawned on her that his displeasure was the result of her decision not to wear the diamond brooch. "Sweet Jesus," she whispered to herself, terrified now that he was about to create a scene and toss off some ghastly insult. Her chest tightened. Without a second thought, she placed her right hand over her heart and held it there.

As Gutakowski droned on, holding him captive with his chatter, Napoleon's gaze shifted back to Marie. His eyes widened slightly at her gesture, and his stern expression melted away.

When supper was announced, Eliza excused herself to find her husband, and Duroc appeared at Marie's side to escort her into the dining room. As they fell into the queue, Marie noticed that Napoleon had been requisitioned to escort the hostess, Justyna Działyński, into the dining chamber.

At the table, Marshal Duroc and Marie were seated near the host and hostess, while Napoleon sat at the far end.

Duroc leaned toward Marie and said, "He's angry that you didn't wear the brooch."

"I told you in the carriage, Monsieur Duroc, that Polish ladies don't wear corsages to suppers. You didn't pass that on?"

"And have him vent his anger on me? Oh, Madame Walewska, I suppose it would have been gallant of me, but alas, I did no such thing. I figured you would be much more persuasive."

The supper seemed to progress at a glacial rate. The food was rich and varied, but Marie couldn't enjoy it. She lifted her fork now and then, pretending to eat, but knowing that she was a curiosity at the table ruined her appetite. She prayed for the night to end.

When the servers brought dessert—plum cake—Duroc leaned in again, whispering: "He expects you at eleven o'clock, Madame Walewska."

The words sent a chill through her. She had tried to put her promise to Napoleon out of her thoughts, but it was always there, like a malevolent specter. That he meant for her to keep it came like a hard slap. If only Anastase had come, she thought, she could easily decline.

Later, when the marshal went to collect her cloak, she noticed Prince Poniatowski watching her from a distance. He had made no move to speak to her throughout the evening. However, his mistress, Henriette de Vauban, approached her now. "Brooch or no brooch, you look lovely tonight, Marie," she said, embracing her. Then, before releasing her, she whispered in her ear, "So much depends on you."

And then she was gone.

34

Marie and Marshal Duroc sat in silence as the carriage rumbled over cobblestone streets toward the Royal Castle. Marie sensed the marshal's nervousness and wondered at the reason. Did he regret his part in this drama? At the entrance on the River Vistula's escarpment, he helped her down and offered her a terse nod.

Trembling, Marie slowly approached the door. She paused, took a breath, and raised the knocker, letting it fall with a resounding bang. The thick, iron-bound door swung open with a loud creak. Marie stepped across the threshold into the castle and was greeted by an expressionless Roustam. He closed the door behind her with a firm, final thud.

Roustam bowed. "If you will follow me."

The mameluke took her on a much shorter path than the one that had led them to the King's Apartment the night before. He halted at a door remarkably close to the riverside entrance and knocked lightly before opening it. "Come along," he said. He led her through an antechamber and into another, larger, room.

Roustam pushed open the double doors, and stepped into the room, Marie trailing. "The Madame Walewska," he announced.

Napoleon rose from a sofa, his demeanor warm yet commanding. "Ah, Marie—welcome!" He nodded to Roustam, who took his leave. "Come, my dear," he said, smiling.

Marie attempted a smile as he approached and greeted her with *la bise*. Her heart raced as she returned the kisses. Dressed in the blue coattails and white breeches he had worn to the supper, Napoleon cut a dashing figure as he took her cloak and bonnet to a chair across the way. With his back to her, Marie deliberately chose to sit in the high-backed chair beside the sofa in order to create a physical barrier between them.

"Hmmm, a dark green cloak instead of funereal black," Napoleon mumbled as he set the bonnet and cloak down. "An improvement, Marie," he mused. However, when he turned back to her, his face clouded. "Won't you sit next to me on the sofa, Marie?"

"I'm fine, Majesty."

"Majesty?" Napoleon's eyes sparkled with a mix of amusement and challenge.

Marie tipped her head to the side. "Napole."

Napoleon dropped onto the sofa. "Good! —Tell me, Marie, are you afraid of me? —Still?"

Marie froze, her breath hitching.

"You are!" Napoleon exclaimed.

Marie read both annoyance and frustration in his expression. She didn't reply. Steeped within her fear of him was another emotion she now realized she had been trying to suppress: attraction.

"Please, Marie, I have only love for you. Do not fear me."

Marie pressed her shoulders against the chair, resisting the show of vulnerability. She met the emperor's gaze. "Marshal Duroc mentioned that you were angry with me."

"Oh, I was *hurt* that you had not worn the brooch. —Why was that?"

"The brooch was cleverly styled into a bouquet, and Polish women do not wear bouquets to supper, Napole. And diamonds! It was too precious."

"Not for you, Marie. Allow me to tell you what I think. I think you were afraid of what people would say. I forget how young you are. In time, you will learn that if you worry overmuch about what people think of you, you'll never leave your bedchamber." Napoleon took a breath. "Now, I heard that you intended to return it. Is that true?"

Henriette de Vauban has been talking, Marie realized. "No," she said, hoping he would accept her word.

"I wonder. Someone convinced you to accept it, I'll wager. Why do you resist me? I am a passionate man. I *will* make you love me, Marie. Do not push me away."

"Napole, you are married, as am I." She had avoided mentioning his marriage at their last meeting, but now it was unavoidable.

"Ha! Love knows no bounds, isn't that what they say? It's true."

"But there are *boundaries*."

"Clever girl, you!"

"I've told you that my first interest is for my country."

"And so, you have no other interest—or love?"

Marie's cleverness faltered. She quickly shifted topics. "Napole, why are we meeting here and not in the King's Apartment."

"These are my private quarters. I prefer the ground floor. The secret entrance on the river gives me easier access coming and going. And the windows in this suite face the courtyard, so I have none of the river noise and a good sense of the goings-on at the castle. I like that."

"I see."

"Come, allow me to show you the other two rooms."

Marie obeyed, following him into another room, slightly smaller, the bedchamber. A few steps in, Marie paused, her guard up, as Napoleon moved across the room. She swallowed hard.

As if sensing her hesitation, Napoleon adopted a chatty tone: "One of the caretakers here told me these rooms once belonged to a favorite lady-in-waiting to Anne of Austria, one of your queens married to . . ." He pivoted to Marie, brow raised in expectation.

"King Sigismund the Bold," Marie offered, yielding to his bit of manipulation. "Centuries ago."

"Indeed," he said. "Come, there is just one more room."

Marie followed him into what had been created as his study. A large desk and table were awash with papers and journals of various sorts. "This is where I do my planning, Marie. That completes the tour." Turning, they retraced their steps, passing through the bedchamber and into the main chamber.

"Very well, Marie, *now* you may pour your heart out for your country. Take your time. When you've done that, perhaps there will be room in your heart for me." He settled onto the sofa. "But first, come sit by me."

Marie felt an ache at the back of her throat. She couldn't swallow. She wanted desperately to refuse but saw this as her chance to tell him everything she had meant to say at Błonie. Nodding, she moved to the sofa. As she seated herself, Napoleon adjusted to face her, his gaze intense.

"Tell me, Marie," he said, in a low voice.

She turned toward Napoleon. She had heard women speak of his fiercely hypnotic stare. It had captured her at Błonie and it still had its effect. She made a deliberate effort to avoid his eyes. "I will begin by telling you that the seeds of my patriotism were sewn by my father," Marie said, her voice steadying. She spoke at some length of her father's faith in the 1791 Third of May Constitution, his loyalty to General Tadeusz Kościuszko when the new democracy was challenged, and his ultimate sacrifice on the battlefield in 1794.

Napoleon lowered his head slightly. "You were very young, then."

"Not yet eight, Napole. But the loss of Father and our country was heavy. Mother was left to struggle to hold onto the estate, and my brothers have left Poland to join up with your effort to bring equality to all of Europe."

"You loved your father," Napoleon observed.

"I'm afraid I've said too much. Forgive me."

"Nonsense! You spoke your heart. I suspect you felt lost in the world when he died so tragically."

"Heroically," Marie corrected.

"Indeed. As for your brothers, they shall be rewarded."

"Our reward will be independence when it comes. Poles are notorious for bickering among themselves. That's why, at Błonie, I wanted to be the first to welcome you to Poland. Despite any factional disputes, the majority of Poles longed for your coming. And we remain grateful."

"Are you here solely to ask for my help and express thanks? Tell me, Marie, are you repelled by me?"

"I am here because I'm told our leaders' pleas have fallen on deaf ears, but that you might hear my voice."

Napoleon shrugged. "The pleas can be bothersome. They pose what I call the Polish Question. Sadly, granting *outright* independence to Poland complicates my ultimate goals, Marie."

"What complications?"

Napoleon tilted his head slightly. "Another time, my Marie." He shifted, moving closer to her, his arm moving around her shoulder. "Politics is a tangled web, and the hour is getting late."

Marie's chest tightened. "Is Marshal Duroc coming at two?" she asked, her voice trembling. "I forgot to ask him."

"No, Marie," Napoleon replied, his smile inscrutable. "Marshal Duroc will not be coming." He pulled her to him now and kissed her.

The sudden realization that she had no means of escape, in tandem with the kiss, triggered a wave of panic. She struggled, pulling away.

"Don't fear, Marie. My bodyguard Roustam sleeps nearby. Should you desire a carriage, he will find my *valet de chambre*, who will see to your rescue. I am not an ogre. Roustam is an interesting fellow. He's Armenian. He was presented to me by the Sheik of Cairo during my campaign in Egypt." Napoleon paused, staring hard at Marie as if trying to assess her level of comfort.

"Roustam tells stories sometimes," he continued, "amusing stories. He knows this Frenchman working in my stables whom I took in as a political favor to his father, who once was employed in the stables of Louis XVI. He was even christened Louis after the king. His mother was the daughter of an officer of the royal kitchens. The story goes that the officer, his grandfather, made a bird cage out of nougat for a special royal celebration, and when it was placed on the buffet table for the fête, it contained a *real* bird, a nightingale. Monks raise them, you know. They sell only the males because they sing. Can you imagine, Marie? Isn't it amazing?"

Marie nodded, more amazed that he was so caught up in telling the story.

"There's more, Marie. The guests began to pick at the delicious nougat and during supper the cage collapsed and the bird flew out!"

Marie gave in to a good laugh.

"Wait!" Napoleon snapped. "Hear the story out! The nightingale flew round and round the room and finding no open window, it landed on Queen Marie Antoinette's head!"

"No!" Marie cried. "Did it sing?"

Napoleon erupted in laughter, and soon the two laughed together, and as their merriment subsided, something shifted in his eyes, something serious. His gaze held her entranced.

Napoleon kissed her on the cheek, a kiss that held some seconds.

Heart thumping, Marie pulled back but the piercing spell of the gray blue held her prisoner. It came home to her now that the painful clenching in her middle could indicate more than fear. It could indicate attraction.

Napoleon kissed her again, on the lips and with passion. He held her close.

Marie drew in breath as if to say something. Words escaped her.

Resistance fell away.

35

MARIE OPENED HER EYES AT some sound. She lay on her back, eyes on the blue canopy above her. He still lay next to her, snoring softly, his heat pressed against her. The memory of the night came back in waves of guilt and shame, yet her heart quickened with the thrill of pleasure and contentment. She felt caught between opposing emotions and dared not move.

But the sound of soft footfalls came now, and then another noise, metallic in nature. Someone was in the room. She sat up at once, goosebumps prickling her arms, mouth dry.

The curtains at the foot of the bed had not been drawn, allowing for access to heat from the stove. A man was bending over in front of the tall tile stove. He snapped closed the brass door with a soft, metallic click. The figure straightened, his dark silhouette against the white porcelain resembling a *wycinanki*. But this was no papercutting. He turned now and took notice of her.

"Oh, Madame, forgive me," he said in a husky whisper. "The emperor is insistent I adjust his stove fifteen minutes before his rising. I am so sorry to have awakened you."

Marie clutched the wool blanket to her breast, unable to respond.

"Forgive me for the circumstances, Madame Walewska, I am Constant Wairy, at your service."

The introduction came at such a peculiar time and place that Marie didn't know whether to laugh or cry. She merely gave a slow nod.

With a bow, Napoleon's *valet de chambre* slipped from the room.

Marie lay back against a pillow. Constant Wairy was known to be a diarist. As such, might she assume he was also a purveyor of royal gossip? I have done it, she thought. I have gone beyond the pale of decorum. What can it matter now?

She would have to deal with the consequences. The thought of returning home gnawed at her. Anastase's reaction loomed large. And society—Poland was not as permissive as France, and that frightened her.

She let that thought go for the moment, uncertain if Napoleon's attention was genuine. How many conquests had he already set aside? Genuine or insincere—might the personal cost to her be worth it if she could persuade him on the *Polish Question?*

Her thoughts were interrupted by a knock at the door. "Your Majesty," a strong voice called, "it's time."

Napoleon stirred beside her, stretching and turning toward her. His gaze met hers. "How long have you been awake?" he asked.

"Since your valet adjusted the stove," she replied, unable to resist a soft laugh.

"Constant was noisy? I'll have him hanged. But—you should have woken me." A glint shone in his eyes. "My Marie, forgive me. I have business with the army." Kissing her hand, he rolled off the other side of the bed and jumped up, grabbing his clothes. "Hurry and dress, Marie. Constant will have coffee and bread for us in the next room." He moved toward the door, stopped, pivoted. "I didn't ask how you slept. How impolite of me. The bed is very comfortable, yes? I didn't tell you that one of the reasons I chose these quarters is because the King's Bedchamber is without a bed."

Marie blinked. That the Emperor of France stood naked chattering like a magpie stunned her. It took a few moments to conjure up a reply. "Really? I haven't seen that room."

"Indeed. The prince told me that King Stanisław was so fond of his bed that he took it with him when he was deposed and sent first to Grodno in Lithuania and then to Saint Petersburg where he lived out his days. Now, you must admit, Marie, that was a well-travelled bed!" Napoleon laughed as he passed into the next chamber.

Marie stared after him and laughed.

The delicious scent of coffee wafted into the room. Marie climbed down from the bed to dress, grateful that her evening gown slipped easily over her head without assistance.

Marie entered the connecting chamber.

"Ah—here she is!" Napoleon said, setting down his coffee cup and rising from his chair, dressed in his greatcoat. "I have to be off in moments. This is my last cup."

He motioned for her to sit, kissed her hand, and drained his coffee. "Constant will see to whatever you need. You'll want to go to Bednarska Street, I imagine." He kissed her hand again and headed for the door.

Marie felt ill. He was giving her short shrift. She'd not spoken a single word since entering. He wouldn't even spare a few minutes to sit with her.

Business with the army? She wondered whether that was true. Across the room, Constant Wairy stood at attention as if he were a footman. How many such scenes had the valet witnessed?

At the door, Napoleon pivoted and called back: "Oh, when you finish, Constant will show you something. I hope you'll like it. *Au revoir!*" He was gone before she could respond.

Despite her request for nothing but coffee, Constant disappeared and soon returned with toast and a boiled egg.

Head down, Marie ate quietly, her mind reeling. Humiliated, she would not look at the valet, who stood nearby, still as stone. She felt exposed, as if on display, her wrinkled gown from the evening supper adding to the discomfort.

When the silence became unbearable, she pushed away her half-eaten breakfast. "I'm finished, Monsieur Wairy."

"Very good, Madame Walewska. If you'll follow me." He moved to hold her chair as she rose and smoothed her gown.

Marie followed him out into the hall, her heart sinking as he turned to the right, toward the secret entrance.

But then, he stopped abruptly.

"Our destination is right here, Madame Walewska," he said, opening a door to a lovely anteroom fitted with chairs and tables of French design. "I apologize. The grates have not been lighted, so the rooms are chilly."

When Marie paused to notice that the windows viewed the River Vistula, the valet gave a little cough. He was already at the threshold of the next room. "This is the main chamber," he said.

Marie hurried to catch up.

The chamber was richly furnished with small tables, gilded chairs, and a painted ceiling depicting Poseidon rising from the sea. The wide windows allowed for the river's reflection to give the illusion that the painted waves were moving.

The layout of the suite so far matched Napoleon's rooms. By now, the purpose of the tour seemed clear. Her heart accelerated. She decided to test the matter. "Monsieur Wairy, I know it's too early for the emperor to review his troops. Was it some other urgent matter?"

"Indeed, Madame Walewska. He is, in fact, meeting with Polish generals on the matter of feeding his Grande Armée, something about flour. I think."

"Oh." If she could believe the valet, Napoleon had not lied.

"Next," he said, "is the Dark Anteroom, so-called because it's windowless."

He ushered her into a shadowy chamber with plush furniture, including a mahogany wardrobe. "For light, step this way, Madame Walewska." Making no announcement, the valet led her into the bedchamber, its theme of royal blue playing out on the walls, furniture, and canopy bed. The river's reflection coruscated upon a dark blue ceiling dotted with painted stars.

Nodding toward a doorway at the upper end of the room, the valet said, "There's a small chamber there that's been used as a dressing room. It could also serve as a chamber for a lady's maid." The valet turned to Marie with a knowing glance. "*If* you wish to have your lady's maid at close hand, Madame Walewska."

And so, there it was! Marie was not being given short shrift. She was being offered a suite in the Royal Castle.

It was almost too much to take in. She thought her heart would burst with colliding emotions.

The moment hung fire.

"His Majesty," the valet continued, "toured the castle yesterday, weighing one apartment after another, only to settle upon this suite as most appropriate for you because . . ." The valet appeared to censure himself.

Marie found her voice. "Because?"

He paused for a moment, sighed, and said, "I'll show you, but when His Majesty shows you, pretend you are seeing it for the first time. Will you?"

"I shall," Marie said, intrigued.

"Come this way, Madame Walewska."

Marie complied, following him back to the Dark Anteroom, where he lighted a chamberstick and motioned her toward the tall wardrobe.

"Now, if you would hold the light for me."

Marie took the chamberstick.

The valet opened the wardrobe door and reached in. He released something, and stepping back, he was able to move the wardrobe diagonally into the room, thus revealing a passage into Napoleon's suite.

Marie saw that the two suites were no longer twins, for the dark chamber opened into Napoleon's bedchamber, the very room where she had spent the night.

"Very clever," she said, at once amazed, amused, and embarrassed.

"A mere bagatelle," the valet said. "There are two more such secret portals, one in your main room behind a bookcase and one in the first antechamber behind a tall tile stove that isn't a stove at all."

Marie gave out with a nervous laugh. "Well, I shall stay out of that antechamber on cold days, you can be sure."

The valet laughed, still managing to say, "Now, remember, you must allow the emperor to show you."

Marie nodded, overwhelmed by the events of the day.

The valet cleared his throat. "Now, I imagine you would like me to call for a carriage?"

Marie's head was spinning. "What—oh, yes. Yes, please, Monsieur Wairy."

Marie stepped into the vestibule of the Walewski residence at mid-morning not knowing what scene might unravel. How would she be greeted? Breathing became uneven.

Her bonnet and cloak were taken by one of the Walewski servants. From the reception room across the hall came the unmistakable rustling sounds and occasional snap of pages being turned. She froze. Anastase was reading the *Gazeta Warszawska,* his morning ritual. She took in a deep breath and entered the room.

To her surprise, it was her mother reading the paper. She had stayed the night.

Madame Łączyńska glanced up from the paper, eyebrows lifting momentarily. "Well . . ." she said, taking a long moment to observe her daughter.

Marie suddenly felt as if she were onstage and in the wrong costume for the scene. She attempted to smooth her rumpled gown, her mind racing to decipher the tone and expression. Her mother was wont to wield that word in a dozen different ways, sometimes as a compliment, sometimes like a sword.

The countess laid the paper in her lap, her blue eyes narrowing in assessment. "So, you didn't wear it—the diamond brooch? You didn't return it, did you?"

"I did not wear it, Mother. Neither did I return it."

"Good! Come and sit down near me."

"I must go upstairs to dress."

"I was just reading about the dinner party at the castle."

"Last night's dinner?"

Her mother nodded.

Marie gasped. "How can that be?"

"I've found that there is always one guest with access to the press."

"They must have sent out runners."

"Ha! That's the sort of comment your father would make."

"Am I—am I mentioned?"

"You are. Not to worry. It's just a comment that you were the young woman with whom the emperor attempted a *contredanse* at Talleyrand's ball."

"Attempted? It says *attempted*?"

Her mother laughed and nodded. "Is he that bad a dancer?"

Marie gave a little shrug and laughed also. "I must change, Mother." Her voice dropped now. "Mother, is Anastase—"

"He's gone out. Marie, he will not be a hindrance to you."

Marie would ponder that statement later, but for now her mind teemed with a host of concerns. She turned to leave.

"Wait, Marie! Benedykt will be here any moment with a hired carriage to take me home. Now, come give me a kiss."

Marie tried to disguise her surprise at the request. Not one to demonstrate or ask for a show of emotion, her mother stood as Marie crossed over to her. Their greeting done, her mother reached out with both hands and held Marie at the upper shoulders. Eye to eye, she said, "Don't allow yourself any misgivings, Marysia. You did the right thing."

Marie felt her lower lip tremble. She fought back gathering tears.

"No weeping, do you hear? Now, go and change. And know that you may very well be able to do something significant, something more than even your soldier brothers could accomplish."

PART FIVE

"She who is worth anything is spoken about."
~Polish Proverb

36

As the January days drew out, Marie's life took on a new rhythm. She divided her time between the Royal Castle and the Walewski townhome. Her mother had been correct: Anastase did not interfere with her comings and goings. He welcomed her with a smile when she arrived home from the Royal Castle in time for lunch, and if he was not out himself when she left later to meet Napoleon, he bid her a pleasant evening.

Karnawał season in Warsaw brought a crush of balls, concerts, and plays, as well as a stream of visiting royals and foreign dignitaries eager to pay tribute to Napoleon. Occasionally, Marie and Anastase would turn up at the same event, but her husband remained civil, even affable. Nonetheless, Marie couldn't shake what her mother called *misgivings*.

Why did it seem like she was the only person who felt that her behavior was unforgivable? Her interlude with Napoleon had been assisted by her brother Benedykt and bolstered by her mother. Just as Teodor wrote words of commendation from his post in the Baltic, so too did Honorata from convent school. Meanwhile, Katarzyna was so frothy with enthusiasm that their mother had to sternly restrain her from revealing the affair to everyone in Kiernozia.

Although Marie took no comfort in Napoleon's lack of guilt over his infidelity with Josephine, Anastase's calm response to her own behavior still baffled her—until one afternoon when Eliza visited and offered insight.

"Oh, Marie, you see the trees, but not the forest," Eliza said. "He was most unhappy when he went unnoticed, but now Prince Pepi and the Governing Commission have taken him in. He attends their meetings and social functions. And—more importantly—Napoleon himself has taken notice, and that comes to him through *you*."

Marie nodded, her throat tightening. Eliza's observation made her realize her husband's reaction stemmed from pride. Anastase was *proud* of her. She felt a fool that she hadn't seen it, and angry that he valued her so cheaply.

At first Napoleon tried to conceal the affair by arriving at events separately while Marshal Duroc accompanied Marie. However, he always wanted her close by so that in little time the elite of Warsaw caught on. Far from condemning her, the countrymen of her class embraced her presence, placing in her their hopes for the nation.

Napoleon reviewed his troops each morning at a nearby parade ground where thousands of Poles watched. Although Marie longed to attend, Napoleon forbade it. Knowledge of their intimacy was reserved for only the highest echelons of society—and kept secret from the common citizen and soldier.

Wednesday, 28 January 1807
"You seem to be in a dark mood today, Marie," Eliza remarked.

They sat on a cushioned bench in an alcove looking out on the large chamber the Potockis used for their cards-and-supper nights. At one of the tables, Napoleon sat with his three partners playing whist.

Marie shrugged. "It's nothing."

"Have things been going well?" Eliza pressed. "He's looking this way. He watches you as if you were going to fly away."

"He does that. It's flattering, but it can become annoying."

Eliza turned her head toward Marie. "Are you losing interest?"

"No, in truth, he fascinates me. Initially, I feared him, but I don't any longer. Once I took him down off the pedestal, I saw that he's as human as you or me. He's interested in people." She laughed. "He loves gossip. He's interrogated me about half the people in this room. Of course, I know only a handful of people well. He's that way with his soldiers, too. He has a good memory for their names, the campaigns they've been on, their injuries. And they return his interest with sheer loyalty."

"What do you talk to him about?"

Marie sighed. "What he calls the *Polish Question*."

"Our future? And?" Eliza pressed.

"And the answer is always the same: 'Be patient'."

"Is that why you're out of sorts?"

"No, Eliza, I'll tell you, but it's not gotten out yet, so be circumspect. Today he received word that one of the Russian armies is on the move toward the French left guard in East Prussia, and one of his marshals has gone against orders, putting the French in jeopardy. I've never seen Napoleon so angry."

"So, you think he'll be off to East Prussia? I thought he was settled here for the winter."

"And he *was*. But this marshal—I think his name is Ney—keeps the emperor in the dark half the time and is slow to follow commands. Now he's put men at risk. Evidently the Russians are not bothered by the winter and the mud. He's waiting for a report, but, yes, I *think* he will be going."

"That's too bad," Eliza said. "Winter is long, but he'll return. He will. He's treated well here. In fact, Anna has had her kitchen create everything French tonight: quiche, crepes, and crème brûlée. Look, the games are breaking up. Good! I'm famished."

"Marvelous," Marie said, choosing not to confide in Eliza her fear that an interruption to her affair with Napoleon could somehow spell the end of it.

The meal was uneventful until Princess Charlotte Sic, a middle-aged woman who had emigrated from France during the Rising, addressed the emperor. "Your Majesty," she began, "have you heard of the novel *Corrine*? Why, it's taken Paris by storm! It's written by Madame de Staël, the woman who wrote *Delphine*. It's quite recent, so perchance you have not heard of it."

A hush fell over the table. Marie—and seemingly, a few others—knew that the emperor hated *Delphine* and its author, Madame de Staël. Marie had learned as much upon meeting the author in Italy. Germaine, as Marie had been asked to call her, told her how Napoleon had personally exiled her from France for fomenting discontent and liberalism with her salon and writings. Despite feeling a twinge of betrayal, Marie had stayed in contact with Germaine via mail and was cautious never to bring up the author or her books to Napole.

"I have heard of it, Madame Sic!" the emperor snapped, his eyes not leaving his plate. "Someone on my staff in Paris had either the temerity or stupidity to have forwarded it to me." He picked at the quiche with his fork, as if forming more to say.

The table was held in suspense. The corpulent princess, who had been absent from France too long to know about the author's exile, sat confused, cheeks blazing red.

Finishing the last of a crepe, Napoleon turned his head toward the princess, and the tension in the room rose. "*Delphine* was a preposterous book," he declared, "and Madame Germaine de Staël nothing short of a traitor to her sex." He paused, his eyes never leaving the woman, and added, "And to look at you, Madame, I would not have thought you much of a reader."

By sheer luck, the princess's humiliation was eclipsed by a profusion of servants delivering the crème brûlée to everyone, and the subject turned.

Marie looked at Anna Potocka, who winked, signaling that she had hurried to have the dessert served at that precise moment.

Friday, 30 January 1807
Marie and Napoleon took a simple supper of fish and potato in her rooms, served by a lone castle servant, Filip. Conversation was light, the mood subdued. Napoleon was about to leave for Willemburg in East Prussia. Marie fought to mask the sadness his impending departure had stirred within her.

Once they were left with coffee and a dessert of billberries from the orangerie, Napoleon brightened. "Ah, Marie, you've worn the diamond brooch," he remarked. "It makes me happy to see it on you. Thank you!"

Marie finished the last of the billberries. She smiled.

"And yet you seem sad, dear Marie."

"It's the berries," she replied, "they're a bit sour."

"Am I to believe that? Allow me to at least think that you are sad to see me leave tonight. Will you miss me a little, my Marie?"

"You should know that I shall, Napole."

"I'd like to think of you here in the castle, Marie. There is no reason for you to return to old Walewski. Marshal Duroc will remain in Warsaw and will be available for anything you need."

Ignoring Napoleon's attempt to control her from afar, Marie shifted the topic. "And the city? Will it be protected?"

"Yes, the city. Nearly twenty thousand troops are assigned to protect it." Napoleon leaned back against his chair. "By the way, Prince Poniatowski called on you earlier today. I assume Józef gave you some final words to relay to me before I depart on this new campaign of mine, did he not?"

Marie realized her movements were being watched. Managing a smile, she said, "He merely mentioned that you asked him to ensure that I am well taken care of in your absence." In reality, she had reduced to one sentence the two-hour entreaty by the prince that she make a final plea to Napoleon for the liberation of Poland.

Napoleon looked askance. "Hmm," he hummed. "I'll not doubt you, but just the same, the moment is at hand for you to remind me of Poland's glorious history, of her heroes and saints. Tell me again of your Queen Jadwiga and how Sobieski led his winged hussars down the Kahlenberg Mountain to save Vienna and Europe from the Turks. And that I should—"

"You're mocking me," Marie interjected.

"Forgive me. It must seem that way. But I do carry your country's plea in my heart, placed there by you. Tell the prince that."

"And might there be a promise in your heart, also?"

Napoleon grinned. "I should have you at the peace table with me on some future day when I meet with Czar Aleksander. The mighty Russia could not help but bend before you." He stood and moved around the table. "Come, stand and kiss me goodbye."

Marie stood.

Napoleon bent down, kissed her, and held her a long minute. When he finally drew back, his eyes locked with hers. "I promise that one day I'll lead your country to independence. Be patient, my Marie."

Marie sat for a long while after Napoleon left, reflecting on their conversation. She recalled Madame de Staël's advice from their Italy meetings: that mastering the art of conversation would help her navigate her relationships with men. Although she couldn't claim much success with her husband, whose narrow attitude toward women had become ingrained long ago, with Napoleon, she felt as if she might be finding her footing.

Madame de Staël! Marie rose at once, recalling that Napoleon had been sent a copy of her new book. She hurried to the bookcase, located the lever inside, and pressed it. She heard something click and felt the bookcase vibrate slightly. With some effort she was able to guide the bookcase toward her, revealing the portal leading into Napoleon's main chamber.

The room was dim. Locating a tinderbox, she lit a chamberstick. Drawing in breath, she entered and moved toward the desk where Napoleon had kept his maps, papers, orders, and letters from Paris.

Her spirits sank. The desktop had been wiped clean, the three drawers, all empty. Of course—why would he leave anything behind? She sighed heavily, both disappointed by the missing book and a reminder that Napoleon might very well not return to Warsaw.

As she turned to go, she noticed some sparks flying up from the fireplace.

She dashed toward the grate, knelt, and retrieved the object of her search. Brushing away the ashes, she found the book was undamaged. In his hurry to pack and leave, Napoleon—who likely wanted no reminder of Madame de Staël—must have tossed it toward the fire with little care—or aim.

The page edges were gold, as was the embossed lettering on the cover that read: *Corrine* by Germaine de Staël.

By the time Marshal Duroc told Marie about Napoleon's 7 February attack on Eylau—where the Russians defended the fortress of Konigsberg—she had already heard from Prince Poniatowski the devastating details. The prince described it as a stalemate, but to Marie, the loss of fifteen thousand Frenchmen dead in the snow felt catastrophic. While the Russians were able to hold the fortress, the Grande Armée, reeling from the cold, headed for winter quarters, not in Warsaw, but in Osterode, East Prussia. Adding to Marie's disappointment was the fact that Duroc had no word of Benedykt, assuring her, however, that the emperor was in good health and steadfast in spirit. He left Marie with a short note from Napoleon:

> *Disregard any bad news, Marie. Russia will pay handsomely. Soon I will set in motion a plan for you to come to me at Finckenstein Castle, near the Prussian village of Kamieniec. Trust me.*
>
> *Napole.*
>
> *Your brave brother Benedykt sends his love.*

She was elated to hear of her brother's safety, but Napoleon's plans for her to meet him at some far-off castle left her with mixed feelings. She'd rather not leave Warsaw; however, knowing he was taking pains for their reunion thrilled her.

Later, her thoughts came back to Kamieniec. Prussian village, indeed, she thought wryly. The village had been the property of the Polish Lithuanian Commonwealth until Poland's three neighbors initiated their first partition. In a sense, she would still be in Old Poland.

37

April 1807

As it turned out, her brother and Napoleon's plans were linked. Marie stood on the stoop of the Walewski townhome, watching Benedykt exit the sleek, dark blue carriage. Napoleon had sent him to escort her to Finckenstein Castle. Love for her brother was tempered by a lingering resentment for the role he was continuing to play between her and Napoleon. And yet, how could she be resentful when she herself had bowed to Napoleon's wishes?

"Hello, Marie," Benedykt said, stepping quickly toward her, his voice cheerful.

"Hello, Benedykt," she replied coolly, avoiding his diminutive.

Benedykt studied her as she approached, seeming to catch her mood and choosing not to bend for a kiss. He took her hand, drew her to the carriage, and helped her aboard.

Marie discovered the carriage was designed for just two passengers. As she settled onto the single, forward-facing bench, she watched through the glass windows as the Walewski servant and the driver hoisted her trunk onto the roof of the carriage.

Benedykt disappeared for ten minutes before emerging from the townhome with something bundled in his arms. When he climbed aboard, seating himself next to her, Marie saw that the bundle was a plush green lap robe made of horsehair. "Why, that belongs to Anastase!"

"Indeed. He sent a servant out to the stable to collect it. He made a point of saying you should have it."

"You—you talked to him?" Marie asked.

"Yes, Marie. He was quite civil." Benedykt held out the lap robe. "Here, cover your lap and knees."

"I have one right here," Marie countered, lifting a dark blue one that had been placed in a corner of the bench. When it unfolded, she saw that it had an intricate circular seal of gold embroidered into it, in the middle of which was the initial N.

"A-ha!" Benedykt piped. "Dueling lap robes! It's symbolic."

"You use that one!" Marie snapped, embarrassed that he had the nerve to voice the symbolism.

"No, while the emperor's one is fancy enough, your husband's will keep you warmer."

Rather than argue, she acceded to the exchange.

"Time to go," Benedykt announced, leaning forward and tapping the front window.

The driver called out to the pair of horses, "Get on with you, now!" The carriage began to roll down the street.

"Glass windows on the sides and at the *front*! You've not seen that before, Marie. Tell the truth. And this beauty has steel springs for a smoother ride."

Marie remained silent.

"He sent the best carriage available. It's a Berline, just like his—without the royal seal and gold fancywork on the outside, of course. He didn't want you to become a target. Why, it has a cooking stove, chamber pots, and dozens of amenities. It's a fine carriage, is it not?"

Marie nodded, staring ahead.

"Oh, and the side panels of the coach are bullet-proof. —You're angry with me, Marie. Why? Because I'm following the emperor's directives?"

"Is that what you call it? Directives? I would call it his *bidding*."

"There! It's out now. You think I've prioritized the emperor's wishes over your well-being."

Marie turned her head to take in his gaze. "Haven't you?"

Benedykt drew his shoulders back. "Like you, Marie, I've placed the future of our country first. For ten years I've followed the Little Corporal with that purpose in mind. The battle at Eylau was the worst I've seen. By sheer luck, I came through it relatively unscathed—though I did take a sword wound to the shoulder."

"Relatively?" Marie pressed.

"It's mending, thank God. I want you to know that when Napoleon called upon me to present you with his note at the Royal Castle, I hesitated, but came to the conclusion that your influence on him could be helpful to the nation."

"But—"

Benedykt lifted a cautioning finger. "And I believed you would welcome this opportunity, that it would be of benefit to you."

"And to you?" Marie sweetened the charge with a pleasant voice.

Benedykt shrugged. "Yes, I've benefited. There's no denying that."

Marie prodded him no further. She placed her hands under the lap robe. "How far is Finckenstein?"

"One hundred and twenty-five miles."

"How long will it take?"

"Six days at minimum if we are lucky with the weather and have rested horses along the way, but it could easily be more. I have possible overnight stays mapped out."

"So long?" Marie sighed, heart sinking. She fell back against the upholstered backrest.

She saw that they were in the suburb of Wola and about to pass through the city's Western Gates. It wasn't too late to change her mind. The landscape ahead would be cold, cloudy, and sodden with spring rains. She instinctively touched the clasp of her cloak, fighting off a shiver that ran down her back.

"I know you have the courage, Marie," Benedykt said, as if he had read her mind.

She dared not look at him. She closed her eyes, and her moment of indecision passed.

"Marie, you're going to him because it's expected, yes? By Prince Józef and a dozen others. You see it as a duty." Benedykt paused for a moment, then said, "But do you know what I think?"

At the side window, Marie kept her eyes on the receding city walls of Warsaw, silent.

"I think," Benedykt continued, "that while expectations and duty motivate you, you have come to care for Napoleon."

Marie turned to face her brother, her impulsive denial dying in her throat. She turned back to the window, her thoughts in turmoil.

———◦∽∽◦———

Later in the day, after mundane exchanges about the slow progress through heavy rains and the quality of horses acquired at relay stations, Benedykt fell asleep.

Marie watched peace come over his face, a face that so often reflected hidden concerns of one kind or another. She had been so young when he left for the Collegium Nobilium and then for Paris. Now, she felt like she was getting to know him anew.

Courage, he had said.

Was it courage, she wondered, or was it merely impulsive, thoughtless daring that propelled her on this journey? She pondered the risks she had taken. This was a step that felt irrevocable. *Am I no better than a camp follower?* she asked herself.

Eliza had already informed her that her dalliance with Napoleon had become the talk of Warsaw's elite, including diarists like their friend Anna Potocka, who viewed Marie as a celebrity, rather than a sinner. But if independence wasn't forthcoming or if the affair ended, would that change their disposition? She prayed that Henriette de Vauban was correct in her assurance that the nobles would close ranks around her.

Marie listened to the incessant rain drumming on the roof as she gazed out at the hilly terrain, absently noting how different the north was from the flatness of central Poland.

Napoleon had promised absolute secrecy in a final note entrusted to Benedykt. "Trust me," he had written. "Hurry, please. I await. You will have your own rooms. My staff, even my Chief of Staff, will remain unaware of your presence. Only my secretary, Méneval, and my valet, Constant Wairy, will have knowledge of it, and they are as faithful as the disciple Peter."

Secrecy—that's all very well, she thought, but what if her presence at the French military quarters should come to light? The scandal would be immense, affecting her family and herself.

Uncertainty persisted. *Why have I done this?*

Was it for Poland's future? There was that, of course. Always, that. But she had to admit something more, something both thrilling and terrifying.

At her side, Benedykt stirred.

Marie thought about what he had said. That she had begun to care for Napoleon.

Marie felt a sudden dizziness, a coldness not from the invasive damp air but from within. Mere attraction had changed.

In the words of her old tutor, Monsieur Nicolas Chopin, Benedykt had *touched the matter with a needle.*

She had fallen in love.

At Pultusk, after ten hours of travel, Marie felt as if her body was still vibrating. Steel springs, Benedykt had boasted, but steel springs could not cushion the bumps and jolts over log roads that had been set into East Prussia's red clay.

They took refuge in a small peasants' house, one in which Benedykt had been bivouacked during the battle with the Russians. The fare was simple, the beds clean, and the elderly couple respectful.

On the second day, the rains abated. This time, it was Marie who kept falling asleep, despite the log roads. At the relay station, they had a midday meal at a small inn crowded with travelers. "Keep your head down," Benedykt warned. "Can't you lower your veil a bit?"

"Not if I am to eat this watery borscht," she said, then fell silent, a sudden weight settling in her chest as she realized that upholding a false identity even in French occupied territory was an unavoidable part of the path she had chosen.

Back on the road, they ventured into a land of lakes and medieval castles. French patrols stopped the carriage six or seven times, always on the alert for any sign of Russian spies.

Marie would pull down her veil as Benedykt stepped out and greeted the officer of the patrol. Her back would stiffen and her temples pulse with fear as curious faces pressed against the windows, but the travel papers signed by the emperor produced the desired effect, and the carriage would be sent on its way.

Days passed.

Marie had counted seven by the time they came to Osterode. Napoleon and his staff had stayed there the week before, and it was still filled with soldiers and army vehicles.

When they stepped down in front of a post inn in the evening, a military courier hurried out to them. "Everything is arranged here for you, Colonel Łączyński," he said, nodding to Marie, who had lowered her veil. Handing Benedykt a letter, he saluted and left.

Her brother waited until the courier was out of sight before handing it to Marie. "It has my name on it for secrecy, but it is for you. Read it inside."

She glanced down and recognized the scribbling on the envelope. Her heart caught. With a mix of anxiety and impatience, Marie waited until after their meal and she was ensconced in a chilly room smaller than a nun's cubicle. Finally, she sat upon the cot and broke the red seal.

My dearest Marie,

Your long, long journey must seem endless, but it is nearly over.

Tomorrow night I'll hold you in my arms. How I long to see you! I hope the trip has not been too hard on you. Your apartment here has been newly decorated. This will be a winter of warmth and love for us always to remember. Till then, my love.

Napole.

His words warmed her. Marie smiled, but the phrase *always to remember* unsettled her. Winter is nearly over, Marie brooded. How often she had longed for spring, but this year it would mean a resumption of the war—and an inevitable separation from Napoleon.

At midmorning, when Marie realized the time, she dressed hurriedly and rapped on her brother's door. He answered in a state of undress. Marie took in a sharp breath. "It's late, Benedykt—we've missed our early start!" She studied his face, noting tired lines and bloodshot eyes. "You were drinking!"

Her brother shrugged. "I ran into some old mates last night."

"Oh, Benny, we'll never get there. I don't want to spend another night on the road."

"We have time, Marie. Don't worry. I *meant* to make a late start. In fact, the matron downstairs is preparing a warm bath for you."

"*Why* did you intend a late start?"

"Because the orders are for us to arrive in the dead of night."

Marie drew in breath. "Oh," she said, her voice flat. Of course, the greatest secrecy was being taken with her arrival. A sense of unease—of shame—overtook her. She shivered, as if she stood at the edge of an abyss.

At midnight, the heaviest rain of the journey pummeled the carriage as they approached Finckenstein Castle. The courtyard was deserted except for a few guards. After Benedykt presented his papers, the driver directed the carriage to a secluded entrance at the rear of the castle.

"Does every castle have a hidden rear entrance?" Marie asked, as Benedykt helped her step down from the carriage and into the rain.

"Most, yes. They were used for sending couriers for help if the castle came under siege."

"And then there is the current usage," Marie said, her tone cryptic. She pulled the cloak's hood up and flashed a brief smile.

Benedykt studied his sister's face "Good to see your sense of humor, Marysia."

"Not to worry, Benny," Marie said as she reached up and lightly touched his cheek. "The choice to come to Finckenstein was mine."

Nodding, he produced a tentative smile.

Marie hurried through the rain toward the recessed door, leaving Benedykt and the driver to lower the trunk. The door swung open, and Marie looked up to see Constant Wairy, lantern in hand. "Welcome, Madame Walewska," he said, "do come in out of the rain."

She followed him into the building.

"The emperor will see you in an hour," Constant said. "He wanted to give you time to get settled in your apartment and refresh yourself. This way, if you will follow me."

Marie obeyed. "This is an enormous building," she offered.

"Two wings off the main, and more than a hundred rooms. It was built by some official from the Court of King Frederick. No sign of a Prussian now, just ninety-two French staff officers."

"*Ninety-two?*" The word took her breath away. "In *this* building?" How, she wondered, is it possible my presence will be kept secret?

"At least that many, thousands more are in outbuildings or camped on the grounds."

Marie fell silent as they climbed from the ground floor to the first level. Her second thoughts about this clandestine adventure were eclipsed by a mounting excitement at the prospect of seeing Napoleon.

"Ah, here we are," Constant announced. "You will use only this door if you must leave, but always listen for voices or footsteps on the stairs, at which you must retreat."

Marie entered the impressive chamber featuring a large bed, its canopy and hangings matching in color to the windows' red damask curtains. More than a dozen beeswax candles lighted the space while a newly-lit fireplace warmed it.

"You won't have to worry about warmth in this devilishly cold April, Madame Walewska," the valet said. "In addition to the fire, you have that porcelain tile stove in the corner. The emperor likes to be warm; some would say almost too warm."

"I see."

"Now, if you will follow me into your sitting room."

Marie obeyed. On one end of the long, rectangular room was a table with two chairs; at the other end were a settee, two cushioned chairs, and a desk. "This door, Madame Walewska," the valet said, gesturing toward a door in the middle of the opposite wall, "connects to the emperor's study, and it's through there that he will come to welcome you in precisely one hour. I'll make my exit now so that you may catch your breath. Is there anything you might need for the moment?"

"No, thank you, Monsieur Wairy."

Constant bowed, pivoted, and slipped into Napoleon's apartment, closing the door behind him.

One hour.

Marie turned and hurried into the other room. Her trunk stood near the door.

Benedykt and the driver had vanished.

The hour crawled by. After washing up and changing, Marie sat embroidering in her sitting room, holding tight to the embroidery frame she had brought from home to busy herself. It was not a pastime she was passionate about. In convent school, she had begun the canvas featuring a purple clematis climbing a trellis, and it was still unfinished. "It's an essential part of a young woman's education," Mother Abbess would say. The class had done dozens of samplers with repetitive designs, usually of numbers and letters. Out of boredom, Marie endured, driving herself to become one of the first to advance to depicting pictures, and upon completing a portrait of her father, the nuns regaled her with compliments. She chuckled to herself. What would the nuns think if they could see her now?

Marie had packed her trunk with care. Even though the most fashionable color of gown was currently white, she recalled Napoleon's insult about white on white—in reference to her nearly translucent skin—and so she had made certain not to include a single gown in white. For this meeting, she wore a gown of deep blue, with simple, straight lines and a well-covered bosom.

In exactly one hour, the sound of wood scraping on stone accompanied the opening of the door to Napoleon's rooms, jolting Marie so that she dropped the needle she was trying to thread.

Napoleon hurried over to her, a rush of warm air from his rooms following, like a perfume. He bent to pick up the needle. "The average woman would drop her kerchief," he said.

"But I—"

He stood before her, lifting his hand to silence her. A tilt of his head, a raised eyebrow, and a questioning gaze soon had them both laughing.

As their laughter subsided, he said, "You're not the average woman, are you?" His gray-blue gaze held hers. "Oh, Marie, I was afraid you wouldn't come. It was selfish of me to ask. But you did! You are so brave, my dearest!"

Brave or foolish?

Napoleon took the frame from her lap and studied it.

"It's petit point," Marie said.

"I recognize that. That's why the needle is so fine—and difficult to thread. Oh, this is lovely work. The purple thread is striking. So many women at the French Court occupy themselves with petit point. But their stitches are not as fine as yours. I think their canvas has only about twenty holes per inch. Yours has—what?"

"Forty-five."

"Forty-five! And your canvas is finer. Is it linen?"

"It is, Majesty."

"There now, we won't start that again."

"Napole, I mean. I haven't embroidered since school, but I thought I'd bring it since I knew I would be confined."

Napoleon winced. "I'm sorry for that, Marie." He set the frame and needle on a nearby side table. Turning back to her, he took both of her hands in his and lifted her from the chair, pulling her close. "I'll make it up to you, I promise." He bent forward, looked deeply into her eyes for a long moment, and kissed her.

Marie melted into the warmth of his eyes, his lips.

Drawing back, he said, "Like me, you love to read. I travel with a rather extensive library, and you are welcome to come take what you like. I think I have every play by Corneille."

Marie blinked at his shift of thought. "Thank you, Napole," she said, reminding herself to keep her novels by Madame de Staël well hidden.

Constant arrived and laid on the table a meal of white wine, crepes filled with jellied raspberries, and salad.

"You refused to play chess with me in Warsaw for reasons I can't fathom," Napoleon remarked, halfway through the meal. "But now I have you all to myself, and I'm certain I can persuade you to a game."

Marie forced a smile. She had evaded his entreaties, not because she wasn't skilled at the game—she and Teodor had played often and she had beaten him any number of times. Her hesitance stemmed from the numerous tales she had heard—and even read—about Napoleon's mediocre prowess at the game and his aversion to losing.

Napoleon studied her face as if he could force an answer. Defeated, he sighed, "I do tire of playing two-deck solitaire, you understand?"

Marie had learned that Napoleon was a swift eater, and so she often left certain dishes untouched on her plate. Tonight, however, she was famished and ate everything Constant had placed on her plate. In Warsaw, he had coached her to pour for the emperor just half a cup of coffee with sugar after meals. This night, Napoleon noticed and absently commented, "Why, that's just how Josephine pours." A moment later, as Marie flushed with embarrassment, he seemed to realize the clumsiness of his remark and offered a weak smile.

With the meal and coffee concluded, Napoleon leaned toward Marie, who sat at his right, and lifted her chin to meet his gaze. "Shall we retire to the other room, Marie?"

The question, laden with promise, made her smile.

38

MARIE AWOKE IN A SWEAT, disoriented by a haunting dream. From a carriage window, she had seen little Antoni in a field of poppies, his high-pitched cries piercing the air as her carriage pulled away. He reached for her, but his image faded until all she could see was an expanse of red.

Gradually, Marie recognized the vibrant red as the canopy over her bed, and her new reality snapped into place. *Sweet Jesus, what have I done?* Her moral beliefs clashed with her actions. She had abandoned her husband who had kept his promises, despite their loveless marriage. Worse, she had deserted her own innocent child.

Her body felt heavy as she turned on her side, toward the window. A slight gap between the panels of the red brocade curtains allowed the gray of early dawn to intrude.

Throwing off the stifling covers, save for a sheet to cover herself, Marie sat up and peered straight ahead. At the foot of the bed, Napoleon sat on a cushioned stool, engrossed in a book. In front of him, the fire roared and sparked in the ornate fireplace. Even at a distance, she felt the intense heat. How does he stand it? she wondered.

"Napole—" she called, her voice weak against the roar and crackle of the fire.

He didn't stir from his reading.

Marie cleared her throat and called again. This time, he turned and a smile cut through his serious demeanor. "Did I wake you, Marie?"

"It was the heat."

"Ah, the heat!" Napoleon rose quickly. Clad only in belted white woolen trousers, he padded quickly to the bedside. "Why, you're drenched, my Marie! It's my fault. I didn't realize—please forgive me."

"No, no, I'm fine."

"I love the fireplace and the heat. The tile stove is not sufficient. I forget myself and keep loading logs onto the grate. Once, sparks ignited the document I was reading. Ha! But I promise to be more mindful. You would have slept on but for my ignorance." He leaned forward, his voice soft. "In your sleep, you look like an angel. Oh, don't deny it. You are an angel sent by God."

"Oh, Napole—"

Napoleon sat on the side of the bed and gazed down at her. "I have to see Constant about a courier from Paris I'm expecting this morning. Don't go anywhere, you hear? Now, let me pull some logs from the fire."

"No, don't do that."

Napoleon flashed a playful smile and gently tugged at the sheet she held to her breast. "And don't dress yet. Constant will be serving us breakfast in bed. I picked up the hedonistic habit in Paris. I do have my odd proclivities, you should know. I must have my hot bath daily, and I can't sleep in a room with doors open." He kissed Marie on the forehead. Then he jumped up and went to her sitting room door, where he paused, his gaze turning back to Marie.

Suddenly, he retraced his steps, climbing in beside her, atop the covers.

Taking her hand, he asked, "Tell me, Marie, did I please you?" His tone was serious, like an old confessor's.

Marie blinked, taken aback. "Why—yes, Napole."

His eyes fastened on her face, as if watching for every nuance of her response. "Did I?"

"Yes," Marie said.

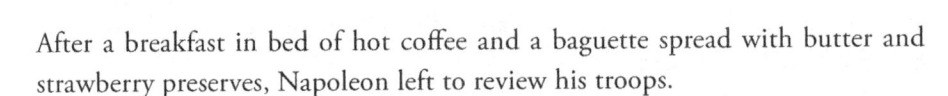

After a breakfast in bed of hot coffee and a baguette spread with butter and strawberry preserves, Napoleon left to review his troops.

Marie went to the window and peeked through the brocaded curtains. She watched him on horseback, head held high under his bicorne, issuing orders to his troops. His men's disciplined attention spoke of respect and loyalty. According to Benedykt, the Polish legions held the emperor in even higher regard than did the French troops, almost to the point of veneration.

A knock came at the door leading to her sitting room. "Come in," she called out.

"Pardon, Madame Walewska," Constant said, "but your bath is prepared."

"I—I didn't know."

"His Majesty's routine is to take his at two in the afternoon. He'll lounge in it for an hour to an hour and a half."

"But . . ."

"Yes, Madame?"

"I'm assuming you have staff that brings up the hot water. Won't there be talk when they have to do bath service twice?"

Constant shook his head. "As instructed, I've already informed them that the emperor will be taking two baths, spaced apart. They know of his peculiarities regarding cleanliness. —Of course, there are already rumors, but they will die away."

"Rumors?" Marie's heart sped up.

"A few soldiers spoke of witnessing a woman in black enter the castle's rear door."

"Oh!"

"Not to worry, Madame. The rumor will fade as long as we keep you secured. Now, please follow me to his rooms."

The valet led her into Napoleon's study, where her attention went immediately to a large copper bathtub at one end of the room. Marie gaped in surprise. "Oh, Monsieur Wairy, I expected a designated bath chamber."

"Oh, there is that, but it has in it a wooden bathtub. The emperor is partial to his own tub."

"His own?"

The valet smiled. "Indeed, Madame Walewska."

"Do you mean he brings this on campaign?"

The valet's smile widened and he nodded. "It seems every great man enjoys his comforts."

Marie laughed aloud. While King Stanisław had a travelling favorite bed, Napoleon had a travelling favorite bathtub. She suspected Napoleon would see the humor in that.

As for Constant Wairy, he tilted his head, his eyes quizzing her, as if expecting her to share what tickled her.

Marie would not chance telling him of the parallel to King Stanisław. A valet's trust was affixed to one man. She merely smiled.

Constant squared his shoulders. "Now," he said, clearing his throat, "that screen will give you privacy and the room will be locked for an hour, so don't fear any intrusion. I'll knock then, and if you don't respond, I'll assume you've returned to your own quarters. The emperor will appear promptly at eleven, and to avoid any chance of interruptions, I'll serve lunch in your rooms."

Marie sank back in the warm water, her mind swirling with thoughts of Napoleon's question: *Did I please you?* What did it mean? She had awakened to that terrible dream of little Antoni. Had he mistaken her gloominess for her reaction to his lovemaking?

The fact was, he *had* pleased her. The months apart had only intensified her longing for his attention, his voice, his touch. She cared nothing for the celebrity of royalty. She did not love an emperor. She loved a man—ambitious, flawed, and vulnerable. Eliza had warned her that one day she might fall under the spell of a younger and more vital man. Her friend could not have imagined it would be Emperor Napoleon Bonaparte.

Her bath finished, Marie slipped into a pink dress. After her marriage, she had enjoyed the luxury of a personal lady's maid. Now, struggling with laces, hooks, and buttons, she keenly felt the absence.

Napoleon arrived at eleven and a lunch of several courses was served in

Marie's sitting room. "Dinner isn't until seven, so eat your fill," he warned. "Did you enjoy your bath?"

"I did," she answered.

"You might think I rise too early, dearest, but my mind is clearest in the morning. And an afternoon bath revives me as if I've had another four hours' sleep." Napoleon placed his hand on hers. "Oh, Marie, I'm so happy you dared to come to Finckenstein. And I daresay, I'll entice you to a game of chess before a single May flower blooms."

"Entice, or do you mean badger? I'm not sure you'll succeed, Napole—but I'm very glad I came to Finckenstein."

Napoleon offered a wide smile. "My secretary will be here in the afternoon, after my bath, to take dictation. You know, I can conduct business equally well, whether I'm at the battlefront or in comfortable headquarters,"

"I'll keep to the other room, then."

"Oh, no. We'll spend enough time apart. I'll dictate here in your sitting room, and you can work on your embroidery."

At four, Marshal Duroc entered, introducing Claude Méneval, Secretary to the Emperor. "The emperor is delayed downstairs giving instructions to a courier," he explained. "He shouldn't be long. I'll leave you two to get acquainted."

With the door closed, the secretary smiled in Marie's direction, a bit timidly, she thought. He went to the other side of the dining table and set there a leather folder, pens, and an inkwell, which he uncorked. Marie resumed her embroidery, occasionally observing him.

He was very thin, rather handsome, with a shock of midnight black hair meticulously combed forward. He appeared awkward, now and then shooting her a quick glance.

Marie set her embroidery aside and cleared her throat. "How long have you been with the emperor, Monsieur Méneval?"

Seated, the secretary began organizing his papers. "Four years, Madame Walewska," he said, without looking up. "He was First Consul then. His brother Joseph recommended me, and suddenly I was invited to supper by Empress Josephine, and the next day . . ." His eyes came up from the table, a flush filling his cheeks.

Marie felt a tightening of her chest at the mention of the empress. Nonetheless, she smiled, ignoring the faux pas. "The next day, you say?"

"Yes—well, the First Consul had me come the next day for dictation. It was a letter to his finance minister, and he spoke too fast for me to follow. I felt certain that the first letter would be my last."

"But here you are!"

Méneval nodded, collecting himself. "He does that, you know. He speaks impossibly fast and once he gets caught up in the message, he'll rise from the chair and start pacing the room, stopping on occasion to take a bit of snuff. I soon found out that he refuses to repeat a single phrase."

"How have you managed for five years, then?"

"I created my own shorthand. I would quickly write down his main ideas, and afterward I would flesh them out, adding his usual interjections and expressions. When he reread the written copy later, he would recognize his style and ideas, and he was happy."

"That's clever, Monsieur Méneval. He tells me you go on campaign everywhere with him, and that you're on call at any hour of the day or night."

The secretary shrugged. "I don't mind. Two hours of dictation is his limit, but for me it's a whole day of work. I enjoy it, however. You—you won't tell him my method?"

Before Marie could respond, the door opened and Napoleon entered.

Wide-eyed, Méneval turned his head toward the emperor. "Majesty," he croaked. Then he looked to Marie, eyes imploring her collaboration.

Marie shot him a smile and the slightest nod.

The dictation of the day's letters began, and Marie returned to her embroidery.

Dictation proceeded exactly as the secretary had described. Napoleon would begin a letter seated, but as he became enthusiastic—sometimes with jubilance or compliments, but more often with criticism and orders—he would jump up from his chair and pace back and forth the length of the room, coming near Marie's chair, the eau-de-cologne he used so liberally tickling her nose. Now and then, he would take a bit of snuff.

One letter took her attention. It was a warning to his brother Louis, whom he had made King of Holland. He urged him to throw off any paternalistic attitudes in governing his people. Instead, he was to act with the same strong and immutable demeanor as he was purported to display in his marriage, knowledge that lent credence to the emperor's interest in gossip. He went on to declare that if Louis's people thought him a "jolly good fellow," he was a failure as a king.

Of course, Marie thought, a king must be stalwart and forceful to be successful. But she was left to wonder about his likening it to a marriage. How much of his philosophy on this matter was sincere? How much merely rhetoric? The question was unsettling.

Constant served Marie and Napoleon a light dinner of fish and preserved peaches at the table in her sitting room. Before leaving the chamber, he said, "Majesty, a few of the generals are asking if you will join them tonight for a game."

Napoleon looked up at Constant, then glanced at Marie. "No, Marie has only just arrived. Not tonight."

"Very good, Majesty."

"We play *vingt-et-un* often at night to pass the time," Napoleon explained after the valet left. "I suppose I shall have to attend now and then, or they will suspect something."

"Do you play for stakes?"

"We do." Napoleon chuckled. "They think I cheat."

"And do you?"

A fork of fish raised in the air, Napoleon paused, allowing only his dancing eyes to answer.

The evening was spent in the sitting room, with conversation interspersed between Napoleon's reading and Marie's embroidery. Marie was halfway through Madame de Staël's novel *Corrine,* but she knew not to bring up her name, much less read in his company the book that Napoleon had thrown upon the fireplace grate.

They retired to bed in Marie's room, snuffing the candle at eleven.

39

THE FOLLOWING DAYS UNFOLDED MUCH like the first, with some variation depending on the state's business. The emperor's locked leather case, arriving from Paris via courier, could arrive at any moment. It had to be opened, answers written, secured, and sent off. Similarly, the emperor exchanged countless letters with officials in Amsterdam, Milan, Rome, Naples, Paris, and a dozen other cities governing his vast empire of seventy million.

At unexpected moments, the realization struck Marie that she was intimately tied to the leader of the age—the leader she had worshipped since school days. It left her breathless.

On occasion, he would still ask if his lovemaking pleased her. She assured him it had.

"There is no woman in the world like you, Marie," he would reply.

Marie often watched him shave. When he finished, he would turn to Constant, who held a gold-rimmed mirror, and ask, "Is it all right?" That Napoleon Bonaparte was asking for validation from his valet, just as he sought approval from his lover, caused Marie to reflect on the contrast: how could someone so unshakable in public reveal such insecurity in private? It was part of his mystique, a side few people ever saw.

Five weeks sped by. Any remnants of regret or guilt about following Napoleon to Finckenstein vanished. Marie was happy, though a sadness lingered, knowing her time there was drawing to a close.

Marie recognized her limited experience with men. She had once thought she could love Arkady—until she learned he was a Suvorov. Soon after, she entered a passionless marriage with Anastase, trying to conform to societal expectations. But now, in Napoleon's arms, she felt a love she hadn't thought possible. She worshipped the emperor, but she loved Napoleon.

One Sunday morning in bed, after they made love, Marie whispered, "Napole, I feel as if we are married."

Napoleon pulled her close, kissed her deeply, and said, "My Polish wife."

Marie looked up at him. "And do you have an array of wives, Napole?" she asked, a lilt in her voice. "In Austria? Spain? Egypt?"

Napoleon blinked. "What? No, my Marie. Never. No woman who has crossed my path could ever hold a candle to you."

As the weeks passed, Marie began to understand Napoleon more deeply. His insecurities about lovemaking that Madame de Staël whispered about rang true. Napoleon revealed past disappointments, corroborating the rumors that women supplied by Talleyrand, while eager to be near power, also spread gossip about his prowess in lovemaking. Madame de Staël had claimed that even Empress Josephine had mocked his virility, calling his lovemaking *bon à rien*—good for nothing. "I can also tell you, Marie," she added, "that Josephine's inability to bear his children left its mark. He wonders if he'll *ever* father a child, whether he *can*."

Napoleon's vulnerabilities only made her love him more.

One day, after reading the last of his daily correspondence in a chair near Marie's, Napoleon suddenly leaped to his feet, fuming with anger. *"Que diable!"* he shouted, startling Marie, who pricked her finger with her embroidery needle.

"Méneval," he barked, "take a letter to Fouché!" Marie knew that Joseph Fouché was his Minister of Police in Paris, and her heart raced at the sudden tension in the room. Napoleon paced furiously, hands clasped behind his back, his voice rising as the secretary scrambled to put pen to paper.

"It's regarding Madame Germaine de Staël," he said, his rapid-fire delivery suffused with anger. "I've had a report, placing the woman in her home city of Geneva. *Bien*! I demand that she be kept there and prohibited from travelling. See it done immediately! She creates unrest, particularly among the women."

Though he offered no specifics, Marie needed none. Her friendship with Germaine, nurtured in Rome and sustained through occasional letters, made the implications clear. Germaine believed Napoleon regarded her as a threat to the patriarchal order he upheld. In addition, she celebrated cultures beyond that of France, particularly those of the German states and Italy. He despised de Staël's progressive views and the sway she exerted through her social circles and writings. "He thinks I should be glorifying him," Germaine had written in her last letter.

The next day, alone with the secretary, Marie reminded him that she had not divulged his note-taking methods to Napoleon.

Méneval appeared lost for words.

"I need a favor," she said. "Monsieur Méneval, May I trust you?"

"What? —Of course, Madame Walewska."

Marie paused, studying the secretary's face. Finckenstein Palace was her prison, albeit a happy one, and with the valet, Constant, too close to the emperor to trust completely, her only choice was his secretary. "I have something I want you to send," she said, handing him a letter addressed to Madame Germaine de Staël.

Méneval's forehead furrowed as he glanced down at it. He looked askance at Marie. Then his eyes widened slightly. He understood.

He paused, slowly nodded, and gave the subtlest of smiles.

Soon after, Napoleon displayed his view of women in a letter he dictated regarding a school for the daughters of the Légion d'Honneur. He insisted their education focus on arithmetic, spelling, sewing, cooking, music, and dancing. He warned, too, against teaching foreign languages, declaring French should be the language of Europe.

Her love for Napoleon was deepening, day by day, so that Marie overlooked his flaws, attributing them to his role as emperor, rather than to her Napole.

Napoleon did not discuss war plans in the letters he dictated in front of Marie, but as spring arrived, she was overtly aware of the inevitability of the war's resumption—and her departure from Finckenstein. Sadness at parting with Napoleon gave way to uncertainty about what lay ahead.

One day, while with Napoleon in his study, there came a loud, insistent knock.

"Who is it?" Napoleon called.

"Berthier!"

Marie stifled a gasp. News of her presence had been kept from the Chief-of-Staff. Napoleon pressed a finger to his lips and gestured for her to hide behind the bathtub screen. She obeyed, settling on a stool beside the copper tub.

"Entre!" Napoleon answered.

Berthier entered and moved quickly toward Napoleon. He started to speak, then hesitated. "*Two* cups?" he asked. "Am I interrupting?"

Marie held her breath.

"Not at all." Napoleon said. "Constant was with me. What is it, Louis?"

Clearing his throat, Berthier informed the emperor that a political plot was afoot among the Polish officers to undermine Prince Józef Poniatowski's position as leader of the Polish Army.

"What?" Napoleon bellowed, his chair scraping the floor. "Is there no end to the squabbles among these Poles? Who are these men? They shall rue the day!"

"There are six, Your Majesty," Berthier replied. "Here's the list."

Neither spoke for a long minute. Holding her breath, Marie listened, aware of her own heartbeat.

'Very well," Napoleon said at last. "I'll speak to you in the morning."

"What—oh, yes, sir."

Once Berthier left, Marie emerged from her hiding place and approached Napoleon, who looked up from the paper, his expression grave.

"Napole, we do have that reputation," she said softly. "Do you know, years ago when two camps of Polish magnates couldn't agree, one side foolishly asked Czarina Catherine to intercede. Once she had her jeweled high heels in rich Polish dirt, she saw no reason to leave."

Napoleon seemed not to hear, his attention drawn back to the paper.

"Napole?"

The emperor's eyes shifted to Marie, dark and penetrating. Wordlessly, he handed the paper to her. "Read it," he said.

Marie glanced down at the neat handwriting.

Six names.

A chill washed over her. There at the bottom, neatly inscribed, was the name of Colonel Benedykt Łączyński.

40

MARIE STEPPED UP INTO THE carriage bound for home, followed by Benedykt, who sat across from her. She was departing Finckenstein much as she had arrived: dressed in black and under cover of darkness, but she carried with her a sense of humiliation regarding her brother's behavior. She stayed silent through the night, her mind drifting to Napoleon's earnest request that she join him in Paris that winter.

At full light, the carriage slowed and was trundling into a relay station when Benedykt blurted, "You're still upset, Marie. Aren't you going to talk to me at all?"

Marie afforded him a little shrug.

"I'm sorry, Marie. I apologized to you and to the emperor."

Tired of averting her eyes, Marie turned her head toward her brother. "Of course, I'm upset. Why did you get involved? To what purpose, Benedykt? Perhaps you thought there'd be a promotion?"

"No, that's not it, really. I just got swept up in it. I was the low man. You saw that I was on the bottom of the list."

"Why were you brought in at all?" A sudden thought struck home, and she drew in breath. "Have you told people about me? Did these plotters think you had influence through me?"

"No, Marie! Please don't put that in the emperor's head. They didn't know you were there!"

"Good. This scandal fuels the emperor's belief that Poles are too often at odds with one another. Now, tell me why the prince was targeted."

"They thought Prince Poniatowski had become too friendly with Napoleon, Marie. They believed the prince would not hold the emperor's feet to the fire when it came to pressing for a timely independence for Poland."

"And you agree?"

Her brother cast his eyes downward. "Yes."

Marie herself could bear witness to Napoleon's evasiveness on the subject of Poland's independence. She empathized with her brother and abandoned her questioning.

The tension dissipated in the remaining days of travel, but as the carriage neared Kiernozia, Benedykt turned to Marie, placing his hand on Marie's. "Are you going to say anything to Mother, Marie? We believed the prince's removal was best."

Marie gazed up into his sad eyes and sensed he wouldn't even stay the night should she inform her mother of his involvement in the failed cabal. She placed her forefinger on her lips. "I cannot fault you for your patriotism."

They arrived home late and after a happy reunion, Countess Eva Łączyńska saw that they had a small meal before they retired.

Before daybreak, Danusha and two new maids served breakfast while the countess fired a quiver full of questions at Marie and Benedykt about the next stage of war with Russia. They could relate little that she didn't already know, except for news of the failed coup, and no mention was made of it. Benedykt made his goodbyes immediately after the meal and left to rejoin his regiment.

When they were alone, her mother looked across the table, her face suddenly serious. "Why did you come here, Marie?" she asked. "Why not go to Walewice? That's your home now."

"I couldn't, Mother. I abandoned my husband."

"He doesn't see it that way."

"He doesn't? He told you as much?"

"Just the other day, Anastase said he longed for your return."

"I can't face him now." Marie flushed, a child again being admonished by her mother.

"You've fallen in love with *him*, haven't you?"

Marie paused, drew in breath, and chose a different thread. "I want Antoni brought here, if that's all right?"

"What? Yes, of course. —But you should go there, Marie."

"No, Mother. Later this afternoon, I'll write Anastase a letter and have our groom deliver it."

Her mother reached across the table and took one of Marie's hands in both of hers. "Listen to me, Marie. Most discerning people understand what you did and that you did it for the good of your country. They will be forgiving, even Anastase. You need to put this—this venture behind you."

"*You* were one of those discerning people who encouraged me, Mother." Marie paused, watching her mother's eyes widen.

Her mother retracted her hands and sat back.

"It's not a little venture," Marie continued. "I can still influence him. And yes, I did it for our country, but one day, I realized I did it for me, too, Mother. You're right. I do care for him."

Her mother sighed, still collecting herself. "You're only twenty, Marie, with so much more to learn. These things run their course, and then they end. You must realize that."

"Before I left Finckenstein, he made me promise to come to Paris this winter."

"I have no doubt he said that, Marysia. It's the kind of thing men, especially soldiers, say at times like that. To think that your interlude can continue is madness, child, madness."

"But, Mother, he *pleaded*."

"I failed you once as a mother, Marie." Tears suddenly appeared at the corners of her eyes. "I regret that. Forgive me." She paused. "Should he send for you, daughter, don't go."

Silent, Marie turned her head away.

"Marie?"

Her head still averted, Marie said, "I will go."

"Look at me, daughter." When Marie turned, her mother wet her lips, steel blue eyes riveted on hers in that old strict way. "And just who is in Paris now awaiting the emperor?"

The question came like a slap and took Marie's breath away. She went cold. In all the days of travel, she had not given Empress Josephine a sustained thought. She knew Napoleon still wrote to her. Marie had seen the letters going into the locked leather cases meant for Paris. On those occasions she pondered what Josephine meant to him. Inevitably, it led to the question: *What do I mean to him?*

"Marie?" her mother pressed.

Marie steadied herself against the back of the chair, staving off dizziness. "He loves me, Mother."

"And so, he might have on the day you parted. But this is now, child." Her mother stood. "Your future is not his future." She cleared her throat. "In the meantime, I'll warn you with my own mother's words: 'Gird well your heart'." She turned and left the room.

Marie sat immobile. With few words, her mother had created fractures in her faith in Napoleon. She recalled reading *Delphine* in convent school and how Germaine de Staël underscored the suffering of women who love inconstant and vacillating men.

Was he as undependable as the men of whom Germaine de Staël wrote? She recalled Delphine's tragic end and shivered.

Katarzyna came rushing into the room, miffed as to why she had not been called for the early breakfast—until her eyes fastened on Marie. She let out a high-pitched yelp and flew into her sister's arms.

"Oh, Kasia, it's so good to see you," Marie exclaimed, holding her sister tight. "Now, let me have a look at you." She grasped her at the shoulders and held her at arms' length. "You are becoming a beautiful young lady."

"Oh! Do you think so?"

"Yes, I do."

"Oh, but not like you."

"Nonsense! When does Honorata finish school?"

"Next month. And then in the fall, I start."

"Are you excited?"

Katarzyna shrugged. "I suppose so. —Marie, are the nuns very strict?"

"Not so very, Kasia, *if you behave*."

"You came alone today?"

"Benedykt was here, but he had to go back to his legion."

"Oh! —Did I miss anyone else?"

"Who?" Marie asked, although she knew very well whom she meant.

"Him! Napoleon—who else?"

Marie laughed. "No, the emperor didn't escort me home."

"I told my friend Agnieszka that you are his favorite. Mother got angry and said I shouldn't say such things. Ha! it was too late."

"She's right. I mean it, Kasia. You shouldn't say such things."

"But it's true, isn't it?"

Marie pulled a serious face. "It's not something to be known, do you understand?"

"Yes, yes, I won't tell anyone."

"Good!" Marie couldn't suppress a little laugh. "You haven't changed a bit, you know. Now listen, if I bring Antoni here for a while, will you help me look after him?"

"What? You're going to stay here?"

Marie nodded.

"Oh, Marysia!" Katarzyna cried and wrapped her arms around her.

20 June 1807

Honorata Łączyńska arrived home from school in time for supper, bringing news from Warsaw. The French had met with the Russian forces at Friedland at the Baltic coast and delivered Aleksander a mighty blow. "There's been no victory like it," Honorata said. "Thirty thousand of the enemy were killed or taken prisoner, twenty-five generals among them!"

"Don't speak so lightly of the dead, Honor," Madame Łączyńska said.

Honorata's eyes went large. "But we've *won*, Mother. The city erupted in celebration. Even the nuns sang victory songs."

"Yes, and we need to pray for Benedykt and Teodor," her mother admonished. "What other news is there?"

"Czar Aleksander has sued for peace."

"Praise God," Marie intoned.

A week later, Teodor sent word that both he and Benedykt were unhurt and that an armistice with Prussia had been signed, with negotiations expected to favor the Poles.

With heightened expectation, Marie, her family, and her countrymen awaited word on whether the lands and peoples Prussia had stolen would be returned. What else could such a victory mean?

41

Hania arrived with two-year-old Antoni and tales of how the bright, blonde-headed child had quickly captured the attention of everyone at the Walewice Palace.

He knew names and could manage short sentences. With someone holding his hand, he could climb three or four steps. He quickly warmed to Marie, often begging her for something that Hania thought to deny him. Sometimes, Marie weakened. In the bosom of her family once again, Marie felt safe and whole. Her heart was full. Or nearly so.

She prayed daily for a letter from Napoleon.

After Sunday Mass one day, the congregation, a good number of grim faces among them, filed out onto the June lawn already abuzz with ominous, even angry, tones. News of some import had arrived in Kiernozia.

The parish priest greeted the family at the bottom of the church steps.

"What is it, Father Albin?" Madame Łączyńska asked.

Noticing Marie, the priest nodded and offered a tight smile. Marie had no time to wait for the priest's answer because Amelia Wozniak grabbed her by the arm and pulled her away. "Marie! It's been so long! Oh, how lovely to see you at last. That's your child with that woman, yes?"

Marie nodded. "Yes, that's Antoni."

"He's beautiful! Now—guess what? *I'm* to be married."

"I'm so happy for you, Amelia. I am! You must tell me all about your future husband, but first tell me what has upset everybody here."

"It's Napoleon, Marie. You haven't heard?"

Marie grasped her friend at the shoulders. "Heard *what*? Is he well?"

"Oh, he's well. They say he has the constitution of a bear."

"What, then?"

"Well, it seems the meeting of the two emperors has gone differently than anyone might have imagined. Napoleon and Czar Aleksander seemed to get along like old boyhood chums. No one knows where it will lead. And no one is happy about it, Marie."

Marie felt herself getting lightheaded.

"It's common knowledge by now," Amelia continued, "that the two have spent a week or more talking, dining together, and riding in the woods. What do you make of it, Marie?"

"I don't know," Marie said. "Please excuse me, Amelia."

Amelia grasped hold of Marie's arms. "Wait, Marie! You turned white as a ghost. Then, it's true! You were with *him*, isn't that right? Dog's blood! The gossip's true—you've caught Napoleon's eye!"

"I can't talk right now, Amelia." Marie kissed her on the cheek. "I'm so glad for you. I really am." She pulled away and hurried to the carriage where her mother and sisters waited.

No one spoke on the way home. Everyone, it seemed, had heard just enough. Could the meeting of emperors have gone so far wrong? The euphoria Poland had experienced upon the news of the Friedland victory was quickly dissipating, it seemed.

What is the future? Marie worried. For Poland? For herself?

At home, Marie spoke to her mother after supper, when they were alone at the table. "Mother, Amelia seemed to know about me."

"Yes? You and the emperor?"

Marie nodded. "Do many people?"

"Things like that don't stay quiet for long, Marie. However, once you return to Walewice and a little time goes by, it'll be forgotten."

Marie fell silent. Her mother was still of the opinion that the interlude with Napoleon would soon end. She, however, remained confident that the summons would come. It had to.

Anastase went to Warsaw often now, and when he returned to Walewice he brought with him the *Gazeta Warszawska* and sent copies over to the Kiernozia estate. Marie, her mother and sisters sat around the dining room table searching through the articles. In this way, they learned the full brunt of the peace terms.

Czar Aleksander had not been asked to give up any of his Polish territories in the west. Not only was he to keep what lands Catherine had taken at the time of Poland's fall, but he was now gifted with the flourishing district of Bialystok that Prussia was forced to cede.

Nonetheless, Napoleon had forced Aleksander to agree to sign off on the creation of a Grand Duchy of Warsaw that was being carved from other previous Prussian-held lands encompassing nineteen hundred square miles and two and a half million Poles.

"A paltry thing that," Madame Łączyńska snapped, her bottom lip protruding. "Yes, it includes Warsaw and our estate here in Mazovia, but this is not the free and independent Poland my sons have fought for."

Marie looked up at her mother, a wave of disappointment washing over her, as well. It was but a fraction of Poland's size prior to the partitions. *Neither is it what I fought for.* After all of his promises, a mere duchy is the result. Did he think that would suffice? And it came from Prussia, not Russia! The czar had yielded nothing!

Later, in her room, she recalled that two years earlier, Napoleon had overseen the dissolution of the Holy Roman Empire, transforming it into the Confederation of the Rhine, a union of thirty-six Germanic states. Clearly, as separate states, Napoleon could exert more control over them. He had even told her as much once. Was he deliberately choosing not to restore the old Poland, keeping it divided to maintain tighter control over it?

More and more, Marie thought Benedykt had been right about Prince Poniatowski's less-than-forceful stance with Napoleon. The members of the failed cabal had had reason to worry. She owed Benedykt an apology.

Before Marie slept, her thoughts turned to Amelia, a deep sadness settling over her as she realized that their paths had diverged, and nothing could undo the distance between them.

July 1807

As Napoleon headed to Dresden to officiate at the signing of the constitution for the Duchy of Warsaw, spirits sank among the Poles, the Łączyński family included. "Oh, my fellow Poles might be complaining of sodden eyes and staring down at empty hands now, but mark me, Marie," her mother said, blue eyes unyielding, "they can be stupidly optimistic and will be once again when the Grand Duchy is in place."

As if to support her tenet, the Provisional Government issued a proclamation the very next day calling for renewed faith in Emperor Napoleon. The moot question: Who else did they have?

The duchy was a veritable political stew created with a Polish administration, French laws, a Prussian currency, and a Saxon king, Frederick Augustus.

As days passed and summer waned, Marie anticipated a letter calling her to Dresden. While she had been as disappointed as her countrymen that hopes for a new Poland had been dashed, that loyalty to France had yielded so little, she still longed to hear from him, longed to see him. The last letter had come immediately after the Friedland victory. Mail days found her moving through phases of nervousness, hopefulness, and ultimately despondency, for she waited in vain.

Her moods didn't escape her mother's observation, either. One day her mother said, "It's a hard thing to accept, Marie, but you must come to realize that the letters have stopped. He is finished."

He is not finished with me.

By the end of July, the papers carried the news that the emperor had returned to Paris in triumph. "He's been received well at home, it seems," her mother said.

15 August 1807

On her name day, the day of her patron saint, the Blessed Virgin Mary, Marie was awakened by Katarzyna's knocking on her door. "Danusha is making *racuchy z jabłkami* for you, Marysia. Hania's already downstairs with Antoni. Hurry, or they'll all be eaten!"

Marie could smell the delicious aroma of the apple pancakes. She hurried out of bed and dressed quickly.

No one spoke when she entered the dining chamber.

And then she saw the package next to the platter of pancakes. She took her seat. It was a square box, a travel box, her name atop it. Her heart thundered.

She looked to her mother, whose expression was inscrutable.

"Don't keep us all waiting, Marie," Katarzyna said. "Are you going to open it?"

Marie pulled the box to her. Her name day occurred on the same day as his birthday. Today he is thirty-eight, she thought. She blushed as she recalled discussing this one morning in bed after they had made love. Her heart beat fast to think he remembered.

"Did he know?" Katarzyna asked.

Marie shrugged.

"Oh, he must have known," Honorata added.

Marie pulled away the heavy paper and lifted the box's lid. She withdrew a triple-stranded diamond and ruby bracelet. Katarzyna and Hania gasped. Antoni was caught by the sparkle and reached out for it, prompting everyone to laugh.

"There's something else," Marie said, but before reaching for it, she dropped the bracelet in her mother's hand, forcing from her a nod of appreciation.

She reached in again and found a gold medallion with his portrait imprinted on it, much in the style of a Roman emperor. This she found more precious. "Today is his birthday," she said. "There's a note," she added in a casual tone.

It was brief, as his missives often were. Her eyes moved over it at once. She had no wish to read it aloud. Napoleon scribbled that she was missed and that in the near future, he would ask her to come to Paris.

Marie looked up at her mother, smiling but wishing that she could tell her that this was the invitation. Her mother's expression was anything but congratulatory as she passed the bracelet back to her. So—there were to be more long days of embroidery, the harpsichord, and reading the plays of Corneille that Napoleon had insisted she take. While her mother doubted Napoleon, her own confidence was restored. In her bedchamber, she stored away the bracelet for her visit to Paris and pinned the medallion on her dress.

September 1807

Countess Teresa Walewska, the favorite of the sisters-in-law, wrote to ask Marie and Antoni to move back to the Walewice Palace, complimenting her on her "heroic efforts" and providing the news that Anastase had left to take the waters at Bad Gastein in Austria, and from there he would press on to Italy for the winter, as was his custom. The letter stunned Marie, who had thought that initiation of divorce proceedings was the more likely news to come from Walewice. Her mother's assessment of Anastase proved nearer to the truth than her own perception.

Still, Anastase's absence from Walewice made no difference. Marie declined the invitation.

In November, Benedykt wrote from his post in Paris that the emperor had left for Italy to induce the pope to side with him against England.

42

Thursday, 24 December 1807
Wigilia (Christmas Eve)

FOUR MONTHS HAD PASSED SINCE the last note from Napoleon. Smiling, she tried to join in the family celebration of the *Wigilia* supper. Everyone stood at their place around the evergreen-laden table singing *Bóg Się Rodzi* (God is Born). Even little Antoni stood wide-eyed, staring at the tip of the spruce tree that had been hung upside down over the food-laden table. They then shared the *opłatek*, the unconsecrated bread wafer.

It was while Katarzyna, home on break, was entertaining everyone at the table with tales of her first year at convent school that the sounds of the arrival of a horseman in the courtyard drew attention. The room went silent as Madame Łączyńska rose and hurried to the door. In just minutes, she led the snow-covered rider wearing Pontiatowski livery through the dining chamber and into the kitchen for warmth and a meal.

Madame Łączyńska returned through the swinging door, her face expressionless. She walked over to Marie and handed her a sealed note.

Marie recognized the irregular, cramped handwriting.

"Hurry and open it, Marie," Katarzyna said. "Is it from him?"

"Yes, Marie, don't just stare at it," Honorata urged. "Open it!"

Marie broke the red seal and silently read the short note. She glanced up and shared silent expressions with her mother, who turned aside, smiled bitterly at Marie's sisters, and said, "Well, girls, I suspect our harpsichord is about to go silent for the rest of the winter."

Late that evening, Marie drew Hania aside. "I'm to travel to Paris, Hania. Now, tomorrow, I want you to take Antoni to Walewice."

The young woman nodded as if she had been expecting the request. Her face darkened with disappointment. Hania had made it clear to Marie that she very much enjoyed her role as lady's maid, as well as guardian to Antoni. Still, she seemed resigned to Marie's order.

"They are good to him there, aren't they, my sisters-in-law and the staff?"

"Oh, yes, Madame. You're going to miss him, yes?"

"Terribly, Hania. Antoni is an angel. I've so enjoyed these months having him with me." Marie battled back tears at the prospect of another separation from her son. She drew in a deep breath. "Now, once he is settled there a few days, Hania, I want you to pack a trunk, not too large of one, mind you."

"Madame?" Hania tilted her head, blue eyes questioning.

"I want you to accompany me, Hania."

Hania's hand flew to her mouth. "To—to Paris?"

"It will be a long and perhaps agonizing journey, but yes, to Paris."

"Oh, Madame!"

"I assume you are in agreement?" Marie knew that Hania had been to Warsaw just once and that Paris was outside of even her wildest dreams.

"Oh, Madame!"

Tuesday, 5 January 1808

A letter from Prince Józef Poniatowski, written in Madame de Vauban's hand, arrived for Marie stating that Napoleon had entrusted him to see to Marie's travel details. The carriage hired by the prince would arrive at Kiernozia at mid-month. She was to be ready for what was likely to be more than a two-week journey. To her disappointment, it would commence only after a two-day stop in Warsaw.

In the early hours of 15 January, Marie, accompanied by Hania, bade a tearful goodbye to her mother and sisters. Despite her doubts about her daughter's future, the countess seemed resigned to the continuing affair with Napoleon, but Marie knew she empathized with Anastase, who had rescued the estate from foreclosure, and that she hoped the marriage would mend and continue. Marie had no such hope.

Once inside the coach as it trundled along the lane toward the main road, Marie brushed away the tears, making room in her heart only for excitement. Half an hour later, the carriage pulled off to the side for a *kulig* to pass from the oncoming direction She and Hania watched it go by. The six or seven sleighs teemed with red-cheeked young people singing songs and calling out gleeful greetings as they passed.

"Oh, Madame," Hania cried. "It seems such fun. They are so happy!"

"Indeed, they are," Marie said, thinking all the while, *Not as happy as I.* She was to see Paris—and Napoleon.

They arrived in Warsaw late in the night to find a soirée at the Royal Castle in full swing. Madame de Vauban showed them to their rooms, insisting that Marie was to dress at once because her attendance was expected.

Marie turned away so as not to display her annoyance. "By the prince?" she asked, certain that Prince Poniatowski would once again entreat her to speak to Napoleon about independence.

"By everyone, Marie."

Hania helped Marie dress in a muted yellow gown. "Hardly a wrinkle, Madame," she said. "You are lucky."

"You're the lucky one, Hania. You can stay in your room across the way and sleep."

"But you will need help after, Madame."

"I will not. You're to sleep. Do as I say."

The gathering was so large that it was held in the Great Assembly Hall, replete with buffet, orchestra, and dancing. No sooner had she entered than the music and dancing stopped—and she was announced. The prince undoubtedly had ordered the honor, one she had never experienced, and one she would rather have done without. A thousand heads turned in her direction. That this was a reception for her came as a shock. A tingling heat rose into her neck, face, ears. She felt as if she were an oddity and longed to turn and make a quick retreat.

But Prince Poniatowski was already approaching her. He took her hand and led her through a sea of faces, some sympathetic, some curious, some cold. He led her to a relatively quiet alcove, fetching a glass of white wine for her as they went.

"What must they think of me?" Marie asked. "I've heard how badly news of the Dresden decision was taken, and rightly so. To be given a tiny Grand Duchy instead of our Poland. They must hate me."

The prince leaned toward her. "Oh, there was great disappointment and anger over the Treaty at Tilsit, that's true. Especially when Russia received the district of Bialystok as a bit of honey from Napoleon. Citizens had provided strong support to the French, and many of their sons joined Napoleon's Polish legions, so they feared retribution."

"And was there—retribution?"

"Yes, the czar's police were cruel. Enthusiasm for the French here plummeted after Tilsit. But now that we have the Grand Duchy fully formed and functioning, albeit under the rule of Frederick Augustus of Saxony, the people's attitude toward Napoleon has mellowed a bit. Besides, Marie, what other hope do we have?"

The next day Marie suffered through tedious and awkward audiences with the men who had been in the Provisional Government and now held roles in the Duchy of Warsaw. Their speeches echoed the vague advice the prince had given her at the end of her reception. She was to continue to exert her influence on the emperor, the resuscitation of Old Poland the goal.

She pledged to do everything she could. But something had changed since that goal was first thrust upon her: she had fallen in love with Emperor Napoleon Bonaparte. This fact she did not communicate to the officials, who would likely think her position badly compromised.

43

Sunday, 17 January 1808

IN THE DARK MORNING HOURS, Marie and a wide-eyed Hania, along with Prince Poniatowski and Madame de Vauban, attended Mass in the castle's Small Chapel. After a brief breakfast, the carriage was loaded and made ready.

"It will take a week to arrive at Dresden," the prince said as Marie prepared to board. "You might want to rest there for two or three days. King Frederick has been made aware of your arrival and will certainly welcome you. He holds a brilliant Court."

This suggestion that she might wish to delay her arrival in Paris to spend it in the Court of the King of Saxony—who now also held the title of Duke of Warsaw—came as a surprise. She nodded, thanked the prince for his hospitality and stepped up into the coach, taking her seat next to Hania.

As the carriage left Castle Square, she thought, *Not three days. Not even two.*

Dresden, Germany
Friday, 22 January 1808

During the carriage drive to Dresden, Marie began tutoring Hania in French, focusing on the conversational approach she had learned from her tutor. The diversion was a welcome one.

The prince had arranged a much simpler carriage than the luxurious Berline Napoleon had provided, so that after six grueling and frigid days of travel, nights at monasteries or poor hostelries, bad food, one broken axle, and countless relay stations, Marie reconsidered the stay at Dresden. She saw her own exhaustion in Hania's appearance.

Arriving at Dresden in the mid-afternoon on Wednesday, Marie was taken on a tour of the grand Dresden Castle. She requested that Hania join them. The guide was Princess Marie Augusta. The lovely princess, just four years Marie's elder, was once considered as a marriage prospect for Prince Poniatowski.

"Why didn't the prince marry her, Marie?" Hania asked, once they were alone.

"The partitions, Hania. Suddenly, in 1795, there was no Poland, and her father wouldn't allow it. The prince suddenly had little to offer. . .. You look tired."

Hania gave out with a little laugh. "I am tired, Madame. As we walked from room to room, I felt as if my derrière was still vibrating on the coach bench."

Marie laughed. "Me, too! Perhaps we should stay another day or two, then. Just think, nights without worries about bedbugs or mice."

"Oh, but Madame, all you've talked about is arriving in Paris."

Marie studied Hania's expression, realizing that Hania knew just why Paris was so close to her heart. It was foolish to think otherwise. "Perhaps we should push on."

"The sooner we get there, the better I'm likely to become in French. I couldn't keep up with you and the princess at all."

"I'm not surprised." Marie said. "However, you will learn." She threw her arms around Hania and hugged her. Taking hold of her then at arms' length, she asked, "So—you are glad you came along?"

"Oh, Madame. *Oui, oui!*"

The two laughed.

At supper, Marie felt blessed that she was the only guest at the royal table. Princess Marie Augusta sat across from her, Queen Amalie to her left, and King Frederick to her right. The king, in his late fifties, wore a serene expression augmented by wide, dark eyes. Over the dessert of *Dresdner stollen*, he took Marie's decision to stay but one night with placidity. "As you wish, Madame Walewska," he said.

"Oh, but we did wish to receive you at Court on Friday, my dear," the queen put in, leaning forward. "Won't you stay till then?"

Marie looked down the table at the plain-faced queen, her brown hair piled impossibly high and topped with tiny flowers, red and white. There was a sadness about her eyes, perhaps a residual effect of at least three stillborn babies. The Princess Marie Augusta was their only child to live to adulthood. Marie froze, uncertain how she would answer.

"Amalie, dear," the king interjected. "The countess no doubt has a mission to complete. Józef has implied as much. I'm certain she's anxious to see it through."

Marie felt a tightness in her neck and shoulders. *Just what does he know?* She managed only the weakest smile at the king and dared not turn her gaze to the queen.

"Now, Madame Walewska," the king continued, "I want you to know that Poland has always been close to my heart. Were it not for the partitions, I would have succeeded King Stanisław. Now, by placing me as Duke of Warsaw last year, Emperor Napoleon did me no great service, but I shall do my best."

The king reached across and covered Marie's hand with his. "Now, what of the future? Might Poland be Poland again one day? If you are to play even the slightest role in a brighter future for your country, Marie, we—Amalie and I—will send you off tomorrow morning with smiles and good cheer."

Marie nodded but could not quite conjure up a smile. At every turn, she was being pressured to bring results.

Thursday, 28 January 1808
Marie ensured they departed for Leipzig early the next morning. They passed through Erfurt, beginning a three-day progress toward Mainz. Between French lessons and stops in towns and military depots, Marie and Hania competed to be the first to spot the French flag. While the flag designs varied, the Imperial Eagle remained consistent, and Marie's heart swelled at the sight of Napoleon's rule stretching from the Russian border on the River Nieman to Paris—a thousand miles of territory.

When the carriage finally rumbled over the bridge on the River Rhine at Mainz, Marie placed her hand over Hania's. "We are in France, Hania. We are truly in France."

Hania drew in a quick breath. "Really, Madame?" Her eyes lit up. "Magnifique, Madame! Magnifique!"

Marie laughed and gave her a hug.

Monday, 1 February 1808
As they set out on the wide and well-traveled highway for Paris. Marie observed that Hania was working at counting something on her fingers. "What are you doing, Hania?"

"Counting the days from Dresden, Madame. I count five—is that correct?"

"It is, but there will be another five along this road."

Hania's shoulders drooped a bit. She sighed. "Oh, Madame."

Marie felt prepared for the final leg of the journey. She looked out at the rolling terrain of white, imagining it in summer. She thought about the French citizens—some thirty-seven million taxpayers, according to Marshal Duroc—who lived and worked under the reign of Napoleon Bonaparte. What do they think of him? she wondered. So many, too, had served in his seemingly endless wars, and countless men had been lost. What did the grieving families think of him? Surely, they must long for peace.

Two days out from Paris, a courier from the capital stopped the carriage and announced that they would be met at the final relay station before Paris.

After he rode off, Hania cried, "Oh, Madame, he spoke so fast! Too fast! I couldn't catch but a word or two."

Marie laughed. "It was good news, Hania. We will be welcomed tomorrow at Fontainebleau."

"Welcomed? *Par qui?*"

Marie shrugged. "We'll see tomorrow, won't we?"

Fontainebleau, France
Friday, 5 February 1808

To the clanging of church bells, both city and country, the carriage left the hard highway and rumbled onto the cobblestone road that ran through Fontainebleau. At the relay station, a familiar face appeared at the coach door's window.

"Marshal Duroc," Marie cried, her hand moving to her throat. She was happy to see the man who had acted as go-between in Warsaw. But, for the Grand Marshal of the Palace to have left his many important duties in Paris to ride some fifty miles to greet them was surprising.

The marshal opened the door and reached up to help her down. "It is a delight to see you, Madame Walewska."

It was only after both she and Hania were on the ground that Marie recognized the soldier approaching them from the front of the carriage, where he had been talking to the driver. Another surprise.

"Benedykt," she said, her voice little more than a whisper.

"It is. I mean, I am," replied her brother, laughing before leaning over to kiss her.

During a modest lunch, Marie learned Benedykt had needed to ask Marshal Duroc's favor to greet her at Fontainebleau. "You see," he explained, "I'm no longer on Berthier's staff."

"Really?" Marie guessed his involvement in the effort to displace Prince Poniatowski was the likely reason, and Benedykt seemed to read her mind.

"The emperor had other ideas for me," Benedykt said, his tone resigned. "I'm now in command of the Third Regiment of Polish Lancers of the Imperial Guard."

"Congratulations!" Marie exclaimed. This was significant. She knew that after Poland's fall, several Polish legions—thousands of soldiers—had been welcomed by Napoleon, who aligned them with the French Army and appointed Polish officers. In essence, they formed a Polish army in exile. Benedykt's new role as commander of one of the emperor's most revered regiments of winged lancers meant that he was now dedicated to protecting Napoleon Bonaparte himself.

Benedykt nodded. "It's a challenge and an honor, but the appointment will most likely keep me at some distance from you."

Marie noticed Marshal Duroc avert his gaze, feigning interest in something across the room. This confirmed her suspicion that her brother had spoken the hard truth. They would be kept apart, but after the attempted coup against Prince Poniatowski, Benedykt would have less access to the emperor's inner circle. She saw the irony: because she was his sister, his punishment for his involvement appeared more like a promotion.

Yes, a challenge and an honor, Marie thought, but one executed with cunning.

After lunch, Benedykt and Duroc rode in front of the carriage as escorts.

Paris, France

Entry into the beautiful city of Paris was more than Marie had imagined. As the carriage rattled along the cobblestone streets, she and a wide-eyed Hania sat across from one another, gazing out at the crowds and stunning architecture. Old, ornate mansions and palaces stood beside simple, classical structures modeled on Roman and Greek architecture.

"They call it the New Rome," Marie said.

"I've never seen so many people," Hania remarked.

"Napole said six hundred thousand people live here. The only city with more is London."

Hania glanced at Marie, raising an eyebrow.

Marie bit her lip, realizing she had casually mentioned Napoleon and used the diminutive he insisted upon. That Hania didn't bat an eye spoke volumes. Servants often knew everything that happened in a household.

The carriage stopped along a wide avenue. From his mount, Benedykt leaned over and opened the coach door. "I leave you here, Marie. I must return to my duty at the Quay Voltaire. Marshal Duroc will escort you to your new house."

The goodbye felt awkward—no private words, no kiss. An odd ache tugged at her chest. She wished she could tell him she now understood why he had taken part in the plot to replace Prince Poniatowski.

Marshal Duroc helped Marie alight in front of a narrow, stone townhome at 2 Rue de la Houssaye in the elite arrondissement of Notre Dame de Lorette. The building had three stories and an attic beneath a steep roof. Upon entering, Marie was met by a staff of five—a cook, two footmen, and two maids—standing at attention.

"The emperor wants you to be comfortable," Duroc explained as he led her on a tour. "He wanted to impress you. Oh, and he has ordered a harpsichord."

"I'm impressed," she replied, laughing, "but my playing will impress no one."

"You are too modest, Madame Walewska. The emperor likes that. It's a rare trait here in Paris."

"I'm merely a tourist from Poland."

"You are hardly that. You're a preeminent guest, specifically invited by the most powerful man in Europe. The people regard him like a Caesar."

Marie was glad she was trailing behind Duroc up the narrow staircase because she knew she was blushing a deep scarlet. Somehow, his words added gravity to her experience in Paris. She wondered, too, whether the staff below had heard him.

Once in the small, formal reception room, Duroc turned to her, his dark eyes narrowing in seriousness. "You know, Madame Walewska, that the emperor will want you presented at Court."

Marie blinked, caught off guard. "At Court?" she stammered. "He told you that?"

Duroc nodded.

Marie squared her shoulders and raised her chin. "Even Caesar did not get every wish."

Duroc laughed. "He did say you're clever."

"Clever or not, I'll not go to Court."

"Is it the empress that makes you hesitate?"

Marie looked away.

"Ah, then," the marshal continued, "I'm merely forewarning you."

Marie turned back. "Forewarned is forearmed."

"Exactly."

"Marshal Duroc—about these servants, five, and there is my maid, too. When the emperor visits, how are we to keep things . . ."

Duroc smiled. "Secret?"

Marie nodded.

"There is no need for that, Madame Walewska. No need at all." He gestured toward the window that looked out upon the wide, busy avenue. "This is Paris."

The next day, a letter arrived, addressed in her mother's familiar hand. It was brief, and the news sudden: Honorata was getting married. How could this be? Marie wondered. Of course, Honor was now eighteen—older than Marie had been when she married Anastase. She remembered how lovingly Honor had helped her prepare for her own wedding, and now she found herself in Paris while her sister's marriage would take place halfway across the continent. Marie couldn't return the favor. She tried to ease the heartache by recalling how Honor had once believed she would never attract a man—a thought now undone. Marie prayed for her sister's happiness.

44

Sunday, 7 February 1808

MARIE LAY ON HER SIDE, her right arm on Napoleon's chest rising and falling slightly as her lover slept. She studied the images of various couples depicted in the blue linen covering the walls. Each pair stood, sat, or reclined beneath a tree, always in a pose of affection. He had told her the textile was distinctly French, calling it *toile de Jouy*. The fashions worn by the couples were certainly French and they were current enough for her to wonder whether the emperor himself had ordered the material.

The thought drifted away. She was happier than she had been in a long while. She had waited months for the reunion. *I must enjoy this.* There would be time later during her stay to bring up the subject of Poland. For now, he seemed thrilled that she had made the journey. This was bliss.

Or, almost so. The experience at Finckenstein Castle surpassed her time here because they had lived together in one residence. Here, in the first week of her stay, she was never certain when he would find time to see her. He arrived at the townhome without fanfare, sometimes in the afternoons, sometimes late at night. She relished the days when he called twice. The unmarked carriage would arrive in front and Constant Wairy would hurry in, ordering the staff to *give way*, and they would scatter like bugs until Napoleon was safely installed in Marie's reception room or bedchamber. If there were to be refreshments or a meal, the valet worked it out with the kitchen help on the ground level and he would see it delivered. Of course, the staff knew the identity of the visitor, but they were not to approach him.

Now, after midnight, Marie prepared herself for a bout of loneliness. In a short while, Constant would knock at the door and say that the carriage was ready to take the emperor back to the Tuileries. Only once did Napoleon stay the night.

He stirred then, pulling her close.

"My Marie," he said, "you've stayed locked up in here like a butterfly under glass. You must move about more in French society."

"Must I? With you?"

"I'm arranging outings to the opera and theater for you."

"With you?" she asked again, though she knew the answer.

"No, Marshal Duroc is to be your escort."

"Ah, I see. The marshal is a handsome man. Aren't you afraid he will win me over?"

His arm went around her and he pulled her close. "Should I be?"

Marie looked up into the gray-blue eyes. Were they intent or were they laughing at her? "No," she whispered, unable to extend the jest.

"Good! Now, about your appearing at Court—"

"I will not, Napole."

"Is it Josephine that makes you say that? She is seldom at the Tuileries Palace. She's most often at the Château de Malmaison. Oh, I was furious when I came back from my Egyptian campaign to find she had bought a rundown manor house for 300,000 francs. She spent as much renovating it, and so she prefers it to the city palace. You needn't be concerned about her, my Marie."

"I just don't wish to put myself forward."

Napoleon kissed her on the top of her head. "You are so different from the others. That is what I liked about you from the first. That is what I love about you now. But I won't have you languish here day after day. There are too many things to do here in Paris."

"I gather that you've suggestions for me?"

"Oh, I have many. There's the opera. Plays aplenty and there's the museum—"

"I imagine you are speaking of the *Napoleon* Museum."

"Why, Marie, have you heard of others?"

"*Are* there others?" Marie asked, pulling a wide-eyed face.

The two laughed.

"Seriously," Napoleon said, clearing his throat, "I would like you to see the treasures I brought back from my Egyptian campaign."

"That sounds interesting."

"Just let Gérard know when you are ready."

"I see. My escort."

"Now, what you must experience is the theatre here. It's outstanding. I've been to plays three times this week. You've heard of François-Joseph Talma, I imagine."

Marie felt a heat come into her face. "I have not." That the sophisticated French culture was alien to her was exactly the reason she shied away from Parisian society.

"He's the greatest actor of the day. We have been friends for years. And right now, he's the hit of the season at the Théâtre Français—and in a play with a *Polish theme*! The title is *Waclaw*. How perfect! You *must* see it. I'll arrange it."

"With my loyal escort?" Marie asked, her tone taunting. She knew that their affair might be the champagne of gossip among the elites, but it was not to be made gruel for the common classes.

"You are naughty," Napoleon said, pinching her upper arm. "Now, how many formal gowns have you brought from Poland?"

Marie clenched her teeth. "Three. I had but one trunk. None of the three are white," she added, smirking.

"Touché! You have a good memory. Just three? Well, that won't do. It won't do at all. I have a friend whom I shall send you to see. His name is Antoine Leroy. He has dressed a good many ladies at Court, my sisters among them."

"You have many friends, it seems."

"Ha! I am the emperor." Napoleon laughed.

Marie had the notion that he was expecting her to join in the laughter. Instead, she asked, "The empress, too?"

Napoleon ignored the question. "Leroy is too busy—and temperamental—to come here, so I shall have you go to him."

"But—"

Napoleon put a finger on her lips, waited several seconds, then kissed her.

Tuesday, 9 February 1808

Light snow was falling when the carriage turned onto Rue de la Loi at midmorning. Clusters of richly dressed men and women moved up and down the wide avenue as if it were Warsaw's Łazienki Park in springtime. Not everyone was bundled up, and the parade of fashion and the stunning facades of the boutiques on either side took Marie's breath away. Each shop was unique but shared a Romanesque style—the painted depictions of arches over windows and doors, faux columns, pediments, and mosaics in muted colors.

As traffic slowed, Marshal Duroc pointed out the boutiques of perfumers, herbalists, pharmacists, jewelers, couturiers, and even musicians for hire. Marie had never seen a street like it. Warsaw's famous street of fashion, *Nowy Swiat* didn't compare.

"Ah, here we are!" Duroc's announcement startled Marie. The carriage came to a halt, and she peered out the window.

Gold lettering on the faux pediment read: *Boutique de M. Antoine Leroy, Créateur de Vêtements*. Marie swallowed hard, suddenly unsure. What would this renowned couturier think of this Polish countess from the provinces? Napoleon's warning about Monsieur Leroy's temperament added to her unease.

A liveried servant appeared from the double doors, hurrying toward the carriage as the marshal stepped outside to offer his hand. Marie drew in breath, and alighted. Mannequins swathed in vibrantly colored silks, satins, and lace stood in the windows, as if in judgment of her. She swallowed hard. There was no going back.

Inside, Marie approached the counter. "I have an appointment with Monsieur Leroy," she said.

"Do you?" The darkly dressed matron did not take her eyes from a scheduling book. "We're running behind today, no surprise to anyone." She looked up now, dark eyes scanning Marie. "Unless you're new, that is. Name?"

"Marie Walewska."

The matron peered down at her bookings. "Ah, yes. You're on time. But, as I said, we're running behind." She nodded toward a woman in blue seated in an alcove. "She's ahead of you. Take a seat there until you're called."

Marie had little time to regret agreeing to the appointment, for Duroc appeared, having stayed behind to talk to the driver. He approached the counter, his brow furrowed. "Do your records show," he inquired in a challenging tone, "who it was that made the appointment for the countess?"

The matron narrowed her eyes at Duroc, assessing his uniform, and paled slightly. "I'll check, Monseigneur." She quickly scanned the book, turning back a page. "It does," she mumbled.

Looking up, she attempted a smile, called a young servant over and whispered something in his ear. He nodded and disappeared.

She looked from Duroc to Marie. "It will be but a few minutes, Countess." She motioned toward the alcove. "If you would care to sit?"

Marie smiled. This was a reminder that she was in France. For decades now, titles in Poland were not used in matters of address. She shook her head.

"Allow me to take your cloak, then," the matron said, already coming out from behind the counter.

Marie drew in breath once the cloak was removed. She wished she had worn something other than the pale green dress she had chosen. Before she could dwell on it, the double glass doors burst open, and a perspiring man with a commanding presence entered.

The couturier was himself a vision of Parisian fashion—dark purple frock coat, embroidered gold waistcoat, white breeches, and dark Hessian boots that now snapped together as if he stood before a superior. "Welcome, Madame Walewska! I am Antoine. Forgive me, I had a late start this morning. I trust you have not been kept waiting." He shot daggers at the matron.

"Not at all, Monsieur Leroy. There is another lady ahead of me, however."

"Indeed?" He waived dismissively toward the alcove. "She'll wait. We'll likely have to order more material for that one." He laughed uproariously, and when no one joined in, he turned to Duroc. "Marshal, the countess is under my wing now. You may return in two hours."

Duroc nodded and bowed to Marie. "In two hours, Madame Walewska." He turned and made his exit.

"Come along, now, Madame Walewska. A private room and your complete transformation await."

The room was small but nicely appointed with plush chairs and a fainting couch.

"Now, Countess Walewska," Leroy said, stepping a few paces away, "let us see what we have." He lifted a tortoise-framed monocle that hung around his neck on a purple ribbon. He examined her from different angles muttering to himself.

Marie felt as if she were a museum piece.

"Magnifique!" the couturier announced. "My friend has found his own diamond mine!" He winked.

Marie could feel her cheeks burning.

"Oh, he tried to describe your complexion, *mon cher*, a sight to behold, indeed! And even in this drab gown, your form shows through. Beneath that provincial bonnet you are a classical beauty worthy of Michelangelo."

Leroy's words made her light-headed with colliding emotions. "Monsieur—" she began, intending to ask if she could sit on the cushioned chair.

"Oh, don't thank me," Leroy snapped. "Have you been presented at Court?"

"No, I—"

"Good! There's much to do here first. I speak of more than gowns that fit and enhance. I speak of coiffures, makeup, posture, and movement. I speak of a transformation."

Napoleon laughed when he heard Marie's recounting of her experience. "Welcome to Paris! As for Leroy, I'll wager he was gambling at the Palais-Royale into the small hours. *That's* why he was late! His passion for the tables runs second only to *haute couture*."

"Really?" Marie looked up from the plate Constant Wairy had just served. She and Napoleon were enjoying a late supper in her reception room.

"You shall have to experience the Palais-Royale, my dove. Before the revolution it housed the royal family, but now the building is a center of politics and culture. You'll see people of every stripe, every class. If you were impressed by the Rue de la Loi, the market stalls and shops at the Palais-Royale will spin your head around."

"And gambling rooms?"

"Oh, yes. I saw to it that the businesses of ill-repute were evicted, but I dared not toss out the gamblers for fear of a rebellion. You can smile, but I'm serious. Gambling gets into the blood of some men, Marie. Like liquor. Antoine is lucky to have his talents and a flourishing business. Every woman of substance in Paris, and then some, are clamoring for his attention; otherwise, he might follow in the paths of unlucky souls who gamble and lose everything."

"Really?"

"Indeed. Why, a pawnbroker's shop is situated in the cellar of the Palais-Royale, amidst a variety of restaurants, where a night's loser might, out of desperation, pawn his fancy coat, last jewel, or silver shoe buckles so that he could return to the tables. If the luck doesn't change, some have been known to acquaint themselves with a pistol, or take a last meander down to the River Seine."

"How sad, Napole."

Napoleon popped a piece of venison into his mouth and shrugged.

45

Monday, 15 February 1808

While Marie bore witness to Antoine Leroy's temperamental side in her subsequent visits to his boutique, the couturier's tantrums—sometimes impish, sometimes outrageously mean—were usually directed at an employee or, on occasion, a customer. Once, while in a fitting room with Leroy, a woman could be heard loudly complaining about being made to wait for her appointment. The couturier shot out of the fitting room and raced to the reception desk, Hessian boot heels clicking loudly as he went.

"Pardon, Madame," Leroy barked, "last week you complained about the price of one of my creations and today you abused my receptionist about having to wait. You wouldn't be here if I didn't mask your frame with something worthwhile, would you? Such a pity that when you took the boat to England, *Le Moulin à Silence* missed her chance. But I won't. You know where the door is."

The Silence Mill? Curiosity got the best of Marie. When Leroy returned, she asked, "*Le Moulin à Silence?*"

The couturier's mood changed abruptly. His face brightened and he laughed. "Oh, my little innocent, Madame Walewska, *Le Moulin à Silence* is the guillotine!"

By now Marie felt relaxed in Leroy's company, for he *had* taken her under his well-dressed wing, showering her with attention and compliments as he saw to her fittings and lessons in make-up and the care and styling of her hair.

"Madame Walewska," Leroy said on her fourth visit, "the pink gown will be delivered before the opera, as I promised. In the same carton you shall find two négligées."

"Two? Monsieur Leroy, I need but one."

"Ha! A third is on the drawing table."

"But it is just for home wear, Monsieur."

Leroy crossed his arms, squinted, and cast a wicked smile. "Ah, but the best entertainment occurs at home. *Non?*" His high-pitched laugh now matched the smile.

Marie felt herself coloring to the roots of her hair.

Wednesday, 17 February

Marshal Duroc escorted Marie to the Théâtre Français to see *Waclaw*, a Polish-themed play starring Napoleon's friend, Francois-Joseph Talma. "He's in his mid-forties and at his prime," Napoleon had said. Marie became absorbed in the lavish production. With his strong, distinctive facial features and a thickening physique, Tamla played the amorous but prattling Polish husband, a character type she recognized from Warsaw society. The character interacted in amusing ways with a French bride who knew her own mind and wasn't afraid to speak it.

Marie was impressed by the fine detail of the costumes and especially the Warsaw setting that seemed so authentic that she found herself not in a theater box but in a suspension of disbelief.

At the end of the play, when Tamla took his third bow alone on the stage, he suddenly looked directly up to their box, smiled, and waved.

Marie sat paralyzed as hundreds of heads turned in their direction. Duroc waved back. "This is Napoleon's box, Madame Walewska. Would you like to meet Talma? I'm certain we would be welcomed backstage."

Still hesitant to be the focus of attention in Paris, Marie declined.

Saturday, 20 February 1808

By the time the carton arrived with the pink dress, Marie had worn each of her three dresses from home at least twice to various events and suppers. Napoleon was present sometimes, and when he was not, she took comfort in mingling with other attendees to whom Duroc introduced her, including officers of the three volunteer Polish Lancer regiments stationed at nearby Chantilly. Despite the enchantment of a bustling Paris, the opportunity to speak her native language on such occasions made her long for Poland.

The cleverly constructed carton stood tall, allowing for the gown and négligées to be safely transported on hangers without danger of wrinkling.

"Oh, Madame," Hania cried as they removed the gown and placed it on the bed. "It's beautiful. Such a delicate pink."

"It is. Monsieur Leroy called it primrose. It's terribly low cut, however. I asked him to add a frill at the neckline to make it more modest. He just laughed."

Hania giggled. She ran her hand over the material. "It's silk."

"It is, and if you bring up that box at the bottom of the carton, I think we'll find that it holds the turban, gloves, and slippers."

Hania went to retrieve the box, but her attention was drawn to the négligées, one blue and one yellow, both very pale. Hania took out the blue one. The full-length *chemise de nuit* was made of a diaphanous silk gauze. She held it out against the light streaming in from the windows. "Ooh la la," she trilled.

Marie sighed. "I don't know whether I'll have the nerve to wear it, Hania."

"Well, Madame, for this, it would have been pointless to ask the monsieur for a frill."

Hania's wit could sometimes catch Marie by surprise. They laughed, sobered, and laughed again.

Upon entering the glittering lobby of the Académie Impériale de Musique, Marshal Duroc helped Marie remove her pelisse and proceeded to the cloak room.

Alone, Marie took in the richness of the surroundings: marble, gold, grand chandeliers, and ceilings painted with angels and saints.

She felt self-conscious. The primrose color and the lines draping from the belted bustline were perfect, but the neckline Leroy had designed was too daring by far. But no one questioned the couturier without being subjected to a tirade. Because the Académie Impériale de Musique was situated on Rue de la Loi, the same grand avenue as his shop, the couturier had insisted on supervising her toilette. "No lady's maid will prepare you like I will, Madame," he scoffed, sending her off with a self-satisfied smile less than an hour before. His staff had done her gown, makeup, and hair—tightly curled and swept forward, capped in the back by a toque.

Despite the crowd, she felt critical eyes and was relieved when Duroc returned to escort her to their seats. They settled into a draped box on the third level, near to the stage, as the theater filled to capacity.

The lights had not yet dimmed when Marie noticed movement in the box across the way, one level lower. An old gentleman was holding the chair for a woman in a highly-embroidered rose gown. Marie recognized it. Her heart raced. She had seen the distinctive gown on a tailor's dummy at Leroy's shop and had commented on it. She knew for whom it was being made.

Marie turned to Duroc. "Monsieur, the woman across the way, in the rose . . ." She paused, tongue-tied.

"Yes, Madame Walewska, that's the emperor's box."

"And that is . . ."

"Yes, that is Empress Josephine."

The theatre lights went down.

The notion that Napoleon's wife sat some yards away unnerved Marie. Nevertheless, when the actors appeared, she tried to lose herself in the story. The main characters in the opera *Le Devin du Village* were a pair of lovers, Colin and Collette, and the title character, the village soothsayer. The story, with its theme of distrust, gave her no relief. Marie felt a tightening at her chest. She fidgeted in her chair and found herself stealing glances at the box across the way.

"Are you all right?" Duroc asked, leaning over to her.

"What? —Yes, fine."

She kept her eyes on the stage until the blessedly short one-act play came to an end.

When the lights came up, Marie and Duroc stood and prepared to exit the box. As Duroc took her arm, Marie had the extraordinary feeling she was being watched.

"One moment," she said, gently pulling free. She turned around.

Empress Josephine and her escort were standing, too. But the empress had her head lifted and was peering through her opera glasses—directly at their box.

On the drive back to Rue de la Houssaye, Duroc sighed, saying, "I'm sorry, Madame Walewska. It was not the best choice of an opera."

It was late into the night when Marie heard the scurrying in the stairway outside her bedchamber. Duroc and the staff were preparing for the emperor's imminent arrival.

Marie pulled on a wrap as much for warmth as for modesty. Underneath, she wore the pale blue gossamer négligée. Wearing it would not have been her choice, but the night before, Napoleon had seen—and been wickedly delighted by—the one in light yellow, and he made her promise that she would wear the one in blue next.

Duroc directed two servants as they set up a late supper on a small table. The task was finished so that when Napoleon entered, they had their privacy.

Napoleon kissed Marie and they sat at the prepared table near the fireplace. Although he plied her with questions about her evening, citing his knowledge of the opera, Marie sensed his mind was elsewhere, and did not mention the empress's attendance or how it affected her.

She bided her time, but finally asked, "Napole, what is it?"

"I'm sorry. Am I being too serious?"

"Something is wrong."

"It's the Bourbons. They're everywhere, it seems, and are thorns in my side. Oh, and my brother Joseph, as well! I want him to take the throne of Spain, but he is hesitating."

"Spain? But you made him King of Naples."

"Yes, Marie." Napoleon sighed. "And now I need him in Spain. Ferdinand has not been true to me. I want Joseph to take that throne."

"You think he can rule both?"

"No, I have de Murat in mind for Naples. You remember Joachim."

"Oh, yes, I remember." Marie recalled the preening marshal's entrance into Warsaw, as well as her friend Anna Potocka's saying that he had tried to seduce her, even while staying as a guest in her household. And it was well-known that he hoped to one day sit on Poland's throne. She would be only too grateful if Napoleon kept him at a distance.

"Enough of politics!" Napoleon blurted. "I do believe you have on the blue négligée under that robe, Marie. Am I correct?"

"It is." Marie felt herself coloring at his sudden shift of focus. She had not been brave enough to sit for the meal in the revealing négligée.

"While the robe is cotton, may I assume the négligée is silk?"

"Yes. Napole, Monsieur Leroy went on at length about how you've saved the silk trade in Lyon."

"Did he?" Napoleon asked. "You know, Lyon was the center of the silk trade before the Rising. The fact that Louis XIV inspired the widespread fashion of Lyonnais silks led to the condemnation of silk by the revolutionaries, who brought down the industry." He paused, adding in a light tone, "Of course, most of its patrons fled France or were sent to Madame la Guillotine."

"A terrible time, Napole. —But luxury is again in fashion."

"Yes, and I've banned trade with England, so should you acquiesce and come to Court, you won't see the Indian muslin worn there. It's an English import. I require formal dress at Court, so you *will* see French cotton, velvet, and silk. Lyon and the entire textile industry are thriving once again, I'm proud to say. You see, Marie, France is everything to me, just as Poland is to you."

I've at least established that much, Marie thought.

"Now, Marie," the night is fleeting, and I have an ardent wish to view the blue négligée."

―⚜―

Napoleon most often dozed off after the lovemaking, but tonight he reached over to the side table for his gold snuff box. After sniffing, he lay quietly, eyes open to the bed's canopy.

"You're in deep thought," Marie said, turning toward him.

"Am I? I suppose I am."

"You're worried."

"This war with England goes on and on, Marie. In an effort to keep the English warships away from Portugal and Spain I invaded them both. It was a miscalculation. Talleyrand tried to warn me—before I dismissed him. You see, the damn priests have raised the patriotic spirit—and anger—of the Spanish people against us. They've raised a significant army. My forces there are now locked in an impossible situation."

Marie lay back, her arms crossed over a churning stomach. She knew where this was leading.

Napoleon continued citing specifics of the situation and looming battles, speaking as if he were talking to himself, gaming out the possibilities.

At long last, he stopped, his head turning on the pillow toward her. "I'm sorry, Marie. I forgot myself. Forgive me."

"Napole?"

"Yes, my Marie?"

"When will you leave?"

―⚜―

Marie helped Hania retrieve one of the trunks that had been stored in an empty room.

"So, you don't mind leaving Paris, Hania?" Marie asked once they had it opened in the center of the bedchamber.

"Oh, no, Madame! I miss Poland. I miss the language. Oh—and I miss the food!"

Marie laughed. "So do I, Hania. So do I."

"But you are sad, too. Yes, Madame?"

Marie tossed off a smile, shrugged, and turned away.

———⁂———

Unwilling to witness Napoleon's departure for the Spanish front, Marie insisted on leaving for Poland at once. She could not bear to watch him leave, knowing there would be months of separation. He begged her to stay, and it was all she could do to deny him.

The driver and four mounted soldiers escorted Marie and Hania out of Paris. Benedykt was not one of them. He had no clearance to leave his command, he told her, suggesting that his orders would take him to the Spanish front, sooner or later.

As the carriage rumbled over the bridge at Mainz, the landscape changed, leaving behind France and the hints of a mild spring for colder air and snow, deeper as they travelled.

With the cold came second thoughts. Should she have stayed in Paris? But why stay without Napoleon? To attend theater and Opera? To become a curiosity? To be fitted for more gowns and négligées? Leroy had tempted her with swatches of rare materials and colors in an effort to convince her—at Napoleon's request, she was certain. Napoleon told her, too, that Josephine was eager to meet her. The idea seemed absurd.

No, without Napoleon, the pull of her homeland was strong.

46

Friday, 25 March 1808

Exhausted from days of travel, yet exhilarated to return to Warsaw, Marie stepped out of the coach in front of the Walewski townhome. She had no desire to return to the family home at Kiernozia, where she would always be seen as the daughter, nor to the Walewski Palace in Walewice, where her sisters-in-law ruled.

Choosing the Warsaw residence posed a risk. Marie had no idea where Anastase was and didn't expect a warm reunion if he was at the townhome. However, she trusted her husband's predictable nature—after visiting Bad Gastein last fall, he had likely gone on to Rome, where he would stay until Easter.

Her assumption proved correct when she found the townhome in an uproar of trunks and bustling staff. Her niece, Józia, had married Adam Walewski, Marie's nephew by marriage. The couple had lived at the Walewice Palace, and Marie had come to like the lovely and high-spirited Józia.

"Oh, Marie!" Józia cried, her face lighting up. She hurried over and crushed her in a hug. "It's so wonderful to see you again! Truly! You look amazing! Paris has done you well." She pulled back to admire her. "I don't think I've ever seen you more beautiful!" Then, blinking as if remembering something, she added, "Anastase isn't here, Marie!" She paused and winked. "But of course, you knew that already. Clever girl. My mother and her sisters admired your sharpness."

Marie felt blood rising into her face. She didn't tell her it had been a gamble.

"I'm thrilled you're here," Józia continued. "We'll go out often, stir up some gossip. The diarists will have to work on Sundays to keep up with us."

After a late lunch, Marie finally understood just why Józia thought they would be worthy of gossip—and why she was at the townhome. Her niece's revelation stunned her. Józia was no longer a Walewska; she had divorced Adam to marry General John Witte.

Marie sat speechless. Józia came from the noble Lubormirski family, and her marriage had been carefully arranged between the two families. "But your family—"

"Ha! They were not pleased. They railed against Napoleon's divorce laws. But what could they do? I fell in love with John. They know my temperament. Oh, I won't travel home for a while. So, that's that. You'll meet John at supper."

"And the Walewski family?" Marie asked, using her open hands to indicate their surroundings.

"Oh, why are we *here*, you mean? Anastase is very generous and on good terms with John. They are both involved in the Governing Commission. As for Adam, our relationship has not changed very much." Józia laughed. "It's almost as if I have two husbands."

James Conroyd Martin

Marie caught the hint in Józia's teasing voice, realizing she was subtly comparing her situation to Marie's.

At supper, General John Witte was as Marie remembered him—serious, reserved, and deeply interested in military and political matters. Yet, despite his somber nature, his heart had been captured by a woman whose interests were far more social and carefree.

Later, Marie pondered the unlikely pairing. Józia was a free spirit whose unique charm could conquer a conventional man.

Still, the idea of having two husbands, as Józia had intimated, was unsettling.

47

Saturday, 24 December 1808
Wigilia (Christmas Eve)

MARIE SAT AT HER DRESSING table, absentmindedly tapping the note from Napoleon that had arrived mid-month. Downstairs, preparations were underway for the *Wigilia* supper. She had insisted on a quiet meal with no guests, but her mother had arrived earlier and wouldn't be deterred. Marie knew she had no choice but to join the celebration soon.

Her gaze drifted back to the letter. Napoleon was still in Spain. Still. The months dragged on, and his letters were few and short. She studied this one, hoping to find meaning between the lines.

Information from Spain did trickle in through Monsieur Jean-Charles Serra, the French Resident Minister in Warsaw, who had visited Marie just two days after her arrival from Paris in March. Napoleon had instructed him to ensure her well-being and report back to him with updates. That Napoleon kept her in his thoughts lifted her at times when she felt low. Her son kept her spirits up, also. Two weeks earlier, she had sent Hania to Walewice to collect Antoni on the pretext that it was for the holiday season and the aunts allowed her to take him.

Through Serra, she learned of both successes and setbacks for the French in Spain, not only against the surprisingly strong Spanish Army, but also against English forces that had landed in several ports. In the effort to reach and take

Madrid, the Polish lancers had lived up to their legendary prowess by opening a pass through the mountains of Guadarrama, so narrow and heavily protected by Spanish artillery that it was thought to be impassable. Serra had no news about Benedykt, whose legion it was that won the day.

Shortly after Marie greeted her mother downstairs, Minister Serra arrived and they sat to supper with John and Józia Witte.

"Where's Antoni?" the countess asked.

"He's upstairs with Hania, Mother."

"And Anastase? In Rome for the winter, I presume?"

Marie nodded, glancing at Serra. He shifted nervously, and she silently confirmed her suspicion that Napoleon had likely instructed Anastase, through Serra, to keep his distance, and her husband had obeyed.

"You have such a handsome grandchild, Madame Łączyńska," Józia trilled. "He's growing so fast. I'm certain his father will be amazed."

Marie's mother shot a curious look at Józia as the table went silent. Everyone had been avoiding mention of Anastase's relationship to Antoni.

Józia looked up from her plate, eyes wide, suddenly aware of her faux pas.

"Quick to steer the conversation away, Marie asked, "Have you heard from Benedykt, Mother?" It was a question at top of mind, but she had been afraid to ask, afraid of the possibilities.

"I have, Marie. A rather long letter arrived yesterday. He is well."

"Thank God," Marie whispered.

"That *is* good news," Monsieur Witte said.

"Oh, we were out this afternoon," Józia chimed, "weren't we, John? And all the capital is abuzz about how *our* legions crashed through those mountains. What mountains were those, John?"

"The Guadarrama, Józia. The pass is called Somosierra."

"Oh, well, it was a lovely victory, thanks to the Poles! We must raise our glasses to toast them." Józia lifted her glass, its fill of red wine nearly gone. "To the health and glory of the victors!" she cried, and everyone followed suit.

The countess took a sip, set her wine glass down, and cleared her throat. "A victory, yes, Józia," she said, "but not lovely, not lovely at all."

The table went silent.

"What did Benedykt write, Mother?" Marie asked.

Her mother sighed. "Benedykt's former superior, Marshal Berthier, warned Napoleon that the pass would be nearly impossible. But the emperor ignored him, and instead of calling on his more experienced Old Guard and infantry, sent in the Polish lancers. Benedykt wrote that they rode up, full of bravado, calling out, *'Vive l'Empereur!'* They carried sabres and pistols—but not their lances, which would've hindered them." The countess took another sip of her wine while her audience sat spellbound.

"Mother?" Marie asked delicately, noticing that tears were forming in her eyes.

The countess squared her shoulders. "Napoleon had Benedykt held back so that he could only watch as the legion moved up the mountain. No more than half survived."

"Tragic," Madame Łączyńska," Minister Serra said. "Too many lost, but those that survived broke through the lines, and the Spanish fell back in retreat."

The countess shot the minister a dark look. "At what cost, Minister Serra? What cost?" She turned to Marie. "Marie, you knew the captain who led the charge, Jan Kozietulski, our neighbor."

"Yes, Mother, a handsome man with blond, curly hair. Is he . . .?"

"He was unhorsed, but survived," the minister interjected.

"Fortune was with him," Józia offered.

The countess turned to her. "One hundred were lost, Józia. One hundred."

Abashed, Józia dropped her eyes.

The countess's challenging gaze darted to Minister Serra.

"Their names will go in the history books, Madame Łączyńska," he said.

As servants brought in desserts, Marie's thoughts turned to her mother's bitter remarks about Napoleon's decision to sacrifice Polish lives. She longed to defend him, but had no words. And yet, Napoleon's decision to hold Benedykt back likely saved his life. She knew he had done it for her. She also knew it had to be humiliating for Benedykt.

She sat quietly, longing for this *Wigilia* celebration to end.

48

Spring 1809

MARIE SAT NEAR THE WINDOW of the reception room, overlooking Bednarska Street, watching as Hania entertained Antoni with a wooden puzzle. She closed her eyes, trying to summon Napoleon's face, manner, and voice, but it was becoming increasingly difficult to do. Each passing month felt like another door closing between them.

Napoleon had left Spain in January, returning to Paris to shore up wavering political support. Any hope of seeing him soon faded with each report from Minister Serra. The French had struggled on the Iberian Peninsula after Napoleon's departure, especially after the arrival of English General Arthur Wellesley, whose military strategy Serra reluctantly admired.

Before Marie left France, Napoleon had voiced doubts about invading Spain and Portugal. "If only I had cut my losses, then," he lamented.

A new coalition formed against the French, consisting of the English, the Spanish rebels, and Austria. Austria had been defeated by Napoleon three times, and yet they were preparing for war again. "Too many French troops are mired in the peninsula," Serra told her.

"And Polish legions are there, as well!" Marie snapped.

The minister nodded. "In the meantime, Emperor Francis and the Austrians have had their nerves restored. We have to pray that Napoleon's bargain with Aleksander holds and Russia checks Austria before they can do damage."

Thursday, 20 April 1809

The damage *was* done. Eight days earlier, Austrian forces had invaded Bavaria, then turned toward the Duchy of Warsaw. "While we didn't expect them to wait to engage Napoleon, no one expected them to turn east, Marie," Serra had told her the day before. He added that General Józef Poniatowski and his forces had gone to confront the much greater Austrian army at Raszyn, some six miles southwest of Warsaw.

"But now they are outside our walls?" Marie shuddered. Warsaw itself was in danger of being occupied. "And Russia?" Marie asked. "What of the French-Russian alliance? Isn't Czar Aleksander nearby with the ability and duty to protect us?"

The minister scoffed. "Aleksander sits on our borders and does nothing. Something's afoot there, I'll wager. Something underhanded."

Before leaving, the minister had turned to Marie and took her hand. "I must tell you something, Marie."

Marie's heart caught. "What? —What, Minister Serra?"

"Your brother is at Raszyn, at the head of seven hundred and sixty lancers."

"My brother? —Benedykt! God help us!" This was the first she knew of his arrival in the Duchy of Warsaw. He had survived Spain, but would he survive the attack on Warsaw?

Marie prayed. For Benedykt, Warsaw, and Napoleon.

At times, she thought she heard the boom of artillery.

The next night, unable to sleep, Marie sat alone in the reception room.

The loud clang of the door knocker startled her just after midnight.

She froze, heart beating fast.

She heard a servant go to the door. Moments later, the butler appeared in the doorway. "Minister Serra, Madame," he announced.

"Good evening, Madame Walewska," the minister said.

Marie lacked the will to rise to receive him. Serra's return visit signaled disaster. "Monsieur?" Marie asked, her voice barely above a whisper. "Please sit."

"We fought to a standstill," Serra said, taking a deep breath. "We were outnumbered—only fifteen thousand of us, while they had double that."

"And, so?"

"General Poniatowski secured a truce. Even the Austrians respect him. Archduke Ferdinand is allowing him to withdraw his forces to the eastern bank of the Vistula. But Warsaw will be occupied by noon tomorrow."

"The prince is simply abandoning the capital to the Austrians?"

"He made a tactical decision, Madame Walewska. He doesn't have the strength to protect the city. Word has it that he'll take the fight south, gathering reinforcements along the way."

"Are we occupied? The city is so quiet."

"Indeed, it's like a graveyard. We are in a grace period. We have but hours."

"God save us all," Marie whispered.

Serra cleared his throat. "Members of the duchy's government are preparing to take refuge at Toruń."

"I see. Is there news about my brother?"

Serra shook his head. "Not yet, Madame."

Marie struggled to hold back tears.

"I promised the emperor that I'd look after your welfare," Serra continued, "so I must *insist* that you go to Toruń."

"Toruń?"

"Yes, the Austrians know of your relationship to Napoleon."

Marie nodded, realizing at once what he meant. "So, I'd be of value to them as a hostage?" Her stomach knotted.

"A carriage will arrive for you just before first light, Madame Walewska. You must be ready. Take only what's necessary."

"I'll have Hania prepare Antoni at once," Marie said.

"No, Madame Walewska," the minister said, his tone sharp. "Send them to Walewice. You must travel alone."

Marie obeyed, reluctantly. She had kept Antoni once he had arrived for Christmas, and now she cringed at having to return him to the aunts.

49

Mid-May 1809

IN TORUŃ, MINISTER SERRA SETTLED Marie in the townhome of an elderly count. "He's not well, nor is he especially companionable. It's best that way, Madame Walewska," Serra advised. "Best to avoid gossip. The staff will see to your needs, and I'll call on you daily."

True to his word, Serra kept her informed. The Grande Armée quickly entered Austria, and Napoleon's legendary strategy outmaneuvered the larger Austrian forces, allowing the emperor to enter Vienna and occupy Schönbrunn Palace on 13 May. Marie couldn't help but enjoy the irony—Emperor Francis had lost his beloved palace while his forces under Archduke Ferdinand occupied Warsaw. She recalled the Polish proverb: "The doorstep of the palace is slippery."

Soon after, Marie received a note from Napoleon, instructing her to come to Vienna as soon as possible.

"When will I be able to leave, Minister Serra?"

The minister shrugged. "Emperor Francis may not have his palace, but he has yet to sue for peace. When he is finally beaten, he'll give up Warsaw and we'll return."

"Why not just go on to Vienna from here?"

Serra shook his head. "You'll need things, I suspect."

"I can make do."

"It's about appearances, Madame Walewska. You'll need something to tell friends."

"A story, you mean?" She suddenly understood. Gossip. "So, I won't be mistaken for a laundress, cook, or mistress?"

"Exactly," Serra replied, grinning.

July 1809

The wait was agonizing, but at last things began to shift. In the first week of July, Napoleon won a two-day battle at Wagram, though at a great cost of lives. Meanwhile, General Poniatowski redeemed himself in Marie's eyes by retaking a large piece of Galicia and the old capital of Kraków. In so doing, he lured Archduke Ferdinand into vacating the capital in order to engage him, thus allowing Marie to return to Warsaw and prepare for her journey to Vienna.

Luck was with Marie upon entering the Warsaw townhome.

"Your husband has been here the past week, Marie," Józia Witte announced, a sly smile tugging at her rouged lips. "But he left for Walewice just yesterday."

"Oh," Marie said, secretly relieved but keeping her voice neutral.

"Your maid Hania is here, however."

"Good." Something had gone right. She had requested Serra to have Hania brought back after she delivered Antoni to Walewice.

Later, as she and Hania packed a second trunk, Józia knocked and entered.

"You're leaving us, Marie," she said, her tone teasing. "But you've only just returned."

Marie turned toward her husband's niece. "I'm going to take the waters at Bad Gastein."

"Are you?" Józia raised an eyebrow, her gaze sharp.

Marie flushed and quickly turned back to her task, aware that Józia, a silly, superficial woman at times, could read a situation at a glance.

"So, that's the story?" Józia asked, tilting her head.

Marie sent Hania downstairs on an errand. Turning to Józia, she asked, "Story?"

"The fiction we're to circulate! You've never shown any interest in taking the waters."

"You've spoken to Minister Serra!" Marie exclaimed.

"No, I haven't, Marie."

"What makes you think—"

"Because," Józia interrupted, wagging a finger, "that's exactly what I'd say in your place. Napoleon is in Vienna, I hear."

Marie laughed. She knew she had been bested.

Józia crossed her arms and grinned. "Oh, Aunt Marie, I know how to make that weak story stronger."

"What? —How?"

"Let John and me come along. I'd love to see Vienna and get a look at Schönbrunn Palace."

Marie didn't have to ask why their coming would improve the story. With Anastase's niece and husband acting as chaperones, no one would question her. She wet her lips. "Will John agree?"

Józia's smile turned wicked. "I have a knack for persuasion. Just wait, I shall have him in the palm of my hand."

"I suspect you will," Marie said, hurrying over to embrace Józia. When she released her and drew back, their eyes met, and they shared a good laugh.

The next day they crowded into a carriage arranged by Minister Serra, who, after an exchange of notes, wrote that he was very pleased that the Wittes would be accompanying Marie. Of course, he was, Marie thought. He'd be able to relay to Napoleon that her relatives provided a perfect cover for her real destination.

They stayed a night in Kraków, where Józia casually mentioned to friends that they were accompanying Marie to Bad Gastein, where, she implied, they would meet up with the Count Walewski.

Four days later, they arrived in Vienna.

The Polish nobility of greater wealth than the Łączyński family often vacationed in Vienna, especially during *Karnawał* season. In their first year of marriage, Marie and Anastase had passed through, but Marie had caught only glimpses of the capital, and she was eager to see the city that had once been saved by King Jan Sobieski and his Winged Hussars from a Turkish jihad against all of western Europe.

The driver had been given two addresses. Marie was to stay in a nearby suburb, while the Wittes would first be dropped off at John Witte's cousin's city center home.

When they arrived, Józia urged Marie to come inside.

Marie smiled. "I think not, Józia. I want to settle in."

"Of course," Józia said "but you must promise to dine on occasion with us, and join us at the theater."

"I promise."

"Do you know how long you'll be staying in Vienna?"

Marie shrugged.

"Marie, tell me, why hasn't he arranged for you to stay at Schönbrunn Palace?" Józia pressed.

Before Marie could respond, Monsieur Witte answered as he helped his wife out of the carriage. "Too many eyes, too many ears, Józia. Now, let Marie get on."

Mödling lay some eight miles south of the city center, Duroc had told her. The carriage slowed as recent rains had caused deep potholes. It was a lovely old town, but eight miles?

As the carriage neared the house, Marie judged it as well built and dating to early in the previous century. When they pulled into the front, Marie noticed a sleek, unmarked carriage parked to the side. Her heart leapt. He was here, she thought. It had been so long.

Upon alighting, she saw Marshal Duroc hurrying down the front steps, a greeting on his lips, and her hopes faltered.

The marshal had read the question on her face. "No, Madame Walewska, the emperor is not here."

"Oh."

"Come inside. It's a beautiful house. Five bedrooms and room for the staff in the attic. You'll have four looking after you."

Moving past her disappointment, Marie grew more intrigued by the house. It had a grand reception room and a dining room with a balcony overlooking vineyards.

"He'll come tomorrow, I have no doubt," the marshal said. "The timing of your arrival was most serendipitous. I had only just stopped by to check on last minute things with the staff."

"Ah, then you had a hand in selecting it?"

Duroc shrugged, slightly embarrassed. "Just the same, Madame Walewska, should he wish to take the credit, you won't contradict him, will you?"

"No, I won't," Marie said, laughing.

Marie sat at the side of the four-poster bed, still groggy from sleep, when the staccato sound of boots echoed up the hall. Her heart sped up.

A knock came at the door, and it opened before Marie could respond.

Napoleon entered, removing his hat as he moved across the room, boot steps muted on the Turkish rug.

"I thought I must be seeing things," Marie said. "I didn't expect you. You review your troops in the morning."

Napoleon pulled her to her feet and embraced her, his scent of eau-de-cologne wafting about them. "I can review my troops anytime," he whispered in her ear.

"Be careful, Napole," she said, laughing, "I'm barefoot."

"So you are, my dearest!" He drew back and winked. "I wanted to whisk you off to the Palace so that we could spend the day together."

"Really? The *whole* day?"

"Yes! Am I not the emperor?" he teased.

"Ah! Then if you'll allow me to dress . . ."

Napoleon put a forefinger to her lips. "Not yet," he said. "First, we lock the servants out." He grinned, his hands brushing her shoulders. "Ah, you wore the blue one. The yellow was lovely, but the blue brings out your sapphire eyes."

Marie recalled little more than the impressive exterior of Schönbrunn on the pass-through to Bad Gastein with Anastase. Today, however, as the carriage rolled down a long chestnut-lined boulevard, she gaped in amazement. The palace loomed ahead, its twin golden imperial eagles glinting in the sunlight atop the gate piers. The wrought-iron gates opened, and they were waved through.

"We're coming into the Parade Court, Marie," Napoleon said. "It's big enough for seven or eight thousand troops."

The light ochre palace swelled in size as they drew closer. "It has nearly fifteen hundred rooms," Napoleon continued, "modeled on Versailles. My rooms are particularly special."

Marie forced a tight smile, irritated that she had been sent to a house miles away.

When the carriage pulled up to an inconspicuous entrance on the east wing, they alighted, hurried into the building, and climbed a stairway to the first floor.

"This is the Hall of Ceremonies," Napoleon said, guiding her into a long room largely devoid of furniture. Its chief features were a grand crystal chandelier, imposing paintings of the Habsburgs, and the Austrian emperor's dais.

He led her through a blue-and gold Chinese-inspired room—his personal reception room—coming to stop in what he called the Vieux Laque Room. "This was Marie Therese's memorial to her husband," Napoleon said, walking up to the large portrait of Holy Roman Emperor Franz Stephan. "She gave him sixteen children and survived him for many years. Of course, she was much younger. She ruled alone for four decades. Quite effectively, they say." His voice dropped to a whisper: "Imagine—a woman. A clever one, at that. When her husband was crowned, she stood in the audience, refusing a crown and showing her independence. No doubt that worked in her favor when the emperor died."

"Because, as a woman," Marie interjected, "Marie Therese couldn't inherit the imperial title. Sad, isn't it, Napole? And yet, within a few short years, she was being addressed as *Empress Marie Therese*."

Napoleon's gaze snapped back to Marie and lingered there, as if deciphering something new. He suddenly laughed. "Perhaps she was more effective than our contemporary Francis who was foolish enough to tangle with me a fourth time." He paused, then pointed to a double portrait at the right. "Two of their sons are there, Joseph and Leopold, and on the opposite wall," he said, pivoting to the left, "is Leopold's wife with several of *their sixteen* children. Is there magic in the number, do you suppose, Marie?"

Not for the mother, she thought. "A coincidence, more likely, Napole," she replied.

Napoleon pondered the painting for a few moments, then shifted back toward the main portrait of Franz Stephan.

As Marie took in the gold-painted French furniture, she heard him murmur, "Dynasty, dynasty, dynasty."

"Is there another room to view?" Marie asked, feeling vaguely uncomfortable.

"What? Oh—yes, my bedchamber!" Napoleon took her hand. "Come along."

Upon entry, he asked, "What do you notice about it, Marie?"

"Aside from the deep red bed hangings, I see that emerald green runs through the wallpaper and the Turkish rug."

"What else?"

Marie surveyed the room again. "Ah! There are no huge paintings of the Royals. Only mirrors, large ones, on each wall!"

"Exactly!" Napoleon took her by the elbow and turned her so they faced the largest gilt mirror. "None of the Austrian royals are here to bother us."

"Maybe you should call it the *Napoleon Room*."

"Ha!" Napoleon turned to Marie and lifted her chin, his gaze drawing her in like a tide. "Brilliant!" he exclaimed, kissing her. He drew back. "We have one last room, Marie," he said. "It's called the Porcelain Room. Come!"

It was a small, narrow room, its walls covered in wooden decorations and dozens of blue and white paintings imitating Eastern porcelain.

Napoleon put his arm around Marie's waist. "This will be your room, Marie, when you are here and I am tending to business—or when you can't bear me any longer! You can use it for letter writing or embroidery. And you have that lovely fainting couch, should you need to lie down. The door on the far wall is locked on this side. Leave it that way so that no one will come in by mistake. Your only exit is the way we came, back into what you've christened the Napoleon Room."

Marie pulled back slightly as he bent to kiss her. "Napole," she said.

Napoleon blinked. "Yes, dearest?"

Marie brought her shoulders back. "Why must I reside in a house so far away, down a muddy road full of potholes? Why can't I stay here?"

Napoleon cleared his throat. "I'm sorry for that, my pet, but we must be discreet."

"But you seemed to care less about discretion in Paris."

"Did I? Well, discretion is the word, Marie. Duroc will see you home later tonight and he'll come for you tomorrow. I'll warn him about the road. Oh, you'll forgive me when you see what I've planned for tomorrow afternoon. Pray for some sunshine."

"But, Napole, why can't it be like it was in Finckenstein? I didn't mind the seclusion. Why—"

Napoleon's finger pressed against her lips.

Discussion about the house in Mödling came to an end.

50

THE DAY WAS WARM AND sunny when the unmarked carriage arrived at the Mödling house. Marie climbed aboard to find Napoleon, not Marshal Duroc, waiting inside.

"This is a surprise," she said, settling beside him and exchanging cheek kisses.

"As will be our destination, my Marie."

"Where are we going?" she asked as the carriage headed north, toward Vienna.

"You'll see soon enough." Napoleon pulled her close.

Marie sniffed the air, taking in the aroma of cooked meat. Looking around, she noticed a luncheon basket tucked under the opposite bench.

The window curtains were drawn for secrecy, but she peeked out every few minutes. The carriage veered off the main road, bumping along a gravel byway, passing through small villages and then into a forested area.

"We're moving toward the River Danube, yes?" she asked.

"Yes, but that's not our destination. We're in the northeastern foothills of the eastern Alps."

Marie's heart caught. "Then we are near Kahlenberg Mountain!"

"We are. At its very foot, Marie." Napoleon knocked on the front side of the carriage, and it slowed to a stop. He stepped out and helped Marie down. The driver had chosen a shady spot on the edge of a vineyard.

"Oh! Thank you, Napole. Thank you!" Marie moved quickly around the carriage and gazed up at the thickly wooded mountainside.

"What are you thinking, my pet?" Napoleon asked, coming up behind her.

"I'm thinking how difficult the hussars must have found the descent in 1683."

"Indeed."

Napoleon spread a red blanket on the ground and set the luncheon basket nearby. "Wait and see what delicious things they've packed for us."

"Oh! I can't eat a bite. I just want to stand here and imagine the hussars flying down the mountainside with their lances—and wings at their back."

"Very well." Napoleon dropped onto the blanket and sat cross-legged. "I know a bit of the history, but tell me what you know."

Marie pointed toward the city. "For two months, Vienna had been under siege by the Ottoman Empire. The city waited for relief as thousands of Turks camped outside its walls, tunneling toward the city. Relief came from the Holy Roman Empire and the Polish-Lithuanian Commonwealth on 12 September. While the imperial forces fought below, King Jan Sobieski led his winged hussars down the Kahlenberg, where they had camped on 11 September."

"You're better than a history book, Marie," Napoleon said. "Prettier, too."

Marie ignored him and continued, "Sobieski had a force of Tatars with him, but below a camp of twenty thousand Tatars had sided with the Ottomans. When they caught sight of Sobieski's winged hussars assembled on the mountain, they broke camp and deserted the Turks. Their leader is said to have warned the Grand Vizier, saying 'Sobeieski wins. Sobieski always wins.' The Grand Vizier, however, remained."

"In for a penny, in for a pound," Napoleon mused.

Marie turned to him. "What?"

Napoleon laughed. "It's from an old play, an English comedy. It means, if you've invested a penny in something, you might as well make it a pound."

Marie afforded the emperor an indulgent smile. "Anyway, as the imperial forces pressed from the north, Sobieski ordered a charge down the mountain. Eighteen thousand soldiers, swords drawn and seventeen-foot lances at the ready. Sobieski himself led three thousand winged hussars."

"I've heard that the wind rushing through their wings made a whistling sound that frightened both the enemy and their horses."

"A few Turks lived to tell that tale, but the *sight* must have been terrifying enough because the heavy cavalry smashed through the Ottoman lines and sent them fleeing, the Grand Vizier in the lead. It was the final blow. Vienna was saved!"

"Sobieski wins." Napoleon clapped his hands together. "Had the allies been delayed even a day, the Habsburg capital would have fallen—and most likely, all of western Europe."

So, despite his levity, he *did* understand. Marie looked up into the heights of the Kahlenberg. "Exactly," she said, conjuring in her mind the descent of the winged hussars. She released a deep sigh as her arms broke out in gooseflesh.

Marie adapted to life at the Mödling house, where her staff attended to her every need. She would arrive at the palace after Napoleon's troop reviews, and they would ensconce themselves in Napoleon's bedchamber for much of the afternoon—though sometimes interrupted by state affairs. After sixteen months apart, their reunion was sweeter and their lovemaking more passionate than ever.

The summer of peace brought balls, plays, and operas. Napoleon himself funded the import of Italian and French singers and actors. Marie, still posing as a relative of the Wittes, attended productions of *Griselda* and *The Barber of Seville* at the Vienna Opera House and the comic opera *Nina*, at the Schönbrunn Palace's own theatre. They took drives along the Danube in the unmarked carriage or disguised themselves—sometimes as peasants, sometimes as gardeners—for secluded walks through the Prater, losing themselves among the paths and flowering alleyways of the public park. Once, coming upon a neighboring vineyard, Marie raced away, forcing the emperor to chase her. She circled back to the flowers before he caught up and the two ended up lying in a patch of lavender, laughing and kissing.

Teodor arrived one day with news: he had been attached to Napoleon's Chief of Staff, Marshal Berthier.

"For how long?" Marie asked.

Teodor shrugged. "Who's to say? I'll be keeping an eye on you, so I was told."

Clearly, Benedykt's involvement in the failed coup against Prince Poniatowski had cost him Napoleon's trust, and Teodor was now her guardian.

As weeks passed and Marie remained in Vienna, attending palace events and parties, often in the emperor's circle, the locals began to notice. She saw their knowing glances and heard whispers behind fans, but she was too caught up in the joy of her love for Napoleon to care. Still, one question lingered: Why did Napoleon care so much about the opinions of Viennese society?

One evening, as Napoleon busied himself with couriers, Marie was reading in the Porcelain Room when she heard a noise from the locked adjoining room. Marie's intrigue overrode Napoleon's caution not to unlock the door.

Day after day, what lay beyond that door had increasingly tantalized her so that she could no longer resist.

The bolt slid easily and just as the door opened, she heard the far door close. Someone had just left. Taking a lighted chamberstick, she stepped inside. The room was filled with exquisite miniatures, busts, and paintings, most of which seemed to be merely stored there.

A noise came from behind, and Marie pivoted to see Napoleon in the doorway, his brow furrowed, eyes narrowing.

"Marie! What are you doing?" He approached her.

Her mouth went dry. "I—I heard a noise, and I became curious. I'm sorry, Napole."

"Did you?" He seemed at once amused but stern.

Marie couldn't read his tone. She had crossed a line and regretted having ignored his warning. For the first time since they had become intimate, he sent a wave of fear through her. She nodded, swallowing hard. "Forgive me, Napole. Someone was in there."

"You are a curious creature, Marie."

She shrugged.

A long moment passed as he studied her.

And then his mouth broke into a smile. "Too curious for your own good, but you could never do wrong in my eyes, my Marie."

Relief washed over her. She touched her heart. "It seems like a storeroom, Napole."

"And so, it is." Napoleon reached out, took the chamberstick from her and held it high. "It's *my* storeroom. These are all the works of masters, and they are mine."

"Yours?"

"Yes, of course! Francis has assembled quite a treasure trove in his fourteen hundred and forty rooms. Here, Marie, look at this sculpture. It's by Antonio Canova and that one over there is of Marie Antoinette as a child. She was maybe six years old, so when she gets to Paris, she'll still have her head." He laughed.

"Do you mean you're *taking* these things?"

"These and a good many others. I have fifteen or twenty such *storerooms*, as you called it."

Marie couldn't suppress a gasp.

"Oh, don't be shocked, Marie. It's the way of things."

"The way of things?"

"War, Marie, war. Tonight, I'll introduce you to Monsieur Vivant Denon. No doubt it was Vivant who was taking inventory when you heard someone in here. He's what I call my 'cultural czar.' He's the Director of the Musée Napoleon, and typically, he'll follow me into a conquered capital to make his choices. He did so in Egypt and now here."

Marie fell silent, remembering Germaine de Staël's account about the looting the French had done in Italy. Even the Madonna from the Sistine Chapel had been carted off.

"Marie?"

"Rome, too?"

"Rome, too. I know a little about art, but his expertise is unparalleled."

"What will you do with it all?"

"Well, Vivant always chooses a few treasures for Josephine. After all, she's the one who suggested I engage him. My museum will take most of it. If not, I'll build an addition."

"The Musée Napoléon?"

"Yes, I intend to make Paris the new Rome."

Marie recalled Madame de Staël's pronouncement that Napoleon had the temerity to create for himself the profile of a Roman emperor: "Just look at the painting he had commissioned for his investiture," she had said. "It's in his stance, in his clothing, even in the coiffure."

"But, Napole, fifteen or twenty storerooms here at Schönbrunn. It's so much to take from someone with whom you're in peace treaty talks." Marie removed her hand from his hold to gesture with a palm upturned. "It seems so, so—"

"Shocking?"

"Yes."

"Greedy? Wolfish?"

In answer, Marie tilted her head slightly.

"Ah, Marie, the victor of the battle chooses his own rewards. And—now that the subject of the treaty has come up, I have news."

"News?"

"Yes, let's sit down, shall we?"

They sat side by side on the settee. Napoleon took one of Marie's hands and pressed it lightly in both of his. "I've not forgotten your most fervent wish, my Marie. The courier today assured me that my demands are likely to be met by Francis."

"What—what did you request?" Marie's heart raced.

"Patience, Marie, let me tell you what we stand to receive." Napoleon cleared his throat. "Austria loses the Duchy of Salzburg to Bavaria and a good number of lands and cities to France, including access to the Adriatic Sea. And Poland? Poland will have Kraków returned, as well as the lands of Zamość. Nearly two million people will fall under Polish governance again."

"Oh, Napole, that's wonderful!"

"I hoped to please you."

"You have!" Marie hugged him.

Allowing some seconds to pass, Napoleon disengaged, saying, "Oh, and lest I forget, Western Galicia will be returned, also."

"Just *Western* Galicia, Napole? The eastern part of the province was ours, also."

"You're not satisfied, my Marie?" Napoleon pulled a pouting expression.

Marie straightened her back and turned toward him. "Eastern Galicia is to remain in Russian hands, then?"

Napoleon nodded.

"You don't want to irritate your friend Czar Aleksander, is that it?"

"Oh—what a foreign secretary you would make! Friend? Not really, Marie. Alas, however, you're right. I don't want to test him at this juncture." Napoleon squeezed Marie's hand. "But, my dear, one day with the help of Austria, and my—*your*—Polish lancers, Russia will be brought to heel. And then, your dream will be realized."

Marie stared into the calm-sea eyes and thought the honesty and determination she saw there sincere. It was enough.

51

September 1809

MARIE SAT WITH THE WITTES in a box at the Vienna Opera House, attending *Il Matrimonio Segreto*. Marshal Duroc had described the opera as a drama spiced with comedy and characters at cross-purposes. From her chair in the third-level box, she could see Napoleon and Duroc in a second-level box across the way. Napoleon occasionally glanced up and flashed a secret smile. If only she were sitting with him—

Józia leaned in close, whispering before the curtain went up. "Marie, since we've arrived in Vienna, no one is more talked about," she said. "Not just men noticing you, either. Downstairs, I heard one woman raving about your *bewitching* complexion."

"Bewitching?" Marie laughed. "Words cost nothing."

"Oh, it's not just your appearance. Marie, you've changed here in Vienna. You have a new vibrancy about you. As if you are perfectly content."

"Not perfectly, but that's very kind of you to say, Józia," Marie said.

The overture began. Marie glanced across the opera house and caught Napoleon's eye. He smiled and winked.

She tried to follow the opera's plot but lost focus after a while. With operas, she sometimes often found herself losing the story but responding to the music, creating her own life events—real or imagined—that played out against the score. Tonight, as the comedic situations escalated, the plot—amidst the ongoing theme of secrecy, a wealthy count takes an unwanted interest in the heroine—Marie suddenly recognized the startling parallels to her own life. Her stomach clenched.

There was no daydreaming with the music after that.

After the opera, they returned to the palace. Marie sat on the settee near the big gold bed with red hangings while Napoleon poured two glasses of wine at a nearby table. Whether they'd spent their afternoons in the luxury of that bed—as they had that afternoon—didn't matter. Napoleon still made time for them in the evenings, before she was bundled off to Mödling.

"*Il Matrimonio Segreto* is an Italian work, Marie, but Domenico Cimarosa based his clever opera on a forty-year-old play entitled *The Clandestine Marriage* by two Englishmen—damn them!"

Napoleon delivered the glass of red wine to Marie and settled in next to her. "Didn't you enjoy it, my dear?"

"I did."

"But?"

"Didn't you notice any parallels?" Marie paused, continuing when he didn't respond. "The interfering count? The secrecy?"

Napoleon was silent for a minute, then shrugged. "Of course, there's your husband—and I suppose you're referring to my desire for secrecy." He paused. "But we will not experience the farcical climax. For that, we may be thankful."

Marie didn't reply. It was an easy answer, she thought, one that did not lessen her unease.

"The opera has nothing to do with us," Napoleon said. "Put it out of your mind." He pulled her close and kissed her, but she drew back immediately. "What is it, Marie? You winced—I saw you. Did I hurt you?"

"No, Napole, forgive me. I'm just tired. Please have Constant order the carriage to be brought around."

At the Mödling house, Marie stepped down from the coach and hurried up to her bedchamber, dismissing the maids. Tossing her cloak onto the bed, she went to the tall, gilt mirror. *Is it possible?* she asked herself.

She gently lowered her gown's bodice and examined her breasts. She drew in a sudden breath at the pain. No wonder she had nearly cried out when Napoleon crushed her to his military coat.

She studied her breasts. They were swollen, the area around the nipples tender, the veins visible. She had experienced this once before—when she realized she was *enceinte* with Antoni.

She had been caught unawares. It was often the case that she would miss one of her courses, something a doctor had once told her could be a result of the time she spent travelling in carriages.

She lost awareness of how many minutes she stood before the mirror. As she turned away, she caught her expression. She was smiling. *Sweet Jesus, there will be no sleep for me tonight.*

Even with having to live away from the Schönbrunn Palace, Marie had been happy, but now, knowing that she was carrying the emperor's child left her elated. She wanted to reach out and embrace the whole world. Still, as the carriage passed through the palace gates the next morning, wheels clattering on the paving stones, her heart beat with uncertainty. How would she tell Napoleon? How would he react?

Marie had been kept up much of the night, both thrilled by the prospect of giving birth to Emperor Napoleon Bonaparte's child—*their* child—and terrified by the complications it would bring to her life, complications that she deliberately left blurry in her mind for the present.

"Are you all right, Madame Walewska?" Marshal Duroc asked.

"What?" The voice startled Marie. She had forgotten for the moment that the marshal was seated next to her. "Yes, fine."

"It's just that you're different today, so quiet, so serious."

Marie afforded the marshal a genuine smile.

Marie's presence at Schönbrunn was less a secret than at Finckenstein, at least among the senior French staff, so that it was Marshal Berthier, who met her at ground level, informing her that the emperor was in consultation with a representative from the Netherlands in the Hall of Ceremonies. "I'll escort you to the emperor's rooms, Madame Walewska, but we must pass through there."

On the first floor, before entering the Hall of Ceremonies, Berthier turned to Marie and put his finger to his lips.

She could hear the emperor's raised voice, and as they crossed the floor, seemingly unnoticed, Napoleon's anger accelerated. Something in her stomach hardened. The timing was wrong, she worried.

"I'll leave you now, Madame Walewska," the marshal said, once they were in the Blue Chinese Salon. "Are you all right?"

That he repeated Marshal Duroc's question added to her anxiety. She had the sensation that things were moving too fast. When she twice assured him that she was fine, he left.

She entered the Vieux Laque Room and sat on the settee that had been placed in front of the huge painting of Emperor Franz Stephen I, Holy Roman Emperor. From a picture on the wall to her right, two of his sons smiled down at her; to her left, his granddaughter-in-law sat rather stiffly with the first three children of a brood that would number sixteen.

She waited. Somehow, and in a way she couldn't explain, the paintings unsettled her. What was it about these depictions of people long dead that had mesmerized Napoleon?

An hour passed.

At last, the door opened, and Napoleon strode into the room, his face calmer than she expected. "Marie! I'm sorry to keep you waiting, my love." He took her hands and guided her to her feet. He kissed her, then pulled back, concern etched on his face. "Are you well?"

"Let's sit down, Napole," she said softly.

They sat together, one of her hands in both of his. "What is it, Marie?"

Marie sat back against the settee. She expelled a long breath.

"Tell me, Marie."

Marie's chest lifted as she drew in a breath and blurted: "I'm going to have a baby, Napole."

Napoleon's face froze. "A baby?" He gasped.

"Your baby," she confirmed. Later, she would ask herself if she was trying to deflect the question some men in this situation might ask, one she couldn't bear to hear. He had to know she was true to him. *He had to know.*

His initial stunned reaction clouded, and he withdrew his hands, twisting away from her. He sat on the edge of the cushion, his back to her.

Marie felt as if she could choke on blind fear at his reaction. "Napole—"

Silence filled the room.

Marie placed her hand on his back. She felt something like shivers vibrating beneath the dark green military jacket. "Napole, are you unhappy?"

Napoleon gave no indication he heard her.

A minute passed. Then, another. The vibrations continued.

Finally, he turned toward her, his eyes red.

"You're crying, Napole," Marie whispered.

"Oh, Marie," Napoleon said, his voice cracking. "You have no idea what this means to me." He reclaimed her hand. "No idea," he muttered, before breaking into sobs.

52

"I'VE SENT TO PARIS FOR Doctor Corvisart, my personal physician," Napoleon announced the next day.

Marie put aside her embroidery and looked up at him from her chair as he paced. "You . . .you don't doubt—"

"Doubt you?" he blurted, swinging around to face her. "That you are correct in your own diagnosis? Oh, Marie, never! But I will have only the best for you."

Marie smiled and looked down. She had practiced several different ways of approaching his uncertainty regarding his ability in the bedroom, but now, in the moment, they all went out of her head. She merely blurted, "You do trust that I've been true, Napole?"

Napoleon fell to his knees in front of her and grasped her hands. "My sweet Marie, I know you've been true." His gaze held hers. "I would know if it were otherwise. I've not met a woman so sincere, so loving, so giving. And don't think I don't know it's been at a high cost to you." He punctuated his plea by squeezing her hands to the point of pain.

She saw that his eyes were wet.

Later, she would think back to his statement that he *would know if it were otherwise*, and her suspicion that he was keeping her under surveillance increased.

In the days leading up to the arrival of Doctor Corvisart, Napoleon kept Marie close. His words to her about the cost she had incurred replayed in her mind. It was true, she thought. And at home there were unknown costs to come. What of the future?

Here in Vienna, the treaty with Austria was about to be finalized. The details had been hammered out so that Napoleon's foreign minister Jean-Baptiste Nompère Champagny had only to wait for the Prince of Liechtenstein to arrive for the signing. At the completion of the treaty, Marie knew she would have to decide her future.

She had two options: return home or follow Napoleon to Paris.

Were she to return to the duchy—a married woman expecting the French emperor's child—how would she be greeted? Recently, Marie heard reports that she was being hailed as a patriot. However, in the main, Polish society remained conservative, unlike the liberal freedom of Paris society. Chances were that she might now be cast as a pariah.

What of Anastase? He had been surprisingly patient with her from the start of her affair with Napoleon. She knew his tolerance stemmed largely from his pride in his favored status and his awe of Napoleon, an awe that would likely fade once he saw his wife carrying another man's child. And then what? He could shame and abandon her.

And Mother? Marie brooded. Her mother had urged her on with the affair, but, convinced that it was fated to end, she attempted to prepare Marie for its dissolution. How would she handle the loss of face, the sheer ignominy? She knew in her heart what awaited her in the land that was once Poland: scandal.

And what if she were to choose France?

Though Paris had long accepted the king's mistresses, Marie knew from her previous visit that the presence of Empress Josephine would weigh heavily on her mind. *How can I show myself—large with the emperor's child—in public, much less in society?*

Ten days later, when Doctor Jean-Nicolas Corvisart arrived in Vienna, Marshal Duroc accompanied him to the Mödling house. It was evening and Marie had already retired when they were admitted to her bedchamber. Duroc introduced the doctor and quickly left the room.

Marie studied the Frenchman—still in his dusty travel clothes—his round face, high forehead and receding gray hair. He was of average height, heavier around the middle, and appeared to be in his mid-fifties.

The doctor began his examination, speaking little except to issue quiet instructions. Marie froze, unnerved by the unfamiliarity of the experience. Doctor Fabianski had never required her to disrobe, and she had successfully delivered Antoni with the help of a midwife.

After the examination, Corvisart closed his bag, stood and smiled. "I can safely relay to the emperor that you are in the best of health."

Marie pulled herself up against her pillow, clutching the covers to her breasts. "And?"

He caught her meaning at once. "Oh! I can assure him that you are indeed *enceinte*, Madame." He smiled again, a secretive sort of smile, the kind that might be accompanied by a wink.

Marie didn't like it.

Later that afternoon, Napoleon informed her, "Corvisart says you must rest for some weeks, Marie. These are important weeks. When you arrive at the palace each morning, he'll examine you."

Marie nodded, still unsettled by the doctor's contemptuous smile—and cold hands. Did he see her as a common courtesan, an opportunist? *If only he could examine my heart—and Napole's.*

"When Corvisart allows," Napoleon continued, "you are to travel very slowly, in the best carriage I can arrange, with slow horses. I suggest you ask the Wittes to accompany you to Paris. They can provide support."

And appearances, Marie thought, realizing for the first time that he *expected* her to choose Paris, rather than Poland.

Marie found great comfort in Hania, who proved very supportive. Having attended Marie through her time with bearing Antoni, she sensed Marie's condition immediately, adding a new French word to her vocabulary: "*enceinte*."

In the following days, Marie endured her morning appointments with Doctor Corvisart, knowing that the remainder of the day would be spent with Napoleon, who showered her with attention.

The more she thought about returning to France, the more doubts filled her mind. Her life had always been in Poland. What would her father, who had passed his love for Poland to her, think of her decision? And what about her mother, to whom she had just shared the news of her pregnancy in a letter? How would she react? Unable to bring herself to tell Anastase directly, she asked her mother to inform him. Together, they had arranged the marriage—together they would decide her future upon her return.

Her thoughts turned to little Antoni, now four. How was he adjusting to life among the Walewska sisters—cool, possessive women—except for Teresa and a niece or two? Did he miss his mother? To think that he might forget her often brought her to tears.

Finally, Marie made her decision: She would return to Poland and face her future.

Napoleon's joy at her company was clear, and so Marie kept her decision to herself. As days passed, her forced smiles and laughter were nothing more than those of an actress. She was miserable, not just because she couldn't tell him, but because she realized how much she would miss him. At Finckenstein, she had told him that she felt as if they were married. He kissed her and called her his "Polish wife." That bond she felt then had only deepened. Now, she couldn't think of Paris or the child she was carrying without thinking of Empress Josephine. Marie never aspired to replace her.

Thursday, 12 October 1809
Today, Marie thought, I'll tell him. After Corvisart's examination, she stood at the window of the Grand Gallery, looking out at Schönbrunn's wide esplanade where the daily review of troops was concluding. The colorful display of the soldiers' order, might, and loyalty to the emperor never failed to stir her.

But, as Napoleon stepped down from his reviewing platform, a young man in plain clothes rushed toward him, his face twisted, mouth moving. He carried something wrapped in cloth.

A bolt of cold fear shot up from her center. Napoleon was in danger, and yet the thousands of soldiers on the esplanade stood motionless. Marie knocked on the window, caring little if she broke the glass, but the effort was as futile as the cry that wouldn't escape her throat.

A soldier, appearing out of nowhere, stopped the youth just a pace or two from Napoleon. Marie recognized the man barring the way as one of Napoleon's generals. She blinked. At his side was Teodor, and together they disarmed the youth of what he had in his hand. The cloth fell away, revealing a large knife, its blade catching the dull sun.

Marie clutched the windowsill and exhaled sharply, relief washing over her.

The afternoon slowly bled away while Marie waited for Napoleon in the Porcelain Room, unable to calm her agitation.

When he finally arrived at dusk, his face clouded with concern. "Oh, Marie, you've been crying." Napoleon sat down beside her on the fainting couch, his arm pulling her to him. "And you're trembling, you are. —What have you been told?"

"Nothing, Napole—it's what I *saw*!"

"You watched?"

"I always watch."

"Oh." Napoleon drew in breath. "It was nothing, really."

"Nothing? He had a knife!"

"It was a kitchen knife, dull as a butter knife."

"I don't believe that," Marie snapped. "He meant to kill you."

"But he didn't. He's just a hot-headed boy—seventeen years old."

"What did he say?"

"He said he had a petition, but his demeanor made Marshal Rapp intervene."

"And save your life! Who is he?"

"We questioned him. He's a young German by the name of Friedrich Staps. His father is a Lutheran clergyman. Ironic, that."

"And he was here to murder you. Don't deny it. He shouted something when he was disarmed. What was it?"

"Ah, that—a bit of bravado. He called out, 'Death to the Tyrant!'"

"The question is, Napole, *why* would he want to take your life?"

Napoleon turned his head away, his eyes dropping to the floor. He cleared his throat. "He said that without my making wars, Europe would find peace. I thought he was insane or an assassin hired by the Bourbons, but . . ."

"But?"

"He's educated and middle class."

That night, Marshal Duroc, not Napoleon's valet Constant, accompanied Marie to the Mödling house. As they rode, Duroc reassured her that new measures were being taken to protect the emperor. Marie had no doubt the comfort came at the suggestion of Napoleon, but she listened politely, and when he finished, she asked, "Marshal Duroc, what's to become of him, the German youth?"

Duroc sighed. "The emperor offered him clemency, Madame Walewska. He thought he was deranged or being manipulated by the Bourbons or the Bavarian secret society known as the Illuminati, but it seems he planned it all on his own."

"Why?"

"Out of patriotism, it seems. He wouldn't ask for forgiveness or even accept a pardon. In fact, he vowed to kill the emperor if given another chance."

"And?"

"On Monday, he'll face a firing squad."

The remainder of the journey to Mödling was made in silence.

Marie lay awake into the late night, haunted by the young man's sacrifice. At seventeen, he had given his life in an attempt to change the course of history. What love and fervor for his country he must have had! Though he had tried to kill the man she loved, her heart bled for him. Recalling how—driven by patriotism—she had boldly chased down Emperor Napoleon at Błonie, she understood the boy.

Marie imagined what Napoleon's late-night thoughts might be. How many more like Staps were out there—young, educated, and disillusioned?

How would Napoleon's quest for a united, enlightened Europe survive if he were assassinated? What dangers lay ahead for him?

What if something happened while she was in the Duchy of Warsaw?

As these thoughts consumed her, Marie realized she could not leave him. She would go to Paris, as he wished.

53

Friday, 13 October 1809

MARIE VISITED THE WITTES IN the early morning. She had already confided in them about her intention to return home—and her condition—so when she told them of her new plans and that Napoleon had suggested they accompany her to Paris, they were delighted, especially Józia.

Upon returning to the palace, Marie requested the presence of Napoleon's secretary, Claude Méneval, in the Porcelain Room. "I've changed my mind about returning home, Monsieur Méneval," she said. "You haven't mentioned my original plans to the emperor, I hope."

"No, Madame Walewska."

"Good." Marie knew this to be the truth; he had observed good faith by mailing her letter to Germaine de Staël, who had thanked her by return post. Had the secretary informed Napoleon, the letter wouldn't have gone out.

After she made arrangements with the secretary for future mail, Méneval stood up to leave. "I'll be happy to see you again in Paris, Madame Walewska. Though I know you'll miss your little boy, now you must consider . . . other things."

Marie looked up from her writing desk and smiled. Her condition had gone unspoken before now, but she knew that he was aware of her frequent morning sickness, as well as the arrival and daily visits of Doctor Corvisart. "Indeed," she said.

Méneval paused, then turned to her. "Perhaps now you'll find France more welcoming, Madame Walewska, once the . . ."

"Yes, Monsieur Méneval?"

The secretary's face went pale. "I mean . . . the emperor's plans."

"His plans?"

"Surely you know about . . ." The secretary looked away, staring as if into an abyss.

"Yes, Claude?" she said, employing his Christian name for the first time.

His gaze returned to her, his voice faltering. "His divorce plans."

Marie gripped the desk, overcome by dizziness.

That evening, with Napoleon sitting at her side, Marie presented him with a gift the Wittes had arranged: a wide band of gold and dark blue enamel, with a lock of her hair beneath a glazed panel. As instructed, the inside was inscribed: "When you have stopped loving me, remember that I love you still."

"Oh, Marie, it's beautiful! And the words—so many!"

She swallowed her disappointment on what he chose to focus. "That's why it's a wide band, Napole, so that two lines of writing would fit."

Napoleon laughed, then grew serious. "But this is more of a memorial ring, dearest."

Marie nodded. "I must confess something, Napole. Up until the assassination attempt, I planned to return to Walewice."

"What?" he snapped, his head pulling back. "To your *husband*?"

"To my *son*, Antoni."

"Oh. —And now?"

Marie met his gaze. "Now, since Thursday, I could not possibly leave you."

He understood. "Ah! Then I have *something* to thank the scoundrel Friedrich Staps for!" Napoleon leaned in and kissed Marie.

The evening passed and he made no mention of a divorce. *Why?*

Saturday, 14 October 1809

Teodor called in the morning, dressed in the dark green of the *chasseur-a-cheval*.

"Why, Teodor, your uniform looks new. And there's something different about your *czapka*."

Her brother squared his shoulders. "Ah! The plume at the front of my headgear is now white instead of the black."

"Yes, that's it! —Meaning?"

"I'm now *Captain* Teodor Łączyński."

"How wonderful!" Marie said, hugging him. As she released her hold, she asked, "Is it . . . is it because of your help with the assassin?"

Teodor shrugged. It could be that or . . ."

"Or what?"

Teodor paused, his complexion reddening. "Or *family connections*."

Marie nodded. "I see. Well, what does it matter?" she said dismissively. "You'll be escorting us to Paris, yes?"

"You'll have four soldiers on horseback to see you safely there, but I won't be one of them."

"But why?"

"Berthier would not agree to have me gone so long, especially with your taking a long, wind-about way."

"Oh! Then—you know about me?"

Teodor's gaze dropped just for a moment. "Yes," he whispered, bringing his deep green eyes to hers.

Marie felt heat rising into her face. She raised a hand to her breastbone. "Oh, Teo, how am I to manage—"

"You will, Marie." He took both of her hands in his. "No tears, now. Listen to me. You will manage, Marie. You *will*. This is your calling. Your family—and Poland—are with you." He bent low and kissed her on the forehead.

An hour later, Marie and Hania left Vienna for Paris, with the Wittes and members of their household following in a separate carriage. The signing of the Treaty of Schönbrunn was to take place in the afternoon. However, the terms would offer no surprise to Marie, for she had read them before boarding the carriage.

Four years earlier, Emperor Francis had already been mortified at Austerlitz when Napoleon forced him to renounce his title of Holy Roman Emperor, Francis II, reducing him to Francis I of Austria. Now, with this treaty, he was compelled to cede western Galicia to the Duchy of Warsaw, further contributing to the restoration of Polish lands. Other losses included additional lands, citizens, soldiers, and a huge amount of cash.

Even while celebrating Poland's gains, Marie sympathized with Emperor Francis's plight, aware that when he returned to Schönbrunn Palace, he would discover much of its artwork and treasures had been seized and sent to Paris in cartloads.

The two-carriage caravan slowly made its way to Paris, passing through Munich, Stuttgart, and Strasbourg. Marie worried for Napoleon, who had promised to leave for Versailles within a day or two of the treaty signing. She knew his carriage—accompanied by a dozen or more Polish officers—would take a more direct route, moving at breakneck speed, and arriving in Paris well before her. With the assassination attempt still on her mind, she prayed for his safe arrival.

The journey through the cities and provinces now under tribute to Emperor Napoleon was long, but the discomforts of the road barely registered. Her thoughts kept returning to Napoleon's divorce from Josephine. Why hadn't he told her? Could it be true? She imagined a dozen reasons for his silence, but eventually convinced herself he might want to surprise her.

She had no illusions about her place— as a member of the *szlachta*, Poland's minor nobility, she knew the French would see her as an unsuitable choice for empress, clearly forbidden—*interdite*. He would not choose her. So be it; the grandeur of a gilt throne was beyond her reach and had never been part of her dreams.

Still, she believed that after the divorce, Napoleon intended to create an opportunity for them to be together. She imagined a life where she would live near the man she loved, bearing his child—*their child*—into the world, and together they would watch him grow. She, like him, was certain the baby would be a boy, a son who would strengthen their bond, bringing them ever closer together.

Although she knew she would have to share him during the day, she dreamed of him lying close beside her in the night. She began making plans to send for Antoni, planning to care for both of her children. The thought of living as a small family brought her immense joy. This, she imagined, would be her life. She would be Napoleon's *shadow wife*, living in his orbit without the majesty she never craved.

54

Monday, 6 November 1809

THREE WEEKS AFTER LEAVING SCHÖNBRUNN Palace, Marie arrived in Paris and settled at the house on Rue de la Houssaye. She learned that Napoleon had arrived a week earlier, yet three days passed with nothing more than a welcome note.

"Oh, I'm sure he's occupied with state matters," Józia Witte reassured her one afternoon.

"And," added John Witte, "I've heard rumors about the divorce. The negotiations are undoubtedly delicate. You shouldn't worry, Marie."

Józia whispered, "Rumor has it the empress is not taking it well."

I should think not, Marie thought. Despite the Wittes' optimism, she remained on edge, her nerves frayed by an intuition that some setback lay in store.

Two days later, in the early afternoon, Marshal Duroc entered the reception room to announce that the emperor had arrived and would come up once the servants had been hidden away.

Within minutes, Napoleon entered, smiling broadly. He hurried over to where she sat at a small luncheon table. "You're here, my Marie!"

Marie noticed the genuine delight in his eyes and resisted the urge to say, *I've been here five days, Napole.* She merely nodded, returning his smile.

"And the journey?"

"It was long."

"But you're here now," he said, initiating the cheek kisses. "You are a gift to me. And—you carry a gift. I can't tell you how precious it is. You are well?"

"I am, yes, Napole."

"Wonderful!" he exclaimed.

"I'm about to have lunch," Marie said. "Will you join me?"

"I can't, Marie. Not today," he said with a grimace. "I have urgent business to attend to."

"With the proceedings?" Marie blurted out.

The gray-blue eyes went wide as he studied her face. "Who told you?"

"Oh, Napole, any number of people could have told me." She would not reveal her source—his own secretary, Claude Méneval.

Napoleon harrumphed. "Secrets don't stay secret long in Paris, especially at Court. Oh, Marie, divorce is difficult. If only you could just snap your fingers and have it done."

Marie did not comment.

"You're not worried, are you? Nothing will change between us." His eyes drifted to her midsection, a forced chuckle escaping. "Well—there is that."

"Yes, there is that. It will be a boy, I'm convinced. The emperor will have his wish."

Napoleon smiled. "May God in heaven hear you! But how could He not? You are the sincerest creature I've ever met." He paused now, cleared his throat, and said, "Marie, I'm sorry for this, but I must go."

Marie didn't ask him to stay, nor when he'd return. She bit her lip, determined not to betray her disappointment, but Napoleon's gaze was too sharp.

He bent, took her hands, and helped her to her feet. "You're in yellow today," he said, kissing her on the forehead. "I love that, and I love you." He pulled her to him, his arms going around her waist in a gentle way, his mouth at her ear. "Goodbye, Marie, my Polish wife." He released her, bowed, and when he raised his head, his eyes were half-lidded. Without another word, he turned and walked toward the door, his boot heels resounding on the wooden planks.

At the door he paused, as if about to turn back—but didn't.

The door clicked shut, and his descending footsteps on the stairs faded, then fell away.

Trembling, Marie braced herself on the table before collapsing into her chair.

She steeled herself against tears, scarcely comprehending the scene that just played out. He spoke like her Napole, with loving and tender words, words she believed in her heart were sincere. And yet—how abruptly he had left her. This, after she had crossed the length of Europe at his bidding and endured days of waiting to see him.

Marie allowed for her breaths to slow, her thoughts to clear. She was well aware that Napoleon's wartime pressures and the divorce proceedings were weighing heavily on him, undoubtedly consuming his time. She wanted to forgive him, but still—.

Her thoughts turned to the empress. She suspected the gossip that Napoleon was avoiding the empress was probably accurate. Even if rumors of Josephine's past marital wanderings were true, she had cast her fate with Napoleon and become empress of a mighty nation. Now, she was to lose it all. To her great surprise, Marie found herself sympathizing with her.

I will not lose him, Marie resolved, sitting back against the chair. I cannot. He had pledged his love. He had. Her hands caressed her middle section. She could feel the life within, the child they had made.

In the days following, Marie waited anxiously, feeling more isolated by the hour. Marshal Duroc called periodically to check on her, offering vague excuses and suggesting that he escort her to plays or operas. She declined. Doctor Corvisart attended to her three times a week, his manner as cool and unnerving as ever.

Weeks passed without another visit from Napoleon.

Marie wondered if he might be regretting his insistence that she follow him to Paris. No matter how liberal the capital, was she an embarrassment, especially during the royal divorce? People would recognize her from the previous stay at the house on Rue de la Houssaye. And—adding to a likely scandal, soon her condition would be evident.

One night, before dropping off to sleep amidst a pelting rain, Marie came to admit to herself that the mistake had been hers. She shouldn't have come to Paris. Her thoughts turned to the duchy. The many difficulties accompanying a homecoming loomed before her, but it was home.

One decision prompted another. Marie couldn't bring herself to return to Anastase at Walewice. She would go to Kiernozia. In the morning, she alerted Hania, whose French had greatly improved.

Marshal Duroc handled the details and placed Teodor in charge of the journey. With her condition in mind, they would travel slowly once again.

When Napoleon didn't object and sent a brief note wishing her a safe journey, the die was cast.

On the day of departure, Marie turned to Duroc, holding her tears at bay, placed a hand on his arm, and asked, "Why has Napoleon been so inattentive, Marshal Duroc?"

The marshal's face colored slightly. He drew in breath and said, "Madame Walewska, the emperor has no wish to be confronted daily with his own conscience."

PART SIX

"One cannot love and be wise."
–Polish Proverb

55

Kiernozia, Duchy of Warsaw
Wednesday, 6 December 1809

MARIE ARRIVED AT THE FAMILY estate on Saint Nicolas Day, dispirited and slightly ill from the journey. She had Hania for company, but missed Teodor, who had escorted the carriage as far as Warsaw. His presence at her homecoming would have bolstered her courage, but he and the other soldiers returned to Paris, leaving Prince Poniatowski to supply escorts to Kiernozia.

Marie was met by a wide-eyed Katarzyna in her usual good spirits, but her mother's mood was difficult to decipher.

After supper, her mother excused Katarzyna from the table and turned to Marie, seated at her right. "Ah, Marie, my heart goes out to you. This affair should have ended long ago."

"I know that was your opinion, Mother."

"But you thought you loved him."

"I *do* love him."

"He sent you away," her mother said, half statement, half question. "And in such a condition."

"It was my choice to come home." Marie said, choosing not to explain fully.

"So—what is to happen?"

"I don't know. Only that I'm to have his baby, as I wrote to you."

"You'll have the child here?"

Marie's stomach tightened. Surely her mother knew that she couldn't bear to go to Walewice. "If . . . you'll have me."

Her mother reached across the table, gently taking Marie's hand. "This is your home, Marysia. Of course, you are welcome."

Marie released a silent breath. The icy reception had softened, and she breathed easier.

Saturday, 9 December 1809

When Marie married, she gave her old room at the front of the house to Katarzyna, and so now settled into the one that had belonged to Honorata, who had married. At midday, Katarzyna knocked on her door. "You have a visitor," she said.

"Who is it, Kasia?"

Katarzyna stepped in, looking around the room. "Do you miss your old room? It's bigger and has a view of the courtyard."

"No, I don't, Kasia," Marie lied. "It's your turn to enjoy it. —Who is the visitor?"

"I don't remember his name. Mother said he's a French Minister, or some such thing, and that you know him."

"The French Resident Minister in Warsaw?"

"Yes!"

"His name is Monsieur Jean-Charles Serra. Tell him I'll be down presently. Address him as *Minister Serra*. Watch your pronunciation, and pay attention to your French class. It's indispensable across the continent. You're fifteen now, Kasia. Time to start doing things properly."

Katarzyna turned to leave but paused at the door, her eyes narrowing with a mischievous glint. "Like you, Marysia?" She laughed and dashed out, closing the door behind her.

Marie froze. Her sister's playful humor now carried a sharp, adult wit. The reproach stung.

In preparing to meet Minister Serra, Marie chose a deep blue gown, thankful that the current style—whereby a ribbon was cinched just below the bosom—made her condition less apparent. Although she realized her breasts had grown fuller, and if Serra were especially observant, that could give her away. Then again, considering that Napoleon had once entrusted him to see to her welfare, he might already know.

The minister stood as Marie entered the reception room. She observed his curious gaze sweep over her, slipper to coiffure. When he leveled his blue eyes at her, she read confirmation in them. He knew.

"The emperor is most concerned about you, Madame Walewska."

Marie nodded. Meeting Serra again felt like *déjà vu;* he was once more the go-between Napoleon and herself.

"He thinks you might be more comfortable at the Walewice Palace."

Marie stiffened. *Comfortable?* The thought of Walewice was unbearable. "This is my family home, Minister Serra. I am most comfortable here."

The minister shifted nervously in his chair. "I understand that. But . . . but the emperor feels Walewice Palace . . . with all its . . . its Walewska aunts and nieces might be more . . ."

"Proper?" Marie interjected with a smile, aware of the irony in echoing Kasia's quip.

Serra paled slightly. "Yes, perhaps, Madame Walewska."

"I'm well cared for here, Monsieur. I have my mother, my sister, and a staff."

"Still, Madame Walewska—"

"And we have a capable midwife nearby."

Serra reddened, clearly flustered. He had skirted the issue while she confronted it directly. He was silent for a long moment. "I see," he finally said.

"So—you haven't brought a note, have you?"

Serra cleared his throat. "I have not, Madame Walewska."

"Well, then," Marie said briskly, "will you see that a letter of mine reaches the emperor?"

"Yes, of course, Madame Walewska. I'll return in a day or two to collect it."

"All that way from Warsaw? That won't be necessary. The letter is upstairs. I won't be a minute."

Marie hurried upstairs, retrieved the letter, and quickly reread her words: how she missed her dear Napole; how unhappy their separation made her; how she longed for their reunion. She assured him she was well in body, if not in spirit, and that their baby would be born hale and healthy.

There had always been a reunion, she reminded herself as she hurried down the stairs. She had to believe there would be one now.

Monday, 18 December 1809

Marie's letter was answered by Napoleon's note, delivered by a Poniatowski servant. She retired to her room to read it.

Madame,

I received your missive with dismay. Of course, I'm happy you've arrived safely and that you are well. As your condition advances, take no chances with your precious cargo. My feelings for you have not changed. Now, you must lift your spirits. Serra writes you've become moody. I won't have it. The future will take care of itself. In your next letter, I must hear that you are cheery and untroubled.

Napole.

Marie's hand tightened on the note as the words seemed to swim before her eyes. While he had signed it *Napole*, the orders in it and use of the word *must* made it sound more like one of the hundreds of letters about civil and military matters she had heard him dictate to his secretary. Was he always fated to be a general? What threatened to break her heart, however, was the salutation.

Madame!

Something had changed.

What is Napole playing at? Why, in the names of the saints, would he encourage me to have our baby at Walewice?

Marie glanced down and realized she had crushed the note in her fist.

56

Kiernozia, Duchy of Warsaw
January-February 1810

THE HOLIDAYS PASSED, AND WITH the new year came the start of the *karnawał* season. Despite the long trip, the French Minister visited Kiernozia twice a week, sometimes bringing a note from Napoleon—messages that conveyed distance and command, leaving Marie depressed and hurt. It was only now that she realized how much power she had held over Napoleon, perhaps from the very first. But now, that power seemed to be slipping away.

At Minister Serra's urging, Marie responded to Napoleon's inquiries about her health with brief, blunt notes—much like his own.

Marie kept Hania at Kiernozia. She loved and missed Antoni, but something in her heart held her back from sending for him. She felt as if she had sinned not just against Anastase, but against what had been her life at Walewice—before meeting Napoleon.

In the first week of February, Countess Henriette de Vauban arrived at the Łączyński estate. Marie found her in conversation with her mother in the reception room. Henriette hurried to embrace her with dramatic cheek kisses, followed by effusive praise and congratulations. Marie's mother took the opportunity to leave the room.

Marie forced a cordial smile, though she could feel her back stiffen. She knew that Prince Poniatowski's mistress was here for a purpose. She had become wary of the woman.

"You look a bit drawn, my dear," the countess remarked once they were seated.

"I'm quite well, Henriette."

"And everything is . . ." The countess's eyes briefly dropped toward Marie's midsection.

"As it should be," Marie replied, more curtly than she intended.

"Well, then . . . Jean-Charles asked me to come. He is otherwise occupied."

"I see." Marie forced a smile. "He's keeping the emperor informed about my health."

After a brief go-round of small talk, Henriette brought up the Treaty of Schönbrunn. "You must be congratulated for any role you played in the restoration of Polish lands, Marie. Prince Pepi is delighted with the return of Western Galicia. I understand you've been corresponding with the emperor. Any idea what his next move is?"

By now, it was clear that Henriette was here on behalf of both prince and minister. "I've always kept Poland's interests in mind, Madame de Vauban."

"Oh, I know that!" the countess blurted, her tone overly solicitous.

Marie managed a smile. "Napoleon plans to add Russia to his holdings. When that happens, he swears Poland will be Poland again." She could tell by the woman's nod and tight smile that this news was no news to her—or to the prince.

"But—is it a promise he is likely to keep? That's a formidable goal."

Marie shrugged.

"I see. Well . . . there's another matter, Marie."

"Yes?"

The countess paused, folding her hands in her lap. "The emperor wishes for you to return to Walewice Palace for the birth of your child."

"So Minister Serra has told me." Marie leaned against the chair's backrest.

"Hasn't the emperor himself written of his wish?"

"I . . . I've not read his last note."

"Oh!" the countess said, raising an eyebrow.

"Madame de Vauban, whether he has put that in writing matters little. I deserted my husband and have no desire to go back. He will not want to see me. Sweet Jesus, I'm carrying another man's child."

The countess compressed her lips. "Oh, not just any man's child, Marie."

Marie nodded.

"Now, I must tell you, Marie, that the French Minister has been in communication with Anastase to pave the way for your return."

Marie felt a knotting in her stomach. "Minister Serra should have consulted me before taking such a step. I won't return. And, why in heaven's name would Anastase want me back? Besides, my husband is in Italy this time of year. He will be there until Easter."

"He's coming home early. Perhaps he's already at Walewice."

"Because of *this*?"

"One doesn't disrespect the wishes of Emperor Napoleon Bonaparte. You must reconsider."

Monday, 19 February 1810

In the late afternoon, Marie was reading in the reception room, wearing a dressing gown, when she heard a carriage on the drive. She hurried to the window, and saw Prince Poniatowski's coach. Her heart raced. Was he here to further direct her life? But it was Henriette de Vauban who alighted from the coach.

Marie hurried upstairs. From the landing, she could hear her mother greeting the countess. Marie noiselessly slipped into her room and bolted the door, scarcely a minute before the knock came.

"Marie, Madame de Vauban has come to see you," her mother whispered. "Please come down." The doorknob rattled. "Why, you've bolted the door. Listen to me Marie, she's come all the way from Warsaw."

"Very well. I'm not dressed for company. Will you entertain her while I change?"

Her mother agreed, and Marie quickly changed into an orange muslin dress and low-heeled silk slippers. She hastened downstairs and crept along the hallway, coming to stand outside the reception room, listening.

"I'm so glad you've come, Henriette," her mother was saying. "I'm afraid for Marie. Her spirits are so low, I'm reminded of the months before her wedding, that is, *before* she agreed to marry Anastase. We had to have Doctor Fabianski come."

"What did he say, Eva?"

"That she had fallen into melancholia and that had set the course for the winter fever. If that's what's happening now, I fear for her . . . and the child."

Marie cleared her throat as if on stage, heard their voices drop away, and made her entrance. After the greeting formalities, Marie settled herself in a chair facing the two women on the settee.

"I've brought a letter, Marie," Madame de Vauban said, "but first . . . have you read the emperor's recent note?"

"I have."

"And his message?"

Marie looked from the questioner to her mother, whose face was full of concern. Marie had not told her of the request. Her gaze returned to the guest. "It was as you suggested, Henriette. His desire is for me to go to Walewice."

"Ah, so—have you given it thought?" Henriette asked.

"I have. My mind is unchanged." Marie turned from Henriette to her mother. "Tell me the truth. Am I a burden here? Will my child be a burden?"

"No, no Marysia, never, but perhaps this *is* something you should consider."

"I have." Marie forced a smile and turned back to Henriette. "So, you've brought a letter. Napoleon doesn't write letters; he writes notes."

Madame de Vauban withdrew a letter from her skirts. "Oh, this is a letter, Marie, but it's not from the emperor."

Marie blinked in surprise. "From the prince, then?"

"No, Marie, it's from your husband."

Marie sat still for several moments, her face flushing.

Collecting herself, Marie accepted the letter and quickly left the room. Grabbing Katarzyna's red cloak from the hall tree, she pulled it on and stepped out into the February cold.

At the top of the stairs, the winter light was dull but good enough to navigate the letter. She read it quickly, then stood dizzily staring toward the snow-covered poplars that lined the drive.

She looked down and read the letter again. Anastase *had* invited her to return to Walewice. But why?

He wrote that she was dearly missed at Walewice. By whom? Marie asked herself. Antoni? Teresa? But by Anastase? It was hard to believe.

"This is Walewice," he had written, "our home and the fitting place for the birth."

Fitting?

Marie pulled the cloak tight, pushed the letter into the pocket, and descended the stairs. She began to walk aimlessly, unmindful of the melting snow that wet her Paris silk slippers.

She found herself in her mother's garden, still and white with winter. This was the path she had walked with Arkady that summer day when the plants were vibrant with life and produce. Now they were gone, just sticks in the ground.

That romance had come to naught. And it was followed by a loveless marriage. And now—when she finally loved someone, true happiness seemed as distant as ever.

Marie placed her hand on her middle. But I have this, she thought. *I have this.*

Marie returned to the house.

Henriette sat alone in the reception room. She stood at once. "Why, Marie, you're trembling with cold. Come over by the fire and sit."

When Henriette stepped closer, as if to take her hand, Marie stepped back. "Why, Henriette? Why would Anastase want me to return? What could Minister Serra have said to him?"

"If we can sit where it's warm, I'll tell you."

They sat across from each other in front of the fireplace.

"Marie, I've been friends with Anastase Walewski for decades. He places great store by what others think of him. Would you agree?"

Marie stayed silent.

"Think back. How did he react when the Provisional Government came together, leaving him on the outside?"

"He was miserable. What made him happy was being invited to their events."

"Exactly. Truth be told, *I* had a hand in those invitations."

"To distract from the attention the emperor was showing me?"

Henriette nodded. "He's a proud man. Now, think again. What is it that might upset his little world?" She tilted her head and squinted, her gaze leveled at Marie's midsection.

"Scandal."

"Yes! Now, how much does he admire Emperor Napoleon Bonaparte?"

"Ha!" Marie spat. "Enough to allow him to romance his *wife.*"

"Indeed. And perhaps enough to agree to a special request from the emperor that he accept your child into the Walewski family as his own?"

"Napoleon asked him *that*?" Marie bristled at the hypocritical standards displayed by men.

"Yes, and together, Minister Serra and I convinced your husband that, despite wounded pride, scandal would be averted, and he would please the most powerful man on the continent."

"All very neat," Marie muttered, "all the way around." With such a plan, she realized not only would both men avoid scandal, but Napoleon could call her back to Paris, child in tow.

Henriette smiled, as if she already knew what Marie would decide.

Monday, 5 March 1810

Two days before the confirmed move to Walewice, a note came from Napoleon via a messenger from Prince Poniatowski. Marie assumed that Madame de Vauban and Minister Serra considered their mission complete and neither had to make the long trek from Warsaw.

Napoleon wrote:

Madame,

I take great pleasure in your decision. Perhaps your dark mood will lift at Walewice. I wish it passionately. Soon I will expect word that you have birthed a hearty boy child. God willing! How I long to see you once again. Never fear that my interest in you wanes. It is sincere. I await the news. Be well.

Napole.

57

Kiernozia and Walewice, Duchy of Warsaw
Wednesday, 7 March 1810

MARIE STEPPED UP INTO THE carriage sent from Walewice, where she was welcomed by her niece through marriage, Princess Dory Jabłonowska.

"I was puzzled," Marie said. "This doesn't look like one of Anastase's carriages."

"That's because it's my personal carriage, Marie, and I was especially keen to ensure your transport arrived without delay."

"I do appreciate it, Dory."

"Now, sit here next to me."

Marie complied while Hania sat across from them.

"I don't imagine everyone at Walewice is keen to see me," Marie whispered.

"You'll be surprised," Dory said. "You're a heroine here, just as I'm told you are at Archbishop de Pradt's receptions."

"I can't believe that, Dory."

Dory smiled. The auburn-haired niece was quite pretty, sociable, and confident. She launched into a monologue about recent Walewski births, marriages, and local events, giving Marie a momentary relief from her anxiety.

After a while, Marie's responses grew quiet.

"I'm tiring you, Marie," Dory said. "I'll let you rest."

Marie waited several minutes before withdrawing the latest note from her bodice. She read it again. No matter how many times she read it, she couldn't fathom what place she had in Napoleon's life. Again, he addressed her as *Madame*. The closeness to him and sheer bliss she had felt at Warsaw's Royal Castle, Finckenstein, Schönbrunn, and during the initial Paris idyll seemed to ebb away by the hour. And yet, his hope that her spirits would be lifted remained uppermost in his notes.

Marie looked up to find Dory's dark eyes drawn to the note.

"It's from *him*, isn't it?" Her niece's gaze moved up and held hers now.

"It is," Marie said, conjuring up a wistful smile.

"You know, you are Poland's Godsend, Marie."

Marie's smile dissolved, and as the carriage turned into the long lane leading to Walewice Palace, she pretended to take interest in the rows of linden trees on either side, still bare of their fragrant yellow flowers and green, heart-shaped leaves.

Minutes later, Marie stood in front of the palace. She was quite large by now, but she waved away a liveried servant's help as she navigated the few steps up to the open double doors, her nerves on edge. What kind of welcome would she receive—an errant wife returning to the husband and home she had willingly abandoned—and big with another man's child?

With the Princess Jabłonowska at her side, Marie stepped onto the marble floor of the colonnaded palace hall to find Anastase's three sisters, several nieces, and dozens of servants lining up at attention on either side. Dory's mother, Jadwiga, the most rigid and sharp-speaking of the sisters, approached Marie with a smile as wide as the River Vistula. "Welcome, Marie! We have all looked forward to this happy day. And now it is here!"

After Jadwiga and Marie exchanged greetings, the other Walewska women swarmed around her, uttering good wishes.

Marie became lightheaded with embarrassment. Her temples throbbed. She had an urge to run away, but the room was spinning around her. She was being treated like a heroine. In truth, she was bringing shame upon the House of Walewski. She longed to say that she was undeserving, but couldn't. She stood speechless, thinking, *What a topsy-turvy world this is.*

In the midst of the crush of female in-laws, Marie collected herself and lifted her eyes to scan the hall. When her questioning gaze came back to Jadwiga, her sister-in-law said, "Anastase has gone to the Warsaw townhome."

A tactful move. "I see. I would like to see my Antoni now."

Sunday, 8 April 1810

Marie sat at her dressing table finishing her morning toilette when Hania entered, a gray cast to her face.

"What is it, Hania?" Marie asked, observing her in the table mirror. "You've only been gone ten minutes. You look as if you've lost your pet kitten."

"It's Minister Serra, Madame, the French Minister."

"He's here? So early and on a Sunday—how odd! Tell him I'll be down presently."

"He's already left, Madame." Hania said.

"Left?" Marie turned toward the servant. "Why do you look so upset? What's that behind your back?"

"It's a Warsaw newspaper, Madame," Hania replied, revealing the folded paper.

"He brought it? The minister?"

Hania nodded. "He did, Madame."

Marie grew dizzy with a sense of dread. *Napoleon is dead,* she thought. *My Napole is dead.* "Bring it here, Hania," she ordered, twisting around with difficulty because of her large middle.

Hania moved forward and handed Marie the paper.

Marie took it into her lap and unfolded the *Gazeta Warszawska*. She stared at the headlines, unable to speak, unable to breathe. The words seemed to move on the page, writhing like worms. At that moment, her world changed forever.

Hania stood there, awkward and uncertain.

Finally, Marie found her voice. "Do you know what it says, Hania?"

"I heard your nieces say some things about it, Madame. They saw me with the newspaper after the minister left and, well, they insisted they see it."

"They read it and then had you bring it up?" Marie asked.

Hania nodded.

"Leave me, Hania. Now."

"Oh, Madame . . ."

"I'm fine. You're certainly not to blame. Now, go."

Marie was already reading again when the door closed quietly behind the maid. However, the words started to move again. She paused, unable to go on. She had read enough.

In a lavish religious ceremony on the second of the month, Emperor Napoleon Bonaparte wed the Austrian Archduchess Marie-Louise.

Despite undoubtedly travelling all night, the French Minister to the Duchy of Warsaw, as well as the Walewska women of the house, had proved too cowardly to tell her of the marriage themselves, leaving it to a maid.

Marie rolled up the newspaper and hurled it across the room, where it crashed into a delicate crystal vase holding spring's first Bridal Wreath flowers.

Only later would she recognize the irony.

It was dark outside when a knock came at the door. "Madame, I've brought you a tray." It was Hania.

Marie cleared her throat. "I don't want anything."

"Madame Jadwiga said you must eat."

"Place it on the floor, then, Hania."

"Will you need help in preparation for bed, Madame?"

"No." Marie heard her footfalls moving away. She pulled herself off the bed, lighted a chamberstick, and went to sit in a high-backed, cushioned chair. She attempted to collect her thoughts. Napoleon and Marie-Louise were married first by proxy in early March. Clearly, plans for this union were in the making when Napoleon wrote his last note. Perhaps the proxy marriage itself had taken place by then. The archduchess was nineteen and even though the paper touted their smiles and happiness at the royal marriage, she must have been frightened at the prospect of marrying Napoleon, a declared enemy of her father, Francis I. He had already lost so much to Napoleon—his Holy Roman Emperor title, countless lands and citizens, and untold riches, as well as art plundered from Schönbrunn Palace. And now the former Holy Roman Emperor was made to sacrifice his daughter.

Marie could spare no tears, neither for Francis, nor his daughter. She kept them for herself.

Why, Napole? Why?

He had always told her that there was no one like her and that he treasured her goodness and faithfulness. And yet he gambled on an arranged marriage with a young woman he had never met.

And then the answer came to her by way of a memory. They had been sitting in the Blue Chinese Room, Napoleon's reception room at the Schönbrunn Palace. Napole stood speaking of the near life-size painting of Franz Stephan. The Holy Roman Emperor had fathered sixteen children with Marie Theresa. Two of their sons were in paintings on the wall to the right, and the wife of one of them, along with a few of *their* sixteen children, looked out from a painting on the wall to the left.

Napoleon had lost himself in the paintings, moving and motioning with great energy, as he often did during dictation with his secretary. And then he whispered something, not to her, but, as if to himself. The same word, three times over.

Dynasty . . . dynasty . . . dynasty.

His marriage was not about love—it was about legacy.

Friday, 4 May 1810

Spring came to Poland and with it, a strong thunderstorm—and the birth of Marie and Napoleon's child: a healthy boy. Sister-in law Jadwiga called it an easy birth. While Marie could not imagine anyone having an easy birth, she didn't argue because it was much easier than Antoni's.

She had two boys now. Antoni was about to turn five and had finally warmed to her again after a period of shyness. Despite their separations, she meant to show him the love she held for him.

Daring not to name the baby after Napoleon, she chose the name of another emperor, Czar Aleksander. The child's flaxen hair and alabaster complexion were gifts from her, but his head shape and facial features were clearly Napoleon's. The reality that little Aleksander was the child of Emperor Napoleon Bonaparte provided consolation, despite his Austrian marriage. It was his first child, and it was a boy, as he had wished. That could not be changed. She smiled to herself.

Marie held back from writing the news to Napoleon. French Minister Serra or Prince Poniatowski would no doubt do so.

Minister Serra had arranged visits from Dr. Józef Ciekierski, a renowned physician from the Warsaw's Institute of Surgery and Gynecology, who had served as consultant to King Frederick Augustus of Saxony and, more recently, to Prince Poniatowski. With his jaw set, the physician had spoken at some length and in a steady, low voice about the state of her kidneys and how nursing could deplete energy and resources needed for the well-being of particular organs. He sternly warned Marie that even though the birth had been uncomplicated, she was in a delicate condition and should not attempt to nurse little Aleksander.

Marie recalled how Antoni had been turned over to the Walewska women and a wet nurse, as if she were merely the instrument that brought the baby into the world. She had been powerless to go against family tradition. She vowed that this time, with this child, it would be different. Disregarding the advice, Marie nursed Aleksander.

———•∽•———

Monday, 7 May 1810
The day set for Aleksander's christening arrived without word from her husband. In early morning, Marie lay in bed, worried that Anastase had chosen not to leave Warsaw for the ceremony. What then? It had been arranged. Serra had assured her of his attendance.

Did he change his mind about recognizing Aleksander as his own? As a Walewski? If such was the case, could she blame him? There was the matter of his will, also. Would Anastase—and his adult children, for that matter—consider Aleksander a threat to the inheritances of the Walewski adult children? Would they think Aleksander the equivalent of a cuckoo's egg, one deliberately placed by the mother bird in the nest of unsuspecting parents of another species?

Just an hour later, there came a knock at the door, and Jadwiga ushered Anastase into the bedchamber. Marie looked up from nursing little Aleksander.

Anastase halted several feet away. "Oh! I didn't know," he blurted. His sister stepped forward and said, "I'm sorry to intrude, Marie."

"No, no, that's all right," Marie said as she finished nursing and covered herself. "Come closer, Anastase."

Her husband obeyed, and bent to kiss her on the forehead. "You have been missed, Marie." He smiled, then turned his attention to Aleksander, who had already fallen asleep. "A fine boy child," he said, nodding. "Came into the world during a storm, I hear. What might that foretell? Marie, your choice of names is fine, but I'll add a couple more. Family names, you know."

Marie lay there paralyzed. She could find no words for the kindness he was showing. She had the urge to ask him if he wanted to hold the baby but quashed it at once. How could she ask him to hold another man's baby?

Seeming to read her unease, Anastase straightened. "I'll visit Antoni now and leave you to prepare for the ceremony. But I want you to know that I will always have your best interest and that of the boys in my heart."

As he left, Jadwiga following, Hania came in to attend to her toilette.

"Why, Madame, you're crying!"

A few minutes before 10 a.m., Marie entered the ballroom, the baby in her arms and little Antoni hanging on to her dress, his big blue eyes wide open at the fuss. She joined the small group of family standing around the Walewski baptismal font that had been brought in. She exchanged kisses with her mother and Katarzyna. "Look behind you, Marysia," her mother said.

Marie turned to see her brother Teodor, who gifted her with one of his monkey smiles. "What a surprise," she cried and hugged him. "Thank you for coming, Teodor," she whispered. "You know you're my favorite, don't you?" She then took her place next to her husband, moving past Doctor Ciekierski, who flashed a warm smile. French Minister Serra was present, too, serious as ever. Men are quick to take their bows, she thought.

Father Jan Wegrzynowicz, a local parish priest, officiated. He read from the prepared document:

"The noble and respected Anastase Colonna Walewski, *Staroste* of Warek, resident of Walewice, and seventy-three years of age, asserts that this child, born on the tenth of May, is to be named Aleksander Florian Józef Colonna Walewski. The high-born Anastase Walewski further asserts that the child is his issue and that of his lawful spouse Marie Łączyńska, twenty-three years of age, daughter of Mateusz Łączyński, *Staroste* of Gostyn."

All that was left to do was the anointing and pouring of water.

Anastase turned to Marie, smiled, took the baby into his arms and held him over the font. The oil and water ritual went smoothly. Aleksander was alert but silent.

After a formal luncheon, Minister Serra departed for Warsaw, accompanied by Anastase.

Her husband had taken part not only willingly, but cheerfully. His behavior was something she devoted a great deal of thought to as she lay in bed that night.

Anastase had just given his name to a child, not his. Why? she asked herself. Was it because he held her interest in his heart, as he had told her? Was her prideful and eccentric husband capable of such unconditional love?

Or was it, she wondered, because Aleksander was the child of an emperor, one he worshipped? Was this not a personal favor and nod to the world's most powerful man? Or did Anastase expect something in return? For him? For his family? For the future of the child bearing the Walewski name?

June 1810

A note from Napoleon, written while in Belgium, and a package containing several yards of Brussels lace arrived via a messenger from Minister Serra, who had sent news of the birth to Napoleon. She knew from the papers that the emperor was on tour with his young empress.

Madame,

You have no idea how pleased I am that you've given birth to a boy. Somehow, we both had known it, yes? I'm no less glad to hear you have come through it in superior fashion. Cheers! Don't doubt me, my Marie.

Yours,

Napole.

Marie did not reply. The next day, when Hania caught sight of the lace, her eyes lit up like diamonds.

"You may have it, Hania."

"Oh, Madame, no. I couldn't."

"You can and you will. Take it now. I don't want to look at it."

September 1810

The summer passed without further word from the emperor. The newspaper was full of information detailing every movement of the newlyweds. Friends and gossipers alike spoke within Marie's hearing of how the emperor was fully besotted with his Austrian conquest.

Marie trained herself to think as little as possible about Napoleon. Instead, she immersed herself in her two children. They would become her life. The boys and the knowledge that she was the mother of Napoleon's child lifted her. It was enough for her.

It had to be, she told herself.

58

Wednesday, 12 September 1810

Marie was awakened by Hania's announcement of a visitor. She sat up in bed, still drowsy. "Who is it?"

"Monsieur Teodor, your brother, Madame."

"Really? How wonderful! Show him up, Hania. At once!"

Minutes later, Teodor entered and approached the bed, his heavy bootsteps muffled by the Turkish carpet. He bent to kiss her on the cheek.

"What a lovely interruption to my life of monotony! That's not to say my boys don't keep me entertained when they're not in the clutches of the Walewska women. Anyway, they can't talk of what's going on across the continent, but you can, Teo."

Marie slid over to the middle of the bed and patted the side for him to sit. "Are you still attached to Marshal Berthier?"

Teodor sat. "I am."

"What are you doing here? Are you on leave?"

He shook his head. "On a mission."

"Really?" She knew at once his mission had to do with her.

From his waistcoat, Teodor withdrew a folded note and handed it to her, its familiar scribbling on the outside causing a flutter in her chest. Half a continent away, Napole was still able to cause that. She broke the red wax seal.

Madame,

How extraordinarily wonderful it is to have word of you by way of your brother. He has heard from your mother that your recuperation is complete. If that is indeed the case, I wish for you to come to Paris at the end of November. Will you do that? Of course, you will! Do not doubt my affection for you, my Marie. Of course, you are to bring Aleksander.

Napole.

Marie stared at the note, the weight of the words sinking in.

Teodor's voice broke her thoughts. "Are you all right, Marie? You're trembling."

"Am I? Are you aware of the content, Teodor?"

"I am. I'm to stay and help with the preparations for your move. And I'll accompany you and the boys, of course."

"Move? Do you mean *visit*?"

"The emperor said *move*, Marie."

Marie had a strange tightening sensation at the back of her throat so that when she opened her mouth to say something, no words would come. She looked toward the window.

Teodor took hold of her hand. "You *will* go, won't you Marie?"

She turned back to her brother, whose green eyes questioned. "I—I don't know, Teo."

Teodor released her hand and stood. He shifted from foot to foot. "There's something else you must know, Marysia," he said, his voice oddly soft.

"What? What is it?"

"The . . . the new empress—Marie-Louise . . ."

"Yes? What about her?"

"She's with child."

Monday, 26 November 1810

By dawn Marie and Hania, along with little Antoni and baby Aleksander, settled into the lead carriage. Accompanying them on the journey to Paris were two of Anastase's adult nieces, Princess Dory Jabłonowska and Madame Tereska Bierzyńska. Although they were years older than Marie, she was thankful that they were a generation younger than Anastase and his sisters. For that reason, she felt more comfortable referring to them as *cousins*, rather than as nieces.

Behind their carriage was a train of vehicles carrying their three personal maids, two nurses, two cooks, several attendants, and a bounty of supplies and luggage. Marshal Berthier had placed Teodor in charge of the preparations, as well as the journey itself. Five additional soldiers completed the escort.

The ten-day journey left Marie with much to think about. What kind of life was waiting for her in France? Napoleon had chosen a dynasty over his love for her. Sometimes at night—at the inn or monastery where Teodor had engaged rooms—she found herself curling into a ball in a bed or on a cot, rocking slightly, heart and mind racing. She slept lightly, facing the door, her senses on guard to noises and movements that might somehow spell some inexplicable danger.

Marie knew the three-year bond with Napoleon had come to an end. During that time in which their love flourished, his marriage to Josephine had already played out. With this new marriage, however, Napoleon was, by all accounts, wholly smitten with his new wife, a woman who very likely was about to give him the heir he so desperately sought.

And yet, he also wanted *her* in Paris. They were linked by those three years, by Aleksander, and by a love that was changing into—what? She didn't know. He had sent for her, and she found it impossible to refuse him.

December 1810

When Marie and her party arrived in Paris, Grand Marshal Duroc welcomed them. It was clear that he would continue in his role as liaison between her and Napoleon. With one child in her arms and the other's hand held by Hania, she entered the house on the Rue de la Houssaye, a place filled with bittersweet memories. From there, Duroc directed three of the soldiers to escort the rest of her entourage to another residence in the *Notre Dame de Lorette arrondissement*.

Before departing, he presented her with a note from Napoleon consisting of a single sentence welcoming her to Paris.

"Marshal Duroc," Marie called, catching him at the door. "When will I see him?"

Duroc glanced at the open note. "He didn't say in the note?"

"He did not."

"Well . . . then," Duroc said haltingly and cleared his throat. "I'm certain it won't be long, Madame Walewska." He bowed, pivoted, and moved down the few steps toward his carriage.

The baby started to cry, and Hania stepped forward and took him from Marie. "Come with me," the maid said to Antoni as she took his hand, "let's go see your new room."

Marie was left standing at the open front door, feeling more alone than ever, when Teodor appeared. A little way down the street, two of his companion soldiers waited for him.

"I'm afraid I must report to Marshal Berthier, Marie." He bent and kissed her on the forehead.

As he turned to go, she grasped hold of his jacket's sleeve. "Teo, tell me, have I chosen properly? *Have I?*"

Teodor's eyes widened with surprise, but then the deep green softened, and he took hold of one of her hands. "You have, Marie. You've made a difference. Know that. Remember that. Father would be so proud." Teodor released her now, gifting her with a wide smile before descending and moving down the street. Without turning around and almost as an afterthought, he blurted, "For Poland!"

Marie was left to wonder whether the exclamation had been meant for his fellow soldiers, who were awaiting him upon their mounts—or whether he was applauding her.

A week later, Marshal Duroc returned with another note from the emperor, one echoing the previous note's welcome and little more.

They took tea in the reception room.

"When will he himself welcome me, Monsieur Duroc?"

Duroc forced a little smile, his gaze reverting to Aleksander, who slept soundly in Marie's arms. "I'm not certain, Madame Walewska. Perhaps soon."

"Perhaps?" Marie felt heat rising into her face. She already regretted having come to Paris. Napoleon was ignoring her. He had a young wife who seemed to have entranced him, one who met his requirements, one who would leave little room for a role for her. *What did I expect? I was a fool.*

"In the meantime, I'm to see you comfortably settled in the city," Duroc was saying. "Doctor Corvisart will visit you on a regular basis." His eyes met hers now. "Your health and that of the baby are of the utmost importance to the emperor, and to me. You shall have access to tickets to any play, opera, or museum that takes your interest. In fact, you will have your own box at the Opéra and the Théâtre Français. You are to have a monthly allocation of ten thousand francs."

Marie covered her mouth at the amount.

"In time, Madame Walewska, you are to be received at Court."

"At Court? But I—"

"The emperor will insist," Duroc interjected. "This is to be your home now, and you are not to be hidden away. It is only right. You are the mother of the emperor's son. Monsieur Antoine Leroy has cleared his schedule Tuesday next for you so that, in his words, you are to become a 'spectacle of fashion and elegance.'"

"And if I don't wish to become a *spectacle?*"

"Forgive me, but dare I say that I know your nature by now, Madame Walewska. You would *never* become that." Duroc's gaze moved around the reception room. "Speaking of style, you've no doubt noticed that this house has been refurbished since you were last here."

"How could I not? The furniture and textiles are *magnifique.*"

"The emperor has also made arrangements for you to have a country villa in Boulogne. Its decorations, as here, were personally chosen by him."

If true, Marie thought, Napole has more time to be picking out furnishings than to visit me, or his son. "Monsieur Duroc," she said, her hand going to that dimpled space at her throat, "this is all too much for me to take in."

Duroc stood to take his leave. "It is the way of the emperor, Madame Walewska."

After his departure, Marie rang for Hania to take the baby.

Once she was alone, she sat taking in the richness of the room's furnishings, replaying in her mind the luxuries Duroc had been entrusted to present. The totality was dizzying. She recalled the time in Kiernozia some four years previous when she angrily threw a fancy box containing a diamond brooch to the floor, insulted that Napoleon Bonaparte thought he could purchase her. And now, he was laying all of Paris at her feet, despite having chosen to marry into a dynasty.

Her thoughts went to the country house Duroc said was located in Boulogne. By now, she knew enough of Paris geography to know that Boulogne was a suburb not far from the emperor's own country residence at St. Cloud.

What does he want of me? What? And am I prepared to give it?

Noon, Christmas Eve 1810

The house was a hive of activity in preparation for the *Wigilia* celebration. Marie felt none of the usual yuletide excitement of previous years. While Antoni played nearby with a set of wooden alphabet blocks, she sat on a settee in the reception room nursing Aleksander, despite Doctor Corvisart's insistence she retain a wet-nurse.

She barely noticed footsteps on the staircase, until a knock came at the door.

"Come in," she called.

Grand Marshal Duroc entered, announcing, "His Majesty the Emperor."

Marie felt as if the breath went out of her. Napoleon stepped in behind the marshal. He had come—unexpectedly.

The marshal's gaze took in her activity and swerved away from her, but Napoleon's eyes locked onto hers. "Marie," he said, a practiced hand signal ordering Duroc to withdraw. "I'm sorry to intrude," he said, his voice soft. "It was thoughtless of me."

Marie shifted her hold on Aleksander and covered herself. The baby seemed content enough, and Antoni was still caught up with his blocks.

Napoleon stood wordless, his bicorne in hand. Typically, he eschewed the more fanciful uniforms of his marshals, wearing instead—as today—the simple green and white of a colonel in the mounted chasseurs of the Imperial Guard as a tribute to the men sworn to protect him. He made no move to advance. "This is the boy? My boy."

"Aleksander. Yes, of course." Marie gathered herself. "Come see him, Napole." How strange it seemed to be speaking to him again. "Come see our child. He's big for six months, I'm told."

Napoleon stepped forward, almost timidly, Marie thought. He dropped his hat on the settee next to her. His black hair was matted and a bit mussed. She noted also that he had put on some weight. He bent to kiss her cheeks.

Marie's heart quickened.

"He's beautiful, Marie," he whispered as he stood over her, staring at Aleksander. "Beautiful."

"He has my complexion and hair, but your face."

"He's falling off to sleep. What color are his eyes?"

"Dark blue," Marie said, although sometimes she thought them black, possibly a feature of his Corsican lineage. She would not voice her suspicion, knowing that Napoleon had begun to distance himself from his connection with Corsica in favor of an absolute French identity. "Napole, let me ring for Hania to take the children."

"No, no, I can't stay. I apologize that it's taken this long to come see you. Duroc has reminded me well enough, and—well, I'm sorry. Tell me, are you comfortable here? Is everything in order?"

"I'm well taken care of, but . . ."

"But?"

"I feel out of place. I intend to return to Poland after the winter." The unplanned words flowed out of her. She had not rehearsed them. And she didn't regret them.

"What?" Napoleon's head drew back. His voice dropped. "I can't allow that, Marie. You are tied to . . . your place is here now."

"Is it?"

"Aleksander is my son and you are his mother. Yes, it is!"

Marie was tempted to remind him that he had called her his *Polish wife*, but she saw that he was tugging on his waistcoat and checking the buttons, a nervous habit that indicated he was anxious to leave.

"We'll talk again, Napole."

"Indeed. I'll allow more time." Napoleon picked up his hat and bowed. "Forgive me, Marie, for the brevity of my visit."

So formal, Marie thought. She attempted a smile, but her lips would not part for a true smile. It was at this moment—at this meeting—that she became aware of how much their relationship had cooled, changed. As he turned and walked toward the door, she determined she would leave Paris as early into the new year as weather allowed.

Napoleon pivoted at the door, cleared his throat, and said, "You know, dearest Marie, that you are holding in your arms the boy who will one day become King of Poland." He clicked his boot heels together and gave her a sly, cryptic smile, the type of smile she had seen him employ when winning at cards or chess. She imagined it as the smile he must wield when his legendary strategy and tactics are proven victorious on the battlefield.

How was it possible that, inside of a minute, his shrewdness would disarm her and vanquish any thought of leaving?

59

Winter 1811

JANUARY PASSED WITHOUT A WORD from Napoleon. Marie remained at the house on Rue de la Houssaye, and though Marshal Duroc visited every other day, by month's end, Marie stopped asking about Napoleon. If it hadn't annoyed him, it had started to irritate her.

In early February, her niece Dory visited. "Marie," she began, once they were seated together on a settee, "when are you going to accept our invitation to one of our salons? We host them twice a week, on Tuesdays and Saturdays."

"Tea," Marie said, nodding to the butler. Her gaze returned to her niece. "My brother Teodor told me about your salons and that you entertain important officials and officers of the emperor's Polish guards."

"French *is* the language of the day, Marie, but you can't escape the Polish cadence among many of our guests. It's like being at home." She eyed Marie intently. "Now, Tereska insists I get a firm answer from you. People are eager to meet you."

"They ask about me?"

"Indeed."

"But I suppose the focus is on Napoleon's marriage and the impending birth."

Dory gave a dismissive wave of her hand. "Well, if it's a boy, yes, but the Parisians haven't taken kindly to the new empress. They had a genuine affection for Josephine."

"So now they pity Josephine?"

"Yes. And Marie-Louise? She's stiff, like a porcelain doll. A cool empress, that one. The French have never been partial to the Austrian Royal House. And here we are, not so many years later, with another Austrian archduchess."

"Ha! —One who is the grand-niece of Marie Antoinette," Marie said.

"Yes!" Dory laughed. "You can imagine the jokes that make the rounds. 'Oh, what a lovely neck she has.' Or 'Such a good head on her shoulders.' That sort of thing."

Marie tried to stifle a laugh. "That's awful."

"It's her hips that really matter. She needs to produce an heir." Dory took hold of Marie's hands. "Enough of her. So, tell me that you will join us this Tuesday?"

"Too soon—perhaps Saturday. I must see Monsieur Antoine Leroy first. I've put him off a number of times."

"Ah, you intend to make an entrance in one of his creations?" Dory teased, eyes sparkling.

Marie's laughter burst forth, light and free. "That's Leroy's intention! Marshal Duroc tells me he wants to make a spectacle of me. Imagine!"

Dory's hand flew to her chest, her eyes widening as she was overtaken with laughter, her giggles ringing out, filling the room. She leaned against Marie for support, unable to catch her breath.

Marie's laughter reignited and their combined amusement echoed back, contagious and unrestrained.

Just then, the door swung open and the butler entered with the tea tray, the interruption only making their laughter harder to repress.

The butler made a quick exit.

"So," Dory said, at last sobering and sitting up, "I shall tell Tereska that my mission was a success! Saturday, then?"

Marie nodded.

After Dory left, Marie vowed to stop casting about in sadness and anxiety. It was time to take charge of a different sort of life, a public one. "Saturday, it is," she said aloud.

Monday, 20 March 1811

Marie sat on a chaise lounge, absently watching Antoni play with the wooden pieces of a favorite puzzle on the floor.

At mid-morning the sound of a cannon boomed. Once, twice, three times—and it still went on. A great cheering went up from in front of the house, and seemingly, from all the streets of Paris. Antoni looked up at her, his eyes wide.

Marie's hand moved to her heart. Marie-Louise had given birth. The booming went on. Duroc had told her that the birth of a girl would merit twenty-one salvoes, but the birth of a boy would dictate a hundred and one.

Marie held her breath as she counted: nineteen, twenty, and twenty-one.

Twenty-two, and the booms continued as the increased shouts in the streets nearly drowned out the explosions. It was a boy. Marie-Louise had done her duty.

Napole had his heir.

Marie felt she couldn't breathe, couldn't navigate her mix of emotions.

The screams of a baby brought her into focus. The door opened, and Hania entered, lips pressed tight in anxiety. "It's the noise, Madame," she said. Aleksander struggled in her clasp, arms flailing and lungs ringing out.

Spring 1811
The day after the birth, Duroc had told Marie, "Even Parisians who despised Napoleon for all his wars are celebrating the birth of his heir." Marie found it strange—her son was now half-brother to the new King of Rome and future emperor, Napoleon Francois Charles Joseph.

Marie sat alone with Aleksander, who slept soundly in her arms after having nursed. Gazing down at the baby, she addressed him with a Polish diminutive, "You came first, didn't you? What will that matter, my little Olek? Your brother might be emperor, but if your papa is true to his word, you will have a future. He's promised Poland to you."

Marie attended the salons hosted by Dory and Tereska and was surprised at how fashionable their gatherings had become, attracting French officials, visiting Polish *szlachta* and magnates, as well as officers of the Imperial Guard, Teodor among them. Also attending were dignitaries from across the continent, who made their way to Paris to bend the knee before the legendary Napoleon.

The attention Marie received made her reflect on her past with Napoleon. Although he claimed to love his *Polish wife*, he chose a young woman, sight unseen and no doubt by way of a pressured agreement with her unhappy parents, so that his wish for a dynasty marriage could be fulfilled.

Just as Napoleon's role had changed—by his own doing—so had her role, but through no fault of hers.

How am I now to shape a life for myself and for my children?

The answer came by way of her old friend and mentor from convent school, Eliza Sobolewska. She and her husband were staying at their second home in Paris while Walenty advised Napoleon about events back in the duchy, some murky business about Russia, according to gossip.

Late one evening, after a salon they had hosted, Eliza and Marie settled into wicker chairs on the terrace.

"It's nearly midnight," Eliza said. "Usually they leave by ten."

"Oh?"

"Do you know why?"

"No, Eliza."

"It's you! Why, the way they flock around you, Marie! From the youngest hussar to the most dignified magnate. They are intoxicated by your youth and beauty. The thing they most comment on is your modesty."

Marie laughed. "So, when my beauty fades and my skin wrinkles, I'll still have something left to draw on? I'll need it."

Eliza laughed.

"Now, Eliza, the truth is, these people find me of interest because of my connection with the emperor, even if it is more in the past. It's simple. I'm good for a bit of gossip."

"Perhaps in some cases, but I think they look up to you as a kind of beacon."

"A beacon?" Marie laughed.

Eliza nodded. "For Poland. Oh, it's more than your face, dearest. Your *words* matter. There's no telling what you might still do. Poland is once more in a game of push and pull for the center of Europe. Czar Aleksander has offended—I should say, *incensed*—Napoleon by opening up Russian ports to England and other enemies of France, as well as placing high tariffs on French goods. More significantly, the czar is amassing a great number of troops on Poland's borders. Poland is going to be pivotal."

"So, war is imminent," Marie whispered. "I dread it. And to think I named the baby after Napole's nemesis."

"You're not a fortune teller, Marie." Eliza took a breath. "Prince Poniatowski is here in Paris going over plans with the emperor. Has he been to see you?"

"No."

"I suspect he will. I tell you, Marie, you have come so far since convent school days. You've become a gifted woman of the world. An influential woman. Napoleon has spoken to me about you. You still hold a place in his heart. Don't think otherwise."

"*He* told you that? I've seen him just *once* since he invited me here to live."

"Not in so many words, but he's spoken of you and your son Aleksander to my husband. He's intent on having you attend Court once Marie-Louise starts receiving again."

"That's—awkward. Unthinkable!"

"It needn't be. The emperor wants you to find your place here in Paris."

Summer 1811

Marie found the words "find your place" deeply haunting. She buried her hurt and set aside her reserve as she made a deliberate decision to conquer Paris's international society. If she was, as Eliza claimed, a beacon for her homeland, then she would embrace her popularity. Or was it notoriety? In any case, she would make her mark. Doing so became her obsession.

Marie maintained weekly fittings with Antoine Leroy, who delighted in creating for her the most fashionable gowns. She held her own salons on Sundays when her large drawing room overflowed with a crush of important people. She had her likeness painted by the most sought-after painters in Paris: François Gérard and Robert Lefèvre.

Napoleon visited now and again. He didn't fail to notice that Aleksander's features resembled his own. "I'm afraid *le garçon* is going to have my large head," he said, laughing. He brought hard candy for both boys, but he was clearly developing an attachment to their child. Little Olek would keep Napoleon linked to her.

One day, he commented on the change in Marie's public persona. "You were always a butterfly to me, Marie," he said, "but now the whole city has taken notice of your flight."

"How do you know that?"

"I have my watcher."

"A—a watcher?"

Napoleon ignored her question. "You must come to Court."

"When?"

Napoleon's eyes opened unusually wide. He had expected an argument.

"You needn't insist, Napole."

After Napoleon left, she sat going over their exchange. What did he mean that he had a *watcher*? Suddenly, it came to her. The same dark-haired young soldier seemed to appear in the background at every salon she held or attended. Once, she had even seen him on Rue de la Loi when she was entering Monsieur Leroy's establishment for a fitting.

Napoleon was having her spied upon! *Why?*

She felt a tightening at her chest.

Court was the center of life for the upper classes in Paris. Leroy created for Marie a sumptuous court gown of turquoise, embroidered at the neck, sleeves, and lower third with navy material studded with amber stones. An orange scarf was wound through her highly piled blond hair.

Court presentations took place at noon at the Tuileries. Marie arrived early. She was among nine or ten to be presented to the royal couple. Third in line, she made her way slowly and solemnly up the parquet walkway at the side of her sponsor, the Duchess of Montebello, wife of a Marshal Lannes, whom she had known in her Warsaw circles. A colorful crowd lined the side, lorgnettes held to a good many eyes, fans to a few mouths. Not too many months before, she would have been trembling in terror, but, while she was a bit nervous, she was fast finding her niche in society.

Coming at last to the bottom of the five-step red dais, Madame Lannes made the presentation. Marie performed the expected curtseys, looked up, and stared. So accustomed to seeing Napoleon in plain or fancy military dress, she blinked in surprise to find him—and the empress—in gold-embroidered red robes with white fur trim. His elaborate gold crown, set with cameos, was fitted with arches rising to a cross at the apex. "Welcome, Madame Walewska," he said in an announcing tone. He turned to his wife.

Empress Marie-Louise affected a smile. "Welcome, Madame. You are from Warsaw?"

Marie recalled Dory's saying the empress seemed like a lifeless porcelain doll. It was an accurate description, especially now, draped to the neck in the robe and bedecked in a silver and gold diadem encrusted with countless turquoise stones and diamonds. "I'm from Kiernozia, Your Royal Highness."

When the empress did not respond in words or expression, Marie felt pressured to say more. "My husband is from Walewice. Both are in Mazovia, central Poland. It's a beautiful land of rivers, forests, and flowering plains. I should say, we *hope* one day it's to be called part of Poland again."

"Indeed. And your husband? He's not here?"

Marie froze. *Sweet Jesus!* Was she aware of the talk? Did she *know*? *How much?* She fought to keep her voice from rising. "The count is taking the waters at Bad Gastein."

"I see," the empress said, her tone flat.

Marie calmed herself, suspecting that the empress was merely bored.

Napoleon nodded, his signal that she should move off to the next drawing room.

Marie had practiced the ritual withdrawal with Madame Lannes so that she flawlessly executed a series of three low curtsies, rotated to her left while carefully managing the train of a Court gown, and moved backwards to the next reception room.

Within an hour, the presentations came to an end.

"Thank you, Madame Lannes, for sponsoring me," Marie said as they left the Tuileries. "I didn't realize how short the occasion would be. Why, I spent more time in Monsieur Leroy's fitting room than here."

The duchess gave a throaty laugh. "It's like that, but many eyes were upon you. This was a test of your manners and grace, and I do believe you carried the day. From here forward, your position in Paris will be unequivocable. Unassailable. Congratulations!"

Marie listened and observed at the salons she hosted and those she attended. Rumors of war were giving way to preparations for it. In response to Aleksander's hostile moves, Napoleon's *Grande Armée* was growing day by day with regiments from nearly a dozen countries. Parisians were on edge, for they recalled the sacrifices of Napoleon's past wars, and now their sons were being called up again in great numbers. Incessant summer rain and the wide scale failure of crops further dispirited the citizenry. For the Poles who frequented the salons, citizens and soldiers alike, a burst of fervor arose for what was called "the Second Polish War." Most of her countrymen in Paris believed that the emperor would at last deliver independence to Poland. Marie knew, however, that not everyone back home in the duchy was of the same mind.

Marie believed in Napoleon. For Poland, she had to believe.

In late July, as Eliza predicted, Prince Poniatowski visited Marie at her country residence on Rue de Montmorency. They sat facing each other in plush floral chairs.

"This is a lovely home, Madame Walewska. Lovely—and so close to the emperor's residence at St. Cloud," the prince noted. Coming from someone else, it might have been a barb, but the prince himself had facilitated her relationship with Napoleon. It was an observation.

"It is," she answered.

"He keeps you close," he said. "Do you see him often?"

"Rarely. He stops to see his son on occasion."

"He tells me the boy resembles him."

"He does. Would you care to see Olek?"

The prince lifted his hand to hold her in place. "No, no, Madame Walewska. I can't stay. I'm preparing to leave for Warsaw tomorrow. There's much to be done."

Marie knew he had been in Paris for four months, yet he waited until now to visit. Something was afoot. She waited for him to continue.

The prince wet his lips. "I'm certain you know we're on the brink of war."

Marie nodded.

"When Napoleon leaves to join his forces, I suspect you'll return to the duchy."

"What makes you think that, Sire?"

The prince cleared his throat. "Let me explain, Madame Walewska. When the czar made plans to oppose Napoleon, Poland was his biggest concern. He hoped to bring Poland to his side. For this purpose, he employed the Russian Deputy Foreign Minister, Prince Adam Czartoryski, whom I admit is a Polish patriot, but one who feels Poland's future is with Russia. Adam proposed to me that Poland could regain her independence if the army of the duchy were to go over to the czar's side."

Marie inhaled quickly, stunned. "And desert Napoleon? Never!"

"You're right, Madame Walewska. That's what I told him in the clearest words possible, soldier's words I dare not repeat." The prince paused, his blue eyes searching Marie's face. "That's where you could help."

Marie sat back against the chair's cushion. "Me?"

"Yes. "You're beloved in Warsaw, even in your absence. Those who've visited Paris speak of your grace and influence."

"Inflated stories, I think, Sire."

"Several diarists have come back and written about you, and you've been featured any number of times in *The Gazeta Warszawska*."

Marie was struck silent.

"Madame Walewska, the emperor feels that in the capital you can sway public opinion in France's favor."

"How?"

"By speaking your mind. You've already become a public figure here. I must admit, Madame Walewska, you've surprised me."

"Ha! I've surprised myself."

"The emperor says his sisters Caroline, the queen of Naples, and Princess Pauline adore you."

Marie shrugged. "His stepdaughter, Queen Hortense of Holland, has also favored me with her friendship. Alas, I've seen more of them than I have of Napoleon."

The prince smiled weakly.

"So, Sire, you're suggesting I return to Warsaw?" Marie asked, shifting the conversation. "When?"

"Not for some months, perhaps into the new year. He'll have someone in Warsaw assist you."

"A spy? He has me watched here in Paris, you know."

The prince showed no surprise. "Not a spy. It will be someone highly placed who can present you to influential figures." He paused, tilting his head slightly. "You know, Madame Walewska, he wants you safe. And the boy."

After the prince left, Marie sat in thought. She would not resist returning to Warsaw or doing what she could to shore up enthusiasm for the French. In fact, her return would also play into her more personal plans.

November 1811

One day, Dory rushed into the reception room at the Boulogne villa, breathless. "You're to have a visitor, Marie—tomorrow!"

Marie stood to receive her. "Yes—is it he?"

"What? Oh! No, it's not Napoleon."

"Oh—well, then, who is it that would make you perspire so?"

"You had better sit down, cousin."

Marie complied. Dory joined her on the sofa and took her hand.

"Enough suspense, if you please," Marie pressed.

"It's—it's Tadeusz Kościuszko."

Marie's mouth fell agape. "You don't mean it!"

"He appeared at our door today looking for you. It seems he has taken up residence here in France, near Fontainebleau."

"Sweet Jesus! So, you told him where I am?"

"Ha! Would I lie to General Tadeusz Kościuszko?"

Marie lay awake long into the night. Although she had grown accustomed to entertaining foreign statesmen, the thought of receiving Kościuszko filled her with dread.

General Tadeusz Kościuszko was the military hero of her youth. His noble insurrection against Poland's occupiers ended at Maciejowice with his imprisonment—and her father's death. Still, after his confinement, Kościuszko refused to align himself with France, passing up the chance to lead Polish legions on behalf of Napoleon, whom he called "the gravedigger of France." Consequently, he fell out of favor in her eyes.

Marie received General Kościuszko in the music room, where the smallness of the room best held the fireplace heat. The general arrived precisely at noon.

He hurried toward her as she rose from her chair. "Oh, Madame Walewska, you needn't rise for me. I may be coming into old age, but I'm still nimble enough to bow and kiss the hand of a beautiful woman."

Marie stood straight, her shoulders pushed back, as he took her hand. She found that she had to look up once he stood erect. She had expected him in a military uniform, but he wore a simple dark coat and breeches, white shirt and waistcoat. The frayed and faded hat he had doffed was the four-cornered hat of the Polish peasant, a faded red with black sheepskin at its base.

"If I do say so, Madame Walewska, you exceed your reputation for beauty."

"And your reputation as a flirtatious bachelor lives up to the palaver of the gossipers and scribblings of the diarists." The words came in a rush, uncensored. Before Marie had time to be embarrassed, his squinty dark eyes widened, and he laughed.

The ice was broken.

Marie's butler served him tea and French biscuits. She studied him as he chatted about the weather, the crop failures, and the plight of the peasants in both France and Poland. He was in his mid-sixties, Marie guessed, and the lines in his face reflected his age, but his dimpled chin and narrow, upturned nose rendered his facial appearance almost delicate.

They both seemed to be avoiding any conversation tilting toward anything military. In time, however, Marie asked him about his experience in helping the Americans secure their freedom from Britain, and that changed the direction of the tête-à-tête. "You used both your engineering skills, as well as your military strategy, yes?"

Kościuszko shrugged. "I helped where I could. They needed guidance in planning fortifications. I like to think I was helpful in gaining their freedom, Madame Walewska. That's the crux of everything, isn't it?"

"It is. Independence is all."

He nodded. "I should have mentioned your father's bravery and ultimate sacrifice at Maciejowice by now, Madame Walewska. Forgive me."

Suddenly choked up, Marie waved her hand in a dismissive motion.

"Over the years I've heard of your own passion for Poland's independence. Mateusz was my friend, and you're very much his daughter."

"Thank you, General Kościuszko," Marie said, finding her voice. Her heart sped up. "You knew him well?"

"Indeed. I've not found a finer soldier—or man. I held him as he lay dying. He refused the wagon for the wounded, told me that others would need it. He knew he had little time. He died with your mother's name on his lips. Eva, isn't it?"

Marie's vision blurred with tears. "Yes," she managed.

"I'm sorry to bring this up, Madame Walewska. I wrote to her, you know."

Marie nodded. "She reads your letter aloud every tenth of October."

"The battle day." The general's pale blue eyes glistened. "How different things would be today if things had gone right for us."

"Perhaps the opportunity will come again," Marie said.

The general averted his gaze and took a sip of his tea, no doubt cold by now.

"Let me call for some more hot water."

"No, Madame Walewska, I don't wish to overstay my welcome."

"Nonsense." Marie caught the general's gaze. "You don't place much faith in Napoleon, General Kościuszko?"

"Ah, Madame Walewska, it saddens me that I don't."

"I know that he respected you highly."

The general looked at Marie with a quizzical intensity, as if in a quandary how to respond. He drew in a long breath and spoke. "Just before the turn of the century and after Napoleon returned from Egypt, he put in a surprise appearance at my apartment on the Rue de Lille. Remember, he was *General* Napoleon then. He saw me as a senior statesman and made a plea for my support. He already had three Polish legions under his banner fighting for protecting

French expansion in Northern Italy and two other regions. He secured their loyalty by promising to force Russia to restore Poland. You were no doubt very young at this time, Madame Walewska."

"I've learned of it in school and on my own, General Kościuszko."

"Then you know many Polish soldiers died fighting for France's territories."

"I do."

The general harrumphed. "In any event, I sensed his bid for my approval was less than sincere. I thought it manipulative, and I had the sense that a power play was in the works. I refused my support. Then, by the end of the century, he staged a coup to become First Consul."

Marie nodded. "And Emperor of the French in 1804."

"His promise to restore Poland, Madame Walewska, became more of an inducement for those who wished only to believe. As it is today."

Until the general said this with edgy urgency, Marie had been on the verge of telling him of Napoleon's promise to her that he would name their son King Aleksander of Poland. Now, she knew he would merely scoff at the idea. She held her tongue.

"You look as if you doubt me, Madame Walewska. I can assure you that he was willing to sign Poland away without blinking an eye in an official offer to marry the Grand Duchess Anne."

"Preposterous! Francis had no room to barter. He had his back against the wall. And I think you mean Marie-Louise."

"Oh!" The pale blue eyes went wide. He appeared stunned. "You don't know, do you?"

"Know? Know *what*?"

"They've kept it from you, have they? I see. It's no wonder, I suppose."

"General Kościuszko, what are you talking about?"

"Prior to his engagement to Marie-Louise, Napoleon bargained with Czar Aleksander for the hand of his young sister, the Grand Duchess Anne. She was his first choice."

"Prior?"

"Yes. Had the czar agreed, Napoleon would have allowed Poland to fall completely into Russia's grasp. The deal fell through when Aleksander's mother, the Dowager Countess Maria, refused to sacrifice her fifteen-year-old daughter to Napoleon."

"You said *prior*, General Kościuszko. When was this offer made?"

"Almost immediately after the divorce from Josephine. French Minister

Champagny began negotiations in December of 1809. By January of 1810, they failed."

Marie was thunderstruck. She had been carrying Napoleon's child while this was going on. It was also about the time the salutation of his notes shifted to read *Dear Madame.* That was when she sensed their relationship change. Her breathing came hard now. She put her hand to the dimpled area below her neck. The room tilted, then spun, round and round. She held to the arms of the chair to steady herself. The general's mouth was moving, and she heard the words he was speaking, but they came through a kind of fog and made no sense. Suddenly, he was at her side, his aged face grimacing in concern, plying her with questions.

Some minutes went by before her thoughts came together. "Thank you, General. I'm fine now. I didn't have breakfast, you see."

"I'm afraid I must leave. I've upset you. I'm so sorry, Madame Walewska. Thank you for your hospitality. Besides wishing to commend your father's heroism, I wanted to see for myself that reports of your beauty are accurate." He bent to kiss her hand, adding, "Indeed, they are."

Marie reached for the servant's bell.

"Oh, don't bother, Madame Walewska," the general said. "I can see myself out."

Marie was left to consider his two reasons for the visit, coming to conclude that there was a third, deliberate, intention: to erode her loyalty to Napoleon.

Winter 1811-1812

For weeks, the visit from Poland's foremost patriot left Marie rattled and in a dark mood. How had Napoleon's overture to Czar Aleksander for his sister's hand been kept from her? It was not public knowledge, but others in her sphere—Constant Wairy, Grand Marshal Duroc, and Prince Poniatowski—must have known. No doubt, they were sworn to secrecy—or were mindful of her feelings. Going forward, Marie was too humiliated to bring up the subject with them. She did ask Dory and Tereska about the overture. They had not heard of it, and they seemed genuinely shocked. Each commiserated with Marie in her own way. It did little to lift her spirits.

On some days, Marie cursed Napoleon. On others—especially when doting on little Aleksander—so like his father—she had to admit to herself that she still cared for him."

"You're still so grave, cousin," Tereska said one day. "Why should you be so offended to find out he plotted twice for what you knew he plotted and attained once?"

"I'm not offended for myself. —Well, yes, some, but what truly offends me most, Tereska," Marie said, her voice going deep, "is that he was willing to barter away Poland!"

She took no pleasure in the fact that the new empress had not found her way into the hearts of the French—or, as the gossip went, that the marriage lacked passion. The verdict on Marie-Louise was that she was cool as ice. Napoleon was caught up completely in the fact that he now had an heir to the throne, and perhaps that mollified any disappointment in the royal bedchamber.

Here was the question Marie anguished over every day: Had Napoleon been humoring her about respecting her wish for Poland's independence all these years? Could he really trade Poland away without batting an eye?

———⋅⋙⋘⋅———

From time to time, Napoleon sent for her and little Olek. Sometimes they would be taken to his office at the Tuileries; other times to a small reception room at the Château de St. Cloud. Napoleon spent most of the short visits playing with little Olek. He seemed to genuinely love children and always had some new ingenious toy for their son. The most recent was a little platform on wheels bearing a drummer and a bell ringer in clown costumes. As the toy was pulled, the porcelain faced figures moved, making music. Marie watched, affecting a smile. While she and Olek were secretly whisked in and out, she knew that the lion's share of his attention went to his heir, Napoleon Francois Charles Joseph.

Once, as they were leaving the Tuileries, Napoleon said, "My Marie, please be a bit happier the next time."

Marie wanted to deliver a sharp reply and pivot away from him, but he had said, *My Marie,* as in the past.

She drew in breath and nodded.

60

5 May 1812

THE MESSAGE ARRIVED BEFORE MARIE awakened. Napoleon directed her to come to his St. Cloud residence. Grand Marshal Duroc would arrive at ten to escort her. She was not to bring Aleksander.

For months, she—and the French people—had expected Napoleon to join his Grande Armée on the banks of the River Vistula. Meanwhile, salons, dances, and theater events continued, though an air of despondency lingered. It was in these social circles that she kept abreast of military matters. Czar Aleksander was in Lithuania's capital, Wilno, personally mustering his troops. He had demanded that the French vacate Prussian and Swedish territories, and all lands east of the River Elbe, an ultimatum that enraged Napoleon. War was imminent.

Upon arriving at St. Cloud, Marie was ushered into the library. Napoleon turned from where he stood at a large desk and nodded. Behind the desk, his secretary, Monsieur Claude Méneval, looked up and gave a hesitant smile. Both men wore serious expressions.

Greetings all around were awkward.

Napoleon cleared his throat. "I leave Paris in four days, Marie."

"I see."

He nodded toward the desk. "With appropriate legal counsel, I had Méneval draw this up. I intended for you to sit here and review it, but I've just now been called away. I must leave at once. I want you here when I sign it, so trust me as to its contents."

Marie glanced from Napoleon to Méneval and then to the document on the desk, which seemed to be several pages long. Her gaze returned to the emperor. "What is it?"

"I'm making provisions for little Aleksander—and for you, too, Marie."

Marie's breath caught. "Provisions?"

Napoleon nodded. "Certain estates in Italy he is to inherit." He turned to Méneval. "Read the name so Marie can verify that I have it right."

The secretary leaned over the desk and read aloud: "'The Naples estates delineated in this decree are hereby granted to Count Aleksander Florian Joseph Colonna Walewski.'"

Marie fell back a step, her hand to her mouth. She had never thought of her little boy in this way.

"Well," Napoleon said, "are the names correct? Your husband certainly put a string of them together, the most unfortunate one being the first."

"*I* chose the name Aleksander, Napole."

Napoleon eyed her sharply for a moment before shrugging. "So be it." He looked down at the desk. "The document goes on to allow for the estates to be passed on to his offspring via primogeniture. If he has no male heirs, it goes to his daughters." Napoleon turned back to Marie. "I've not forgotten you, Marie. Méneval, tell her, in short, just the important parts."

"Yes, Sire." Méneval glanced from Marie to the document and read: "'Until the young Count Aleksander Florian Joseph Colonna Walewski comes of age, his mother, the Countess Marie Walewska, is to be the full beneficiary and may make use of the income as she sees fit. Upon the count's coming of age, he is to pay her a yearly pension of fifty thousand francs.'"

"And?" Napoleon was pulling at his waistcoat and checking his buttons.

Méneval continued, "'Should Count Aleksander die without a descendant, the entail will return to the Bonaparte private domain, but Countess Walewska is to retain all monies resulting from the estates—until her death'."

Napoleon picked up a pen, inked it, and signed with a flourish. Handing the pen to Méneval, he said, "You'll sign as a witness."

After the secretary signed, Napoleon kissed Marie on the cheeks and hastily made his exit.

Marie shot a questioning glance at Méneval, who nodded, his lips compressed. The two had come to understand one another.

"I believe he's going to the Tuileries. It's the empress, Madame Walewska. She's vexed."

"Oh—about his departure for the front?"

"I don't know. The empress is often vexed."

Marie chose not to pursue that thread. The empress's temperament was already the talk of the salons. "Marshal Duroc is downstairs waiting for me. I must go. —But, Claude," she added, "about this document—"

The secretary instantly interjected, "The emperor has left you a very rich woman, Madame Walewska. Your son's endowment consists of sixty-nine farms in the Naples region, with an annual income of one hundred and seventy thousand francs."

Marie nodded and bit her lip. She had meant to ask whether Napoleon had dark thoughts about the coming confrontation, but she now realized that the document itself held the answer.

"Oh," Méneval added, almost as an afterthought, "in addition to any Polish titles your son might bear, other documents are being drawn up that will name Aleksander a Count of the French Empire. The emperor will sign them before he leaves—or on the road."

Marie stood stunned, her mouth slightly open as she processed the secretary's words. She suddenly realized why Napoleon had insisted that she return to Walewice for Aleksander's birth, and why he had somehow convinced Anastase to swallow his pride and be named the baby's father. Had her son been born out of wedlock, Napoleon wouldn't have been able to make him a Count of the French Empire.

As the carriage trundled back to the Boulogne villa, Marie sat, shoulders curving forward, head bent. The revelation of astounding wealth and the honor afforded her son were overshadowed by the reality that Napoleon thought such a document might be necessary. Had she just bid her love goodbye for the last time?

Seated next to her, the astute Marshal Duroc left her to her own thoughts.

When he escorted her to the villa's door, he handed her a calling card. "It is the emperor's wish that you work in tandem with the duchy's French Minister in fostering support among Warsaw's elite."

"I see. Oh, I know Minister Serra quite well."

"If you look at the card, you'll see the duchy has a new minister. It's the Archbishop of Mechelen, in Brussels, Abbé Dominique de Pradt. He's to look after you."

"An archbishop?"

"Tallyrand expected that *he* would get this appointment, and his partiality to Poland would have made him a good choice, but Napoleon thought this particular religious connection would carry some weight in your very Catholic country."

"Ah, as opposed to a secularized clergyman like Talleyrand," Marie said. "So, I'll be expected to attend countless religious events."

"I don't think so, Madame Walewska. "I must admit that I recommended him to the emperor as his chaplain in 1804. From there, he was appointed archbishop and now French Minister to the duchy."

"Why do you say *admit*, Marshal?"

"Oh, well, there have been some tales circulating about him. Be on your guard, Madame Walewska." Duroc bowed and turned to leave.

Marie had no opportunity to pursue his cryptic remark.

Monday, 29 June 1812

Marie and her two boys, along with Hania, departed Paris for the duchy, accompanied by her niece Dory, who was to stop in Spa, Belgium, to take the waters. From there, Marie planned to pass through Dresden before heading to Warsaw. A second carriage followed, carrying servants, including Dory's lady's maid.

As the carriage rolled through Paris, Marie watched the city pass by in silence. Napoleon had left for the Grande Armée four days after signing the entail papers. That was the last she had seen him.

Once out of Paris, with the boys asleep—Aleksander beside her and Antoni tucked in between Hania and Dory on the opposite bench—Marie spoke quietly. "Dory, I'll miss having you nearby in Warsaw."

"I don't intend to live in Spa, cousin. I'll find my way to Warsaw soon enough."

"Good."

"What is it, Marie? There's something on your mind. You've been so serious since we left."

"There is. Your mother Jadwiga has written to me."

"Yes? —About me?"

"No, no, not at all. It's about her brother."

"Uncle Anastase? Oh! She wouldn't write unless it's something serious."

Marie nodded. "She's written a number of times. It seems the Walewice estates have fallen on hard times because of the economy and dropping farm prices."

"Oh, surely they'll rebound, Marie."

"She also cited my husband's heavy spending habits. Did you witness any of that?"

Dory lowered her gaze. "Yes, I did. We all did. Sometimes, when he came back from wintering in Rome, my mother would declare, 'It's time to lay out a fine supper for the return of the prodigal *father*.' That was before he came to the table, of course."

Marie couldn't find it in herself to laugh. "Your mother writes that Walewice is heavily mortgaged."

Dory's hand flew to her mouth. "No! Is it really *that* bad?"

"Yes," Marie said, forging ahead. "I told you about the provisions the emperor has made for Aleksander."

"Yes! How fortunate! So, you and the boys will land softly."

"That's no guarantee. Those monies from those estates in Naples could be eaten away in very little time. Remember, Anastase is Aleksander's legal father. Oh, I'm the administrator and will hold the purse strings until such a time as Aleksander here reaches adulthood, but the laws of communal property will give Anastase rights equal to mine—"

Dory cut in. "I hate to speak badly about my uncle but, by that time, Aleksander could very well be a pauper without a *złoty* to his name."

They lapsed into a thick silence.

"What can you do, Marie?" Dory asked a few minutes later, her tone tentative. "There's no talking to him about his spending."

"I have a plan."

61

Warsaw
July 1812

MARIE ARRIVED IN THE GRAND Duchy of Warsaw to learn that Napoleon had caught up to his multi-national army of 500,000 as they crossed the River Nieman into Russian territory. Her friend Eliza delivered the news.

"Napoleon's calling it 'The Second Polish War'," Eliza said. "He insists it will establish peace for fifty years. At one of his suppers, the Archbishop de Pradt read an excerpt from one of the *Bulletins de la Grande Armée* sent from the warfront."

"Did the excerpt happen to mention Poland's independence?"

Seated across from Marie, Eliza lowered her eyelids a bit and shook her head. She brightened at once. "But that did not put a cork on our boys' enthusiasm for the emperor. Prince Józef leads a force of forty thousand and a Polish regiment of lancers continues to escort the emperor."

"My brothers Benedykt and Teodor among them, no doubt. So—independence was *implied*, then."

"As you say, Marie, but then came the strange news. The Russians moved into the interior, choosing not to take a stand. They all but left Wilno and all of Lithuania tied up in a bow for the French."

"Really? Strange, indeed."

"And ominous." Eliza stood up. "I'm sorry, dear, I must fly."

Marie rose and reached for her friend's hand. "First, the abbé—tell me, what is he like?"

"The abbé? Oh, Marie, it's better for you to decide for yourself."

That, too, is ominous, Marie thought.

"A divorce?" Anastase gulped air, his head shaking. "You've just arrived home and dare to present me with *this*? Why should you wish such a thing?" His chin trembled. "Why?" His voice cracked as he spoke, and he slumped back in his chair.

Marie had hoped he was at Walewice so that she could delay the conversation until she had more time to prepare, but she found him at the Warsaw townhome. Sitting across from him in the reception room, she saw no sense in prolonging the inevitable and broached the subject. "I'm sorry, Anastase, you know as well as I that our marriage has come apart. It's not your fault. It's mine. I want to be free. And it's better for you to be free of me."

"No, Marie! I won't have it!" he commanded in a hoarse voice.

Marie remained calm, though she was shaken. She had seen his anger before, directed at servants, but seldom at her. "Anastase," she said evenly, "I'm afraid you must."

"*Must*?" Her husband's brow lowered, nearly obscuring his eyes. Do you mean the *emperor* wishes this? Is that it?"

Marie considered saying yes, playing on his reverence for Napoleon, but decided against it. She had a more personal truth to share. "You care for me, I know, Anastase. You've been patient with me. I ask that you recall my state of mind when I was induced to marry you. I was depressed. —And I was not yet eighteen."

"I do remember, Marie," Anastase muttered, his anger softening. "But even if you were unduly influenced, as you imply, that doesn't justify a divorce! What of the children?" He paused, face reddening as the rage returned. "And the scandal! Can you imagine? The House of Walewski has never suffered such a scandal."

Marie knew better, yet held her tongue. As long as the appearance of their marriage continued, he could keep up pretenses, ignoring his wife's affair with Napoleon Bonaparte. He could lend her out—but not give her away.

"And you, Marie. Such shame and disrepute are worse for the woman!" Anastase took a breath. "—Besides, you can go through all the legal entanglements, and it's likely to be denied."

"The laws have changed, Anastase. I think I can manage it. Times have changed. We—both you and I—can bear the scandal."

Anastase snarled. "What about the boys?"

"The emperor has made provisions for Aleksander." She knew not to reveal the extent of Napoleon's largess.

At the mention of Napoleon, Anastase became quiet, then took a different direction. "And for Antoni? You mean to take him?"

"Yes. We will have enough to manage, the three of us."

Anastase paused. Something seemed to shift behind his milky blue eyes. "No, Marie, should I agree to this divorce business, I would insist you set up a trust for Antoni with the funds I provided for you as part of our marriage agreement. You *do* still have those funds?"

"I do. They are untouched and have increased in interest. I'll do as you say."

Her husband used the arms of the chair to push himself up. "And *if* I agree to a divorce, I will want to see Antoni often. I'm leaving for Walewice tomorrow. When I return at the end of the week, I'll have an answer for you."

---

18 July 1812

Marie didn't wait for Anastase to return from Walewice. Her friend Zofia Gronska confidentially provided her with a recommendation for an attorney, and she immediately began the process of filing for divorce in both the ecclesiastical and civil courts.

In reply to her letter outlining her concerns about Anastase's likely mismanagement of Aleksander's inheritance, her mother's response was reassuring. She and Benedykt would testify in court, stating that Marie had been coerced into the marriage while in poor physical and mental health—and under the age of eighteen.

The grounds for the divorce were truthful. However, what mattered most to Marie was the public acknowledgment from her mother and brother that they had wronged her by pressuring her into the marriage. Though their admission would come late, it would still be timely. She was grateful, but also bitter.

Anastase returned exactly one week later. Hania had eaten with the children in the kitchen earlier, so it was just husband and wife at the supper table. While he sat at the table's head, Marie sat near, on the lengthwise side, as usual. He appeared red-faced and addled. She worried that he planned to contest the divorce.

When the maids returned to the kitchen once the main course of fish and potato pancakes was served, Anastase turned to Marie with a glowering expression. "So, you couldn't wait, Marie. You've already begun the divorce process."

Marie went cold. She gave a slow nod. How did he know? "I—I thought I would get it started. I wasn't sure how long the process would take."

"You couldn't wait a week?"

Marie didn't answer. She cut into the fish, yet couldn't bring the fork to her mouth. Some minutes went by.

Anastase drank down the last of his wine. "You're wondering how I found out, Marie. Yes? Well, this morning I stopped to see Archbishop de Pradt for advice as to how likely the request would be accepted in the church court. It seems the request had already crossed his desk. I was humiliated, Marie."

That the French minister would be notified took her by surprise. Evidently, his role as archbishop somehow mattered. She wondered whether the priest at the ecclesiastical court sought his advice, or perhaps Abbé de Pradt actually had to ratify the request—or deny it. "I'm sorry for that, Anastase. I am." She wanted to ask him what de Pradt had told him, but dared not.

Anastase watched her, as if trying to decide whether her apology was sincere.

At that moment, the serving maid entered to clear the dishes before bringing the dessert. Noticing that neither Marie nor Anastase had touched their main course, she curtsied and made her retreat, empty-handed.

Anastase sighed. "Just a few years ago, a divorce wouldn't have been possible, but now, thanks to the Napoleonic Code, it's allowed. Isn't that convenient? Add to that the fact that Abbé de Pradt owes his position to the emperor, and I can already imagine the outcome in both the ecclesiastical and civil courts. If I were to contest your request, it would only make things more public—and ultimately, my effort would be futile. The abbé suggested as much. So, you'll likely have your way, Marie. You and Napoleon Bonaparte."

Marie remained silent, careful not to allow her response to betray her pleasure.

"The squat little man also told me that, in his capacity as French Minister to the duchy, Napoleon has entrusted him and *you* with building up support for the French cause here. Did you know about this?"

"I did. I haven't met him yet."

"Oh, he's eager to meet you. He expects to see you at his Saturday reception. He was a bit overwrought, however, because he's told people that you're to be the guest of honor, but you haven't replied to the several notes he's sent."

Marie would not inflame things further by telling her husband that the prelate's three notes were brash and flirtatious, nothing like one would expect from an archbishop.

"So—do you plan to attend, Marie?"

"I don't think I have a choice, Anastase."

Anastase grunted, pushed back his chair, rose, and left the room.

Evidently, her husband had not been invited.

Abbé Dominique de Pradt had been given the Brühl Palace—a grand rococo masterpiece—for the tenure of his new position as French Minister. Marie felt a flutter of nerves as she stepped from her carriage and joined the well-dressed guests making their way toward the entrance.

Inside, eighty or ninety guests sipped wine and chatted in small groups. Marie soon realized she was causing a stir. Conversation ebbed, and then a buzz spread through the room. She felt a multitude of eyes on her. Her stomach clenched.

To her relief, Anna Potocka broke through the crowd and greeted her warmly. "Marie, I'm so glad you're here," she said.

The two embraced. Anna directed her to an alcove away from the crowd. "Would you like some wine?"

"Not now, Anna. —Is your husband here?"

"Oh, my lord, no." Anna laughed. "He's had enough of Abbé de Pradt. When he was granted the Brühl Palace, he was unhappy with the interiors and had them completely redone. But where was he to stay during the undertaking? The man is so frugal. When he hinted at his problem to my husband, the

Polish reputation for hospitality prevailed, and Aleks offered him our ground floor."

"Much as you did for Prince de Murat all those years ago," Marie said.

"Exactly. And while the abbé didn't make any improper advances like the prince, I made certain to keep my door locked."

The two shared a laugh.

Anna suddenly grew serious, raising her fan to her face. "Here he comes, Marie."

Marie looked up to see the abbé approaching. He had an olive complexion and unremarkable features. His graying hair was short in front, but rolled at the sides and back. A large gold cross, encrusted with rubies and sapphires, hung from his neck, swaying gently against the black cassock.

"Ah, my guest of honor," the abbé said, his voice high and gravelly. "I see you're already acquainted with Madame Potocka. The Polish women here are extraordinarily beautiful, but Madame Walewska, you surpass them all." He extended his hand, and Marie knelt to kiss his ring.

"You're too kind, Your Eminence," Marie replied.

Anna added with a smile, "We Polish women have been a state secret, Your Eminence, but now with so many men off fighting for the French, we're more visible."

The abbé, still eyeing Marie, responded: "Remember, Madame Potocka, your men are fighting for the resurrection of your nation."

"If only we could trust in that," Anna said.

The abbé turned to Anna, his small, black eyes narrowing. "Do you doubt the emperor?"

"I didn't say that," Anna said, smiling neatly. "However, we Poles would like more than an implied commitment."

The abbé harrumphed. "Supper will be announced momentarily, ladies. Madame Walewska, you are to sit at my right at the head table. Anna has already requested the seat next to you. Until, then." He bowed slightly and disappeared into the crowd.

Anna turned to Marie, her voice low. "You've caught his eye, Marie, quite literally. He could hardly take his gaze off you. And not just your lovely face."

Marie blushed, glancing down at the décolletage of her pink supper gown. "I argue with Monsieur Leroy every time he leaves so little material for my bosom. He seldom relents."

Anna laughed. "Well, you're wearing the latest Parisian style. Every woman here is jealous, you can be sure."

Marie hesitated, then whispered, "I've come back to Warsaw to help the archbishop build support for the French—but also . . . I've filed for divorce, and it turns out the archbishop has influence in the ecclesiastical courts."

Anna's eyes widened. "You did what? Really?"

Just then, supper was announced.

"Too much to explain now," Marie said, relieved. "I'll tell you the details another time. Let's go in, shall we?"

The dining hall sparkled with crystal, gold, and fine paintings. "For a square little man unimpressive to the eye," Anna muttered, "he certainly knows how to decorate."

The abbé waved them over to the middle of the long head table, where Marie was made to stand until all the other guests had seated themselves. That done, he announced her as his hostess for the many suppers he was planning. The room responded with applause. Marie flushed with embarrassment and breathed a sigh of relief once the abbé nodded for her to sit.

Servers poured into the hall now, bringing appetizers—pickled herring, delicate crepes, and fragrant bean soup. The abbé loudly commented on each dish, sometimes praising, sometimes criticizing. He boasted about the chef he had left behind in Malines and bemoaned the lack of his favorite French dishes. Twice, he publicly scolded a servant for minor mistakes, a display unthinkable in Polish households.

What disturbed Marie most, however, was the way he repeatedly placed his right hand on her left hand, holding it there for long moments. After a few such gestures, Marie tried to keep her hands in motion, pretending to eat. At times, he would turn to her and use a lorgnette to slowly sweep over her form, like a searchlight.

The archbishop raised his voice. "I must say," he announced, "that the bean soup reminds me of a story about Madame de Pompadour. She favored beauty spots on her face, you see. One day, one spot chose to rebel and it took a little dive into her bean soup."

He paused, waiting for a response. Marie thought she could read more puzzled faces than amused ones.

"You'll never guess what Madame de Pompadour did!" he exclaimed. "She spooned it up from the broth, and cried: 'Look, friends! What good luck—a raisin!' and ate it before anyone could get a good look!"

The story brought polite laughter.

Anna leaned over to Marie. "He told the same story twice at Wilanów. And it won't be the last of the Pompadour anecdotes."

True to form, the abbé continued, "Did you know that Madame de Pompadour believed a woman fears the end of her youth more than the end of her life? And she certainly proved it! On her deathbed, she asked her Creator to wait while she called for her rouge pot, and with her last strength, she painted crimson circles on her pallid cheeks—and promptly died!"

The audience's reaction did not improve.

"Isn't it strange, Marie," Anna whispered to Marie, "that a prelate should be so obsessed with a king's mistress?"

Anna's comment struck home. She froze in place, her thoughts on her relationship with Napoleon. She had little time to dwell on it, for the archbishop again placed his hand on hers. She turned in his direction to find him smiling at her.

"I must say, this is a happy task, my dear. The emperor has placed you in my charge."

Marie's back stiffened. Duroc had said the abbé was *to look after* her. For the cleric now to say she was in his *charge* chilled her. "We . . . we are to bolster enthusiasm for the French." She took a breath. He had not removed his hand. "I'm glad to help in any way I can."

"Thank you, Madame Walewska," he said, "I merely ask that you attend my receptions and mingle with my guests. You'll see that you are held in high regard." He smiled again. "I've no doubt you'll speak highly of the emperor and his cause."

Marie cringed. How could she endure many more nights by his side, listening to his rants and suffering his unwanted attention? She attempted to pull her hand away, but his grip tightened.

"I know about your divorce filings," the abbé whispered near her ear, his tone sharper now. "I can be of service in both the ecclesiastical and civil courts, Madame Walewska, especially in the ecclesiastical offices, keeping in mind the conservative clergy here who don't much care for the Napoleonic Code—the new divorce laws, in particular."

A flutter of anxiety gripped Marie. Did he mean her divorce could be in jeopardy? "My mother and brother Benedykt will speak for me."

"I don't think they need to do so in person. They've been asked to submit statements."

Was he trying to make the process easier? Or was something more sinister at play?

"May I call you Marie?" he asked, his voice smooth. "In return, you must call me Dominique." Without waiting for a reply, he withdrew his hand and faced the front again. He waved for more wine, then leaned toward her and whispered, "Only in private, mind you."

The abbé drained his glass and stood to address the guests. "I've just received another *Bulletin de la Grande Armée*," he announced.

The dining hall fell silent.

"From Wilno, the Grand Armée has trekked the three hundred and fifty miles to Vitebsk," he continued, pausing for effect. "And now comes the most marvelous news!" Another pause. His gaze moved over the large chamber. "Once again, the Russian Army has withdrawn without a fight!"

A murmur ran through the room, but Marie noticed that not all the faces at the supper tables were smiling. Some guests were, like her, puzzled by the *marvelous* news.

Why would the Russians draw back? Was it fear to engage—or a strategy?

Later, Anna pulled Marie aside. "What happened? What did he say to you earlier, Marie? You turned white as a nun's wimple."

"It seems," Marie said shakily, "that should my divorce go through, I'll find myself beholden to Abbé de Pradt." She went on to describe the abbé's overture.

Anna took Marie's hands in hers. "Listen to me, dearest. Attend his receptions to play his game, but never accept an invitation to be alone with him. Oh, I saw how he clung to your hand, how he looked at you."

Marie braved a smile. She had already charted her path forward: she would avoid any situation whereby she would have to address him by his Christian name.

While Marie waited for the civil and ecclesiastical divorce decrees, she joined Countess Anna Potocka and other friends in the effort to prepare Warsaw hospitals for the wounded. As they had done in 1806, they requisitioned additional beds from private homes, gathered food supplies and medicines, tore bandages, and sewed sheets.

The Archbishop de Pradt held his supper receptions for the society of Warsaw almost nightly. Whether the grand furnishings of the palace, fine dining, and imported liqueurs won the more recalcitrant of his guests over to the side of the French, Marie couldn't determine. She found the majority of her fellow citizens just as joyful and hopeful as they had been years before, when Napoleon's star began to rise. They flocked to the abbé's receptions to indulge in gossip and to hear the latest news from the front. The emperor's *Bulletins de la Grande Armée* came regularly and seemed to arrive with unfailingly good news and optimistic outlooks.

After her daily hospital tasks, Marie performed her duties as the abbé's hostess, moving among the duchy's officials, society women, high-ranking military men, and diplomats. Their cordiality toward her came as a surprise. Whether they were aware of her role in Napoleon's life, they nonetheless showed her respect and paid her what seemed to be sincere compliments.

On occasion, the packets with the *Bulletins* contained the briefest of notes to her from Napoleon. They always began with *Madame*, but they cheered her, despite the formality. One day, the packet included a letter from Teodor. Marie waited until she went home before reading it. In it, her brother described the attempt to cross the River Niemen and how the wooden bridges had been burnt by the retreating Russians. In his impatience to allow for engineers to create three pontoon bridges, the emperor sent an urgent message for the Polish Young Guard to find a place to ford the Wilia, a tributary of the River Niemen.

Teodor's company was half an hour into the search when the lead company could be heard whooping and shouting, no doubt overcome with thoughts of being the first forces on Russian ground—and of pleasing the Little Corporal. In catching up to them, Teodor saw that fifteen or twenty of the Young Guard had directed their horses head-on into the surprisingly dangerous rapids.

Teodor's company called out for them to halt, but those heedless soldiers—still unaware of their plight—heard nothing, for they were crying out in their pitifully callow voices, *"Vive l'Empereur!"*

In moments, however, the bottom dropped away, and the raging river ripped them from their horses, sweeping them downstream. A number were lost.

"Oh, Marie," Teodor wrote, "such was my initiation to war."

Marie swiped at her eyes. No mention of the debacle had been made in the *Bulletin* that reported the crossing.

More improper notes from de Pradt had started coming the morning after the first reception Marie attended. With the simple salutation, *Marie*, the archbishop wrote to thank her for her "sterling" presence, praising her beauty and charms. How wonderful it would be for her once she was free. How the two of them could dine alone, go for walks and drives. One day's note varied little from that of the previous day. All were signed *Dominique*.

More than one had a postscript assuring her that the divorce should pose no problems. Was he suggesting that she might meet obstacles? Or was he attempting to make her feel a sense of indebtedness to him, should all go smoothly?

Marie became unnerved. The success of the divorce seemed a kind of bargaining chip.

Saturday, 29 August 1812
During the evening reception, Marie thought Abbé de Pradt his pompous self, but unusually cheerful. After the main course of fish in white sauce, he stood to read the latest *Bulletin*, this one from the Russian city of Smolensk, where the Grande Armée had succeeded in driving out Russia's Second Army. He read Napoleon's dispatch with the excessive flair of a bad actor: "'I have come once and for all to finish off these barbarians of the North. The sword is now drawn. They must be pushed back into their ice, so that for the next twenty-five years, they no longer will meddle in the affairs of civilized Europe.'"

Marie believed Napoleon's intentions were clear: the Grande Armée would continue its advance, moving deeper into Russia. She questioned whether this wasn't a Russian strategy.

Almost as if to answer her thought, a deep, ominous voice from one of the distant tables cut through the conversation. "Winter is not far away, and winter in Russia is not to be trifled with." The remark instantly dampened the initial festive reaction.

Abbé de Pradt cast the speaker, a usually taciturn duchy official, a fierce glare but chose to ignore the comment.

Later that night, Marie read a letter from Teodor that had come with the emperor's packet. The Russians had retreated, he wrote, but their own bombardment of Smolensk left it burned to its foundations. Worse, French losses numbered some fifteen thousand.

The letter went on to reveal that the peasants, who despised the French, burned their own crops to starve the invading troops. Soldiers went hungry. In addition, the crushing heat of summer brought with it louse-borne typhus and water-related diseases like dysentery.

Marie was stunned by the sheer horror of what Teodor revealed. She felt only dread for what the next packet from the East might bring.

She crossed herself and said a prayer for her brothers, for Napoleon, and for Poland.

Marie was awake when Hania entered the bedchamber in the morning. She had not slept.

The maid handed her a large, official-looking envelope. Marie felt a warm rush to her face as she took it. Hands trembling, she opened it, quickly scanning the contents.

She let out a sigh of relief. Her pulse slowed.

Hania stood at the foot of the bed, her face folded into a question.

"It is what I'd hoped for, Hania." Marie smiled and sat up. "We'll leave for Kiernozia today. We'll take the boys, of course. Start packing at once."

Hania's eyes widened with understanding. She curtsied and withdrew.

Marie pushed her covers away and sprang from bed.

The divorce was final.

It had been finalized on the 24th of the month, and yet Abbé de Pradt had never even hinted that it was a *fait accompli*. Nonetheless, his signature was there among several belonging to ecclesiasts and duchy officials.

A shiver ran up her back. Now that she was free, there was no telling how bold his advances might become. Oh, he was short and thickset, but she had felt strength in his grip. She feared now that his sense of entitlement would make him reckless.

No matter, she would not attend another reception. Her plans to retreat to her family home seemed all the more important.

Kiernozia, Duchy of Warsaw
Tuesday, 1 September 1812

Marie's mother set down the last of the letters Teodor had sent to Marie, her face pale. "Marie, Teodor's description of events is horrifying. And you say none of this information was included in the emperor's *Bulletins*?"

Marie shook her head. "The *Bulletins* radiated only success and hope for the next interaction with the Russians. They were often giddy with optimism."

The two sat alone at the table as servers cleared away the supper dishes.

"We must trust your brother. Compared to his news, the *Bulletins* are all bluster."

Her mother might as well have said that Napoleon was all bluster. Marie was glad that she hadn't, but she knew it was the same sentiment. It tore at her heart. After a moment, she asked, "Don't you get any word of the Eastern campaign here in Kiernozia, Mother?"

"We don't, at least nothing current. Anastase was inclined to send the papers over from Walewice now and then, but that was before . . ."

"Before the divorce? Oh, Mother, I'm sorry. I know you thought it wrong of me, as does my Catholic conscience, but I had to think of Olek's future. I explained in my letter how Anastase might squander the assets Napoleon arranged."

Her mother gave a dismissive wave of her hand. "I understood. I saw to it that statements from me and Benedykt were forwarded to the court."

"Thank you for that, Mother."

"And you say Anastase *might* squander the inheritance? Sadly, I agree. *Probably* is more the case. As they say, money is round and rolls away. I don't fault you. You were right to take precautions, Marysia."

Marie's vow to herself to abstain from the de Pradt suppers did not take long to weaken. Each day that passed without news of Napoleon and her brothers heightened Marie's anxiety. She desperately missed the letters from her brother and especially the occasional personal note from Napoleon that the *Bulletins* packet contained.

The passage of a week heightened her anxiety, as did the lack of activity. She admitted to herself that she craved being at the heart of the politics of the day. Guilt shadowed her, too. Warsaw was to be the main site of evacuation, as it had been in 1806, and she came to feel she had shirked her duty and deserted her friends, who were there each day preparing the hospitals. Most importantly, however, she was not there to bolster Polish allegiance to the French, as Napoleon had requested.

Her mother saw through to her discomfort. "You want to return to the capital, don't you, Marie?"

"I—I do."

"Then what's holding you back?"

Marie swallowed, feeling the back of her throat go dry and tighten.

"What is it?" her mother urged.

"It's Archbishop Dominique de Pradt. That's *who* it is."

"What?"

Marie went on to explain the abbé's forwardness and her dislike—no, fear—of the man, detailing his inappropriate touches, as well as the tenor of the many notes.

"You have these notes?"

Averting her eyes, Marie nodded. "I dare not show them to you."

"Ah, I see. Never mind that. These indiscreet scribblings may very well rescue you from his advances, but it will take some fortitude and a bit of cleverness."

"How?"

"Patience and I'll tell you. You said the archbishop has an obsession with Madame de Pompadour. Well, I know one of her anecdotes, should you find a use for it."

"Really? It's one of hers?"

Her mother winked. "So, they say. Who's to know? For our purposes, it is."

Warsaw
Thursday, 10 September 1812

As soon as Marie entered the dining hall of the Brühl Palace, Archbishop de Pradt descended upon her. "What in the name of God made you leave Warsaw, Marie? And without a word to me?"

"Oh, I'm sorry, Abbé de Pradt. I was in a hurry. It was thoughtless of me."

"I count on you to help manage these suppers." He took her hands in his. "They are your people, after all."

"That's exactly the reason, Abbé de Pradt."

"What?"

"Gossip has arisen among *my people*." Marie made a point of lowering her gaze to his hold on her.

The abbé's head retracted slightly. He understood and dropped her hands at once. "About us?"

"Yes. I couldn't allow it to go on. People were saying you were treating me like a queen—like *your* queen."

"That's nonsense. The emperor placed you in my charge."

"Of course, but perception is everything, isn't it Abbé de Pradt?"

The abbé produced a false smile. "Come to my table, Marie. We'll talk during supper."

He reached for her elbow, but Marie pulled back. "I'm afraid not, Abbé de Pradt."

The abbé pivoted toward her. "What?"

"You see, the Countess Anna Potocka and another friend from the hospital, Countess Zofia Gronska should arrive any minute, and I have promised to sit with them. Don't you see it's best?"

"Why? This gossip thing? No, I don't. There's a *Bulletin* to read tonight, and I want you there beside me."

"That will only fan the flames, Abbé de Pradt. And there is the matter of the notes to me."

"What?" My notes . . . to you?"

Marie nodded.

"Well, what of it? They are perfectly innocent."

"Oh, but my mother didn't think so—no, not innocent at all."

"Your mother? You showed them to your mother?"

"It was an accident, Abbé de Pradt. She came upon them by accident."

"And read them? All of them?" His brow lowered in suspicion. "By *accident*?"

Marie nodded, drawing in a breath as her lie took shape. "You see, she believes Napoleon is still in love with me."

"Do you believe that?"

"He continues to have me watched—he did so in Paris, and even here. His notes invariably say, 'Do not doubt me.'"

At this, something shifted in the abbé's black eyes. Marie recalled that two of Napoleon's notes had appeared to have their seals broken and then resealed, so as to conceal the breach. The look in his eyes betrayed him now. However, Marie shifted focus. "Mother thinks I should show them to the emperor. She believes he'd be most interested."

The abbé paled. "You wouldn't, would you, Marie? As I've said, the notes were innocent. And to trouble the emperor needlessly? You know, as well as I, that the weight of the world is already upon his shoulders."

Marie pressed her lips together, feigning indifference.

"Oh, Marie," he said, his voice cracking with panic, "we must destroy them—if someone like your mother could so grievously misconstrue them. Where are they?"

"That's the problem, Abbé de Pradt. I left Kiernozia in such a hurry that I forgot them."

The abbé's eyes narrowed as he gave her a hard, lingering look. He was suddenly suspicious. "Don't play me for a fool, Marie. What's your game here? What does your mother intend to do?"

"Nothing, Abbé de Pradt. At least, not until she hears from me."

"Hears what?"

Marie straightened, deliberately pausing before delivering her prepared speech. "She'll hear that I'm allowed to sit where I wish at your suppers. That no cleric behaves as if he's above God. And that no more notes with . . . seductive intentions make their way to me."

The abbé's jaw dropped. "So, we're getting down to business, are we? You, Marie, are quite the shapeshifter." Anger flared in his eyes. "I'm reminded of the proverb, 'Where the devil can't manage, he'll send a woman.'"

"Is that meant for my mother—or for me?"

"What?" His breath seemed to hitch, his eyes flickering. "Oh, I meant nothing by it. —Forgive me, Madame Walewska," he said, returning to a formal address.

"You are forgiven, Your Eminence. My mother told me the most delightful Madame de Pompadour maxim about the hedgehog. Do you know it?"

The archbishop produced a false smile. He shook his head.

"Then it's a new one for your collection. Madame de Pompadour said that the hedgehog gives up its quills only when the wolf loses its teeth."

Marie sat two tables removed from de Pradt's head table, with Anna Potocka and Zofia Gronska.

"How did you manage this, Marie?" Anna asked.

Marie shrugged and offered only a smile.

After supper and over a dessert of elaborate French pastries, Abbé de Pradt reported the news from the latest *Bulletin*. It celebrated French victories, including a monumental battle at Borodino that cleared the path to Moscow, a mere seventy-five miles away. Napoleon called it "a battle of giants."

The packet had included a letter from Teodor, which Marie read in the privacy of her bedchamber that night.

Yes, the Russians had retreated, leaving the road to Moscow open, but the French losses were massive, nearly equal to the number of Russians lost. "So the victory was not a decisive one, Marysia," Teodor wrote. "And I can only wonder why the road to Moscow lay before us like an invitation to dance."

Marie wondered, too, and knew that the question had to be uppermost in the emperor's mind. Despite the news, she began to nurture the dream of reliving a winter idyll with Napole in Moscow, as they had experienced in Finckenstein and then in Schönbrunn. His notes, short and few in number as they were, sustained her.

62

WEEKS PASSED WITHOUT A NEW *Bulletin de la Grande Armée*. Word had it that the horsemen carrying them had been intercepted by Cossacks working in league with Czar Aleksander.

Marie kept busy at the hospital. Abbé de Pradt mended his ways in his behavior toward her, so she did not miss a reception. The grand affairs at the Brühl Palace continued uninterrupted, overflowing with citizens desperate for news of the war in the east. Nearly everyone had loved ones who had followed Napoleon into battle.

And yet, the silence from the front became deafening.

Warsaw
Mid-October 1812
Marie had no idea how the news reached Abbé de Pradt, but at one of his receptions, he announced in deceivingly light tones that the French had experienced "some difficulty" upon taking Moscow. According to other sources in Warsaw, the Russians had burned Moscow to its foundations prior to abandoning it to the French.

To her left, Anna Potocka whispered, "He's probably had a bulletin that he dares not read."

Marie couldn't find her voice, but Zofia Gronska said, "My God, anyone who might have imagined Napoleon watching his troops' formation from the emperor's apartment in the Kremlin was cruelly disappointed."

Marie felt as if the room were spinning, as if her body were collapsing in on itself. She had imagined just that, and more. The dream of an idyll with Napole in Moscow evaporated like mist at noon.

With false smiles and sanguine rhetoric, the abbé attempted to hold the line on morale, but the ensuing suppers turned into fatalistic, gloom-ridden affairs.

Old, experienced soldiers spoke in grim tones of Napoleon's "winter blunder," predicting that a retreat was inevitable—though, by now, they warned it might be too late. Word had it that the czar had left neither shelter nor food supplies for the Grande Armée. Soldiers who had made it back from the earlier battles let it be known that the French were woefully unprepared, lacking warm clothing and sturdy boots. The Russian winter would fall on Napoleon's multi-national army like a hammer of ice.

November-December 1812

Some silent weeks later, Marie witnessed a crest-fallen Abbé de Pradt announce at supper that Napoleon had called for retreat in the third week of October. Napoleon had sent Czar Aleksander an offer suggesting peace talks, only to wait in vain for a response. Five weeks he waited. Five weeks lost.

Master strategist Napoleon had been outplayed.

Marie tried to keep her spirits up by working longer hours at the hospital, where she heard firsthand accounts from wounded soldiers returning from the battles at Borodenko and Smolensk. Sitting at their bedsides, Marie wrote letters in Polish or French to their loved ones. She cried with and for the men so maimed in body and mind. In some cases, the letters were sent to a family in place of a dying soldier. She was sick with anxiety about her brothers Teodor and Benedykt. Had they survived? Were they wounded? Were they at some cold, foreign hospital, or worse? Was some nurse at their bedsides offering medical aid and support?

How many soldiers would be lost in the Grande Armée's retreat?

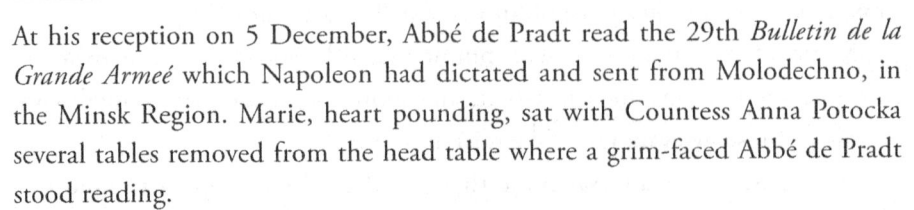

At his reception on 5 December, Abbé de Pradt read the 29th *Bulletin de la Grande Armeé* which Napoleon had dictated and sent from Molodechno, in the Minsk Region. Marie, heart pounding, sat with Countess Anna Potocka several tables removed from the head table where a grim-faced Abbé de Pradt stood reading.

The Bulletin described the retreat from Russia: battles at Maloyaroslavets, Vyazma, and Krasnoi had cost thousands of French lives, with many more—mostly stragglers—taken prisoner. As the Grande Armée advanced toward Lithuania and Poland, they reached the River Berezina which had unfortunately thawed. With Russian forces closing in and another army waiting on the west bank, disaster loomed. Napoleon claimed a victory, however, because the French managed to distract the enemy long enough to set up pontoon bridges, saving tens of thousands of veteran soldiers, Napoleon's generals, his war chest, and artillery. But the cost was high: 25,000 French died, along with countless civilians.

The dispatch was worded in such a way the losses were impossible to gloss over. Abbé de Pradt grew quieter with each loss, but brightened when he read Napoleon's final words: "'Onward to Wilno! His Majesty's health has never been better.'"

No letter from Teodor was included in the packet. What was she to think?

Avoiding her friend Anna Potocka and the crush of supper guests, Marie hurried out of the Brühl Palace into the cold night. What could she tell them? That the war was lost, and with it, the dream of reestablishing Poland gone? That even the Duchy of Warsaw was likely to fall? Though Marie was relieved that Napoleon had survived, her heart ached with worry for her brothers.

The news of the retreat spread quickly through the duchy, reaching even small villages like Kiernozia. Marie received a letter from her mother, reporting she'd had no word from either Benedykt or Teodor in weeks. Between the lines, Marie could sense her mother's panic, an anxiety she shared.

Marie was torn. Her mother hadn't asked her to return home, but the desire was clear. She wanted to comfort her mother, but at the same time, she hoped to see Napoleon as he passed through Warsaw on his way west.

Using Molodechno as the Grand Armée's last known location, one of the

Walewski grooms calculated that Marie could travel to Kiernozia, stay for two days, and return in time, should Napoleon come through Warsaw. She decided to leave the next day.

Hania was shocked when Marie told her she planned to go alone. "But, Madame, there are rumors of Russian Cossacks chasing the French. Who's to say they won't arrive here in Warsaw before the French? They leave quarter to no one. I'd rather face a pack of wolves. Please, let me and the boys come with you."

Marie reluctantly agreed. Though it would slow her travel, Hania's concern was justified.

9 December 1812

By midnight, the Walewski carriage arrived at the Łączyński manor home. Tired and drawn, Countess Łączyńska invited them in, waking servants to prepare a meal. The boys had fallen asleep during the journey, so Hania took them upstairs to bed.

At the dining table, the countess made small talk, allowing her daughter to finish her bowl of that evening's *bigos*.

"That was delicious," Marie said, wiping her mouth. "*Bardzo smaczne!* They have a similar hunters' stew in France, but it's nothing like ours."

"Do they?" her mother replied. "You surprised me, Marie. I didn't suggest that you come."

"No, but I wanted to," Marie said, "Like you, I'm worried for Benny and Teo."

Tears welled in the countess's eyes. "When did you last hear from Teo?"

"Early September, I think. His letters came with the emperor's packets, but some have been lost due to Cossack attacks."

"And the latest one, about the retreat? Was there nothing from Teodor?"

Marie swallowed hard. "No, Mother," she whispered, "nothing."

Her mother sat in silence, breathing heavily. Finally, she met Marie's gaze. "You'll stay a few days, won't you?"

"Two days, just two. But, Mother, may I leave the boys here?"

"Of course." The countess's eyes narrowed in appraisal. "You want to get back for *him*, yes?"

Marie flushed. Her mother was as perceptive as ever. "There's no guarantee he'll come through Warsaw, Mother."

"But it's likely, isn't it?"

Marie shrugged, feeling exposed. "Perhaps."

"Very well, Marie, two days. Let's get you up to bed."

"I *am* tired, Mother," she admitted. As she shifted in her chair, her mother grabbed her hand, holding her at the table. "The duchy is lost, Marie. The emperor is finished. There's no future for Poland, or for you, my darling."

Marie noticed now for the first time how her mother's blue eyes had paled, but the intensity in them stirred painful memories. "You give me advice in the form of a warning now, Mother. If only you had said something before I married Anastase." She stood, forcing her mother to release her hand. She hurried to the door.

"Wait!" the countess called.

Marie stopped at the door but did not turn around.

"Marysia," her mother said, her voice breaking, "I did say something then. I asked for the greatest sacrifice of you. . .. I was wrong."

Marie stood in the doorway for several seconds, her heart racing, and then continued to the stairs.

That her mother didn't elaborate upon her apology the next day was no surprise, but it was a relief. What more could be said on either side that wouldn't ignite one's temper or open a sluice gate of tears?

By late afternoon, Marie turned her attention to two-year-old Aleksander, who had come down with a bad cold. She blamed herself for taking him on the cold journey. She could not leave him. She postponed her departure.

By the fourth day, Aleksander seemed better. Relieved, Marie set her departure for the next day, knowing she might've already missed Napoleon at Warsaw.

Late that evening, a knock sounded at the door. Marie peeked out of the reception room to observe the maid admitting someone, a man. The two spoke in low tones. Suddenly, the man's eyes came up over the maid's shoulders, and his gaze above a dark beard met hers.

"Marie!"

The maid stepped aside, revealing a soldier in a torn and dirtied greatcoat. Although Marie didn't recognize him at first, his voice was unmistakable. She stood. "Teodor?"

"Indeed, it's me!" the soldier replied, rushing forward to embrace her. "There, now," he said, pulling back to study her. "No tears, please."

Marie smiled. "Very well, Teodor. Oh, my Teo! We were so worried." She hugged him again. "However," she added, drawing her head back and staring at his noticeably gaunt face, "I won't speak for Mother's reaction."

"Tears, you mean? I don't think I've ever seen her cry."

"Once, Teodor—at Father's—"

"Oh, then. You're right, Marysia. —Where is Mother?"

"She's gone to bed, but I'll get her up in a bit. Come sit with me here. Now, what about Benedykt?" She paused, trembling. "Is he all right? Safe?"

"I don't know, Marie," Teodor said, as he settled next to her on the couch. "He was with Prince Pepi's rearguard, keeping the damn Cossacks at a distance, or trying to."

"He's in harm's way, then."

Teodor's face darkened. He nodded.

"And you?"

"I'm with the emperor's Young Guard. We left the Grande Armée, or what's left of it, a good distance behind and headed to Warsaw."

Marie's hand went to her throat. "Warsaw? *When?*"

"We arrived on the tenth. Napoleon was disappointed to hear from Archbishop de Pradt that you'd come here."

"The tenth? I left on the eighth—Sweet Jesus! Two days! I missed him by two days. I'll go back tomorrow. Will you go with me?"

"No, Marie."

"No?"

"It was a short stay. Napoleon was dressed in such a manner that he wouldn't be recognized. Over his uniform he wore a gold-braided green velvet cloak and a huge black sable hat. You would have taken him for a wealthy merchant. He met with Archbishop de Pradt, Count Potocki, and a few others of the duchy government."

"And Prince Pontiatowski?

"Prince Pepi is having a leg wound attended to, but as expected, he has stayed with his slow-moving army returning to Warsaw. With diminished numbers, I might add."

"Bless the prince! But Napoleon. Are you saying he left Warsaw? For Paris? Without you?"

"No, he and Marshal Caulaincourt climbed aboard a sleigh, and we accompanied them to Łowicz. That's where I've come from."

Marie gasped. "Łowicz?" Her heart seemed to swell. "That's no more than thirteen miles! I can see him tonight!"

"No, Marie."

"Then, tomorrow, first thing."

Teodor shook his head.

"Why not? *Why*? —Oh, Teodor, tell me he's coming here!"

"Well, he did have it in mind to do so, but—"

"But what?" Marie demanded.

"Marshal Caulaincourt dissuaded him, saying it would be bad for morale should it get out that he left the straggling Grande Armée to . . . well, to meet *with you*."

"With a *mistress*, you mean!"

Teodor ignored her comment. "It's more than that, Marie. There's a movement afoot in Paris to stage a coup d'état. It's urgent they get there as quickly as possible. They've already left."

"A coup! . . . But they left without you?"

"I have my orders."

"Yes, tell me, Teodor."

"I'm to accompany you and Napoleon's . . . that is, Aleksander, to Paris."

Marie's heart raced. "Paris? Again?" Marie straightened against the back of the couch. "Now?"

Teodor nodded.

"Why? —And I have *two* sons, Teodor."

"Of course, Antoni is to go, as well."

"And you say he did mean to come to Kiernozia?"

"He did."

Marie's heart leapt. So, he didn't come, she thought. *He had meant to come!*

"Let's not wake Mother," Teodor said.

"All right, though she might be a bit cross in the morning."

"I'll be here to see her first thing."

"Teo, tell me what happened in Moscow. Some are calling it a victory despite the retreat. Was it? Sweet Jesus, the Grande Armée that had passed through Warsaw boasted some 600,000 men." Marie tilted her head, eyes questioning. "And now?"

Teodor's face darkened. "I suppose it could be considered a victory when we gained Moscow, but when the czar ignored Napoleon's peace entreaties, it was one disaster after another. The Russians left the city in ashes so that food and shelter was in short supply. Once a retreat was decided upon, winter was waiting in the wings. Napoleon called it *General Winter*. So, you see, Moscow was a Pyrrhic victory."

Teodor paused, as though reconsidering whether to say more. After a moment, he continued. "What followed, Marie, was sheer horror. The main forces quit Moscow on the eighteenth of October—though we were not allowed to call it a *retreat*. After the battle at Maloyaroslaverts, Napoleon and his generals chose the northern route to Smolensk, which was already stripped of supplies, instead of the southern one. Benedykt became furious at the decision."

"What—Benedykt was there with you? Safe? You didn't say!"

"Oh, I'm sorry, Marie. That was the last time I saw him."

"He was still in command of his regiment of Polish Lancers?"

"Yes. A command of noticeably fewer lancers, but he seemed well enough."

Marie grew dizzy as Teodor went on to detail how the soldiers had previously shared their dwindling foodstuff, putting in shares for a common soup, but as mere survival became their focus, they hoarded any ingredients in their possession.

He's alive. Benny's alive! Marie's expelled a deep breath. He had survived up to that point. It was something good they could tell their mother in the morning.

"Marie . . ."

"What—yes?"

"You're lost in thought. The details are too terrible. I shouldn't say anything more."

Marie looked into Teodor's face and read the pain imprinted there. "No, you should, Teo. Please do tell me the rest. I want to know."

Teodor nodded. "Because we took the same route we came, we passed the Borodino battlefield with its many thousands of corpses torn to pieces by wolves and carrion crows. Despite the sight and stench, no one could look away. I realized, Marie, that war meant more than courage and glory." He drew in breath. "We were now a starving, ragtag army with Cossacks and peasant bandits biting at our backs. Before we reached Smolensk, snow began to fall and the roads iced over. The horses were without winter shoes and thousands of them either slipped and fell on the ice or dropped dead of starvation or cold. We passed soldiers that had become white sculptures gathered in a circle around what must have been a fire that had for a time warmed and coaxed them into an eternal sleep. We finally made it to Smolensk, only to find it depleted of supplies. The soldiers and stragglers that survived did so by eating horseflesh and blood soup. . ... That's all I mean to tell you now, Marie."

Listening to her brother's account of the war left a burning in the back of her throat and a bitter taste in her mouth. Marie couldn't find words that wouldn't sound trite. She reached out and placed her hand over his.

Reading Teodor's face had never been difficult. His green eyes widened slightly now, and he forced a smile. His complexion had gone ghostly white against the black beard. He paused, perhaps as much for his own sake, as for hers.

Before they retired for the night, Teodor asked, "You will come, then, Marysia? To Paris?"

"I don't know, Teo. I don't. But tell me this, when Napoleon left his Grand Armée for Paris, how did his men react?"

"For the most part, their faith in him never wavered. The emperor stayed with them until the last rough river crossing, his talent to inspire intact. The soldiers, such as they are, assume he will return with a new army."

Later, Marie stood at the window of her room, peering out into the dark night. "Napole, Napole," she whispered, "what is it about you that commands such loyalty?"

In the morning, Marie entered the dining chamber to find her mother already reunited with Teodor. As she sat down, her mother turned, wiping away tears with both hands. She met Marie's gaze and said, "Of course, you must go to Paris, Marie."

"What? —Why?"

"Because you can't stay here. Czar Aleksander knows who you are. He'll send soldiers—or Cossacks—to ferret you out. You would be of *considerable* value to him."

"Then, you think—"

"Oh, the Russians will come for us. It's just a matter of time. I just pray it's not another Praga."

Could it be? Marie went cold as she recalled how thousands of ordinary citizens had been slain as the Russians advanced on Warsaw's suburb. She turned to Teodor. "So—the duchy is lost?"

"For now, we must assume so," Teodor mumbled.

Her mother placed her hand over Marie's. "And I want Kasia to go with you. She's just eighteen; she can't be here when the Russians arrive. Do you understand?"

Marie swallowed hard. "Yes."

"Kasia doesn't have your figure or beauty, Marie, but she has good humor, and she acquitted herself well enough at her convent school studies. I think you'll be glad to have the company."

"What about you, Mother? You should come to Paris!"

"And leave the estate to whom?"

Her mother's tone left no room for argument.

"Besides," she added, "I must be here when Benedykt returns home."

The carriage carrying Marie, Teodor, Katarzyna, Hania, and the two boys entered Warsaw. Upon reaching the Royal Castle's Great Courtyard, Marie and Teodor alighted and entered the Guard Room, where an elderly general relayed the latest news: the Grande Armée, once 610,000 strong, had been reduced to just 110,000 soldiers.

Teodor stiffened but showed no surprise. Marie drew in a sharp breath. "What about Prince Pepi's V Corps?" she asked.

The grizzled old soldier straightened his back. "As it happens, Madame Walewska, he has just returned."

"Thank God! How many Poles have returned?"

The general compressed his thin lips together as if he wished to withhold his answer. "Eight hundred that were armed, Madame Walewska. No doubt thousands of stragglers who were left behind have been taken by the Russians."

Marie stared at the old general, her mind unable to fathom his answer. She knew Napoleon had requested 40,000 Poles, and that was the number the duchy had produced.

"Is the prince here?" Teodor asked.

"No," the general said. "I'm sorry. He has a leg wound and is being cared for by Count Potocki at his residence at Wilanów."

Marie and Teodor thanked the general and returned to the carriage.

In little space of time, the carriage was moving into the Court of Honor of the Wilanów Palace, an impressive yellow edifice, with wings on either side.

At the window, Katarzyna's eyes went wide. "Is it true, Marie, that King Jan Sobieski once owned it?"

"It is. He built it." Marie noted the wonder on her sister's face. She was glad to reacquaint herself with the good-natured Kasia on the long journey to Paris. What better way than a trip of ten or more days in an enclosed coach?

Despite the duchy's despair, Aleksander and Anna Potocki warmly welcomed the group and arranged a late supper. Once Hania and the children were taken to the kitchens, Marie, Teodor, and Katarzyna were ushered into a large reception room crowded with friends of the Potockis, officials of the government, and a group of soldiers gathered at the far end.

Prince Józef Poniatowski was reclining on a chaise lounge, still dressed in a bedraggled uniform, one trouser leg torn up the side, revealing a well-bandaged limb. Standing nearby, Countess Henriette de Vauban looked up, nodded and smiled at Marie. The prince saw her now, too, and his face lit up. "Come close, Marie," he said. "I'm not dying. I merely twisted my leg when my horse slipped on the ice. Unfortunately, my horse got the worst of it. And, Teodor, good to see you again in better circumstances."

Marie introduced him to Kasia, whose nervous curtsey would need a bit of practice.

"Forgive me, Marie," the prince said, "but you must bend for me to kiss you."

When Marie leaned down, they exchanged cheek kisses. Before she could rise, he whispered, "You are Poland's heroine, Marie."

She stood, hot blood coming into her face. "I am not."

"Now, Madame Walewska," the prince announced, his tone strangely smug, "you must meet the soldier patiently standing behind you."

Marie pivoted to find Benedykt grinning at her. All breath went out of her. Her brother took her into his arms and held her. "Mother believed," she whispered. "Oh, Benny, I dared not."

Teodor and Katarzyna hurried forward and the four huddled in an embrace amidst tearful greetings.

Before the supper was announced, one of the guests asked the prince to recount his experience during the Moscow campaign.

The prince drew a deep breath and spoke from the heart. "So many died," he said. "So many—French, Italians, Saxons, Poles, and more. The emperor faltered this time and faltered badly. His decisions no longer amazed us. He hesitated, wavered, and often made the worst choices. The army was cut to pieces in battle after battle. Meanwhile, blood-thirsty Cossacks and enraged peasant partisans attacked us like relentless wolves. Many of the brave men who survived these attacks perished from hunger, typhus, or the cold. Brave men, I say! For them, the greatest disappointment was not to die in battle."

The prince scanned the room, then shrugged. "I won't stay long in Warsaw. After everything I've said, it may seem impossible—but the Polish Army is to be reformed, and I will lead it again."

A few gasps in the audience preceded a long moment of complete silence.

How is it possible? Marie wondered.

"Imagine," the prince resumed, his voice gaining strength, "amidst the chaos in Moscow when entire units succumbed to the temptation of looting, not one—*not one!*—of my men deserted his post!"

At that moment, Lord Potocki stepped forward to inform the prince that some of his soldiers had just arrived from Wilno and were requesting to see him.

Prince Poniatowski rose, wincing in pain. With the aid of a crutch, he maneuvered through the double doors into the adjacent room. Madame Anna Potocki gestured for the other guests to follow.

Marie and her siblings fell in line.

Her brothers, who had seen war firsthand, and Marie, who had bound wounds in the hospital, were nonetheless shocked by the sight of the gaunt, bandaged soldiers. Marie placed an arm around Katarzyna, whose blue eyes were pooling with tears.

Few of the soldiers still wore the colorful uniforms in which Warsaw had proudly sent them off. They were but skeletal figures, draped in filthy clothes and ragged furs. Several stepped forward, saluted their general, and placed their regimental eagles at his feet. Upon retreat, Napoleon had ordered every unit to destroy its staff, flag, and eagle to prevent them from falling into enemy hands. Yet, despite his command, these young soldiers had secretly hidden their eagles. Prince Poniatowski stared at them, his eyes pooling with tears. "Only one is missing," he said softly. "Only one."

He saluted his men, unabashed as tears rolled down his cheeks.

"No, it's here, General Poniatowski," a soldier said. "Kazimierz has it. He's ashamed because it is no longer intact."

A haggard and frightened soldier—no more than a boy—was pushed forward. He placed the final eagle before his commander.

Katarzyna leaned in and whispered to Marie, "Its head is missing."

A flush of crimson had spread across the soldier's face, and his voice trembled. "A bullet took its head, General Poniatowski. I am so sorry."

For a moment, the prince was speechless. Collecting himself, he said, "God bless you, Kazimierz," motioning the boy to come closer. Like a priest, he placed his hand on the soldier's blonde head. Then, looking up at the rest of the young men, he called out, his voice both loud and quivering: "God bless you all!"

The ragged band of brothers stood at attention, and cried, "Long live Poland! Long live Poland!"

The next afternoon, Marie bade goodbye to Benedykt, who intended to stay with the reconstituted army. She boarded the carriage with Katarzyna, Teodor, Hania, and the boys, and departed for Paris. Aleksander's monies from the Neapolitan estates had grown considerably so that before leaving Warsaw, Marie arranged with her banker to advance Prince Poniatowski many thousand francs and sovereigns for the purpose of reestablishing the Polish Army. The farms in Naples that Napoleon had bequeathed to little Aleksander were producing the predicted 170,000 francs annually.

63

Paris
February 1813

MARIE SAT ANXIOUSLY WITH LITTLE Aleksander in a waiting room at the Château de Malmaison, near the left bank of the River Seine. What possible reason could have prompted former Empress Josephine to request an interview? Although each was well aware of the other, they had never met.

Twenty minutes later, they were shown into a library consisting of three small connected rooms featuring glassed-in bookcases of mahogany. The empress sat at a round table in the middle room. She stood as Marie was announced. Well into her late forties, she was petite and still pretty. Her dark hair was dressed close to the head with curls framing the forehead and sides, and her dress of pale pink muslin, though simple in its drape and design, was undoubtedly a creation of M. Antoine Leroy.

Even though her own dress was of a similar design, its stronger lemon color made her think she had overdressed for the occasion. Marie curtsied, realizing at once that she hadn't thought how to address a former empress, managing only, "Madame Bonaparte." Embarrassed, she busied herself placing Aleksander in a chair.

The empress must have noted her uncertainty and said, "Call me Josephine, if you will. In turn, I will call you Marie, and we shall be fast friends."

Marie nodded and smiled, hoping to hide her surprise. After all, Napoleon had forbidden the empress to visit him in Poland and, according to him, when word got back to her of his *Polish conquest*, she became irate.

The empress stepped around the table now, her white slippers visible as she moved quickly toward Aleksander. "Mon chéri," she cried. "Mon chéri! Oh—he's beautiful!" She bent to lift the wide-eyed boy's hand. Holding it captive, she said, "Why, he's so like him. His face is his father's face. Of course, his hair is light like yours, but it will darken, and I see that bit of red in it, like that the emperor has in his black hair." The empress released the boy's hand and looked up at Marie. "You must have noticed that?"

Marie flashed to the intimate moment with Napole when she had noticed it. The thought nearly made her faint. She swallowed hard before replying, "I have."

The empress stood, her eyes still on Marie. "It escapes most people's notice. How old is Aleksander now?"

"Olek will be three on the fourth of May."

The boy sat watching. He had promised Marie that he would sit quietly.

"I shall send him something." As the empress returned to her chair, she asked, "You have another child, a boy?"

"Yes, Antoni will be eight next month." Glancing about, Marie struggled to find something to say. "These rooms are very beautiful . . . Josephine."

The empress sat and motioned for Marie to do likewise. "The rooms are small, but they house more books than you would imagine. The emperor oversaw the makeover. You know, I purchased Malmaison while he was on campaign in Egypt. Oh, he was incensed, I can tell you." The empress gave a little laugh. "It was done on credit. But he came around."

Marie smiled. The empress's low voice was at once musical and powerful. Marie thought her inflection, like the pale-yellow cast of her complexion, was rooted in her Martinique Creole lineage.

"I'll give you a tour the next time you come to visit."

That a return visit was expected came as another surprise. Marie nodded.

"Hortense has kept me informed of your rising star here in Paris. It was she who suggested we meet, my dear."

"I see." Hortense, the empress's daughter by her first marriage, had married Napoleon's brother Louis, King of Holland, thus making her Queen Consort of Holland. A society gadabout, Hortense befriended Marie as a matter of course.

"Hortense says the general tenor of the city is dark and gloomy these days. Do you find it so, Marie?"

"I'm afraid it is, owing to the . . .well, the Grand Armée's lack of success."

"Less dancing, I'm afraid, and more talk of war. But I'm glad you returned to Paris. I do admire you, Marie. You gave the emperor what he most longed for." The empress nodded toward Aleksander. "He's providing for you and the little one, I trust?"

"He is—but he has yet to visit."

"Ah! If you feel ignored, know that his attitude toward marriage is rather that of a traditionalist. His focus is on another now, and on another son." The empress paused, eyes narrowing. "I can see the hurt of that in your face, my dear. But your child will hold him close to you, I think."

Marie could merely nod.

"You're just twenty-five, Marie?"

"Twenty-six."

"You're so young and beautiful, my dear. You must *engage* life, do you hear?"

"I'm sorry, Josephine. I find it hard to be truly happy these days."

"You will in time, do you hear? Now, will you come see me again? With the boy? Each week? It would mean so much to me." The empress released a great sigh and looked toward the window. Outside, the sky was darkening. A full minute must have passed before she turned her gaze back to Marie. "It's as if a billowing of clouds presaging some catastrophe is moving toward

France . . . and the emperor." The empress hesitated, blinked. Her face had paled. "Oh, I would like to see you, Marie. *Will* you come?"

"If you wish it . . . Josephine."

"I do."

In the following weeks, Marie made the attempt to engage life. It was a quieter life than her time last spent in Paris. Antoni and Aleksander happily filled some of her daytime hours. While balls were fewer and salons more sedate, she nonetheless entertained, visited friends, and attended theater and opera in new clothing creations by M. Leroy. She deeply missed her mother, but kept her sister and brothers nearby.

The empress proved correct in that their son would keep him close. That their relationship had changed, however, became more evident with each meeting. An awkwardness, like some invisible screen, stood between them. Marie longed for their old intimacy—a touch, a kiss, a whisper of love. Josephine was also correct on the matter of his marriage: Napoleon had become surprisingly conventional, presenting himself to Marie merely as an attentive friend. Still, when he showered attention on Aleksander, she could sense in the room the warmth and even passion of their past attachment. Sometimes, he would glance up from the boy, the affection glowing in his eyes. But was that ephemeral closeness becoming the bane of her happiness? Each time he departed, she lifted her chin, her lips pinched to keep them from trembling, and suffered his kisses light against her cheeks. Even after he left, with her love—and her pride—crushed like a flower, she resisted tears.

As the weeks passed, Marie kept her word, regularly bringing Aleksander to her meeting with the former empress. Each week, it seemed as if there were new clouds for Marie and the empress to discuss—or attempt to ignore.

In her homeland, Prince Poniatowski pieced together a new army, even as he was forced to withdraw from the duchy and regroup in Krakow. Empress Josephine wondered aloud whether he might accede to overtures to shift sides to Russia, but Marie remained adamant that he would never desert Napoleon. "Josephine," she said, "changing loyalties is not the Polish Way."

Crises came fast. Marshal de Murat, in command of the severely weakened Grande Armée, left his command to return to Naples. His replacement,

Empress Josephine's son, Eugène de Beauharnais, was forced to retreat before the Russian line. Jean-Baptiste Bernadotte, the Swedish Crown Prince and French marshal, turned coat, betraying Napoleon and forming an alliance with England. And, amazingly, the many-times defeated Prussia rebounded with increased strength and a new alliance with Czar Aleksander.

In preparing to join his troops, Napoleon named Empress Marie-Louise his regent, so sure was he that he would hold onto the loyalty of Austria—and his father-in-law, Emperor Francis. However, Josephine confided in Marie that Napoleon had heard talk that Francis was secretly negotiating with the czar. "He doesn't believe anything will come of it, Marie," the former empress said, "but I'm not convinced."

Marie made no comment.

April-May 1813
Napoleon left Paris without making a final visit to Rue de la Houssaye. With his new force of three hundred thousand recruits, mostly pitifully young, Napoleon rejoined his Grande Armée at Erfurt, Germany, at the end of April. Just days later, in moving on Dresden, he routed the Prussian and Russian enemies at Lützen, near Leipzig, and after occupying Dresden, he scored a second victory at Bautzen in late May. The news of each was met with rejoicing in Paris. A few days later, across the table in the library, Empress Josephine revealed to Marie the crucial news about the victories that had been withheld from the initial reports.

The Lützen victory was a shallow one because Napoleon had too few cavalrymen to pursue the enemy, and his foremost cavalry commander, Marshal Jean-Baptiste Bessières, was brought down by a sniper. "That's not the worst of it," Josephine said to Marie. "At Bautzen, Marshal Gérard Duroc was killed—disemboweled by a cannonball ricocheting off a tree—while riding next to the emperor. Napoleon so deeply grieved his loss that he halted all action and retreated into his tent. You knew him, also, didn't you, Marie?"

The news—and the image—struck like a thunderbolt. Marie nodded dumbly. She went cold to her core. Of course, Napoleon was devastated. Grand Marshal Gérard Duroc was the emperor's closest advisor and intimate friend. For years, he had been at his side, responsible for the emperor's personal security whether in France or on campaign. He had also been entrusted with any number of the most delicate and crucial negotiations.

Even in the carriage on the way home, Marie held her tears at bay so as not to alarm Aleksander, who sat beside her, playing with a wooden chariot the empress had given him. Gérard Duroc had been a constant in her life since that day she had boldly gone to meet Emperor Napoleon's carriage. He had been her confidant on the very day she followed through—trembling—on the first assignation with the Emperor Napoleon Bonaparte at Warsaw's Royal Castle. He was her connection—often unappreciated by her—to Napoleon for six years. She was bereft and could only imagine Napoleon's sense of loss. She recognized that, like herself, Gérard Duroc was one of the few who loved Napoleon for himself.

Alone in her room, rather than tears, she offered prayers for Duroc, prayers poisoned by the disturbing thought that a ricocheting cannonball could just as easily have struck her Napole.

Marie took time to compose her heartfelt condolences in a note to Napoleon and dispatched it at once.

64

DESPITE THE TWO VICTORIES AND an armistice that might pave the way for peace, the ground beneath Napoleon's empire shifted unpredictably. In negotiations, the allied powers demanded that France be dismembered, with his conquests—including the Grand Duchy of Warsaw—relinquished.

Old compatriots turned on Napoleon one after another. In Spain, British Commander Arthur Wellesley bested King Joseph Bonaparte. And then on 12 August, came the coup de grâce: Austria's Emperor Francis, who had suffered multiple defeats at Napoleon's hands, joined the enemy alliance and declared war on his son-in-law.

Napoleon had sacrificed Marie for his dynastic marriage, and Marie found it a bitter pill, but the thought that he was now hoisted by his own petard brought her no comfort. She grieved for him.

One day, as Marie stood ready to leave the Château de Malmaison, Josephine reached out to detain her. "Stay a moment, will you, Marie?"

Marie turned to Josephine, eyes questioning.

"My heart breaks for you, my dear. Napoleon married the wrong Marie.

You don't speak of your sorrows, but I see them. You still love him, as do I. I encourage you to seek a new path—find other interests." Josephine paused, studying her. "I doubt that you lack interest from men of substance these past months, am I right?"

Marie gave a small shrug. "Ah, so you think I should return their *interest*, as you say?"

"I do."

"I have no desire to do so, Josephine. Even if I did, any suitor would be discouraged by Napoleon. He has me watched—he knows my every move."

Josephine raised an eyebrow. "I'm not surprised. Fouché, his Minister of Police, seems to be in everyone's lives."

"At Napoleon's orders. —Your life, too?"

"Yes. . .. Listen, there is one man Napoleon would not object to."

Marie nodded, feigning curiosity.

"Philippe Ornano. He's a soldier. I believe you've met him."

Marie caught her breath. "I have, but how do you know that? Do you have spies, too?"

Josephine smiled and gave out with a self-conscious laugh. "I know him. He's spoken highly of you, very highly. He's Corsican, with an Italian look."

"And just why would—" Marie began.

"Napoleon turn a blind eye to him?" Josephine asked, finishing her question.

"Exactly," Marie replied, tilting her head.

Josephine smiled, more assuredly. "Philippe is a *cousin* of Napoleon's."

"Oh!" Marie paused, collecting herself. How odd, she thought, to imagine Empress Josephine as a matchmaker. "I see, but that means nothing to me. I have no interest, as I've said."

"One day, Marie, I hope that you will take an interest."

Having no wish to extend the conversation, Marie forced a smile; whether it humored the empress she cared little.

October 1813

Heart racing, Marie hurried into the entrance hall of the Château de Malmaison. Former Empress Josephine's request to visit came two days before their usual meeting, and she had asked Marie not to bring Aleksander. Marie could only infer that there was news. And that it was not good.

The last she had heard, Napoleon was leading the Grande Armée toward Leipzig, preparing for a decisive battle against the Russian, Austrian, and Prussian forces.

Her face grave, Josephine embraced Marie as she entered the library. She had never done that before. "Thank you for coming, dearest. How is little Olek?"

"He's fine, Josephine." Marie waited, uneasy.

"Good . . . well, then, shall we sit?"

Josephine gestured to a chair, but instead of sitting across from Marie, she settled beside her, where Olek usually sat.

"Has the battle at Leipzig been lost?" Marie blurted, her voice sharp with worry.

Josephine sighed. "It went on for four days. We lost over seventy thousand men."

Marie could feel her pulse thrumming at her temples, sensing there was worse to come.

Josephine pressed her lips together, locking eyes with Marie. "Your health seems more and more delicate, Marie. Did the trip to Belgium help?"

Marie had no wish to discuss her trip to Spa, where she took the waters. "I'm fine, Josephine." She waited.

Josephine nodded, then spoke softly. "The troops were forced to withdraw from Leipzig," she said, "but someone detonated too soon the explosives on the last surviving bridge over the River Elster so that instead of holding back the enemy, our rearguard was held back."

"Napole was with them, yes? Has he been captured, or—? Tell me!"

"No, no. Napoleon has more lives than two cats. He had already crossed. It was your Polish Old Guard that was held back."

That Napoleon was safe did not stave off fear and dizziness. *The Old Guard.* Marie had recently received news that Benedykt was being held prisoner in Italy, but Teodor was in the latest campaign with the French. "My brother—Teodor! Is he—"

"He's safe. Napoleon made a point of saying so. No, Marie, it's Prince Poniatowski. He was killed in the river crossing."

"What?" Marie's breath caught before she could say more. She sat stunned. "Prince Pepi?"

Josephine nodded, her face soft with sympathy. "Napoleon asked me to tell you in his stead. The prince was important to you, he said."

"Sweet Jesus, he was important to Poland. I can't imagine him gone. Did Napole say how?"

"He'd been wounded three times during the retreat from Leipzig, yet he pressed on after all bridges were down, directing his horse into the river. His own men begged him to stay and surrender to the Russians."

"Oh, he wouldn't do that, Josephine."

"No, Marie. At mid-river he was hit again and unhorsed. The River Elster took him. A childhood friend of his related the details to the emperor. He said that a gypsy had once warned the prince to beware of magpies. And Elster is—"

"German for magpies," Marie blurted. "I know."

In the days that followed, Marie slept little. She mourned Prince Józef Poniatowski as one would mourn a family member. As a child, she had admired him as a hero, and her friends at school had adored him, as well. His death felt like the end of Poland's dream of resurrection. Had Poland been reconstituted, Pepi, as the nephew of the deposed King Stanisław, would surely have been her king.

Marie's health faltered, her grief deepening over Poland's lost hopes and the one-time promise that Napoleon could recreate Poland under the aegis of a new order for Europe and the establishment of rights for every man.

December 1813

Assisted by a footman, Marie climbed up into the carriage. Upon his return to Paris, Napoleon had requested her presence at the Tuileries—a surprising summons, given his worsening situation. After Leipzig, he lost the support of the German states, Holland, and Northern Italy. As bidden, she traveled alone. Josephine's premonition about an impending catastrophe seemed to be coming true.

At the Tuileries, she was shown into Napoleon's office, where the emperor and Monsieur Méneval greeted her without ceremony. Seven months had passed since she had seen him. She noted his appearance—he had gained weight and the lines in his face were deeper, though he still exuded a semblance of invincibility.

"We need to make some changes, Marie," Napoleon said.

"Changes?"

"Yes. It's about Aleksander's inheritance. We've heard that the King of Naples is about to defect."

"The king—de Murat?" Marie recalled de Murat's flamboyant entrance into Warsaw and his rumored ambitions for Poland's throne. His betrayal didn't surprise her.

Napoleon nodded. "When de Murat defects, it's all but certain that Aleksander's farms will be confiscated. However, Méneval is drawing up documents for a pension of 50,000 francs annually for him." He motioned for the secretary to speak.

"In short, these funds will originate here in France, Madame Walewska," Méneval said. "To be specific, they will accrue from France's register of pensions together with navigational duties collected from the nation's canals."

"I understand," Marie managed, overwhelmed by the knowledge that in these perilous times such care was being taken to look out for Aleksander's welfare.

"There you have it, Marie," Napoleon said. "I have a man looking for a new house for you, as well."

Marie blinked at the news. "That's all very well, Napole, but I'm happily settled at Rue de la Houssaye."

"Nonsense!" Napoleon turned toward her. "I'm thinking of your future, Marie, and the future of our son. You'll need more room, stables, and lodges for servants." He leaned down, brushing his lips against her cheeks. Straightening, he clicked his heels, and held her gaze, his gray-blue eyes soft and warm. "We'll get word to you soon."

Late January 1814

The house found for Marie, a square two-storied edifice, featured a courtyard in the front and garden in the back. By the time she signed the papers and moved into 48 Rue de la Victoire, Russian and Prussian armies were crossing the River Rhine into France, and the Austrian army was descending through Switzerland. Having defeated the French in Spain, British Commander Wellesley, with his combined forces of British, Spanish, and Portuguese, was approaching from the southwest of France.

"What forces does Napoleon have to stand against this tide?" Josephine asked during one of their visits. "He's patched together an army of 100,000 to protect the homeland but, by all accounts, they are boys, not soldiers. And many of those conscripted have avoided service. I can tell you that France is tired of wars."

Marie listened, her stomach tight with anxiety, heart breaking. The end was near. Still, she allowed no tears through these, the final days of the campaign.

Château de Fontainebleau
14 April 1814
Dressed in a dark cloak and one of Leroy's veiled hats, Marie sat in a small library that adjoined the bedchamber where Napoleon lay. She had arrived the day before, traveling over forty-five miles in cold, driving rain. The Château de Fontainebleau had been a hunting lodge and holiday escape for many French kings. She recalled how, in happier times, Napole occasionally enjoyed respites there.

Three days earlier, the Treaty of Fontainebleau, forcing Napoleon to abdicate, stipulated that he be banished to the island of Elba.

Hours passed, and still, she had not seen him.

Her old acquaintance Constant Wairy had greeted her, saying the emperor was ill. The reunion with the valet, though bittersweet, offered no solace. He ignored her request to see Napoleon, instead settling her in an upholstered chair with tea and a crackling fire. Nonetheless, the frigid air in the nearly deserted château seeped through the woolen cloak.

During the night, Constant periodically checked on Napoleon, often retreating to a nearby gallery, where Marie heard him pacing. She suspected he couldn't bear to watch her grieve.

At one point, she pressed him: "How is he? May I see him? Please!"

The valet took up a chair across from her, his voice heavy. "You know, even his enemies spoke of his genius in battle, Madame Walewska. However, he was not present at the battle for Paris, and it was here at Fontainebleau that we heard that Marshal August Marmont surrendered the city at the end of March. The emperor was outraged and wanted to continue the fight, but his marshals would not have it and urged abdication. Then, within hours, we heard that the King of Prussia and Czar Aleksander and their armies made a triumphant ride down the Champs Élysées." Constant blinked, catching himself. "You came from Paris, so you know about the surrender, of course."

"I do—and it was one of Napoleon's favorites, Talleyrand, who presented the czar with the key to the city. The Judas!"

Constant drew in a deep breath. "I didn't know that, Countess Walewska, but I do know the emperor's marshals are slipping away, one by one."

Marie pressed again, her voice trembling. "How is he, Constant? You're keeping something from me. Tell me, please."

Constant averted his gaze. "I'm afraid I have no good news, Madame Walewska." His gaze came back to her now. "The emperor signed the abdication papers, and—last night . . . he tried to take his life."

Marie gaped in disbelief. "Suicide?"

The valet nodded.

Marie shifted in her chair, taking a moment to collect herself. "How?"

"Poison."

"That phial he carried into battles?" Napoleon had spoken lightly of a mixture of belladonna, opium, and hellebore, but she couldn't imagine his putting it to use.

Constant nodded again.

Marie's breaths came fast and she looked away.

"There, there," Constant consoled. "It made for a night of violent sickness, but he survived it. He's in some feverish other world, Madame Walewska. I dare not admit anyone, not even you. Not until he comes to his senses."

Marie's voice caught. "He may not wish to come back," Marie said. "He's lost everything, Constant, even France." She could scarcely believe that a man with so much ambition and drive could be so broken.

"He has lost it all," Constant murmured.

"What of Marie-Louise and their son?"

"She's been informed of his—his circumstances. "I'm not certain what her plans are—although I've heard that her household is being packed up."

"That sounds ominous," Marie whispered. "My God, he's lost everyone."

"Not everyone," Constant said, his sad gaze on her.

At dawn, Marie pressed Constant to check on the emperor again.

She was standing at the bedchamber door when the valet returned, blocking her path. "Did you tell him that I'm here?"

"I did, Madame Walewska. If he did hear, he didn't understand."

"I can't stay any longer, Constant. I'll be recognized and it will not serve him well." Marie took a step toward the bedchamber door. "Just allow me a moment—"

Constant raised his hand, palm out. His expression hardened. "He would never forgive me if I allowed you to see him like this."

Not long after sunrise, Marie ordered her carriage and left the Château de Fontainebleau. With the armistice signed, the roads were clogged with troops and vehicles so that the journey back to Paris stretched into the night. As they neared the city, the driver informed her that Cossacks had been employed by the enemy to patrol the roads surrounding Paris. As the carriage neared the gates, she could hear rough language being hurled at her driver, directing the carriage into a long line leading to a checkpoint. She shivered. She knew well enough the reputation of the Cossacks.

Fifteen minutes passed as she worried what to tell them. Upon hearing a woman's high-pitched, desperate scream, her heart raced and worry shifted at once to fear. She was in real danger.

Her attention was drawn now to a double line of soldiers on horseback slowly passing the stalled carriage. She thought she was seeing things. Catching her eye first was a two-pointed pennant with the familiar crimson over white. The soldiers were dressed in well-worn battle dress of dark blue with scarlet fabric and brass buttons on the front of their jackets. Their four-pointed *czapki* were much the same caps as Benedykt's the last time she had seen him. The men were Polish, members of Napoleon's Imperial Guard! One column was passing so close to the carriage that she thought she could touch the horses' flanks.

"Pomacy!" Marie called for help in Polish. Throwing formality to the wind, she thrust her head and right arm out the window. "Please help us get through this check point!" she cried, waving her arm.

One soldier, tall in his saddle, drew up, halted his horse and leaned down. "Madame?"

"We are being detained, and I'm afraid they won't let us through. Can you help? Please?"

Another soldier, capless, drew up and the two went into conference. A minute later, the second soldier called to the driver in French: "Where are you coming from?"

Marie heard him say, "Fontainebleau," and wished he hadn't. *God help me, if he gives that answer to the Cossacks.*

In the meantime, the last of the double column passed the carriage. These two soldiers were her lifeline.

The driver's answer, however, seemed to impress the tall soldier. He leaned down again. "Madame—?" It was a single-word question.

Marie drew in breath, held it a moment, then said, "Madame Marie Walewska."

The soldier's eyes widened and his forehead seemed to push up into his *czapka*. He nodded. Straightening, he said something to his companion, who, after a quick glance into the coach with wide blue eyes, directed his horse forward. He leaned down again. "Madame Walewska will wait for my superior, if you please."

Marie was about to say she had no choice when the carriage lurched forward. The line of vehicles was moving toward the checkpoint. She felt her heart contract.

"Halt!" the soldier barked at the driver. The carriage ground to a stop. Suddenly, another soldier appeared outside the carriage.

After a few words were exchanged between the two soldiers, he dismissed the tall soldier. Dismounting his horse, he removed his *czapka*, revealing a mass of blond curls in need of washing. Looking up into the coach, he said, "Madame Walewska, I am Jan Kozietulski, Commander of the French Third Regiment of Scouts of the Imperial Guard, at your service."

"Commander, I recognized you immediately. You've been to my salon—at least twice."

"How kind of you to remember me, Madame Walewska."

"Of course, I would. You were at the Battle of Somosierra, and you know my brother Benedykt."

He smiled. "I do."

"The Prussians are holding him in Italy."

"Ah, but with the armistice signed, he should be released soon."

"Really?" Marie's heart lightened.

The commander nodded. "I'm certain of it."

"You were quite the hero in Spain, Benedykt said. You bravely charged between Napoleon and Cossack assailants. Oh, you needn't blush. You saved the emperor's life!" Marie spoke with such feeling for Napoleon that she noticed something shift in the commander's eyes. Of course! He was aware of her relationship to Napoleon. She felt herself flushing.

"And today," Commander Kozietulski said, "I shall have the pleasure of coming between the Cossacks and *you*, Madame Walewska. We will see you safely into Paris. Your destination?"

"Forty-eight Rue de la Victoire." Marie nodded, smiling. "Dziękuję, Commander Kozietulski. Dziękuję."

Upon arrival at her new Paris address in the ninth arrondissement, Marie set about writing a farewell letter to Napoleon. The return to the capital saddened her, for she saw that a great number of the citizenry now sported white cockades and that white pennants abounded among the National Guard, symbols of the Bourbon restoration. That the resurrected King Louis XVIII had been held back from a triumphal entry because of a case of gout made for jokes among the staff of the household, but it gave Marie no comfort. She noted how quickly and enthusiastically crowds turned their allegiance from Napoleon, just as many of his closest allies—de Murat, Metternich, Talleyrand—had done.

Marie paid a groom and driver a handsome sum to deliver the letter to Fontainebleau at once. She was surprised when Napoleon's reply came the next day. She prayed that his recovery was complete.

> *Madame,*
>
> *I was buoyed by your thoughtful letter, Marie, and devastated to learn I had missed you here at Fontainebleau. Forgive me. How is your health? Perhaps the waters in Italy would be of benefit. Should you go, you could see, too, what might be done about Aleksander's farms. Know that I desire to see you and your son. Be well. Think of me with tenderness, undeserving as I might be. Never doubt me.*
>
> *Napole.*

20 April 1814

In the dead of night, Marie left Paris for Fontainebleau in a carriage with Aleksander, Dory, and Katarzyna, hoping to arrive in time to see Napoleon depart for Elba, even if it was merely to view the event among the crowds seeing him off. However, the effort was in vain. The roads leading to the palace had been barred by those executing the treaty. They were forced to turn back.

Katazyna sat crying softly.

"Perhaps it's best," Dory said. "It would have been too sad to have watched it."

Marie stared out the window at the receding Fontainebleau Forest. She couldn't speak until the carriage rolled into Paris.

The next day, she would learn that the agreed number of the Imperial Guard allowed to accompany Napoleon into exile had been set at 400, but so many had volunteered that the number was increased to 1,000. Among them were 120 Polish soldiers, whose faith had not faltered.

Paris
10 May 1814

Commander Jan Kozietulski's prediction proved correct. Colonel Benedykt Łączyński arrived at the house on Rue de la Victoire safe and unharmed. "Thank God," Marie cried, throwing her arms around her brother. He was eight years older than she, having spent most of her childhood years pursuing his military career, so he was not as close to her as Teodor, her constant childhood companion. Still, she was sincerely glad to see him. Even though the part he had played in persuading her to marry Anastase still vexed her at times, they had bonded in recent years. And his willingness to support her in the divorce went some distance to redeem him in her eyes.

Later in the day, when he inquired about her health, she changed the subject, instead informing him of the uncertain situation with Aleksander's entail in Italy.

"I've gotten to know Italian quite well, you know. Let me go to Naples, Marie. I can assess the situation. I can inquire as to its status and perhaps gain an interview with de Murat. He knows me."

Marie blinked back her surprise. "Really? You would do that?"

"I would. You and your boys will need your future secured."

Benedykt returned almost two months later with grim news. "King de Murat wouldn't see me, Marie. But his secretary told me that he had already begun plans to cancel the entail."

Marie wasn't shocked. "He might have been too ashamed to see you, Benny. What can you expect from a turncoat? I suspect Napoleon will not be surprised."

"Perhaps he'll listen to you, Marie, if you go."

Marie nodded, offering no objection. She was already planning a trip to Italy, but not to beg the self-serving de Murat. She had received a letter from Elisa Bonaparte Bacciochi, Napoleon's sister and a French royal princess, inviting her to Bologna and confiding in her that Napoleon was plotting a reunion with her and little Olek at Elba. Elisa's residence would provide a staging post from which the plot would unfold.

Instead of mentioning the plan to Benedykt should he frown upon it, she said, "I'm in your debt for attempting to see de Murat, Benny, but may I ask another favor? –A *great* favor?"

Her brother paused, his forehead wrinkling. "You know I have to leave for Poland at once and catch up to my legion. I took a leave in order to go to Italy."

"I know that. I do, and I am in your debt."

"Nonsense. What is the favor, Marie?"

"Will you—will you bring Antoni with you to Poland and return him—for the time being—to his father at Walewice. Hania will accompany him."

Benedykt's mouth dropped a bit, and his eyes narrowed as if suspecting a hidden motive. Despite his reaction, he agreed without questioning, and for that Marie was thankful.

Two days later, Benedykt and Antoni left for Walewice. At eight years old, Antoni was eager to travel with his military uncle, though, as the carriage pulled away, his expression turned serious, and he looked back at Marie, seeming to realize she wasn't coming along. Marie waved until the carriage was out of sight, feeling a pang of doubt. Had she done the right thing? She spent several days in despondency, wondering if her son would think she loved Aleksander more than him.

She cheered herself by vowing to bring him back as soon as circumstances permitted.

65

1 July 1814

Accompanied by Teodor, Katarzyna, Aleksander, and two maids, Marie reached Bologna via Lyons, Geneva, and Genoa. Arriving in the early evening on a hilltop overlooking the center of Bologna, they came upon the most impressive façade in the city. Having recently been stripped of her holdings and title as Grand Duchess of Tuscany, Elisa Bonaparte, along with her husband, had been given temporary use of an apartment in the colonnaded structure. The butler ushered them into the dining hall for supper, explaining that the princess was "seeing to her newborn son."

After the meal, Marie was escorted to a small sitting room where their hostess awaited. Elisa Bonaparte stood for the exchange of kisses, saying, "It's so good to see you again, even in my reduced circumstances. I trust the meal was palatable. The chef is new."

"*Deliziosa*, Princess Elisa. We are indebted to your hospitality."

"Nonsense! I know how much you mean to my brother."

Marie felt herself blushing.

"Please, come sit," the princess said, nodding at an upholstered chair across from her. "And please, call me Elisa. You must be tired after that long journey—and in this blistering heat."

"I'm fine, Elisa."

Marie had met Napoleon's sister before, but this was the first time she fully took notice of her. Dark-haired and with a rather long face and features strikingly like Napoleon's, the princess was thirty-five and quite pretty.

"You've recently had a child," Marie said. "You're nursing him? I wasn't allowed to nurse my first-born, but I did nurse Olek—in spite of my doctor's advice."

"Really? I had no choice, Marie. I traipsed from one city to another pleading my case for what was once mine, but the new powers had no mercy. I gave birth to my son enroute home so that there was no chance to find a wet nurse. Oh, well, we've been lucky. We'll be lucky again."

Marie felt awkward. "This is a beautiful villa," she said, already regretting her words, remembering at once that it was not hers.

"Oh, it's lovely, isn't it?" Elisa's tone was light. "It's newly constructed. It belongs to Antonio Aldini, one of my brother's ministers. He was, at any rate. We are here because of his generosity."

Marie was impressed. Despite losing lands and titles with the changeover in Italy's power structure, she appeared cheerful, resilient, and in control. For the time being, Elisa retained the title of French royal princess.

"Have you—have you seen him, Elisa?"

"I have not, but I receive reports regularly."

"I've been worried for him. The last time I tried to see him, they wouldn't allow me. He had attempted . . ."

"Ah, I know. However, he's past those dark thoughts. In his brief four months on Elba, Napoleon has put his energy and ingenuity to work. He's recreating that mountainous island with its poverty-stricken population into a little kingdom with new fisheries, vineyards, and sanitation. The island's hundred thousand citizens adore him."

The news lightened Marie's heart. She had spent those four months in trepidation, worried over in what frame of mind she would find Napoleon.

Elisa nodded, seeming to take note of Marie's reaction. "And you will be glad to know, I trust, that the emperor is excited to have you visit."

"How is it to be arranged?" Only now, accompanied by a quickening of her heart, did it come home to Marie that she might actually succeed in seeing Napoleon.

"Oh, he has a network of agents here in Italy and in France. His agent in Florence has arranged a house for you in the hills above the city where you'll find relief from the summer temperatures. I have the directions. You're to wait there for him. His name is Jean Baptiste Cipriani." Elisa paused, as if hesitant about saying more. Smiling tentatively, she added, "Marie, as beautiful as you are, I think you are tired after all your travels. On your way to Florence, I recommend you take the waters at Lucca so that you will be in the best of health when you see my brother."

Florence, Italy
Late July 1814
After taking Elisa's advice and resting at Lucca, Marie arrived in Florence feeling refreshed. Jean Baptiste Cipriani appeared at the modest hilltop villa the day Marie's entourage arrived. He was fit, with dark, wavy hair above black darting eyes. All business, he informed Marie that despite her impatience to sail to Elba, the emperor ordered that Teodor was to come see him at once.

"Be patient, Madame Walewska," Cipriani said, smiling. "The time will come for you to make the little voyage."

Marie detected a glint in his eye, a knowing look that was both humiliating and maddening.

Marie regretted yet another delay.

On 1 August, Marie saw her brother off on a ship named the *Abeille*, entrusting him with a letter for Napoleon.

Teodor returned on the ninth, carrying Napoleon's welcome reply.

> *Marie,*
>
> *Thank you for your kind letter. Before coming here, go to Naples to see what might be accomplished about Aleksander's affairs. That done, I shall be glad to welcome you and the little boy to Elba. Teodor tells me of his progress. I shall be glad to give him a hug and a kiss. Until then, Adieu–*
>
> *In affection,*
>
> *Napole.*

Marie exhaled and looked up from her chair to where Teodor stood. "Will you send word to Cipriani that we can sail as soon as he can make arrangements."

Teodor averted his eyes. His body seemed to stiffen. "I'm afraid to disappoint you, Marie, but the emperor has given me a mission that might take two weeks."

"What? Why would he do that? The princess said he has an entire network of agents to do his bidding."

"Just the same, I have an order."

"Two weeks. I don't intend to wait for you. Tell Cipriani that I'll go ahead at once, and you'll join me later."

"No, Marie. His orders are clear. You're to wait for my return and we are to sail together."

"But two weeks! —And your return from *where?*"

"It wouldn't be a confidential mission if I were to tell you, now, would it?"

"Teo, we have not kept secrets from one another, have we?"

"We have not, but what if the fellow who signed that letter asked you to keep a secret, would you do it? Truth, if you please."

"Ha! Checkmated by my own brother!"

The two laughed.

"You will hurry back, I trust." Marie sighed. "Teodor, tell me what to expect upon my arrival on Elba."

"It's very beautiful, Marie. You'll like it. So will Olek. First, you'll see a ruggedly magnificent coastline with hills and mountains rising up behind it. We'll dock at the bay of Portoferraio, export center for the island's iron trade. Grand Master Bertrand boasts that Napoleon has greatly increased iron's production and sale. Above the town, you'll see fortifications built by the Medicis."

"I'm certain we'll find all that interesting. His sister has spoken of some of his improvements. But tell me now about *him*. About Napoleon. —How is he?"

"Oh—yes." Teodor tilted his head slightly. "He is in good health although he . . ."

"What?"

"He's put on some weight, Marie."

"I see. Much?"

"It's noticeable."

"He has a chef?"

"Oh, yes, a good one. Napoleon might reside in a plain two-level house, but he keeps the old rituals of a military and civilian household staff as he did at the Tuileries."

"I'm not surprised."

"While I was there, preparations were being made . . ." Teodor paused suddenly, glancing at his sister as if he regretted his words.

"Preparations for what, Teodor?"

"Well, his birthday is—"

"The fifteenth of the month, I know."

Teodor leveled his eyes at Marie. "He's preparing to receive his mother for his birthday."

The news gave Marie a start. "His mother—Madame Mère?"

Teodor gave a slow nod. "Does this complicate your visit, Marysia? I was hesitant to tell you."

It took some moments for Marie to respond. She immediately suspected Napoleon had delayed her sailing until after his mother's arrival and the birthday festivities. "I've met Madame Letizia Bonaparte a few times in public settings and once at his sister Pauline's. I overheard her compliment me, but I'm certain gossip has found its way to her. Sweet Jesus! Will his mother be staying?"

"Who knows the whims of an emperor's mother? However, I don't think you'll have to meet her there. Bertrand wants to keep you a secret."

"From Napoleon's mother?"

"From everybody."

"Oh. How does he hope to manage that?"

"The people around the emperor are nothing else if not loyal, no worry there. Madame Mère will be residing in Marciana Alta, a village high in the mountains overlooking a marina below. And you'll be well away from the citizens of the island."

"All hundred thousand? Where?"

"We will reside some two miles' distance still higher up from Marciana Alta, at a shrine called Madonna del Monte."

"I'm to stay at a *shrine*? You're joking, Teodor!"

"Well, no. Besides an ancient church, it has a hermitage where you will stay."

"I see. We go by carriage, I assume?"

Teodor nodded. "For the most part, but once we arrive at Marciana Alta, we take ponies up through an old mules' path to within a mile of our destination. Then we must change to a narrower path used by pilgrims."

"So, we walk?"

"I'm afraid so. I'm told the hermitage is historically interesting. Napoleon will entertain you there."

"I see. No one lives there now?"

"Some six monks still reside there, but Bertrand had convinced them to occupy the cellar."

Marie felt a tightening at her chest. "Teodor, this sounds more and more outlandish. It seems great pains are being taken to hide me away. I don't like it."

"Are you having second thoughts, Marie?"

She stared at her brother, thinking—knowing—that this plan was not Bertrand's. She paused for a long minute, took in a breath, and said, "No, I'm not."

Later, in her room, second thoughts lingered. On the one hand, anger welled up in her over the secrecy, but when she thought of Napoleon, what he had lost and how vulnerable he must feel, the anger dissipated.

When Marie rose the next morning, Teodor was gone.

August dragged on painfully for Marie, its suffocating heat only intensifying her impatience.

On the twenty-eighth, Teodor finally returned and arranged with Cipriani for the group to sail from Livorno to Elba on the night tide of 31 August. The day before their departure, after Aleksander was tucked into bed, Teodor took a chair across from Marie in the reception room.

"What is it, Teo?" Marie asked. "You have that faraway look on your face. I know you too well—something's bothering you."

Teodor managed a tight smile. "You haven't asked about the mission."

"No, you made it clear you'd keep the emperor's confidence."

Teodor nodded and looked away.

"So—you wanted me to question you?"

Teodor brought his gaze back to her, the green darkly serious. "It's just that—well, I think you should know about it."

Marie sat forward, her back stiffening. "Why is that, Teodor?"

"The emperor gave me two letters to deliver when I left the island."

"One for me, and one for—?"

"A woman in Aix-les-Bains."

"Oh? All the way to France? —Who is she, Teodor?"

"The Duchess of Colorno."

"Who?"

"It's a false name meant to conceal the identity of Empress Marie-Louise."

"What?"

"I couldn't *not* tell you before we leave tomorrow."

"But if Napoleon has agents for such missions, why would he choose you?"

"I asked him that. He said I would be the most unlikely person to carry the message, that his enemies would be expecting him to try to contact her through known agents."

"Ha! Well, I daresay he was right. So! —One letter for his wife and one for me." Marie felt as if her cheeks were afire. One for his shadow wife, she thought.

Marie felt a thickness in her throat and let some moments pass before she collected herself and spoke: "Teodor, you don't know what was in her letter?" she asked as if fearful of the answer.

"I do know. It was his request—order, really—for her to go to Elba and to bring their son."

"Oh!" Marie suddenly felt weak, dizzy. "Then *I* cannot go."

"No, wait, Marie. I know what was in the letter because the empress saw that I was given refreshment and told to wait in an adjacent room, should there be an answer. As I sat alone, I heard a conversation between her and a gentleman about Napoleon's request."

"And?"

"She has no intention of going to Elba."

"No?"

"After their conference, her secretary came to me and told me there'd be no reply. He was the loose-lipped type. When I casually asked him who the gentleman was, he told me a good deal. He was General Adam Neipperg, an Austrian count who had been assigned to escort the empress to Vienna."

"So—she's leaving France."

"Her father is calling her home, along with her son. She's leaving Napoleon, Marie."

Marie's hand went to the dimpled area at her collarbone. A jolt ran through her. "Sweet Jesus! You're certain of this?"

"I am—and that's not all of it."

"It's enough for me." Marie felt as if she were floating on the news.

"Listen to me. When I asked the secretary about the man's identity, he arched one eyebrow and tilted his head in a way I could not misread. Immediately thought back to the conversation between the general and the empress and realized there was a sense of *intimacy* between them."

"Perhaps you're reading too much into the circumstances."

Teodor cocked his head. "I'll wager that I'm not. But—Marie, Napoleon can't learn any of this."

"He'll learn soon enough of her desertion."

"Yes," Teodor said, his voice steady but trending lower. "But he can't know that I discovered the contents of his letter, much less what else I learned in Aix-les-Bains about the relationship between the general and the empress. You won't tell him, will you?"

"Oh, Teo. Of course not." Marie stood abruptly, went to the window, and gazed out into the night.

"Marie?"

Marie drew in a long breath and pivoted toward her brother. "We should retire now, Teodor." Without waiting for a response, she moved swiftly toward her bedchamber, a sense of calm enveloping her.

In her room, she sat at the desk and wrote a letter to Anastase, asking him to send Antoni and Hania to Elba in October. She wanted both sons with her, now that her stay on Elba was likely to be extended, as was her intention. She prayed that Napoleon would be delighted with her proposal that she remain on the island.

Though their relationship had evolved—physical passion waned over the years, and his unyielding pursuit of a dynastic marriage shattered what had once been a magical idyll, even if interrupted by his wars—Marie still loved him deeply. No longer would she fear his death in battle or by assassination. Elba could offer what Paris could not: a refuge with the privacy of Finckenstein and the intimacy of Schönbrunn, where she had conceived Aleksander.

Her heart soared.

PART SEVEN

"Life does not grant us what we wish, but what it has for us."
~Polish Proverb

66

The Tyrrhenian Sea
31 August 1814

THE NIGHT WAS WARM. MARIE sat on a deck chair, provided by the ship's commander, Captain Bernardi, and gazed up at the star-dotted sky. The pitch and roll of the waves and the creaking and groaning of the timbers kept her alert and exhilarated.

Henri-Gatien Bertrand had greeted them upon boarding and escorted them to small but comfortable cabins. Napoleon had long forgiven him for his flirtation with Marie at that supper in Warsaw. Neither he nor Marie mentioned it. Despite Napoleon's exile at Elba, Bertrand remained Grand Marshal of the Imperial Household, and now commanded the *Abeille*, a two-masted brig with a special additional gaff sail on its main mast. Among Bertrand's current duties was sailing across to Italy for provisions, furniture, and equipment—but Marie suspected there were also secret messages exchanged with Napoleon's allies and agents.

Marie was reminded of the letter entrusted to Teodor, directing Empress Marie-Louise to join Napoleon at Elba, and wondered about his reaction when he learns she has abandoned him. Gossip in Paris had characterized her as pretty, but doltish, an idle woman with a roving eye. Might he be able to forget her—even though she had a young son who would always be a link between the two?

Marie sat alone, lost in thought. Teodor had gone to explore the brig and chat with the captain and crew, with whom he had become familiar on his previous trip to and from Elba. Katarzyna, looking pale but determined, had taken the sleepy Aleksander below to their cabin.

Later, as the sea grew rougher, the ship began to heave and sway, sending cold spray onto the deck, its sting prompting her to go below, though she had little hope that her excitement would allow for any real rest.

---◦◦◦---

1 September 1814
By midday, the novelty of the ship had worn off for most of her party, except for Aleksander, who ran around pestering the crew with questions about the ship, the sea, and its creatures. He dragged Marie to the stern several times, hoping to spot sharks or swordfish, but they saw only schools of smaller fish.

---◦◦◦---

By the time Teodor came to Marie's cabin to announce they were nearing the entry of Portoferraio, dusk had fallen. Marie's heart quickened. "We're ready," she said.

Teodor caught her gaze with a questioning look.

"I am," she said, lifting her chin.

Several crew members appeared, collected the luggage, and followed the group to the deck. Aleksander, wearing a blue frock coat and short white trousers purchased for the occasion, darted toward the railing, his curly blond head topped by a naval cap the captain had given him.

"Stay with us!" Katarzyna called after him, but he ignored her and ran ahead, forcing her to hurry after him.

Captain Bernotti approached. "We'll anchor at San Giovanni in a few minutes," he said, smiling.

"San Giovanni?" Teodor questioned. "Isn't the dock at Portoferraio the usual dock?"

"It is," Bernotti replied, the smile fading. "We *are* in the Bay of Portoferraio. You'll be able to see the town across the way momentarily." In responding to the questioning looks of both brother and sister, he kept talking. "San Giovanni is a small village. The emperor requested that we disembark there."

"I see," Marie said, pulling her navy-blue cloak closed as the night breeze lifted the long white veil of her Leroy-inspired hat. "So, it's more remote, secluded?"

"Well, yes, Madame Walewska, it is at that," Bernotti admitted.

Marie sensed a tightening in her middle. *And so it begins, the hiding away. Have I miscalculated?*

Grand Marshal Bertrand escorted Marie and her party as they stepped onto land and into an olive grove. The mountainous interior of the island rose up in a dark, hulking outline behind it.

"Secluded, indeed," Teodor muttered.

At the grove's edge, a carriage drawn by four black horses, its lanterns dark, waited. Behind them, Captain Bernotti followed the group toward the carriage. Several of his crew followed, baggage on their backs.

Katarzyna held tight to the hand of the excited Aleksander as they followed. "Mother, look at the horses!" the boy exclaimed, his excitement breaking the night's quiet. As they drew closer Marie recognized the carriage as Napoleon's imperial coach, wondering at once whether Napole was about to step down from the coach to welcome them. Her breath went out of her.

As if he read her thoughts, Bertrand said, "I'm afraid you must make do with me as your escort for the first leg of our journey, Madame Walewska. The emperor awaits you at the tiny town of Procchio."

Baggage was lashed to the roof as the party stepped up into the coach. Marie and Katarzyna, with Aleksander wedged between them, sat facing forward, Bertrand and Teodor on the opposite bench.

In no time, Bertrand knocked at the roof, and they were off at a good pace, the carriage grinding and rumbling as it made the ascent.

Any wish that the motion would lull Aleksander to sleep was in vain. An hour into the rattling and jolting journey, he crawled onto Marie's lap, crying out, "I want to see out the window!"

Marie sighed and lifted the leather shade.

Aleksander pressed his nose to the glass. "I can't see anything," he whined. "It's too dark, Mother."

Marie turned and looked out. "It is, Olek," she said.

At that moment, the carriage lurched to the left, jolting its passengers as it continued to climb. Marie held tight to Aleksander.

Bertrand coughed softly and spoke in his Parisian French, "It's a fortunate thing he can't see out into the night, Madame Walewska. The mountain road is extremely narrow." He paused, his voice dropping to little more than a whisper as he added, *"Une chute abrupte."*

Katarzyna gasped. "Drop-off?"

Her French was improving, Marie thought, wishing for once she hadn't understood.

The grand marshal gave an uncertain nod, perhaps regretting his description.

Katarzyna clasped and held Marie's hand. In squeezing her sister's hand in return, Marie gave courage to herself. "I told you this would be an adventure, Kasia, did I not?"

The carriage leaned and lurched again. "Oh!" Katarzyna cried out.

Not long after, Aleksander drifted off to sleep despite the roughness of the ride.

Another hour passed and the carriage slowed and the road smoothed out. Shouts rang out from ahead.

"This must be Procchio," Bertrand said.

Marie lifted the shade. Outside were riders armed with torches.

Then came a booming voice: "The Emperor!"

The door was flung open and Napoleon stood there on the drop-down stair, leaning in and kissing Marie's hand. He wore a uniform she had not seen before, blue and white, with little ornamentation.

As he stepped into the coach, Katarzyna, wide-eyed, quickly moved across to the other bench.

Napoleon took Katarzyna's place, rubbing his son's curls in the process. Aleksander stirred but didn't awaken.

Napoleon nodded to Bertrand, dismissing him.

As Bertrand wordlessly exited the coach, Napoleon nodded hello to Teodor and Katarzyna, explaining, "Regretfully, half of your journey is ahead of us, and it is the harder half. At Procchio, a smaller carriage is waiting. You see, the road from there is indeed narrow and we need a vehicle better able to maneuver it."

Marie's pulse sped up. The worst was still to come. Across the way, even in the shadows, Katarzyna's fear was clearly etched on her face.

They soon reached the road's end at Procchio, whereupon Napoleon alighted from the coach. When Teodor handed Aleksander down to a smiling Napoleon, the boy came fully awake, crying, *"Papa Empereur!"*

"Yes, my boy," Napoleon said, and tweaked Aleksander's nose.

Watching the father-son interaction, Marie quashed her uncertainty about having undertaken the venture.

The second carriage was quite small, its size necessary to navigate what was little more than a mule's track leading still farther up the mountain. At Marie's side, Napoleon held his son upon his lap on the forward-facing, hard bench. Katarzyna and Teodor shared the opposite bench, Katarzyna's expression attuned to every bump.

Marie turned to Napoleon. "This is a new uniform," she said.

"New to me, but it's the uniform of the Elba National Guard. This is my kingdom now, so it's appropriate. Thankfully, it's made of cotton drill so that its lightness is fitting for this Mediterranean climate."

This carriage—with but a single horse—had only just begun to move when Marie felt Napoleon clasp her hand. He held it all the way to Marciana Alta.

"Ah, here is where we make another change," Napoleon said.

"I suspect your mother must be fast asleep at this hour," Marie said.

Napoleon dropped Marie's hand and shifted in his seat toward her, his eyes wide and brow furrowed.

It was an impulsive comment, one she immediately regretted. He had to be wondering how she knew about Madame Mère's presence on Elba. She shot Teodor—her source—a sidelong glance to find him staring back incredulously. No—he was scowling. *Sweet Jesus!*

Napoleon faced forward now and finally responded: "I'm certain she is sleeping soundly, at that," he said with a finality that closed the subject.

Marie swallowed hard.

The carriage fully stopped, and a soldier appeared at the door to help the party exit.

To Marie's relief, the subject of Madame Mère was dropped.

"Aleksander, would you care to ride with me?" Napoleon asked, ruffling the boy's blond locks. "My pony is very tame."

"Oh, yes, *Papa Empereur!*" the boy cried.

Ponies for the other three had been ordered by Bertrand, as well as mules for the baggage, and some eight or ten soldiers to carry torches and attend to the mules and luggage. In half an hour's time, they set off on the narrow incline.

Following the torches of two mounted soldiers, Napoleon led the party on a brown pony, holding Aleksander, who would occasionally call back to Marie, whose pony followed Teodor's. Then came Katarzyna with mules and soldiers following.

Marie noted that the soldiers wore the Napoleonic uniform of the Polish soldiers who had so enthusiastically followed the emperor into exile. Her heart swelled with pride and gratitude. Loyalty runs deep in the veins of a Pole, one of the nuns had told her.

A mile's distance from the shrine, they came upon soldiers standing guard. They dismounted, surrendered the ponies, and began the final climb on foot along a path of granite slabs that led into a forest of chestnut trees and dense, scented evergreen shrubbery. They passed fourteen stone shrines, each adorned with paintings inset to mark the Stations of the Cross, and a votive candle dispelling the dark.

The uphill climb grew steeper, and as it did, Marie noticed that—despite the light-weight uniform—forty-five-year-old Napoleon, walking ahead with Aleksander, was slowing, his breathing labored. He had gained weight, too, just as Teodor had said.

Nearly an hour's ascent on foot—four since disembarking from the ship—brought them onto the terrace of the shrine Madonna del Monte.

"I feel like a pilgrim," Katarzyna said.

"I think we are pilgrims, indeed, Kasia," Marie replied.

Led by Napoleon, the party set about exploring.

The twelfth-century, tan-colored church stood protected by ancient chestnut trees with weathered and eerily gnarled trunks. Opposite its façade stood a semicircular stone structure that featured three masks pouring water from their mouths. "Come drink and slake your thirst," Napoleon ordered. "It was a long climb. This is a sacred spring coming down to us from Monte Capanne, the highest mountain on Elba." Cupping her hands, Marie drank from the middle mask, one eye watching Napoleon lift Aleksander to drink from the one at the far left.

To the right of the church stood the hermitage, a low ochre-colored building of mossy, weathered stone, into which soldiers were now entering with the baggage. A large white tent had been pitched near the Church. The emperor's emblem—consisting of the initial "N" and topped with a crown—hung over its entrance.

"I adore this place," Napoleon announced, "I discovered it one day out riding and hiking. The views are exceptional! Why, I can see my Corsica from here. There's not much of a moon tonight, but we have a good many stars. Tomorrow in the daylight, however, the views will amaze you."

Marie noticed Napoleon whispering something to Teodor, whose eyes narrowed as if in confusion. Slowly, he nodded his head in response.

"Before we sit down to supper," Napoleon said, addressing everyone, "go into the hermitage where my valet Ali is waiting to show you to your rooms. Or should I say *cells*," he added, with a chuckle. "Refresh yourselves and then come out to be seated here under the stars. Go, now!"

As they walked toward the hermitage, Marie turned to her brother. "What did he say to you, Teodor?"

"He said that after supper I'm to return to Marciana Alta and take command of the guards keeping watch over Madame Mère."

"What? Why would he do that?"

"It's done, Marie. My valise is already there and I'm to have an escort."

"Then you don't have a cell here."

"No, I'll clean up in Aleksander's cell, but I won't have a change of uniform."

"I don't understand why—"

"I do, Marie. He wants me out of the way."

Inside the hermitage, Marie was glad to see Mameluke Ali bow to them. He had been second valet to Napoleon for many years. She hadn't known him well, only that he was decidedly French, but when he was accepted into Napoleon's household, he was made to wear the Ottoman costume and take the name "Ali," after the mameluke he replaced. Once Katarzyna and Aleksander had been shown to their cells, Marie detained the valet at the doorway to her room. "You have been with him for many years, Ali. I thank you for that."

"Thank you, Madame Walewska. You know that his first valet, Constant Wairy, left his service after the abdication?"

"Yes, I was shocked to hear it. I knew Constant well."

"Louis Marchand was chosen to replace him."

"I see." Marie wondered why Napoleon had not promoted Ali to first valet. Why had he not been rewarded for his loyalty? Her empathy for Ali made her feel a quiet awkwardness between them, as if his unacknowledged loyalty weighed heavily on the moment.

Ali smiled, seeming to sense her discomfort. He cleared his throat, lowered his head to capture her gaze, and said, "The emperor worships you, if I may be so bold as to say." With that, he bowed and moved away.

Marie entered her cell, a narrow room featuring a pine wardrobe, a prayer bench, and a small table with two chairs. It was what she would have expected of a monk's cell, except that the bed was wider than she would have imagined. She thought of the monks whom Bertrand had confined to the cellar beneath her. Perhaps it belonged to a corpulent abbot, she thought, noting also that on the iron bedstead's thin mattress were new linens and a fine blanket. Candles on the mantle above the fireplace and on the table had been lighted.

Marie stepped toward the bed, where her leather valise had been placed. She withdrew a dress of gray taffeta and set to work trying to lessen the wrinkling. Finally satisfied, she stepped into it, tightening the cinching below her bosom. She finished her toilette, counting herself lucky to have brought a small table mirror, for the cell had none.

Supper was served under the stars and attended by valets Ali and Marchand, who offered a white bean and egg soup flavored with wild garlic, quail stew, and grilled sea bass. To Marie's surprise, it was Napoleon himself who poured the native wines, both red and white, and carved the roast lamb and goose. He hummed as he carved, smiling at his guests and appearing to be delighted with the tasks.

"I need to monitor how much I eat," Napoleon announced, "I'm becoming as round as a butter plate." He chatted about the features of the island and promised to take Aleksander fishing. Marie had not seen Napoleon so ebullient in years.

By the time the dessert of watermelon and apricot galettes was served, Aleksander was drifting off to sleep. Katarzyna took him to bed, returning shortly afterward.

An hour later, Ali suddenly appeared and nodded to Teodor, who excused himself, mumbling something about duty calling him to Marciana Alta.

Napoleon kept Marie and Katarzyna engaged with light-hearted conversation for half an hour, then escorted them to the entrance of the hermitage. There, he gave them cheek kisses, fragrant with wine, promising them an exciting day ahead.

Marie looked in on the sleeping Aleksander, kissed him lightly, and retreated to her own cell. She sat at the table, slightly dizzy from the wine, replaying the evening's events in her mind. When, she wondered, would there be time alone with Napoleon? She longed to tell him she'd come prepared to stay, with plans to send for her things from the Paris house. She would tell him, too, that Antoni was to arrive in October. And there was the matter of her jewels—she had brought them, knowing that the allied powers weren't supplying Napoleon with the promised funds to support his soldiers and improve life for the Elba citizens. She would insist he accept them, even if he was proud enough to refuse.

Just as Marie slipped into her nightdress, a knock came at the door. It was not Katarzyna's light tap, but a firm, impatient rapping. She felt a surge of anxiety, well aware there was no lock, nothing to bar the door.

She approached and listened.

Another rapping startled her. Her hand went to her throat.

"Marie," came a voice she recognized.

She opened the door.

There stood Napoleon, smiling boyishly in his purple brocade dressing gown.

Marie stood, unable to think, unable to move.

"Will you invite me in, my Polish wife?"

Marie stepped aside as he entered, his purple slippers bearing the "N" emblem kicking out below the hem of the gown.

Marie lay awake, listening to Napoleon's soft snoring. His appearance at her door had not been a complete surprise. And yet, it had. She had come to Elba to support a loved one at his lowest. He had not allowed intimacy since their time at Schönbrunn, when she conceived Aleksander, now a lively four-year-old. Throughout those four years, she had set aside her heartbreak and lived for their son and the hope that Napoleon would one day play a pivotal role in restoring Poland. It had been enough to be near him, to know he meant to take care of her beloved Aleksander, enough for him to end his letters with "Never doubt me." She hadn't expected passion, not after all this time. And yet, if she were honest, she thought, upon hearing from Teodor that Marie-Louise had abandoned her husband, a flicker of curiosity had been ignited within her. Only now could she admit to herself it was a longing.

He moved now, the length of his body touching and warming hers, setting off a flutter in her chest. His heart was hungry; she had sensed it soon after he entered the carriage, when he took her hand in his. She felt it at the supper table as well. He appeared happy in his new domain, reduced as it was. And he seemed very glad to have her here.

Marie thought she could be happy here at Elba, also. The specifics of how this new chapter might unfold eluded her, however. She could manage only emotions now. The rigid and exact details of day-to-day life here had to be left to the future. She allowed herself the thought that Bertrand was keeping her presence on Elba secret only at the order of the man sleeping next to her, but the events of the evening eclipsed that thought. Love and possibility intervened.

Napoleon had fallen asleep happy, she was certain. Now she meant to do the same. She recalled his promise to their son that he would take him on a fishing excursion, just the two of them. Olek's face had lighted up in wonder. Marie was thrilled to see him bond with his son. Still, she had to stifle a little laugh. She had seen Napoleon addressing great armies on grand palace esplanades and imagined him taking them into war on great battlefields, their lives in jeopardy, but the thought of Napoleon wielding a fishing pole in hand . . . well, she could not conjure it.

In time, she felt herself drifting off . . ..

2 September 1814

Marie awoke to find Napoleon pulling on his dressing gown and cinching the cord around his waist. Soft early light shone through the curtainless window.

"I have things to attend to today. Forgive me, my Marie."

She couldn't help but smile. He hadn't called her that in so very long. She sat up, pulling the sheet to cover herself. "I'll forgive you . . . this once, Napole."

Napoleon laughed, leaned in to kiss her, and left.

Marie stepped out of bed, drawing the sheet around her, and went to the window. She watched Napoleon as he moved away from the hermitage. No one else seemed to be up and about.

In just moments, he vanished from sight, his tent no doubt his destination. There, the fine-feathered bed he had boasted about at supper no doubt remained unmussed.

Marie started to turn away from the window when she heard voices. Below, two servants appeared, each carrying a basket of fruit, vegetables, and other food items. They were not soldiers. They were clearly local citizens—and they were coming from the direction Napoleon had taken.

Marie felt a spike of fear. *Had they seen him leaving the hermitage?*

She dressed slowly. If Bertrand had gone to great pains to keep her visit secret, why had Napoleon taken such a chance as to be seen leaving the hermitage in his dressing gown? People were not fools. Others had observed, as well. While he trusted the soldiers who had accompanied him to Elba, what of the local members of the National Guard? While the way to the Madonna del Monte site was barred to pilgrims during Marie's visit, what of those servants who were in the employ of the church? Were they as close-mouthed as Napoleon's loyal guards?

Marie was not worried for herself. She was not afraid of gossip. She had gotten quite used to it. In certain circles in Poland and in Paris, people knew of her relation to the emperor. In fact, for some in Warsaw, it seemed a badge of honor earned because of her supposed influence on Napoleon regarding Poland's possible independence.

Marie was worried for Napoleon. Undoubtedly, he wanted their rekindled affair to remain clandestine because he had managed to create his dynastic marriage to an Austrian archduchess and had no wish for gossip to undermine it in any way.

A light knock came at the door, jolting her into the present.

Katarzyna said, "Aleksander and I are dressed and ready, Marie."

Held in the shade under a blue canopy, breakfast proved a veritable feast of fresh fruit, imported French cheeses, prosciutto, boiled eggs, and croissants. Ali poured tea, coffee, and Marie's choice, hot chocolate.

As Marie scanned the scene, a flash of red caught her eye. A woman in a scarlet headscarf peered out from a corner of the church. Marie's first thought was that she was a kitchen worker, but by the time she turned in her chair to get a better look, the woman had vanished. Marie smiled to herself. The emperor's lavish breakfast would likely seem very curious to the locals. And yet, the specter of gossip rebounded. What was there to keep this woman or the servants here from revealing what they've witnessed?

After the meal, Napoleon led Marie, Katarzyna, and Aleksander into the church, taking on the role of tour director, pointing out exquisite old frescoes and a painting on granite behind the altar depicting the Madonna's Assumption. Marie found it mesmerizing. They knelt briefly at the sanctuary where dozens of votive jars—unlighted—were placed, with many little notes no doubt requesting heavenly favors. Marie imagined them written by fishermen's wives, praying for their husbands' safe return from the sea. Napoleon helped Aleksander to light one of the candles.

Exiting the church, Marie asked Napoleon why no other candles had been lighted.

"No other pilgrims have been here."

"Because *we* are here?"

"Precisely." Napoleon shrugged. "Marie," he continued, changing the subject, "in the church Aleksander asked if we were to go fishing today. I'm afraid I spoke too soon about any fishing venture. At this altitude, there is no fishing, of course, and the coast is a good distance away now." He took her hand in his. "This time is ours, my dear."

"Perhaps another day?"

Napoleon's smile was more of a grimace. He shook his head. "Too many people."

His reaction was what she expected. *Too many curious people at the coast.*

"I stayed in the boy's good graces, however. While I take you sightseeing, Ali is going to teach him to ride a pony."

"By himself? Oh, I don't—"

"Now, don't worry. Ali will see to his safety. And we can ask your sister to go along. She'll enjoy the outing. Meanwhile, you and I will climb to a favorite overlook of mine."

As Napoleon led the way up the mountain toward the lookout point he had mentioned, Marie briefly considered confiding in him about the risks of exposure from unexpected sources. But she held back, knowing that his agents would soon inform him that Empress Marie-Louise was returning to Vienna, not to Elba. Once that news reached him, how careful would he have to be in keeping her presence—and Olek's—a secret?

When word of his wife's abandonment does come, she dared to think, *perhaps her own star would rise—*

She would not be the one to tell him.

"Here it is!" Napoleon exclaimed, interrupting her thoughts.

They had come upon an unusually shaped rock formation. "It's like a chair," he told her. "Now, come sit by me." He set down a lunch basket and laid out a gray blanket.

Once settled at his side, Marie put away her thoughts and became absorbed in the magnificent panorama. Dotted with islands, the Tyrrhenian Sea stretched out in vivid blues, with the waves gently crashing onto the shore below more of a luminescent turquoise.

Napoleon pointed left now, out to sea. "There is my birthplace, my Marie. There is Corsica."

"Why, it's quite large, Napole."

"It is. Many times larger than my tiny kingdom here. And, you know, had not French warships taken it in 1768, the history of the world would be much different."

Marie squeezed his hand. She did know. He had told her several times that he was born a year after the conquest and so was granted French citizenship.

After he pointed out other Tuscan islands, they had lunch, talked, and kissed.

They returned to the Madonna del Monte terrace where an idyllic afternoon played out. Teodor came up from Marciana Alta for supper, completing Marie's little family. To accompany cake and a variety of tarts that night, Napoleon insisted everyone drink his favorite wine, a red made from the Aleatico grape, grown and vinified on Elba. He poured it himself.

Marie retired, a bit inebriated, but sated and happy. She was at one with the world.

A little after midnight, a knock came at the door.

This time, the visitor's appearance was met with anticipation, rather than surprise.

67

MARIE AWOKE FROM A DEEP sleep to some noise. She turned and lifted her head. Napoleon's place at her side was empty. Then she heard a light knocking.

"Marie! Marie! May I come in?" It was Teodor.

"A moment!" she cried, pulling herself out of bed and reaching for her dressing gown.

When she opened the door, her brother stood there, his face creased and red with worry. She took his hand and drew him inside. "What is it, Teodor? What has happened?"

"I—I don't know where to start."

"Sit down." Marie motioned to the hard wooden chair. "Take a breath," she said, standing close to him. "Start at the beginning, Teodor."

Teodor nodded, collecting himself. "Well, Bertrand had arranged for me to stay at the home of an old couple. Today, they were all aflutter about something when I was called to have breakfast with them. They were bickering whether to place a candle or a lantern in the window tonight. It was odd. I remembered seeing several houses lit up last night, so I asked them if it was some holiday here on Elba. The old man looked at me, surprised, and asked, 'You haven't heard, young man?' The woman gasped and said . . ."

"Said what, Teodor?"

"She said, 'Why, the empress has arrived! She's at the Madonna del Monte, along with the King of Italy.' She meant—"

"Empress Marie-Louise and her son, of course," Marie managed to say, gripping the table for balance. She stumbled backwards and sat hard upon the other chair. Her heart thundered in her chest. "So—they think I am the empress? Sweet Jesus. It's widespread this—this mistaken gossip?"

Teodor nodded. "At the entrance to the pilgrimage path, I met the emperor's doctor who had ridden up from Portoferraio dressed in his best suit of clothes, I'd wager. His name is Fourreau de Beauregard. We kept company along the way of the Stations of the Cross. He said not a house in Portoferraio lacked a welcoming light in the window. Oh, Marie, how could this have gotten out? How?"

"Any number of ways, I imagine," Marie said, sighing. "His soldiers might have been quiet, but many have taken notice—servants, citizens, even the driver." She paused, then said, "Like me, Marie-Louise is blonde and Aleksander is but a year older than her son and he's the image of Napole. Why should we be surprised at the mix-up? Did you take the doctor to Napoleon?"

"I did. The emperor was under the breakfast canopy. He—he had Olek on his knee."

"Kasia already had him dressed and out? Really! I *have* overslept. So—he thought Olek the King of Italy?"

Teodor tilted his head and gave a little shrug. "It's what they're expecting, Marie."

"Yes, it is. And it's what *he* is expecting."

Before Teodor could respond, there came a knocking at the door. Teodor shot Marie a questioning glance that told her it was likely Napoleon on the other side. It was her thought, too. She nodded toward the door, and Teodor jumped up and pulled it open.

Grand Marshal Bertrand entered, his usually neat hair windswept. "Pardon my intrusion, Madame Walewska."

Marie stood, heart pounding. "What is it?" she asked.

"I'm afraid I bring unhappy news."

"Yes?" Suddenly, Marie somehow knew exactly what he was going to say before he said it.

Bertrand paused, wetting his lips. "The emperor has asked that you prepare to leave the island."

"I see." Marie stiffened, a dizziness washing over her.

"Perhaps you should sit, Madame Walewska."

"I'm fine."

Bertrand winced. "It seems the Elba's citizens have concluded—"

"That the empress is here. Isn't that correct?"

"It is."

"And the emperor doesn't want word to reach the mainland—and Marie-Louise, does he?"

"Among other reasons."

"Other reasons?"

"Madame Walewska, the populace here on Elba is very conservative. The women especially identify with the emperor's wish to be reunited with the empress and their child. For them to learn of your presence, well, you see it is a tiny kingdom and one whose citizens the emperor must win over."

Marie's tone turned businesslike. "When are we to leave?"

"We've sent word down to Captain Bernotti to ready the *Abeille* for tomorrow's morning tide."

"Tomorrow?" Marie asked. "So—we're to spend the night descending the mountain?"

Bertrand averted his gaze, his face flushing with embarrassment. "I'm afraid so, Madame Walewska."

"And the plan?"

"Horses, a carriage, and mules are being sent for. You will have to negotiate the pilgrim's path through the Stations of the Cross first. But at Marciana Alta, the carriage will take you on a new road that leads up from there and then down to Porto Longone, in a bay somewhat east of Portoferraio where the *Abeille* will be waiting."

Silent until now, Teodor asked, an edge in his voice, "East? How *far* east, Grand Marshal?"

Bertrand pursed his lips, then said, "Twenty or twenty-two miles, Teodor."

Teodor drew in a deep breath. "But—why? Why extend the journey down?"

"Ah," Marie interjected, "*seclusion* is why, Teodor. Isn't that right, Marshal Bertrand?"

Bertrand's lips tightened again, this time allowing no words to escape.

Marie strode over to her open valise and withdrew a reticule of red velvet embellished with beading. Pulling the drawstrings tight, she brought it to the Grand Marshal. "See that the emperor gets this," she said, adding, "only after the ship has sailed."

Bertrand squinted at her, silently quizzing her.

"It's a little joke between us," she lied.

The marshal took hold of the purse from the bottom and nodded. "Yes, Madame Walewska."

"When should we be ready?" Marie asked.

"Three hours," Bertrand answered, avoiding eye contact. He brought his heels together, bowed, and turned. He stopped at the door and turned back, as if remembering something. "Oh, Teodor, he asked that you stay." No doubt unused to anyone denying an order from the emperor, Bertrand left without waiting for a response.

Marie left Aleksander in Teodor's care and took Katarzyna for a walk up the mountain, following the route Napoleon had taken for their lunch the previous day. When Katarzyna had learned of their imminent departure, she'd burst into tears, worried about trusting their lives to the coach driver on the narrow mountain road. Marie hoped to calm her.

By the time they reached the overlook with the stone chair, her reassurances had done little. "Look, Kasia, there's Corsica! And see the other islands in a semicircle? Napoleon says that legend has it that when Venus was born, she rose from the Tyrrhenian Sea, fully grown. The story goes that her necklace broke and seven pearls fell into the sea here. From those pearls, Elba and six other islands were formed."

"Really?" Katarzyna enjoyed reading and had a special love for mythology. Looking out at the wide panorama, she said, "I'd not heard of that, but I knew she was born fully grown." She began sharing further details about the Roman goddess.

Marie felt a small victory in easing her sister's nerves.

Minutes later, however, Katarzyna cried, "Oh, Marie, look!"

Katarzyna had shifted and was now facing southeast. She pointed. "There! Do you see, Marie? Do you see?"

Marie did see. The sky in that direction was darkening. She held her breath and watched, praying the storm was moving away. It took little time to realize her prayer would not be answered. The storm was moving with some speed toward Elba, its angry black clouds a foil for intermittent flashes of lightning.

"Come along, Kasia," Marie said, taking hold of her sister's hand.

"Where is Napoleon?" Marie asked Bertrand as they assembled for the walk down the granite slabs toward Marciana Alta.

"He's completing a document that you're to take with you, Madame Walewska," the marshal replied.

"It's to the King of Naples, Marie," Teodor added, "about Aleksander's properties."

"He's an optimist," Marie said. "If de Murat can change sides and betray his own brother-in-law, what makes Napoleon think he will be generous toward me? Are we to wait?"

"It's best we start down," Bertrand said. "The emperor will catch up to us."

The rain began to fall shortly after their procession started, but the canopy of chestnut trees kept them relatively dry. As they descended through the fourteen Stations of the Cross, Marie noticed Teodor glancing behind every so often. She knew he was looking to see if Napoleon would make it in time to say goodbye. She shared his concern but kept her eyes forward, focusing instead on Aleksander at her side. "Are the mules still with us, Teodor? she asked, her tone teasing.

Her brother grunted in response to the quip.

When they reached Marciana Alta, the rain intensified, hastening them toward the small carriage that had brought them to the pilgrimage just two days earlier. Soldiers unloaded the luggage from the mules and lashed it to the roof, while the driver and footman helped Marie's little family into the coach, crowding together on the forward-facing bench. Aleksander claimed a window seat.

433

The time came to say goodbye to her brother. Teodor peered up into the coach. "I could still come with you," he said, his voice trembling, tears mixing with the rain.

Marie shook her head, holding back her own tears. "Your duty is here."

Teodor stepped back and closed the door.

The wind outside began to pick up, howling and shaking the carriage.

No goodbye from Napoleon. *Has he arranged it so?*

The driver and footman had only just taken their positions when the grand master's commanding voice overrode the storm: "The Emperor!"

The door flew open, and Napoleon stepped up on the footboard and thrust his upper body into the coach. Water ran off the sides of his bicorne until he doffed it. He was breathing hard, his eyes fastened on Marie. "I'm sorry for this, Marie," he shouted over the storm. With effort, he lifted a leather dispatch case and placed it on the floor. "Take these papers to de Murat. Make your case for the boy, Marie."

The light was fading, but Marie met his gaze, silent and resolute.

A flash of lightning lit the coach interior, revealing a strange, frantic grimace on Napoleon's face.

Outside, thunder crashed and the horse neighed, hoofs pawing the earth. Katarzyna gripped Marie's hand.

A shout came from Bertrand, causing Napoleon to snap to attention. "I'll—I'll detain you no more. Adieu, Katarzyna. Adieu, my boy Aleksander." He turned and looked up at Marie. "Au revoir, my Marie." He replaced his hat, drew back, and stepped down.

The door slammed shut, resounding with finality.

"Papa Empereur!" Aleksander cried out.

"Hush, Olek," Marie whispered in his ear. "He's gone."

Seconds later, Bertrand could be heard bellowing an order to the driver. The carriage lurched forward, carrying them into the unknown.

The heavy slamming of the coach door rang in Marie's mind, and time seemed to stop. A sharp ache of loss gripped her chest, pulling her back to the moment her father's casket was placed in the family mausoleum, its iron grillwork clanging shut—and sealed. *So very final.*

"We're not going down—we're going *up!*" Katarzyna's shout rang with fear, breaking through Marie's thoughts.

"We are, Kasia," Marie said, shaking free of the memory. "Don't worry. We're taking a new road, but we must go up first to connect with it."

"But why?"

Marie then explained that they would be sailing from Porto Longone, instead of Portoferraio, admitting it would be a longer journey, but saying no more about it.

Aleksander kept the window shade open. Marie allowed it, lacking the energy to curb his curiosity. His facial features might bear the imprint of the emperor, but his inquisitiveness, she knew, could be traced to her.

The rain became torrential, punctuated by lightning and thunder, as the carriage bumped along the uneven road. After half an hour, the carriage stalled. Five minutes elapsed, rain drumming relentlessly on the roof. They could hear the strained voices of the driver and footman competing with the storm.

Aleksander stood at the window as if mesmerized. Marie hesitated, then leaned over to glance outside. Through the swirling rain and mist, a flash of lightning illuminated a fir tree, its trunk bent over a washed-out stretch of road, roots clinging to the edge of a dark abyss.

Marie gasped.

"What?" Katarzyna asked, her voice sharp with concern. "What is it, Marie?"

The carriage began to move again, slowly beginning its descent, sparing Marie from answering.

Her own heart raced, a chilling fear settling in as she realized they teetered on the brink of a violent death.

The journey dragged on, the carriage jolting with each pothole, hour upon hour. Marie prayed for the strength of the wheels.

Twice, they had to disembark and cling to the mountainside as the driver and footman delicately negotiated the horse and carriage over the narrowest stretches of road. Urging Katarzyna and Olek not to look down, Marie assured them with a resolute, yet light, tone that they were experiencing an authentic adventure, one they would boast about to friends someday. They were in her charge, and she meant to keep them safe.

Olek looked around in wonder, while Kasia's pale face and wide, darting eyes betrayed her panic.

Finally, they reached Porto Longone. In preparing to disembark, Marie picked up Napoleon's dispatch case and opened it. A sheaf of documents tied with a red ribbon lay inside, but there was something else, something a bit heavy. She reached in and felt the beaded reticule she had left for Napoleon. It was still weighted with her jewels.

Napole's pride, she thought. Was it his concern for her and Olek that prompted their return—or was it the arrogance that comes before a fall?

"What's in it?" Katarzyna asked.

"What? — Oh, nothing, Kasia, nothing."

The *Abeille* was anchored offshore, and they were led to an open-sided shelter where the port's commandant welcomed them. She recognized him immediately. He had been pointed out to her at one of the salons in Paris. Like so many who followed Napoleon, he was young, still in his thirties when he joined the 120 Polish Lancers who had volunteered to follow Napoleon into exile.

"I'm Captain Paweł Jerzmanowski, Madame Walewska, here to see you safely aboard." He bowed and kissed her hand. "We have a meal prepared, if you will allow me to escort you to the harbor house there."

"Oh, no, Captain Jerzmanowski, I am determined to be on our way. Captain Bernotti will have something aboard for us to eat. The outbound tide must be imminent, yes?"

"Yes, Madame Walewska, but it is my duty to ask you to delay this journey. This storm could be merely the forerunner of the true force about to confront us. Madame, you must trust me. We had a storm last week that sank a good-sized cargo ship that dared to cast off."

Almost as if to underscore his forecast, the wind surged violently, howling with a sudden intensity. Marie smiled nonetheless, and raised her voice. "Captain, we wish to go on. Is that smaller boat there meant to ferry us out to the *Abeille*?"

"Yes, Madame, that's the *Abeille*'s tender."

Marie turned to her sister and directed her to take Aleksander to the waiting boat.

Katarzyna's eyebrows rose, registering skepticism.

Before her sister could say anything, Marie ordered, "Go now, Kasia!"

Katarzyna obeyed, hurrying into the torrent, drawing Aleksander along with her. The driver and footman followed with the valises.

"Madame Walewska, stay a moment. Please reconsider sailing now. I've spoken with the harbormaster. He has given a severe warning against proceeding."

"Have you spoken to the captain? Captain Bernotti."

Captain Jerzmanowski grimaced. "Yes, I have."

"And?"

The captain tilted his head. "He'll obey the emperor's orders."

"To sail with the morning tide? And if we miss it? I assume it would be perhaps a twelve-hour delay?"

The captain gave a slow nod. "That is correct, Madame Walewska."

"We'll leave at once."

Captain Jerzmanowski continued to plead with her to postpone the sailing, the ever-increasing force of the gale lending support to his argument. Marie remained undeterred.

The downpour's loud din kept her from hearing the approaching hoofbeats until the rider was nearly at the shelter.

She recognized her rain-battered brother at once as he dismounted, and having no wish to have the captain influence Teodor with his warnings, she excused herself and went to meet him at the entrance. "Teodor, what is it?"

Breathless, he said, "It's the emperor, Marie."

Marie's hand moved up to her throat, touching the fibula that held her wool cloak closed. "Napole?" she asked.

Teodor nodded.

"What's wrong? Tell me!"

"He sent me on ahead. He's following on that white horse he kept near his tent." Teodor took Marie's hand in both of his. "He's coming to stop the sailing. He's had a change of heart, Marysia. He means to talk to Captain Bernotti himself."

"A change of heart, you say?" Marie muttered, withdrawing her hand.

"Yes, Marie, yes!" Teodor placed his hand on her shoulder. "You're not to go. He's worried for you."

"I see," Marie said, pulling away and turning to look out at the *Abeille*."

Several moments passed.

Finally, she looked up at her brother and said, "They're holding the tender for me, Teo. The worst of our journey is behind us. No—I must go. I'll not yield, Teodor." Marie laughed. "You know how I am."

Teodor could manage only a tentative smile. "I'm afraid that I do."

"Kiss me goodbye, then. They're waiting in the rain down there."

"Please wait for the emperor, Marie. Please. Listen, he doesn't know Marie-Louise is not coming to Elba. He doesn't know his marriage is over. Perhaps if you tell him—"

"No! Leave him to his illusions. Mine have burst on their own." She stared at her brother for several beats, holding her tears at bay. "Oh, Teo, a tardy change of heart is no change of heart."

Teodor held his sister's gaze. "I could still come with, Marie. If you need me—"

"No, Teodor, stay. *He* might need you." Marie drew her brother's face to her and kissed him.

Marie stood at the stern of the *Abeille*, impervious to the rain as the high tide drew the ship farther and farther from the harbor. She gave one last wave toward the shore, hoping her brother could see her. Just as she was about to go below to join Kasia and Olek, a motion onshore drew her attention. She shielded her eyes and squinted.

It was a rider just arriving at the port's shelter, the white of the horse against the black of the sky like a ghostly *wycinanki*.

Marie drew in a quick breath, pelting rain lashing her face. Pivoting now, she went below.

HISTORICAL NOTE

NAPOLEON LIKELY SPENT SEVEN OR eight days worrying and wondering whether his "Polish wife" and their son survived the dangerous sea crossing.

Finally, Captain Bernotti sent a message from Livorno stating that the *Abeille* and her passengers had arrived safely. It included no note or message from Marie. The personal debacle for Marie at Elba effectively ended the romantic relationship between Marie and Emperor Napoleon Bonaparte.

Marie's business sense regarding Aleksander's confiscated properties prevailed, propelling her to Naples, where she must have charmed Napoleon's sister, Queen Caroline, and brother-in-law, King Joachim de Murat. They saw to it that their nephew, who so resembled Napoleon, had all of his Italian estates returned to him, as well as a considerable sum in arrears.

Marie wintered in Naples, and in January of 1815, news came that Anastase Walewski had died. Although she must have wished a reunion at Walewice with her first-born son, Antoni, she was likely deterred from going by the fact that the duchy was now a Congressional Kingdom ruled by the Russian czar and fought over at the Congress of Vienna. In April, Marie returned to Paris.

Having escaped Elba with a thousand men and plans to retake France, Napoleon had actually arrived in Paris before her, on 20 March, easily routing the Bourbon King Louis XVIII.

It seems Marie and Napoleon did not meet until 11 June, just days before his battle with the allied forces at Waterloo, when she granted his request to appear at the Elysée Palace in Paris, the official residence of the French head of state. At the meeting, the once-and-current emperor gave her specific and sound advice on how to manage her French shares in the canals of Loing that he had previously arranged. She would follow his advice, assuring the future for her and her sons.

Napoleon's defeat by Wellington and allies came on 18 June with the decisive Battle of Waterloo.

Three days later, again at the Elysée Palace, Marie and Aleksander, together with Queen Hortense and Marshal Bertrand's wife, kept Napoleon company as he burned state papers and waited for his final exile to the island of Saint Helena. The crowds outside still cheered him, crying out *"Vive l'Empereur!"*

Marie and Aleksander met Napoleon for the last time at the late Josephine's Château de Malmaison, now owned by her daughter Queen Hortense. Napoleon embraced his son, who years later would remember the emperor's tears, if not his words. The deposed emperor and Marie talked privately for an hour, at the end of which Queen Hortense attested to Marie's deep sadness and tears.

For Marie, nine years came to a close.

General Philippe Ornano, Napoleon's Corsican cousin, had met Marie in about 1807. His attraction to her, immediate and long lasting, was unrequited for years. Still, with Napoleon's knowledge and tacit approval, he occasionally squired her around Paris.

After Napoleon's cruel behavior toward Marie on Elba and the news of Anastase Walewski's death, Ornano took up his pursuit of Marie with renewed hope. He proposed marriage, most likely a number of times. Marie finally accepted, and they were married in Brussels on 07 September 1816 and settled in Liège, Belgium.

By the following January, an *enceinte* Marie made the difficult journey to Poland to consult with her gynecologist at Warsaw's Institute of Surgery and Gynecology, Dr. Ciekierski who, out of concern for her kidneys, had warned her years before against nursing baby Aleksander. She had not obeyed.

Now, seven years later, the doctor confirmed kidney disease, complicated by the pregnancy. He told her that if she nursed this baby, she would lose her life.

Marie returned to Liège, and on 9 June 1817, Rodolphe-Auguste d'Ornano was born in good health. Again, Marie ignored the doctor's orders and nursed her third child.

Marie's health deteriorated during the summer. Her husband honored her wish to die at her Paris home, where they arrived in November. With her three sons and husband at her bedside, Marie died on 11 December, four days after her thirty-first birthday.

On the island of St. Helena, Napoleon learned of Marie's marriage and, later, her death. For comfort, his supporters would note, he kept Marie's image next to Josephine's.

Napoleon would live three and a half more years, dying at the age of fifty-one.

DUCHY OF WARSAW AFTER NAPOLEON

In 1815, the Congress of Vienna created the Kingdom of Poland, or Congress Poland, a purportedly semi-independent state placed under the sovereignty of the Russian Empire. Over time, Russia increased its control, prompting uprisings in 1830 and 1863, which were forcefully put down.

Independence remained an elusive dream until the end of WWI, in 1918.

READING GROUP GUIDE

1. What is your idea of unconditional love? How do Marie's feelings for Napoleon compare and/or contrast with that concept?

2. Before falling in love with Napoleon, Marie, under pressure and with a political goal in mind, bowed to his will. How far would you go if it were for the greater good?

3. The proverb for Part One is "Children are what you make them." How might that apply to Benedykt, Teodor, and Marie?

4. The fate of one's country often influences the shaping of lives—and the character of its citizens. How has Poland's fate played out in the inner lives of the Łączyński family?

5. How are the changing attitudes toward women and their place in the world demonstrated in this early nineteenth century story?

6. At what points in her life does Marie show growth?

7. What is your overall takeaway regarding Napoleon? In general? In regard to his relationship with Marie?

8. Poland disappeared from the map of Europe in 1795 and did not regain independence until 1918, following World War I. And yet, Poland's culture—its language, faith, and traditions—survived the 123 years. Might Napoleon be credited with establishing the semi-independent—but short-lived—Duchy of Warsaw, thereby sustaining hope for a free Poland?

9. Pertaining to Marie's life, how true/appropriate is the proverb for Part Six: "One cannot love and be wise."?

I hope you enjoyed Marie's story. All of the main events and relationships are true to her life. It took writing this novel for me to feel as if I understood her. I hope I have brought her to life for you.

This author would so appreciate it if you would write a little review on Amazon, B&N, KOBO, i-books, Smashwords, Goodreads, or whatever your source might be. It really does make a difference.

You might want to wander around my website, or even subscribe to my infrequent newsletters while you're there.

https://www.jamescmartin.com

Follow/add me on **Goodreads:**
https://www.goodreads.com/author/show/92822.James_Conroyd_Martin

If you enjoyed Napoleon's Shadow Wife, you'll enjoy traveling back to sixth-century Constantinople with **Fortune's Child, A Novel of Empress Theodora.** The BBC rates Empress Theodora as the 35th most important woman in History.

"A meticulously researched historical account presented in the form of a thrilling political drama."
—KIRKUS REVIEWS

FORTUNE'S CHILD

A NOVEL OF EMPRESS THEODORA
THE THEODORA DUOLOGY BOOK ONE

JAMES CONROYD MARTIN
AUTHOR OF THE POLAND TRILOGY

Made in the USA
Monee, IL
20 May 2025